Sydney

"All you've got to do is decide to go
and the hardest part is over.

So go!"

TONY WHEELER, COFOUNDER – LONELY PLANET

THIS EDITION WRITTEN AND RESEARCHED BY
Peter Dragicevich

919.441
D 2012

Contents

Plan Your Trip — 4

Welcome to Sydney 4
Sydney's Top 10 6
What's New 13
Need to Know 14
Top Itineraries 16
If You Like... 18

Month by Month 21
With Kids 24
Like a Local 26
For Free **28**
Beaches **31**
Eating **33**

Drinking & Nightlife ... 36
Entertainment 39
**Gay & Lesbian
Sydney** **41**
Shopping **44**
Sports & Activities ... 46

Explore Sydney — 48

**Neighbourhoods
at a Glance** **50**
Circular Quay
& The Rocks 52
Sydney Harbour 68
City Centre &
Haymarket 82

Darling Harbour &
Pyrmont 98
Inner West 105
Surry Hills &
Darlinghurst 117
Kings Cross &
Potts Point 130

Paddington &
Centennial Park 138
Bondi to Coogee 149
Manly 159
**Day Trips from
Sydney** **166**
Sleeping **179**

Understand Sydney — 191

Sydney Today 192
History 194
Food Culture 200

The Arts 204
Architecture 209
Sporty Sydney 213

Survival Guide — 217

Transport 218
Directory A–Z 223

Index 237

Sydney Maps — 246

Left: **Sydney Harbour Bridge (p55)**

Above: **Art Gallery of NSW (p84)**

Right: **Sydney Opera House (p54)**

OPERA HOUSE ARCHITECT: JØRN OBERG UTZON

Manly
p159

Sydney
Harbour
p68

Circular
Quay &
The Rocks
p52

Kings
Cross
& Potts
Point
p130

Darling
Harbour
& Pyrmont
p98

City
Centre & Haymarket
p82

Inner
West
p105

Surry Hills &
Darlinghurst
p117

Paddington &
Centennial
Park
p138

Bondi to
Coogee
p149

Welcome to Sydney

Book a window seat for your flight to Sydney: day or night, it sure is good-lookin'. Scratch the surface and it only gets better.

Show Pony

Brash is the word that inevitably gets bandied around when it comes to describing the Harbour City, and let's face it, Sydney is one hot mess! Compared to its Australian sister cities, Sydney is loud, uncompromising and in-your-face. Fireworks displays are more dazzling here, heels are higher, bodies more buffed, contact sports more brutal, starlets shinier, drag queens glitzier and chefs more adventurous. Australia's best musos, foodies, actors, stockbrokers, models, writers and architects flock to the city to make their mark, and the effect is dazzling: a hyperenergetic, ambitious marketplace of the soul, where anything goes and everything usually does.

Making a Splash

Defined as much by its rugged coast as its exquisite harbour, Sydney relies on its coastal setting to replenish its reserves of charm; venture too far from the water and the charm suddenly evaporates. Jump on a ferry and Sydney's your oyster – the harbour prises the city's two halves far enough apart to reveal an abundance of pearls. On the coast, Australia ends abruptly in sheer walls of sandstone punctuated by arcs of golden sand. In summer they're covered with bronzed bodies enjoying a climate that encourages outdoor socialising, exercising, flirting and fun.

After Dark

After a lazy Saturday at the beach, urbane Sydneysiders have a disco nap, hit the showers and head out again. There's always a new restaurant to try, undercover bar to hunt down, hip band to check out, sports team to shout at, show to see or crazy party to attend. The city's pretensions to glamour are well balanced by a casualness that means a cool T-shirt and a tidy pair of jeans will get you in most places. But if you want to dress up and show off, there's plenty of opportunity for that among the sparkling lights of the harbour.

On the Wild Side

National parks ring the city and penetrate right into its heart. Large chunks of the harbour are still edged with bush, while parks cut their way through the skyscrapers and suburbs. Consequently native critters turn up in the most surprising places. Great clouds of flying foxes pass overhead at twilight and spend the night rustling around in suburban fig trees, oversized spiders stake out the corners of lounge room walls, possums rattle the roofs of terrace houses, and sulphur-crested cockatoos bleat from the railings of urban balconies. At times Sydney's concrete jungle seems more like an actual one – and doesn't that just make it all the more exciting?

Why I Love Sydney

By Peter Dragicevich, Author

My visits to Sydney were becoming increasingly frequent before I decided to up sticks and move to the city in 1998. Sure, it was the glitzy side that first attracted me – the sense that there was always something thrilling going on somewhere, and if you turned the right corner, you could be part of it. That sense remains, but I've discovered much more to love: the lively food scene, endless days at the beach and the way Sydney's indigenous and convict history is so often hidden in plain sight.

For more about our author, see p272.

Bondi Icebergs pool (p151)

Sydney's
Top 10

Sydney Opera House (p54)

1 Striking, unique, curvalicious – is there a sexier building on the planet? Seeing such a recognisable object for the first time is always an odd experience. Depending on where you stand, Jørn Oberg Utzon's Opera House can seem smaller or bigger than you think it's going to be. It confounds expectations but it's never disappointing. Most of all, it's a supremely practical building and what goes on inside (theatre, dance, concerts) can be almost as interesting as the famous exterior.

👁 *Circular Quay & The Rocks*

Sydney Harbour National Park (p73)

2 Spread out around the harbour, this unusual national park offers a widely varied set of experiences, all with a blissful harbour view. In this park, it's equally possible to separate yourself from civilisation or be surrounded by traffic. It incorporates harbour islands, secluded beaches, ancient rock art, lighthouses, untouched headlands and, right in the middle of the city, a historic cottage. You can kayak into otherwise inaccessible beaches or cycle along well-tended paths. Pack a picnic and disappear along its bushy trails. SOUTH HEAD CLIFFS

👁 *Sydney Harbour*

SEVEN OSBORNE / FOX-FOTOS.COM ©

The Rocks (p52)

3 Australia's convict history began here with a squalid canvas shanty town on a rocky shore. Its raucous reputation lives on in atmospheric laneways lined with historic buildings, more than a few of them still operating as pubs. Sure, the place is overrun with tacky, overpriced stores and package tourists, but there are some great museums here as well. When it all gets too much, head through the convict-hewn Argyle Cut (p60) to the less frantically commercial Millers and Dawes Points.

⊙ *Circular Quay & The Rocks*

Bondi Beach (p151)

4 An essential Sydney experience, Bondi Beach offers munificent opportunities for lazing on the sand, lingering in bars and cafes, carving up the surf, splashing about in the shallows and swimming in sheltered pools. Every summer the world comes to Bondi, and what a wonderful world it is. The tightly arranged beach towels form a colourful mosaic, and a walk to the water can reveal a multitude of accents and languages. After dark, the action shifts to accomplished Italian restaurants, quirky wine bars and bustling pubs.

⊙ *Bondi to Coogee*

Sydney's Eateries (p33)

5 Eat to the beat of a city that's shaken off its colonial yoke, broken free of the tyranny of meat-and-two-veg and fallen in love with the flavours of the multitude of cultures that inhabit it. Sydney's dining scene has never been more diverse, inventive and downright exciting. Sure, it can be pretentious, faddish and a little too obsessed with celebrity chefs, but it wouldn't be Sydney if it weren't. It's assuredly not a case of style over substance – Sydney's quite capable of juggling both.
CAFE SOPRA (P63)

✕ *Eating*

Sydney Harbour Bridge *(p55)*

6 Like the Opera House, Sydney's second-most-loved construction inhabits the intersection of practicality and great beauty. The centrepiece of the city's biggest celebrations, the bridge is at its best on New Year's Eve when it erupts in pyrotechnics and the display is beamed into lounge rooms the world over. The views it provides are magnificent, whether you're walking over it or joining a BridgeClimb expedition up and over its central rainbow of steel.

⊙ *Circular Quay &*
The Rocks

Art Gallery of NSW *(p84)*

7 The Art Gallery of NSW's stately neoclassical building doesn't divulge the exuberance of the collection it contains. Step inside and a colourful world of creativity opens up, offering portals into Sydney's history, the outback and distant lands. There's certainly nothing stuffy about the place. All are welcome (including children, who are particularly well catered for), admission is free, and free guided tours help to break down any lingering belief that art is the province of a knowledgable elite. SOL LEWITT'S WALL DRAWING #1091: ARCS, CIRCLES AND BANDS (ROOM) 2003

⊙ *City Centre & Haymarket*

Royal Botanic Gardens (p50)

8 Although the bustle of the city couldn't be closer, these spacious gardens are superbly tranquil – the only visible traffic being the little road-train that whisks people around and the purposeful procession of ferries on the harbour. Whether you're content to spread out a picnic on the lawn or you'd prefer to study the signs on the botanical specimens, it's an idyllic place to hang around for an hour or two.

◉ *Circular Quay & The Rocks*

Aboriginal Rock Art *(p152)*

9 It inevitably comes as a surprise to stumble across an art form that's so ancient in such a modern city, yet Sydney is built on top of a giant gallery. Until recently not much attention was paid to such things and much was covered over or destroyed. But with the dot paintings from distant deserts being celebrated, Sydney-siders have started to wake up to the treasure trove in their own backyard. Look for it on headlands around the harbour, and on the coast and in nearby national parks.

⊙ *Bondi to Coogee*

Taronga Zoo *(p76)*

10 A day trip to Taronga Zoo offers so much more than the zoo itself: running the gauntlet of didgeridoo players and living statues at Circular Quay; the ferry ride past the Opera House and out into the harbour; the cable car from the wharf to the top gate; the ever-present views of the city skyline as you make your way between the enclosures. And to cap it all off, the zoo is excellent too.

⊙ *Sydney Harbour*

What's New

Small Bars

In the last edition of this book we noted that the laws had changed, making it easier for smaller bars to get liquor licenses. We're pleased to report that this has resulted in idiosyncratic new venues flourishing all over Sydney. Best of all are the faux speakeasies, hidden down alleyways (Shady Pines Saloon, Baxter Inn) or even behind fake shopfronts (Stitch). Sydney's bar scene has never been better. (p38)

Mordant Family Wing

Circular Quay's Museum of Contemporary Art was already one of our favourite buildings before this modern $53-million extension was grafted on. (p58)

White Rabbit

Wealthy philanthropists are to thank for Sydney's exciting new free gallery, devoted to Chinese art from the new millennium. (p107)

Eveleigh Farmers' Market

Carriageworks has been pushing artistic boundaries for a few years now, but it's really come into its own with the opening of excellent farmers' and artisans' markets. (p111)

Vivid Sydney

Sydney's most exciting new festival has been illuminating Sydney's most illustrious buildings for only a few years, but it's already a firm favourite on the city's calendar. (p22)

Dugongs

Injured in the wild and unable to be freed for their own safety, this pair of rehabilitated marine mammals are the accidental new stars at Sydney Aquarium. (p100)

Madame Tussauds

She may have been dead for over 160 years, but that hasn't stopped her expanding her empire to Sydney. Is world domination by waxy celebrities inevitable? (p100)

Westfield Sydney

The opening of giant malls often kills established shopping strips, but Westfield's newest offering has done the opposite, injecting new life into Pitt St. (p95)

The Star

Nearly a billion dollars was sunk into rejuvenating Pyrmont's Star City casino. In the process it dropped the 'city' and gained a crop of fancy new restaurants. (p103)

For more recommendations and reviews, see **lonelyplanet.com/ sydney**

Need to Know

Currency
Australian dollar ($)

Language
English

Visas
The only visitors who do not require a visa in advance of arriving in Australia are New Zealanders. There are a variety of visa options (p227).

Money
There are ATMs everywhere and major credit cards are widely accepted.

Mobile Phones
New Zealand and European phones will accept local SIM cards. Quad-band North American handsets will work but need to be unlocked to accept a SIM.

Time
Eastern Standard Time (GMT/ UTC plus 10 hours).

Tourist Information
Sydney Visitor Centre – The Rocks (☑9240 8788; www .sydneyvisitorcentre.com; cnr Argyle & Playfair Sts; ⊙9.30am-5.30pm; ⓡCircular Quay)

Your Daily Budget
The following are average costs per day:

Budget under $190
➡ Dorm beds $23–$48

➡ Hanging out at the beach or free sights

➡ Free hostel breakfasts; burgers or cheap noodles for lunch and dinner; all up $15

Midrange $190–$320
➡ Private room with own bathroom $100–$220

➡ Cafe breakfast and lunch $15 each

➡ Two-course dinner with glass of wine $45

Top end over $320
➡ Four-star hotel from $220

➡ Three-course dinner in top restaurant with wine $120–$200

➡ Opera ticket $150

➡ Taxis $50

Advance Planning
Three months before Book accommodation; make sure your passport, visa and travel insurance are in order.

One month before Book top restaurants; check to see if your visit coincides with any major events and book tickets.

A week before Top up your credit cards; check your bookings are in order and that you have all booking references.

Websites
Destination NSW (www.sydney .com) Official visitors' guide.

City of Sydney (www.cityof sydney.nsw.gov.au) Visitor information, disabled access and parking.

Sydney Morning Herald (www .smh.com.au)

Time Out (www.au.timeout.com/ sydney)

Urban Spoon (www.urbanspoon .com)

Lonely Planet (www.lonely planet.com/sydney)

WHEN TO GO

The peak season is from Christmas until the end of January, which coincides with summer school holidays and the hot weather. Spring (September to November) is dry and warm.

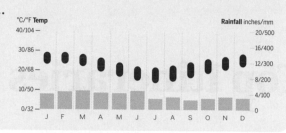

Arriving in Sydney

Sydney Airport Taxis to the city cost up to $50 and depart from the front of the terminals. Airport shuttles head to city hotels for between $6 and $14. Trains depart from beneath the terminal but charge a whopping $17 for the short journey into the city.

Central station Country and interstate trains arrive in Haymarket, at the heart of the city. Follow the signs downstairs to connect to local services or head to Railway Sq for buses.

Sydney Coach Terminal Long-distance coaches stop in front of Central station.

Overseas Passenger Terminal Many cruise ships pull in here, right in the centre of Circular Quay. The train station is nearby.

Barangaroo Smaller ships dock immediately north of King St Wharf, where there are connecting ferry services.

For much more on **arrival,** see p218

Getting Around

If you're here for a week, a MyMulti1 pass will get you most places you'd want to go on trains, ferries, buses and trams. Otherwise buy off-peak return tickets

➡ **Train** Generally the best way to get around, with reliable and reasonably frequent central services.

➡ **Bus** Buses will get you to all the places that trains don't go, such as Bondi and the Eastern Beaches, Vaucluse and Balmoral Beach.

➡ **Light Rail** Connects Central station, Pyrmont and Glebe, but nowhere else you're likely to go.

➡ **Ferries** An excellent way to see the harbour and the best option for getting from the city to Manly, Watsons Bay, Taronga Zoo and Balmain.

For much more on **getting around,** see p218

Sleeping

Sydney is not a cheap city to stay in, and the strong Australian dollar provides no relief for international visitors. This is particularly true for midrange travellers; even many of the hostels charge over $100 for a private room with its own bathroom.

You're best to book well in advance, both to secure your top choice of accommodation and to take advantage of cheaper rates. Weekends are usually busier than weekdays, although the reverse can be true for some of the most business-focused places.

Websites

➡ **Wotif** (www.wotif.com) Bookings, including 'mystery deals'.

➡ **Trip Advisor** (www.trip advisor.com) Unvetted, user-generated ratings for a wide range of accommodation.

➡ **Lonely Planet** (www.lonelyplanet.com/sydney) Traveller forum and listings.

For much more on **sleeping,** see p179

Top Itineraries

Day One

Circular Quay & The Rocks (p52)

 Why postpone joy? Start at Circular Quay and head directly to **Sydney Opera House**. Circle around it and follow the shoreline into the **Royal Botanic Gardens**. Have a good look around and then continue around **Mrs Macquaries Point** and down to Woolloomooloo.

> ✕ **Lunch** Grab a pie at Harry's Cafe de Wheels (p132), a Sydney institution.

City Centre & Haymarket (p82)

 Head up to the **Art Gallery of NSW**. Take some time to explore the gallery then cross **The Domain** and cut through **Sydney Hospital** to Macquarie St. **Parliament House** is immediately to the right, while to the left is the **Mint** and **Hyde Park Barracks**. Cross into **Hyde Park** and head straight through its centre, crossing Park St and continuing on to the **Anzac Memorial**.

> ✕ **Dinner** Catch a cab to Porteño (p121); it doesn't take bookings.

Surry Hills & Darlinghurst (p117)

 After dinner, if you haven't booked tickets for a play at **Belvoir St Theatre** or a gig at the **Gaelic Club**, take a stroll along Crown St. There are plenty of good bars and pubs to stop at along the way.

Day Two

Bondi to Coogee (p149)

 Grab your swimming gear and head to the beach. Catch the bus to **Bondi** and spend some time strolling about and soaking it all in. If the weather's right, stop for a swim. Once you're done, take the clifftop path to **Tamarama** and on to **Bronte**.

> ✕ **Lunch** Detour slightly up to Bronte's excellent Three Blue Ducks (p156).

Bondi to Coogee (p149)

 Continue on the coastal path through **Waverley Cemetery** and down to **Clovelly**. This is a great spot to stop for a swim or a snorkel. Continuing on you'll pass **Gordons Bay** and **Dolphin Point** before you arrive at **Coogee Beach**. Stop for a drink in the beer garden of the **Coogee Bay Hotel** then jump aboard a bus back to Bondi Junction. Shopaholics can have a brief whirl around **Westfield**.

> ✕ **Dinner** Fortify yourself for a Cross blinder at Fratelli Paradiso (p134).

Kings Cross & Potts Point (p130)

 Everyone needs at least one trashy night up the Cross. Start with cocktails at **Jimmy Lik's** or **LL Wine & Dine** before dinner. Back it up with a tipple at **Gazebo Wine Garden** after. Then **Sugarmill**, **Kings Cross Hotel**, **World Bar**...

Day Three

Sydney Harbour (p68)

 Take the scenic ferry ride from Circular Quay to **Watsons Bay**. Walk up to **The Gap**, to watch the waves pounding against the cliffs, then continue on to **Camp Cove** for a dip. Take the **South Head Heritage Trail** for sublime views of the city and the whole of the upper harbour.

Lunch Pull up a pew with a view at the Watsons Bay Hotel (p78).

Circular Quay & The Rocks (p52)

 Head back to Circular Quay and spend the afternoon exploring The Rocks. Start at the **Museum of Metropolitan Art** and then head up into the network of narrow lanes to **The Rocks Discovery Museum**. Continue through the **Argyle Cut** to Millers Point and wander up **Observatory Hill**. Pop into one of Sydney's oldest pubs (maybe the Lord Nelson or Hero of Waterloo) and then cut down to **Walsh Bay** and double back under **Sydney Harbour Bridge**.

Dinner Book well in advance for Sydney's top restaurant, Quay (p62).

Circular Quay & The Rocks (p52)

 If last night was your trashy night, make this your glamorous one. Book a show at **Sydney Opera House** or Walsh Bay, or head straight to **Opera Bar** to be mesmerised by the lights sparkling on the water.

Day Four

Darling Harbour & Pyrmont (p98)

 Have a stroll around the waterfront and settle on whichever of the big attractions takes your fancy – perhaps the **Australian National Maritime Museum**, **Sydney Aquarium** or **Wild Life Sydney**. Each of these will easily fill up an entire morning.

Lunch For a cheap bite, pop up to Central Baking Depot (p91).

Sydney Harbour (p60)

 Jump on the river service at King St Wharf and take an hour-long cruise upstream as far as **Sydney Olympic Park**. Take a stroll around **Newington Nature Reserve** until the next ferry arrives to whisk you back. Stop at **Cockatoo Island** for a look at its art installations and the remnants of its convict and shipbuilding past. From here you can either catch a ferry to **Balmain**, or head straight back to Darling Harbour or Circular Quay.

Dinner Head to Bloodwood (p111).

Inner West (p105)

 After dinner stroll up to King St, **Newtown**, and cruise the late-night bookshops and bars. A short pub-crawl could include **Jester Seeds**, **Corridor**, **Bank Hotel**, **Zanzibar** and **Courthouse Hotel**. Or continue on to the **Sandringham Hotel** to catch a band, or to the **Imperial** for the Priscilla drag show.

If You Like...

Parks & Gardens

Royal Botanic Gardens
Well-tended lawns, interesting botanical collections and ever-present harbour views make this Sydney's most beautiful park. (p56)

Hyde Park A shady avenue of trees, lit with fairy lights at night, makes this an inviting place for a stroll. (p85)

Chinese Garden of Friendship A traditional arrangement of streams, ponds and paths to soothe the city's stresses. (p100)

The Domain Its extensive lawns are used for large-scale public gatherings, while Mrs Macquaries Point offers unforgettable city views. (p86)

Centennial Park Formal bits, wild bits and a whir of joggers, cyclists and horse riders circling the central avenues. (p140)

Nielsen Park A tucked-away, leafy, harbourside park with a blissful shark-netted beach. (p73)

Rushcutters Bay Park Mature trees, tennis courts and yachts bobbing in the marina – and only moments from the chaos of Kings Cross. (p140)

Blue Mountains Botanic Gardens, Mt Tomah The Royal Botanic Gardens' cold-climate collection, including rhododendrons and lots of mature trees. (p168)

Victoria Park At the foot of the university, Victoria Park's formal paths and swimming pool are popular with more than just students. (p107)

Hyde Park Barracks (p85)

Museums

Australian National Maritime Museum Half the museum is moored outside; clamber through a submarine and into the hold of a tall ship. (p100)

Nicholson Museum The university's museum of antiquities is such a hidden gem that most Sydneysiders have never heard of it. (p107)

Sydney Jewish Museum An affecting little museum tracing the history of Judaism in Australia but mainly devoted to the Holocaust. (p119)

The Rocks Discovery Museum A warts-and-all primer for Australia's first proper neighbourhood. (p58)

Susannah Place Museum A reminder that history is as much about the people who lived in slum houses as those who lived in palaces. (p58)

Australian Museum The grand dame of Sydney museums, with historic collections of minerals and bones and an interesting Aboriginal section. (p119)

Museum of Sydney Telling a tale of one city through interactive displays and antique objects. (p89)

Sydney Observatory Capping Observatory Hill, this historic sandstone building has displays of astronomical equipment and indigenous star lore. (p60)

Justice & Police Museum A small museum devoted to the darker side of life in the former convict town. (p57)

Art

Art Gallery of NSW Where the state stashes its greatest treasures; locals are well represented. (p84)

Museum of Contemporary Art Bringing edgy art to the heart of the city. (p58)

White Rabbit A fascinating private collection of contemporary Chinese art, free to all. (p107)

Australian Centre for Photography Not limited to traditional photography, the ACP displays digital, video and multimedia work as well. (p140)

Artspace On the bleeding edge (sometimes literally – ew) of Sydney's art scene. (p132)

SH Ervin Gallery Venerable Millers Point gallery hosting interesting exhibitions of Australian art. (p62)

Object Gallery A small gallery devoted to beautiful things housed in the modernist chapel of a defunct hospital. (p119)

National Art School Students' work is displayed within the slightly spooky sandstone confines of the old Darlinghurst gaol. (p119)

2 Danks Street A collection of reputable commercial galleries sharing a roof with an excellent cafe. (p124)

Brett Whiteley Studio The Art Gallery of NSW keeps this small Surry Hills studio as a memorial to one of Sydney's most accomplished artists. (p119)

Historic Buildings

Vaucluse House William Wentworth's Vaucluse mansion is a rare surviving colonial estate on the harbour's edge. (p73)

Elizabeth Bay House Another harbourside home, built in a gracious Georgian style in the heart of Lizzie Bay. (p132)

Hyde Park Barracks Convict architect Francis Greenway's beautiful prison, housing a fascinating museum. (p85)

For more top Sydney spots, see
➡ Eating (p33)
➡ Drinking & Nightlife (p36)
➡ Entertainment (p39)
➡ Shopping (p44)
➡ Sports & Activities (p46)
➡ Beaches (p31)
➡ Gay & Lesbian Sydney (p41)

Old Government House Part of a cluster of important remnants of the early colony lingering in Parramatta. (p75)

Queen Victoria Building The most unrestrained and ornate survivor of the Victorian era. (p87)

Martin Place A stretch of grand bank buildings and the High Victorian former General Post Office, the most iconic building of its time. (p87)

Town Hall The Victorians may have seemed buttoned up, but not when it came to their buildings, as this exuberant Town Hall attests. (p89)

Elizabeth Farm The farm may be a distant memory, but the grand house still stands; it's Australia's oldest surviving home. (p75)

Victoria Barracks Still used by the military, these Georgian army barracks can be visited on free guided tours. (p140)

Experiment Farm Cottage Emancipated convict James Ruse's farmhouse is a testament to a turning point in Australia's social history. (p75)

Religious Buildings

St Mary's Cathedral Beamed in from Gothic Europe, the grand

Catholic cathedral is awash with colour when the sun hits the stained glass. (p85)

Great Synagogue A mismatch of architectural styles, maybe, but a beautiful one. (p86)

St James' Church Francis Greenway's elegant, understated church is perhaps his crowning achievement. (p85)

Mary MacKillop Place The final resting place of Australia's only Catholic saint, with a small museum about her life. (p76)

Garrison Church Regimental flags brighten the cool interior of this sturdy sandstone church. (p60)

St Andrew's Cathedral Based on York Minster, the city's Anglican cathedral stakes its place in Sydney society next to the Town Hall. (p89)

St Patrick's Church With many Catholics on the convict ships, this handsome sandstone church was the centre of a tightknit community. (p59)

Sze Yup Temple A surprising find on the edge of Glebe, this small Chinese temple is perpetually wreathed in incense. (p107)

20th-Century Architecture

Sydney Opera House One of the world's most recognisable architectural treasures enhances the beauty of the harbour. (p54)

Sydney Harbour Bridge The city's favourite coathanger, the bridge manages to be simultaneously practical, sturdy and surprisingly elegant. (p55)

Australia Square In 1968 this distinctive tower block raised the city's skyline to new aesthetic heights. (p89)

Anzac Memorial Art deco sensibilities lend grace and beauty to this solemn monument. (p85)

Governors Phillip & Macquarie Towers Completed in 1993, the metal 'milk crate', as Governor Phillip Tower is known, added bling to the skyline. (p89)

Wildlife

Taronga Zoo A thoroughly modern establishment, housing its animals in spacious enclosures with million-dollar views. (p76)

Sydney Aquarium Well laid out and fascinating, with giant sharks, rays and, most unusually, dugongs. (p100)

Wild Life Sydney Bringing the outback to the heart of Darling Harbour. (p100)

Oceanworld A slimmed down, cheaper version of Sydney Aquarium, great for entertaining the kids on rainy days in Manly. (p161)

Views

Sydney Tower Eye Towering over absolutely everything, there's no better place to get an overview of the entire city. (p87)

Orbit Order a cocktail and enjoy the vista from the rotating bar at the top of the Australia Square tower. (p93)

Mrs Macquaries Point Jutting out into the harbour, offering the best ground-level views of the Opera House and the city skyline. (p57)

Observatory Hill Trudge up from The Rocks to this grassy knoll and gaze over Walsh Bay to the inner harbour. (p60)

Sydney Park The hill at the centre of this Inner West park offers an intriguing perspective of the city and, in the other direction, Botany Bay. (p110)

Waverley Cemetery A great spot for gazing out to sea and shouting 'thar she blows' whenever you spot a whale. (p152)

Industrial History

Powerhouse Museum The building once generated power for the tram network and is now a shrine to technology. (p107)

Cockatoo Island The detritus of defunct shipyards lends a sculptural quality to the island landscape. (p72)

Walsh Bay Elegant Edwardian warehouses, once part of a bustling port, now housing theatres, restaurants and apartments. (p60)

Woolloomooloo Finger Wharf The wool bales may have gone, but the winches and girders remain. (p132)

Carriageworks Cavernous brick train sheds converted into an edgy arts precinct. (p108)

National Parks

Sydney Harbour National Park Preserving the wild side of the city on numerous headlands and islands. (p73)

Blue Mountains National Park A vast swath of forested wilderness guarding the city's western flank. (p171)

Royal National Park Secluded rivers and beaches amid bush and heath, to the city's south. (p174)

Ku-ring-gai Chase National Park This large untamed area to the north completes the circle of wilderness enclosing the city. (p177)

Lane Cove National Park Encircled by suburbia but rich in wildlife nonetheless. (p163)

Month by Month

TOP EVENTS
....

New Year's Eve,
December

Sydney Mardi Gras,
February/March

**National Rugby League
Grand Final**, September/
October

Sydney Festival, January

Tropfest, February

January

**The peak of the peak
season with school
summer holidays in full
swing, taking advantage
of the long, hot days. On
average this is the hottest
month.**

☆ Sydney Festival

Sydney's premier arts and
culture festival (www
.sydneyfestival.org.au)
offers three weeks of music,
theatre, visual art and
'happenings' around town.

☆ Flickerfest

Bondi's international short-
film festival (www.flicker
fest.com.au) offers shorts,
docos, animation and
workshops, and runs over
10 days in mid-January at
Bondi Pavilion.

☆ Australia Day

On 26 January Sydney-
siders celebrate with picnics,
barbecues, fireworks on the
harbour and, increasingly,
much nationalistic flag waving and drunkenness.

☆ Ferrython

Part of the Sydney Festival,
this delightfully insane
Australia Day contest sees
a fleet of bespangled ferries
race around the harbour.

☆ Big Day Out

The biggest day on the alt-
rock calendar, this touring
festival (www.bigdayout
.com) hits Sydney Olympic
Park on Australia Day.

February

**Almost as hot as January,
but the kids are back at
school, so the beaches are
less crowded. From mid-
February the Mardi Gras
influx arrives.**

☆ Chinese New Year

This three-week Chinatown-
based celebration (www
.sydneychinesenewyear
.com.au) arrives with a bang
(literally) in either January
or February; dragon danc-
ers, dragon-boat races etc.

☆ Tropfest

The world's largest short-
film festival (www.tropfest
.com) is enjoyed from picnic
blankets in The Domain on
the last Sunday in February.

☆ St Jerome's Laneway Festival

A one-day music festival
(www.lanewayfestival.com
.au) held in Rozelle, featuring the hippest international
indie acts just as they're
breaking.

☆ Sydney Mardi Gras

A three-week gay and les-
bian festival (www.mardi
gras.org.au) culminating
in a massive parade and
party on the first Saturday
in March.

March

**March kicks off with the
Mardi Gras parade. The
temperature is still balmy,
but it's traditionally
Sydney's wettest month.
Smells like wet drag queen.**

☆ St Patrick's Day

On March 17 (www.stpat
ricksday.org.au) Sydney-
siders add an 'O' to their
surname and get blotto on
Guinness in The Rocks.

April

As autumn progresses, showers are frequent, but it's not particularly cold. People make the most of the four-day Easter weekend and the two-week school holidays.

✾ Royal Easter Show

Ostensibly an agricultural show, this two-week fiesta (www.eastershow.com.au) features carnival rides, showbags and sugary horrors; held at Sydney Olympic Park.

✝ Sydney Carnival

Sydney's biggest horse-racing carnival (www.ajc .org.au) spans six weeks in March and April. Lawn parties attract arrogant princesses in big hats and drunken blokes in ill-fitted suits.

☆ Sydney Comedy Festival

Wise guys and gals take to the stage at numerous venues for three weeks from late April (www.sydney comedyfest.com.au).

May

Average high temperatures finally dip below 20°C and rainfall remains high, but Sydneysiders take it as an opportunity to dress up and pull out the novels.

🔒 Fashion Week

The gaunt, pert and pubescent tread the catwalk around Circular Quay wearing local designer duds (http://australia.mb fashionweek.com).

☆ Sydney Writers' Festival

Readings and discussions with writers from Australia and overseas; runs for a week in mid-May (www .swf.org.au).

✾ Vivid Sydney

A three-week festival (www .vividsydney.com) of 'light, music and ideas' brightens up Sydney with light installations and multicoloured buildings.

June

Sunshine hours shrink to their lowest levels (an average of 5½ per day) as winter kicks in. The rugby league season keeps passions running hot.

✝ State of Origin Series

Rugby league fans consider this series of three matches between Queensland and New South Wales (NSW) the pinnacle of the game.

☆ Darling Harbour Jazz & Blues Festival

Free jazzy jamboree (www .darlingharbour.com) over the Queen's Birthday long weekend in June.

☆ Sydney Film Festival

This excellent, highly re-garded film festival (www .sff.org.au) screens art-house gems from Australia and around the world.

✾ Yulefest

The Blue Mountains in winter is about as close to a traditional northern-hemisphere Christmas as Sydney gets (www.katoom ba-nsw.com/yulefest.html).

Katoomba holds a Winter Magic Festival (www.winter magic.com.au).

July

The kids escape from school for the first two weeks of Sydney's coldest month, where the daily highs rarely strike above the mid-teens and the lows are in single figures.

◉ Biennale of Sydney

In even-numbered years this two-month international art festival (www .biennaleofsydney.com.au) showcases the bold, the brilliant and the downright mind-boggling.

August

August is chilly but dry – perfect for a run to the beach, but once you get there, you won't be tempted to get in.

✝ City to Surf Run

On the second Sunday in August, 80,000 people run the 14km from Hyde Park to Bondi Beach (www.city 2surf.com.au).

September

Spring brings warming weather and sunny days. September is traditionally Sydney's driest month and daily highs scrape back above 20°C.

◉ Festival of the Winds

Bringing spectacular kites shaped like animals and aliens to Bondi Beach on the second weekend in September.

☆ Queerdoc

The world's largest queer documentary festival (www.queerscreen.com.au), held on the second weekend in September.

October

The pleasant spring weather continues. Workers get the Labour Day long weekend to enjoy it, while school students get the whole first week.

✕ Crave Sydney International Food Festival

A month of food-focused events (www.cravesydney .com), including night noodle markets in Hyde Park and Breakfast on Bondi.

✲ Manly International Jazz Festival

Held on the Labour Day long weekend; the music ranges from traditional to fusion and contemporary.

✶ National Rugby League Grand Final

The NRL season (www.nrl .com.au) culminates with this clash on the Sunday of the long weekend. Sometimes falls in late September.

✲ Sydney Design

Sixteen days of exhibitions, events, talks and markets devoted to young designers' wares; it moves around but is currently scheduled for late October (www .sydneydesign.com.au).

November

November is a great time to visit Sydney. It's usually the sunniest month, averaging nearly eight hours of rays per day, with temperatures warm but rarely scorching.

◉ Sculpture by the Sea

In late October/early November, the cliff-top trail from Bondi Beach to Tamarama transforms into an exquisite sculpture garden (www.sculptureby thesea.com).

☆ Graphic

A weekend devoted to graphic storytelling and art, presented by the Sydney Opera House (www.sydneyoperahouse .com). Features pop-culture luminaries from the music, film and art world.

December

Hello summer! Decembers in Sydney are hot and dry, and for the first three weeks the beaches are free of school holidayers. From Christmas onward things go crazy.

☆ Homebake

This one-day music bash (www.homebake.com.au) in The Domain is a showcase of the best Australian and New Zealand bands.

✲ Bondi Christmas Bash

Sydney's international family of travellers traditionally descends on Bondi Beach on December 25. There's usually a party in the Pavilion.

✶ Sydney to Hobart Yacht Race

On Boxing Day, Sydney Harbour churns with competitors and onlookers for the start of the arduous yacht race (www.rolex sydneyhobart.com).

✲ New Year's Eve

Watch the harbour bridge erupt with pyrotechnic bedazzlement during the annual fireworks displays over Sydney Harbour (www. sydneynewyearseve.com).

With Kids

With boundless natural attractions, a climate favouring outdoor activities and a laid-back inclination, Sydney is a top spot for kids. In summer there are plenty of beaches to keep everyone happy, and when it rains, there are many indoor institutions geared to the junior tourist.

Sydney Aquarium (p100)

Attitudes

Australians are generally tolerant towards children, and while they may not be fawned over as much as in places like Italy or Vietnam, they're not likely to receive a frosty reception either. Most cafes and restaurants are welcoming of well-supervised children, and many have high chairs and special children's menus.

Parents' rooms are the norm in larger shopping centres, offering a discreet space to change a nappy or breastfeed. Most Sydneysiders are relaxed about mothers breastfeeding in public but some continue to disapprove of the practice.

The only place you may come across a blanket ban on children is in some of the quieter B&Bs and boutique hotels.

Beaches

The calm waters of Sydney's harbour beaches are great for kids to splash about in. If you're particularly paranoid about sharks, head to the netted areas at Redleaf Pool, Shark Beach, Balmoral and Manly Cove. But don't feel like you need to stick to the harbour beaches. Most of Sydney's surf beaches have free saltwater pools, meaning that dad can paddle about with the toddlers while mum goes body-surfing.

Parks & Wildlife

Sydney's not short on places to let the kids off the leash. Right in the middle of the city, Darling Harbour's Tumbalong Park (p100) has one of Sydney's best playgrounds. Once you're done you can hitch a ride on the road train (p104) to Wild Life Sydney (p100) and Sydney Aquarium (p100). Better still is the ferry ride to the excellent Taronga Zoo (p76).

Active Pursuits

Bondi's Let's Go Surfing (p151) offers surfing lessons for kids aged seven to 16 – but watch out, you may find that your offspring are suddenly much cooler than you are.

Bike tours are another good way to expend excess energy and prise the teens away from the iPad; try Bike Buffs (p67), Bonza Bike Tours (p67) or Manly Bike Tours (p165). Otherwise you can hire bikes (kids' bikes are widely available) and lead your own pack around Centennial Park (p148) or Sydney Olympic Park (p108).

Sydney Harbour Kayaks (p80) welcomes fit 12-year-olds to its tours, as long as they're accompanied by an adult.

Wet-Weather Lifelines

The museum of most obvious interest to youngsters is Ultimo's science and technology-focused Powerhouse Museum (p107). There are plenty of hands-on experiments to partake in, trains and big chunks of machinery for budding engineers, and an interactive Wiggles exhibition on the bottom floor (watch out for the ear worms!).

If the thought of dragging Johnny around an art gallery fills you with dread, you may be surprised by how child-friendly the Art Gallery of NSW (p84) is. Its *Gallery Kids* program includes free shows on Sundays, tailored discovery trails and self-guided, child-focused iPod tours. You can even book a Tour for Tots.

Twelve-year-old girls are likely to be quite distracted by Rihanna and Lady Gaga at Madame Tussauds (p100), giving mum (or dad) the opportunity to surreptiously siddle up to Hugh Jackman. Directly next door, the Sydney Aquarium (p100) is a fascinating place to fill a few hours finding Nemo, sea dragons, disco-lit jellyfish, dugongs, and gargantuan rays and sharks.

Kids at the House

Cue 'cool dad' eliciting groans from all as he slips into Ali G mode and insists on referring to the Opera House's excellent youth program as 'Kids in da House'. Events include Baby Proms, where proper ballet dancers strut their stuff and put the littlies through their paces (bring your own tutu), Creative Play sessions and children-focused performances. The schedule shifts up a gear during school holidays.

NEED TO KNOW

→ Items such as baby food, formula and disposable nappies are widely available.

→ Mothers have a legal right to breastfeed in public.

→ For an extra cost, car-hire companies will supply and fit child safety seats (compulsory for children under seven).

→ Most accommodation providers can provide cots, but it pays to arrange them in advance.

Family & Children's Tickets

Most sights, entertainment venues and transport providers offer a discount of up to 50% off the full adult rate for children, although the upper age limit can vary widely (anything from 12 to 18 years of age). Many places also let under fives or under threes in for free. Family tickets are common at big attractions, generally covering two adults and two children.

Babysitting

Some of the big hotels offer babysitting services. Otherwise agencies can send babysitters to your hotel, usually for a four-hour minimum (per hour from $20) and a booking fee (from $23); try Nannies & Helpers (www.nanniesandhelpers.com.au) or The Wright Nanny (www.thewright nanny.com.au).

Resources

Scan kiddie shops for copies of *Sydney's Child*, a free magazine listing activities and businesses catering to ankle-biters, or check the online family-events calendar at www.webchild.com.au. For more general information, snag a copy of Lonely Planet's *Travel with Children*.

Like a Local

In most parts of Sydney, locals are firmly in the majority, even at that perennial tourist favourite Bondi Beach. Ditch the tour group, unstrap the bum bag (don't ever call it a fanny pack!) and step away from The Rocks – before you know it, you'll have blended right in.

ANDREW WATSON / GETTY IMAGES ©

Surfer heading to Manly Beach (p161)

Dining Out Like a Local

Unless it's a very special occasion locals don't dine at Circular Quay or The Rocks. And unless they barely venture into the central city or have out-of-towners to entertain, they shun Darling Harbour as well. Those in-the-know head to reliable Surry Hills or to that just-opened place that everybody's been talking about in one of the hip inner suburbs or near the beaches. For those seeking cheap eats, Chinatown is the standby, or they'll rock up to their tried-and-true neighbourhood favourite or local pub.

But above all, locals head to cafes. Oh, the comfort of settling into the reliable local where staff make a decent flat white without bubbling the milk, serve consistently good food without charging the earth and always have a newspaper to read. For many urban Sydneysiders, brunch has replaced religious services as the main weekend ritual. And if not brunch, then yum cha.

Drinking Like a Local

Australians have a bad reputation for binge drinking, particularly when they're overseas, but generally you'll find Sydney pubs and bars pleasant places to be. Sure, Kings Cross can be unpleasant on weekends, but that is precisely the neighbourhood that soon-to-be-vomiting types gravitate towards. Licensing laws punish venues that serve drunks, so you're more likely to see this kind of behaviour on the streets than in the bars themselves.

The British-style local pub survives throughout the city, although you're less likely to see cross-generational family groupings in them than you would in the 'mother country'. The local passion for sport and the monopoly of coverage by pay-TV operators makes the pub a popular place whenever the local side is playing.

Hipsters gravitate to the new crop of small bars in Surry Hills, Darlinghurst and the city, while those wanting to give their glad rags an airing might make for a cocktail bar with a harbour view.

Shopping Like a Local

The advent of the mega-mall has killed many a neighbourhood shopping strip. Once exclusively the province of supermarkets, midpriced chain stores and bain-marie food courts, malls like giant Westfield Sydney and Westfield Bondi Junction have added designer boutiques and fancy dining to the mix. Paddington, the former go-to neighbourhood for fashion, is still holding on...just. For a day of shopping escapism, the central city is still the destination of choice. But you won't find locals shopping in The Rocks or Darling Harbour.

Beach-Going Like a Local

By and large, Sydney's beaches are full of locals – even Bondi. Australia has one of the highest skin-cancer rates in the world – nearly four times greater than the USA's. Consequently sunbaking is less popular than it used to be, and many locals will head to the beach early in the morning or late in the afternoon to avoid the worst of the sun. Once they get there, they'll lather up in extremely high SPF sunscreen and cover the kids in protective clothing. Sydneysiders aren't overly bothered by the possibility of shark attacks. The last fatal attack in the harbour was in 1963; surfers face more of a risk.

Local Obsessions

Sport

Enough already! Sports coverage takes up half the news broadcasts, a fair chunk of the daily paper and most of the weekend TV programming. Tribal affiliations run the deepest in rugby league, so knowing who to barrack for will stand you in good stead. If you're in the Eastern Suburbs (particularly the beaches), it's the mighty Roosters; in Surry Hills, Redfern or Erskineville, the Rabbitohs; in Balmain, the Tigers; in

NEED TO KNOW

The city's premier eating guide is the annual *Good Food Guide* put out by the *Sydney Morning Herald*. The book awards 'chef's hats' in much the same way as Michelin awards stars: a 'three-hatted' restaurant is the pinacle of good dining. The *SMH* also publishes *Good Cafe Guide* and *Good Pub Food Guide*.

Cronulla, the Sharks; in Parramatta, the Eels; and in Manly, the Sea Eagles.

Food

Sydney foodies constantly read reviews, gossip about what's hot and what's gone off the boil, and hang out for the annual update of the *Good Food Guide* so they can religiously work their way through the places they haven't been to. Switch on the TV and chances are it'll either be a food or a sports show.

Property Prices

Did you hear how much an unrenovated one-bedroom terrace house went for last week in Erskineville? Don't worry, you soon will. With housing affordability extremely low, property obsession is at an all-time high.

Celebrities

Sure there are some fair-dinkum stars that live in Sydney, but Sydneysiders are just as fascinated by the personal lives of chefs, football players, radio jocks, former reality-TV contestants, all of the above's ex-partners and stylists, their local crime boss...

Keeping Fit

How much do you bench? I hear that jogging on the sand does wonders for the butt. Have you tried sweaty yoga yet? How's the diet going? You lost 5kg by switching to low-carb beer!? Can't talk, I'm off to jog around The Domain in my lunchbreak.

For Free

In Sydney, many of the very best things in life really are for free – especially in summer, when lazing around in the sun is one of the city's priceless pleasures.

PHILIP QUIRK / GETTY IMAGES ©

Southern right whale in Sydney Harbour (p68)

Beaches

This ain't the Mediterranean. There are no tightly arranged lines of deckchairs awaiting your paying pleasure at Sydney beaches. Lazing on the beach is part of the Australian birthright and one that's freely available to anyone who cares to roll out their towel. Many of the beaches have ocean pools carved out of the rocks on their headlands and almost all of those are free as well. And if you forget to bring sunblock, ask the surf lifesavers. Chances are they'll give you some. For free. In between patrolling the beach. Also for free.

Parks

A climate like this encourages enjoyment of the great outdoors and if you can manage to drag yourself off the beach, there are plenty of parks to enjoy. Aside from those national parks that have vehicle entry fees, entry to parks is free as well. Noteworthy examples are the lovingly maintained grounds of the Royal Botanic Gardens (p56) and the capacious spaces of Centennial Park (p140).

If you've got kids, there's an excellent free playground at Tumbalong Park (p100) in Darling Harbour. Also check out the cute little Neild Avenue Maze (p140) in Paddington.

Wildlife

Contrary to popular stereotypes you're unlikely to see a kangaroo bounding down George St. There are, however, plenty of native critters to be spotted if you know where to look. Mrs Macquaries Point (p57) is a good place to see sulphur-crested cockatoos. Keep an eye on the sky for the twilight flyover of swarms of bats (greyheaded flying foxes, to be exact).

Water dragons can be spotted sunning themselves in Lane Cove National Park (p163) and in the bush around Parsley Bay (p73), while you might be lucky enough to come across a goanna on the Manly Scenic Walkway (p162).

Whales pass along the coast between May and December and it's surprisingly easy to spot their spouts from the tops of cliffs – grab a perch at Waverley Cemetery (p152) and keep an eye out for the whale-watching boats. Snorkelling is rewarding both in the harbour and on the coast. One of the best spots is Gordons Bay (p152), where a free underwater nature trail has been set up.

Free Art

If you're an art fan on a tight budget, you're in for a treat. Most of Sydney's big public galleries are free and there are dozens of commerical galleries in Paddington, Woollahra and Danks St in Waterloo, which welcome eager browsers.

At the top of the heap is the Art Gallery of NSW (p84) and the associated Brett Whiteley Studio (p119). As well as free admission to a wonderful repository of art, it offers kids free IPod tours and Sunday performances. The Museum of Contemporary Art (p58) comes a close second; special exhibitions are charged but most rooms are free. Rounding out the top three is White Rabbit (p107), a private collection of contemporary Chinese art, also generously displayed for free.

Other excellent free galleries include Artspace (p132), the Australian Centre for Photography (p140), Sherman Contemporary Art Foundation (p140), Object Gallery (p119) and the student galleries at the University of Sydney (p107) and National Art School (p119).

Free Museums

Although the big museums have admission charges, many of the smaller ones don't. One of the very best of these is Sydney University's Nicholson Museum (p107), with its fascinating collection of antiquities.

The Rocks Discovery Museum (p58) provides an excellent (and completely free) introduction to Sydney's oldest neighbourhood, and you can follow this up with a visit to the free archaeological displays at nearby Cadman's Cottage (p58) and The Big Dig (p59). Up the hill, Sydney Observatory (p60) has interesting exhibits, although you'll need to pay for astronomy sessions.

You'll also find a small military museum hidden away within the Anzac Memorial

(p85) in Hyde Park, and a Rail Heritage Centre within Central station (p90). In Manly, the Manly Art Gallery & Museum (p161) and the museum at the old quarantine station (p161) on North Head, are both free.

Free Tours

Free guided tours are offered at the Art Gallery of NSW, the Royal Botanic Gardens and at the historic Victoria Barracks (p140) in Paddington. It doesn't cost a cent to wander the streets, and with that in mind we've put together a series of walking tours in our neighbourhood chapters to guide you on your way. Additionally, Walsh Bay (p60) offers a downloadable self-guided shuffle around its historic wharves.

While they're only completely free to the most hard-hearted, both I'm Free (p97) and Peek Tours (p67) offer three-hour walking tours of the inner city, which the enthusiastic guides work for tips.

Free Classical Music

Lunchtime is the right time to enjoy the talent of classical musicians for nothing – particularly Wednesday lunchtime, it seems. The Sydney Conservatorium of Music (p58), St James' Church near Hyde Park and St Andrew's Cathedral all offer regular Wednesday concerts. St Andrew's also has lunchtime performances on Mondays and Fridays, and the Town Hall has lunchtime organ recitals monthly. Both the city's cathedrals (St Andrew's and St Mary's) have excellent choirs and organists, which can be heard performing at selected services.

Free Pub Entertainment

On any given night of the week you can catch a band for the price of a drink at any of dozens of pubs around the city. Of course, things ramp up towards the weekend. There are too many to list here (we've flagged the best options in the Drinking & Nightlife sections of our neighbourhood chapters), but hot spots include The Rocks, the city centre, Darling Harbour, Newtown, Annandale, Balmain, Surry

Customs House (p57), Circular Quay

Significant Structures

Many of Sydney's most beautiful old buildings are open to the public, including the Customs House (p57), the Mint (p86), the State Library (p86), Government House (p56) and the Town Hall (p89). For added entertainment, visit Parliament House (p86) on sitting days. Window-shoppers can get free thrills perusing the exquisite Queen Victoria Building (p87) and the Strand Arcade (p95). And then, of course, there are the churches: St Mary's Cathedral (p85), St James' Church (p85) and St Andrew's Cathedral (p89) being the best of them.

While you can't just go traipsing through the Opera House (p54) if you're not on a tour or watching a performance, you can scramble all over it. Then you can walk over that other great icon of the city, the Sydney Harbour Bridge (p55), and wander through the sinister clown gate of Luna Park (p76; entry is free, rides are charged).

Hills and Kings Cross. Plenty of pubs also enlist DJs on the weekends, blurring the line between pub and club but with the added advantage of having no cover charge (usually).

Pub quiz is a tried and true tactic to get punters through the doors midweek, while some establishments offer more unusual incentives (life-drawing classes, crab races, poker or snooker comps, comedy, drag shows and the like).

Free Bus

Jump on bus 555 for a free loop around the inner city.

Free Wireless Internet

Unlike many countries, where free connections aren't hard to come by, you'll have to try a little harder for a cheap hook-up here. McDonald's, Starbucks and public libraries are a good bet, along with some shopping centres, cafes and bars.

Cheap Alternatives

For views, put on some snazzy threads and zip up to Blu Bar (p64), on the 36th floor of the Shangri-La hotel, or Orbit (p93), on the 47th floor of the Australia Square tower (Orbit has the advantage of rotating). They're not cheap bars but a cocktail will cost less than the price of visiting Sydney Tower.

Rather than booking an expensive harbour cruise, grab a ferry to Manly to explore the outer harbour and a Parramatta River service to head upstream.

Dining Discounts

While there's no such thing as a free lunch at Sydney's fine-dining restaurants, you can save a pretty penny at some of them if you know when to go. Marque (p121) in Surry Hills offers set three-course Friday lunches that are half the price you'll pay for the regular menu. Guillaume at Bennelong (p62) and Aria (p62), the two closest restaurants to the Opera House, both offer cheaper pretheatre menus.

Beaches

Whether you join the procession of the bronzed and the beautiful at Bondi, or surreptitiously slink into a deserted nook hidden within Sydney Harbour National Park, the beach is an essential part of the Sydney experience. Even in winter, watching the rollers break while you're strolling along the sand is exhilarating.

Beach Culture

In the mid-1990s an enthusiastic business-woman obtained a concession to rent loungers on Tamarama Beach and offer waiter service. Needless to say, it didn't last long. Even at what was considered at the time to be Sydney's most glamorous beach, nobody was interested in that kind of malarkey.

For Australians, going to the beach is all about rolling out a towel on the sand with a minimum of fuss. And they're certainly not prepared to pay for the privilege. Sandy-toed ice-cream vendors are acceptable; martini luggers are not. In summer one of the more unusual sights is the little ice-cream boat pulling up to Lady Bay (and other harbour beaches) and a polite queue of nude gentle-men forming to purchase their icy pops.

Surf lifesavers have a hallowed place in the culture and you'd do well to heed their instructions, not least of all because they're likely to be eminently sensible and in your best interest. It's not coincidental that the spark for racist riots in Cronulla a few years back was an attack on this oh-so-Australian institution.

Ocean Pools

If you've got kids, shark paranoia or surf isn't your thing, Sydney's blessed with a string of 40 man-made ocean pools up and down the coast, most of them free. Some, like Mahon Pool, are what are known as bogey holes – natural-looking rock pools where you can safely splash about and snorkel, even while the surf surges in. Others are more like swimming pools. Bondi's Icebergs is a good example of this kind.

Surfing

Sydney has been synonymous with surfing ever since the Beach Boys effused about 'Australia's Narrabeen' in 'Surfin' USA' (Narrabeen is one of Sydney's northern beaches). For updates on what's breaking where, see www.coastalwatch.com or www.realsurf.com.

Beaches by Neighbourhood

⇒ **Sydney Harbour (p68)** Lots of hidden coves, getting progressively better the further from the city you go.

⇒ **Bondi to Coogee (p149)** High cliffs frame one golden-sand surf beach after another.

⇒ **Manly (p159)** Straddling harbour and ocean with beaches to suit all requirements.

⇒ **Royal National Park (p174)** Isolated, often empty beaches with great surf breaks, but unpatrolled and sometimes dangerous.

⇒ **Northern Beaches (p176)** A steady succession of great surf beaches stretching for nearly 30km.

NEED TO KNOW

If you're not used to swimming at surf beaches, you may be unprepared for the dangers.

➡ Always swim between the red-and-yellow flags on lifesaver-patrolled beaches. Not only are these areas patrolled, they're positioned away from dangerous rips and underwater holes. Plus you're much less likely to get clobbered by a surfboard.

➡ If you get into trouble, hold up your hand to signal the lifesavers.

Lonely Planet's Top Choices

Bondi Beach (p151) Australia's most famous and best ocean beach.

Shark Beach (p73) The pick of the harbour beaches, hidden within leafy Neilsen Park.

Clovelly Beach (p152) Despite the concrete, this is a magical swimming and snorkelling spot, and has great bars.

Whale Beach (p177) Peachy-coloured sand and crashing waves, near the top of the Northern Beaches.

Lady Bay (p73) Discreetly tucked under South Head, this is the best of the nude beaches.

Best Harbour Beaches

Camp Cove (p72)

Balmoral Beach (p78)

Store Beach (p161)

Parsley Bay (p73)

Manly Cove (p161)

Best Ocean Beaches

Bronte Beach (p152)

Palm Beach (p178)

Manly Beach (p161)

Tamarama Beach (p152)

Bilgola (p177)

Best Ocean Pools

Mahon Pool (p155)

Fairy Bower Beach (p161)

Giles Baths (p154)

Ross Jones Memorial Pool (p154)

Bondi Icebergs (p151)

Best for Surfing

Curl Curl (p163)

Narrabeen (p177)

Tamarama Beach (p152)

Cronulla (p156)

Garie Beach (p175)

Best for Snorkelling

Gordons Bay (p152)

Bundeena (p175)

North Bondi (p151)

Camp Cove (p72)

Freshwater (p163)

Best Hidden Beaches

Store Beach (p161)

Parsley Bay (p73)

Washaway Beach (p163)

Reef Beach (p163)

Bilgola (p177)

Best for Cafes

Bronte Beach (p152)

Manly Cove (p161)

Balmoral Beach (p78)

Palm Beach (p178)

Freshwater (p163)

Best for Bars

Watsons Bay (p72)

Manly Cove (p161)

Coogee Beach (p152)

Manly Beach (p161)

Best for Picnics

Parsley Bay (p73)

Bronte Beach (p152)

Watsons Bay (p72)

Tamarama Beach (p152)

Coogee Beach (p152)

Best for Public Tranport

Manly Cove (p161)

Manly Beach (p161)

Cronulla (p156)

Watsons Bay (p72)

Redleaf Pool (p74)

Eating

Sydney's cuisine rivals that of any world city. Melbourne makes a big deal of its Mediterranean melting pot, but Sydney truly celebrates Australia's place on the Pacific Rim, marrying the freshest local ingredients with the flavours of Asia, the Americas and, of course, its colonial past. For more information, refer to the Food Culture chapter.

Where to Eat

Sydney's top restaurants are properly pricey, but eating out needn't be expensive. There are plenty of ethnic eateries where you can grab a cheap, zingy pizza or a bowl of noodles. Judicious ordering can even land you an affordable meal at some of Sydney's superchef restaurants – try brunch at bills (p125) or share vegetarian dishes at Billy Kwong (p122). Cafes are a good bet for a solid, often adventurous and usually reasonably priced meal.

Cooking Courses

If your relationship with food goes beyond mere hunger, several seminars enable you to expand your culinary repertoire while slipping some fine food and wine under your belt.

One of the city's best providores, **Simon Johnson** (☎8244 8220; www.simonjohnson.com; 24a Ralph St, Alexandria; course $55-130), runs the excellent 'Talk Eat Drink' series, featuring two-hour classes with leading chefs at its base 5km south of the city centre. They're usually held on Thursday or Saturday morning from 10.30am.

The Sydney Fish Market (p101) attracts 13,000 people per year to its fish-focused 'Sydney Seafood School' sessions. Courses start from $85 and run from 11am to 3pm on weekends and from 6.30pm to 8.30pm about three nights per week.

For a less high-falutin' experience, **Bar-Be School** (☎1300 227 745; www.bbqschool.com.au; 491 Willoughby Rd, Willoughby) runs a series of three sessions for a hefty $299 (or single sessions for $120), where you mull over the finer points of barbecuing meat, seafood and veggie skewers, and then eat the results. The three-hour classes are held in various locations from 11.30am or 3.30pm on Saturday and Sunday.

Drinking & BYO

Most of Sydney's licensed restaurants have a respectable wine list, with an understandable emphasis on Australian product. There's almost always at least a handful of wines sold by the glass as well, and better establishments have sommeliers who can

---

SELF-CATERING

Coles and Woolworths have supermarkets everywhere, many with attached bottle shops. Some are open 24 hours or until midnight. Excellent providores, with a handful of branches, include Simon Johnson and Fratelli Fresh (p135). Paddy's Markets (p97) has a large produce section, while the Eveleigh Farmers' Market (p111) and EQ Village Markets (p147) are better for fancy fare.

NEED TO KNOW

Opening Hours

Cafes and restaurants generally open seven days a week. If they do close, it's usually on a Sunday night or Monday. In this book, opening hours are listed in individual reviews only when they vary significantly from the standard opening hours, as described below:

➡ Cafes: 8am–4pm.

➡ Restaurants: lunch noon–3pm, dinner 6–10pm.

Price Ranges

We've classified our eating reviews using the dollar symbols below, based on the cheapest main meal or its equivalent offered in the establishment.

$	under $12
$$	from $12 to $30
$$$	over $30

Reservations

Most restaurants take reservations for lunch and dinner. Book at least a week ahead for the best restaurants, although you might sneak in with less notice, particularly for a midweek lunch. For 'iconic' restaurants, such as Quay and Tetsuya's, book a month ahead. Conversely, some Sydney restaurants don't take bookings at all; if you're prepared to wait a couple of hours, you'll snaffle a table.

Tipping

Tipping isn't compulsory in Australia, but if the service is passable most folks tip 10% (particularly at better restaurants). If anything gets on your goat, you don't have to tip at all. Tipping isn't expected at cafes where you order and pay at the counter, but there's often a jar where customers can sling loose change.

help you make the best possible food and wine match. Restaurant prices are usually about double as much as you'd pay in a bottle shop (liquor store).

Sydney is blessed with enlightened licensing laws that allow you to BYO (bring your own) wine and sometimes beer to those restaurants with a BYO licence. You'll usually be charged a corkage fee (even if your bottle's got a screw cap) at either a per-person or per-bottle rate, but it's generally cheaper than choosing off the wine list.

Eating by Neighbourhood

➡ **Circular Quay & The Rocks (p62)** Sydney's best and priciest fine-dining restaurants, many with a harbour view and a famous chef.

➡ **Sydney Harbour (p78)** A handful of gems make the most of harbourside locations in this amorphous area.

➡ **City Centre & Haymarket (p90)** Ranges from expense-account fine dining to all-hours dim sum; Chinatown is truly pan-Asian.

➡ **Darling Harbour & Pyrmont (p103)** Touristy and overpriced, with some notable exceptions.

➡ **Inner West (p110)** Affordable multicultural eateries and serious coffee temples, with the odd fine-diner thrown in.

➡ **Surry Hills & Darlinghurst (p121)** Sydney's gastronomic heartland, with chefs pushing boundaries in all directions for a mainly local clientele.

➡ **Kings Cross & Potts Point (p132)** Chilled-out neighbourhood cafes in leafy streets and a frantic strip of all-night takeaways.

➡ **Paddington & Centennial Park (p142)** Gastropubs, chic cafes and white-linen restaurants lurking along tree-lined back streets.

➡ **Bondi to Coogee (p155)** Cool cafes catering to surfers and beachside brunchsters, and a handful of prominent ocean-gazing establishments.

➡ **Manly (p163)** Plenty of average family-focused eateries and a clutch of good cafes and switched-on restaurants.

Lonely Planet's Top Choices

Quay (p62) Inventive fine dining with the best views in Sydney.

Porteño (p121) Delicious slow-cooked meat and bucketloads of atmosphere.

Three Blue Ducks (p156) The sort of creative cafe fare that Sydney excels in.

Chat Thai (p92) Reasonably priced, loaded with flavour and constantly buzzing.

Sepia (p90) Japanese-influenced fine dining at the top of its game.

Best by Budget

$
Spice I Am (p122)
Mamak (p92)
House (p121)
Danks Street Depot (p124)
Le Monde (p121)

$$
Spice Temple (p91)
Longrain (p121)
Rockpool Bar & Grill (p91)
North Bondi Italian Food (p155)
Bar H (p121)

$$$
Marque (p121)
est. (p91)
Tetsuya's (p90)
Universal (p124)

Best by Cuisine

Modern Australian
Marque (p121)
est. (p91)
Rockpool (p62)
Four in Hand (p142)
Bentley Restaurant & Bar (p122)

French
Guillaume at Bennelong (p62)
Bistro Moncur (p143)
Felix (p91)
Bathers' Pavilion (p78)

Italian
Pilu at Freshwater (p164)
Icebergs Dining Room (p155)
Otto Ristorante (p135)
Cafe Sopra (p124)
North Bondi Italian Food (p155)

Chinese
Spice Temple (p91)
Billy Kwong (p122)
Bar H (p121)
East Ocean (p92)
Golden Century (p92)

Thai
Longrain (p121)
Spice I Am (p122)
House (p121)
Sailors Thai Canteen (p63)

Latin American
El Capo (p123)
Norfolk on Cleveland (p123)
Guzman y Gomez (p112)
El Loco (p123)

Best Cafes
Single Origin Roasters (p122)
Le Monde (p121)
Deus Cafe (p110)
fouratefive (p122)
Danks Street Depot (p124)

Best Bakeries & Patisseries
Adriano Zumbo (p103)
Central Baking Depot (p91)
Black Star Pastry (p111)
Bourke Street Bakery (p122)
Sonoma (p143)

Best Seafood
Pier (p78)
Boathouse on Blackwattle Bay (p110)
Fish Face (p124)
Golden Century (p92)
Kingfish Bistro (p112)

Best Tapas
Bodega (p122)
Ash St Cellar (p91)
Bloodwood (p111)
Firefly (p63)

Best Local Chains
Adriano Zumbo (p103)
Cafe Sopra & Fratelli Fresh (p124)
Sonoma (p143)
Guzman y Gomez (p112)
Sabbaba (p156)

Drinking & Nightlife

In a city where rum was once the currency of choice, it's little wonder that drinking plays a big part in the Sydney social scene – whether it's knocking back some tinnies at the beach, schmoozing after work or warming up for a night on the town. Sydney offers plenty of choice in drinking establishments, from the flashy to the trashy.

The Sydney Scene

Sydneysiders are generally gregarious and welcoming of visitors, and the easiest place to meet them is at the pub. Most inner-city suburbs have retained their historic corner pubs – an appealing facet of British life the colonists were loathe to leave behind. The addition of beer gardens has been an obvious improvement, as has the banning of smoking from all substantially enclosed licensed premises.

Until recently NSW licensing laws made it hard to set up small wine bars and hole-in-the-wall cocktail lounges, but a recent relaxation has seen a blooming of such establishments, particularly in the city centre.

Poker machines ('pokies' in the local lingo) are the scourge of Sydney pubs, changing many a lovely local into a circus of flashing lights, beeps, whistles and hypnotised gamblers. It's a brave licensee who forgoes this cash cow in favour of a more pleasant drinking environment, but bigger complexes at least have the luxury of hiding them in the corner.

The cheapest places to drink are at the Returned & Services League (RSL) clubs. In a tourist-friendly irony, locals are barred unless they're members, but visitors who live more than 5km away are welcome (you'll need to bring proof).

What to Wear

Sydney can be flashy, but it's also very casual. Men will nearly always get away with tidy jeans, T-shirts and trainers. Thongs (flip-flops, jandals), singlets (vests) and shorts are usually fine in pubs in the daytime, but incur the ire of security staff after dark. Women can generally wear whatever the hell they like, and many take this as an excuse to wear as little as possible.

Live Music & DJs

Since the 1950s Sydney has been hip to jazz, and in the 1970s and '80s, Aussie pub rock became a force to be reckoned with. Although Sydney fell into a house-induced haze in the '90s, live music is making a comeback. You can catch bands any night of the week in dozens of inner-city pubs. Check

A NIGHT ON THE TILES

Most of Sydney's older pubs are clad in glazed tiles, often with beautifully coloured art-nouveau designs. Why? Prior to drinking law reform in the mid-1950s, pubs shut their doors at 6pm, before which after-work drinkers would storm in and chug down as many beers as quickly as possible – the six o'clock swill. Publicans discovered pretty quickly that it's easier to hose slopped beer, vomit and urine from glazed tiles.

the free street mags (*Drum Media, Brag*) and Friday's Metro section of the *Sydney Morning Herald* for listings.

Sydney's obsession with dance music was born out of the gay scene's legendary shindigs: Mardi Gras, Sleaze Ball and numerous other megaparties. The cross-over into mainstream culture in the 1990s coincided with the worldwide house and hip-hop explosion and a flood of Ecstasy tablets.

If you feel like tying one on, you'll have no problems finding a place to do the tying. As well as a few world-class clubs, plenty of upmarket bars have DJs and dance floors. This isn't New York or London where you can party any night of the week, but if you just can't control your feet, there are plenty of options from Wednesday through Sunday.

Drinking & Nightlife by Neighbourhood

➡ **Circular Quay & The Rocks (p64)** Historic pubs and glam harbour-facing bars galore.

➡ **Sydney Harbour (p78)** Great old pubs in Balmain and a handful of prominent venues scattered about elsewhere.

➡ **City Centre & Haymarket (p92)** Fancy watering holes for after-work execs, and hip speakeasies in back alleys.

➡ **Darling Harbour & Pyrmont (p104)** Big brash booze dens full of suburban kids and suited city slickers.

➡ **Inner West (p112)** Diverse venues catering to students, bohomians, politicos, punks, lesbians, gay dudes and live-music lovers.

➡ **Surry Hills & Darlinghurst (p125)** Gay bars, hipster havens, schmickly renovated pubs and interesting little backstreet bars.

➡ **Kings Cross & Potts Point (p135)** Legendary late-night locale for all things seedy, shady, trashy and boozy.

➡ **Paddington & Centennial Park (p143)** Upmarket old pubs and classy wine bars for would-be fashionistas.

PLAN YOUR TRIP DRINKING & NIGHTLIFE

NEED TO KNOW

Opening Hours

➡ Pubs and bars: roughly 11am–midnight; later on weekends and in livelier areas; some open 24 hours.

➡ Clubs: 10pm–5am Wednesday to Saturday; most are busiest after midnight.

Beer Sizes

Traditional Sydney pubs serve middies (285mL) and schooners (425mL), while pints (570mL) are the domain of Anglo-Celtic theme pubs. Australian pubs abandoned pints long ago because beer would go warm in the summer heat before you'd finished your glass. Arm yourself with this invaluable local insight and order a schooner instead.

Tipping

Tipping in bars is very unusual, so you should feel under no obligation to do so. The only possible exceptions are where there has been a considerable amount of table service (more than just delivering drinks and clearing empties) or where fancy cocktails are concocted.

Door Policies

➡ It is against the law to serve people who are intoxicated and you won't be admitted to a venue if you appear drunk.

➡ If security staff suspect that you're under the legal drinking age (18), you'll be asked to present photo ID with proof of your age.

➡ Some gay bars have a 'no open-toed shoes' policy, ostensibly for safety (to avoid broken glass), but sometimes invoked to keep straight women out.

➡ **Bondi to Coogee (p156)** Big, boozy beach bars full of Brit backpackers, Irish larrikins and Latin lovers.

➡ **Manly (p164)** Large pubs with water views for a post-beach refresher or a weekend rave-up.

Lonely Planet's Top Choices

Stitch (p92) A modern-day speakeasy hidden beneath the city's streets.

Pocket (p126) Alternative music, hip decor, comfy couches and table service.

Hinky Dinks (p126) *Happy Days* are here again in this 1950s-themed cocktail bar.

Baxter Inn (p92) Whiskies by the dozen in a back-alley hideaway.

Bank Hotel (p113) Snazzily renovated pub catering to multiple Newtown subcultures.

Best Cocktails

Victoria Room (p126)

Eau-de-Vie (p126)

Shady Pines Saloon (p126)

Zeta (p94)

Grandma's (p93)

Best for Beer

Lord Nelson Brewery Hotel (p64)

Redoak Boutique Beer Cafe (p94)

Bavarian Bier Café (p94)

Australian Hotel (p64)

Opera Bar (p64)

Best Wine Bars

Wine Library (p143)

10 William Street (p143)

Bambini Wine Room (p92)

Gazebo Wine Garden (p137)

The Winery (p126)

Best Views

Orbit (p93)

Blu Bar on 36 (p64)

Opera Bar (p64)

Icebergs Bar (p157)

North Bondi RSL (p156)

Best Outdoor Drinking

Beresford Hotel (p125)

Opera Bar (p64)

Courthouse Hotel (p113)

Manly Wharf Hotel (p164)

Ivy (p93)

Best Historic Pub

Hero of Waterloo (p64)

Lord Nelson Brewery Hotel (p64)

Courthouse Hotel (p113)

Old Fitzroy Hotel (p137)

Exchange Hotel (p79)

Best Small Bars

Grandma's (p93)

Hive (p114)

Shady Pines Saloon (p126)

Jester Seeds (p113)

Corridor (p113)

Best for Glamour

Establishment (p93)

Ivy (p93)

Waterbar (p137)

Zeta (p94)

Marble Bar (p93)

Best for Kooky Decor

Ruby Rabbit (p127)

Shady Pines Saloon (p126)

Grandma's (p93)

The Winery (p126)

Tio's Cerveceria (p126)

Best for Live Rock

Annandale Hotel (p113)

Sandringham Hotel (p113)

Oxford Art Factory (p126)

FBi Social, Kings Cross Hotel (p135)

Good God Small Club (p93)

Best for Live Jazz & Blues

Basement (p66)

Venue 505 (p126)

Vanguard (p113)

Empire Hotel (p113)

Hero of Waterloo (p64)

Best Clubs

Good God Small Club (p93)

Chinese Laundry (p93)

Soho (p136)

Arq (p127)

Home (p104)

Best Sunday Sessions

Beresford Hotel (p125)

Watsons Bay Hotel (p78)

Clovelly Hotel (p157)

Gazebo Wine Garden (p137)

Kit & Kaboodle (p136)

Entertainment

Take Sydney at face value and it's tempting to unfairly stereotype its good citizens as shallow and a little narcissistic. But take a closer look: the arts scene is thriving, sophisticated and progressive – it's not a complete accident that Sydney's definitive icon is an opera house!

Theatre

Sydney doesn't have a dedicated theatre district, but that doesn't mean theatre lovers miss out. The city offers a vigorous calendar of productions from Broadway shows to experimental theatre at venues across the inner city.

Classical Music

There's a passionate audience for classical music in Sydney. Without having the extensive repertoires of European cities, Sydney offers plenty of inspired classical performances – offering the perfect excuse to check out the interior of those famous harbourside sails.

Dance

Dance and Sydney's body-focused audiences go hand in hand (and cheek to cheek). Australian dancers have a reputation for awesome, fearless physical displays. Performances range from traditional ballet with tutus and bulging tights to edgy, liberating 'physical theatre'.

Opera

Despite its small population, Australia has produced some of the world's best opera singers, including Dames Nellie Melba and Joan Sutherland. The Opera House may be the adored symbol of Sydney, but supporting such a cost-heavy art form is difficult. New and more obscure works are staged, but it's the big opera hits that put bums on seats.

Cinema

Most suburbs have mainstream cinemas, while art-house cinemas hover around the inner city. Movie listings can be found in Sydney's daily newspapers, or check out www.yourmovies.com.au.

Entertainment by Neighbourhood

➡ **Circular Quay & The Rocks (p65)** Sydney's principal arts neighbourhood, containing the Opera House and Walsh Bay precinct.

➡ **Sydney Harbour (p79)** Ensemble Theatre and Starlight Cinema, both in North Sydney.

➡ **City Centre & Haymarket (p94)** Several major concert venues and theatres scattered about.

➡ **Darling Harbour & Pyrmont (p104)** Lyric Theatre and a giant IMAX Cinema.

➡ **Inner West (p114)** Edgy theatre stages and concert venues.

➡ **Surry Hills & Darlinghurst (p128)** Some of Sydney's most interesting theatre companies are based here.

➡ **Kings Cross & Potts Point (p137)** Pub theatre at the Old Fitzroy.

➡ **Paddington & Centennial Park (p144)** Arthouse cinemas.

➡ **Bondi to Coogee** Theatre and cinema at Bondi Pavilion (p151).

NEED TO KNOW

Business Hours

➜ Box Office: usually 9am–5pm Monday–Friday plus two hours pre-performance.

➜ Cinema sessions: 10.30am–9.30pm.

What's On Listings

➜ Friday's Metro section of the *Sydney Morning Herald* and online at www.smh.com.au.

➜ **What's On Sydney** (www.whatsonsydney .com)

➜ **What's On City of Sydney** (http://whatson. cityofsydney.nsw.gov.au)

Ticketing Agencies

Moshtix (☏1300 438 849; www.moshtix.com. au) Handles ticketing for smaller and independent concerts, theatre and festivals. Outlets include Red Eye Records and Coogee Bay Hotel.

Ticketek (☏132 849; www.ticketek.com.au) Sydney's main booking agency for theatre, concerts and sports. Outlets include Metro Theatre, Westfield Sydney, Westfield Bondi Junction, Enmore Theatre and Sydney Olympic Park.

Ticketmaster (☏136 100; www.ticketmaster.com.au) Sells tickets for music, sports, arts and theatre events. Outlets include State Theatre, Sydney Entertainment Centre, Capitol Theatre and Lyric Theatre.

Lonely Planet's Top Choices

Sydney Opera House (p54) Don't miss the chance to see the House in action.

State Theatre (p94) We don't care what's on, visiting this beautiful place is a joy.

City Recital Hall (p94) The city's premier classical-music venue.

Metro Theatre (p94) The best place to watch touring bands.

Belvoir St Theatre (p128) Consistently excellent productions in an intimate setting.

Best Theatre Companies

Sydney Theatre Company (p66)

Company B (p128)

Griffin Theatre Company (p128)

New Theatre (p114)

Bell Shakespeare (p66)

Best for Musicals

Capitol Theatre (p95)

Lyric Theatre (p104)

Sydney Theatre (p66)

Seymour Centre (p114)

Best Classical-Music Companies

Opera Australia (p65)

Sydney Symphony (p65)

Australian Chamber Orchestra (p65)

Musica Viva Australia (p95)

Australian Brandenburg Orchestra (p95)

Best Venues for Free Classical Music

Sydney Conservatorium of Music (p58)

St Andrew's Cathedral (p89)

St James' Church (p85)

Town Hall (p89)

St Mary's Cathedral (p85)

Best for Dance

Sydney Dance Company (p65)

Bangarra Dance Theatre (p65)

Australian Ballet (p65)

Performance Space (p114)

Best Cinema Experiences

Sydney Film Festival (p22)

Tropfest (p21)

Open Air Cinema (p66)

Moonlight Cinema (p144)

Bondi Openair Cinema (p151)

Best Cinemas

Hayden Orpheum Picture Palace (p79)

Chauvel Cinema (p144)

Palace Verona (p144)

Dendy Newtown (p114)

Hoyts Entertainment Quarter (p144)

Best Live Rock & Pop Concert Venues

Enmore Theatre (p114)

Gaelic Club (p128)

Hordern Pavilion (p145)

Sydney Entertainment Centre (p95)

Oxford Art Factory (p126)

Gay & Lesbian Sydney

Gays and lesbians have migrated to Oz's Emerald City from all over Australia, New Zealand and the world, adding to a community that is visible, vibrant and an integral part of the city's social fabric. Locals will assure you that things aren't as exciting as they once were, but Sydney is still indisputably one of the world's great queer cities.

Social Acceptance

These days few Sydney dwellers even bat an eyelid at same-sex couples holding hands on the street, but the battle for acceptance has been long and protracted. As recently as the early 1990s, several murders were linked to hate crimes, and a stroll up Oxford St could result in a chorus of abuse from car windows. Sydney is now relatively safe, but it still pays to keep your wits about you, particularly at night.

The Birth of Mardi Gras

On 24 June 1978 a Sydney icon was violently born. There had been other gay-rights marches – in 1973 activists were arrested in Martin Place – but this one was different. Two thousand people followed a truck down Oxford St in a carnival-type atmosphere, encouraging punters to come out of the bars to join them.

After harassing the participants for much of the route, the police corralled the remaining marchers in Darlinghurst Rd, Kings Cross, beating and arresting 53 of them. Worse still, the names of all of the arrestees were published in the *Sydney Morning Herald* and many of them lost their jobs.

The following year 3000 people joined the march, dubbed the 'Gay Mardi Gras', and in 1981 the decision was made to move the event to summer. The parade still has a serious political edge; more than just a protest, the parade is considered by many to have helped transform Australian society into a more accepting place for lesbians and gay men.

Mardi Gras Today

Sydney's famous **Mardi Gras** (www.mardigras .org.au) is now the biggest annual tourist-attracting date on the Australian calendar.

PARTY TIME

Ain't no denying it, Sydney puts on a good party. By good, we mean big, lavish and flashy. Some party animals treat it like a professional sport, spending months preparing for the big fixtures, which can resemble endurance events.

While Mardi Gras is the city's main Gay Pride festival, Darlinghurst's Stonewall Hotel organises a mini festival around the traditional Stonewall commemorations in late June. Catering to more niche tastes, **Harbour City Bears** (www.harbour citybears.com.au) runs Bear Pride Week in late August, while **Leather Pride Week** (www.sydneyleather pride.org) is a moveable feast, but is usually held in winter.

NEED TO KNOW

Gay & Lesbian Press

Aside from *DNA*, all of the following are available for free from gay and lesbian venues, and from many gay-friendly cafes and shops. You won't have any trouble stumbling over them in Darlinghurst or Newtown.

➡ **Star Observer** (www.starobserver .com.au) Weekly newspaper.

➡ **SX** (www.gaynewsnetwork.com.au) Weekly newspaper.

➡ **DNA** (www.dnamagazine.com.au) Monthly glossy gay men's magazine, available from newsagents.

➡ **LOTL** (www.lotl.com) Monthly lesbian magazine, aka Lesbians on the Loose.

➡ **Cherrie** (www.gaynewsnetwork.com .au) Monthly magazine for lesbians.

➡ **AXN** (www.gaynewsnetwork.com.au) Monthly magazine for gay men.

Further Resources

➡ **AIDS Council of New South Wales** (www.acon.org.au)

➡ **Pinkboard** (www.pinkboard.com. au) Gay bulletin boards and information, including classifieds, venue guide and blogs.

➡ **Same Same** (www.samesame.com. au) News, events and lifestyle features.

➡ **Gaydar** (www.gaydar.com.au) Gay personals site.

➡ **Gay Sydney Hotels** (www.gaysyd neyhotels.com) Accommodation site.

Legal Matters

NSW's gays and lesbians enjoy legal protection from discrimination and vilification, and an equal age of consent (16 years). They can't legally marry, but they do have de facto relationship rights.

While the straights focus on the parade, the gay and lesbian community throws itself wholeheartedly into the entire festival, including the blitzkrieg of partying that surrounds it. There's no better time for the gay traveller to visit Sydney than the three-week lead-up to the parade and party, held on the first Saturday in March.

On the big night itself, the parade kicks off around sunset, preceded by the throbbing engines of hundreds of Dykes on Bikes. Heading up Oxford St from Hyde Park, it veers right into Flinders St, hooking into Moore Park Rd and culminating outside the party site in Driver Ave. The whole thing takes about 90 minutes to trundle through, and attracts up to half a million spectators ogling from the sidelines.

For the best views, make friends with someone who has an apartment above the street. If you're forced to stand on the street with all the plebs, bring a milk crate (oh so suddenly scarce) to get a better view. The gayest section of the crowd is between Crown St and the first part of Flinders St. If you're running late, the crowd thins out considerably near the end – although by this stage the participants' enthusiasm is on the wane. Another fun option is to volunteer as a marshal: you'll need to attend a few meetings and arrive hideously early on the day, but you'll get the best view and a discounted party ticket for your efforts.

You can also buy a ticket for the Glamstand, positioned at the end of the route. Not only is this a handy option if you're heading to the party, but you'll also have toilets and bars at your disposal and entertainment while you wait.

The legendary Mardi Gras Party (tickets $147 through www.ticketek.com.au) is an extravaganza in every sense of the word. With around 16,000 revellers, it stretches over several large halls, and showcases the best DJs and lighting design the world has to offer.

Gay & Lesbian Sydney by Neighbourhood

➡ **Sydney Harbour** Some of Sydney's most popular gay beaches including Lady Bay (p73) and Obelisk (p78).

➡ **Inner West (p105)** The fabled lesbian homeland, also popular with gay men.

➡ **Surry Hills & Darlinghurst (p117)** Sydney's main gay 'ghetto', with most of the bars, clubs and gay-targeted businesses.

➡ **Kings Cross & Potts Point (p130)** No gay venues but loads of gay guys live here.

➡ **Paddington & Centennial Park (p138)** The home of the Mardi Gras Party and lots of well-dressed dudes.

➡ **Bondi to Coogee (p149)** The beautiful boys gravitate to North Bondi.

Lonely Planet's Top Choices

Sydney Mardi Gras Is there another city that embraces its pride festival with more fervour?

Cabaret Bar (p114) Lavish drag performances in the depths of the Imperial Hotel.

Beresford Hotel (p125) Sunday afternoons see an infestation of the bold and the beautiful.

North Bondi (p151) Staking a claim to a stretch of Sydney's most iconic beach.

Arq (p127) One of the city's best nightclubs, gay or straight.

Best Regular Parties

Fag Tag (www.fagtag.com.au) Organised takeovers of straight bars, usually in summer – lots of free fun.

Toy Box (www.toyboxparty .com.au) Sydney's most popular daytime party, held periodically at Luna Park.

Daywash (www.johankhoury .com) Regular day parties (usually noon to 10pm on a Sunday) held at Chinese Laundry.

Love Muscle (www.johan khoury.com) Luring lots of sweaty, shirtless muscle with top-notch DJs – what's not to love?

In the Dark (www.inthedark .com.au) Runs various parties, including Homesexual and Queer Nation (both at Home) and DILF (who's your daddy?).

Best Lesbian Hang-Outs

Bank Hotel (p113)

Sly Fox (p114)

McIvers Baths (p154)

Exchange Hotel (p127)

Best Gay Bars

Oxford Hotel (p127)

Imperial Hotel (p114)

Palms on Oxford (p127)

Midnight Shift (p127)

Stonewall Hotel (p127)

Best for Drag Shows

Imperial Hotel (p114)

Midnight Shift (p127)

Sly Fox (p114)

Stonewall Hotel (p127)

Best Gay-Friendly Straight Bars

Bank Hotel (p113)

Sly Fox (p114)

Green Park Hotel (p127)

Courthouse Hotel (p113)

Darlo Bar (p127)

Best Gay & Lesbian Beaches & Pools

Lady Bay (p73)

Obelisk (p78)

McIvers Baths (p154)

Redleaf Pool (p74)

Andrew 'Boy' Charlton Pool (p97)

Best Gay-Friendly Hotels

Medusa (p186)

Arts (p188)

Manor House (p186)

Adina Apartment Hotel Sydney (p186)

Simpsons of Potts Point (p187)

Best for Shopping

Bookshop Darlinghurst (p129)

House of Priscilla (p129)

Sax Fetish (p129)

Gleebooks (p115)

Better Read Than Dead (p115)

Shopping

Brash, hedonistic Sydney has elevated shopping to a universal panacea. Feeling good? Let's go shopping. Feeling bad? Let's go shopping. Credit-card bills getting you down? Let's go shopping... Many locals treat shopping as a recreational activity rather than a necessity, evidenced by the teeming cash-flapping masses at the city's weekend markets.

Service

Retail service in Sydney is generally reasonable, although travellers from the USA might find it a bit laid-back at times. Sycophancy isn't the Australian way, but nor is snobbiness. You shouldn't face condescension if you rock into a boutique in your thongs and a singlet, but nor will you be treated like a princess just because you've splashed $5000 on daddy's credit card.

What to Buy

Want something quintessentially Australian to take home? Head to The Rocks and dig up some opals, an Akubra hat, a Driza-Bone coat or some Blundstone boots. Aboriginal art is globally popular.

Sydney has a thriving fashion scene, and a summer dress or Speedos won't eat up luggage space. Ask at CD stores or bookshops about local bands and authors, or grab a Sydney-made DVD. Hunter Valley wine makes a great gift – check your country's duty-free allowance before buying.

Shipping Goods

Check with your airline about excess baggage rates – it may be cheaper than shipping a parcel. For standard parcel-post rates, enquire at any **post office** (www.auspost .com.au). For big items, such as art or cases of wine, some vendors arrange shipping for a fee. Shipping companies operating out of Sydney are listed in the **telephone directory** (www.yellowpages.com.au).

Sales Taxes

Sales taxes are included in the advertised price. Apart from the 10% goods and services tax (GST), the only other sales duties are on things such as alcohol and tobacco, which are best bought at duty-free shops, such as those at the airport. The GST-tourist refund scheme (p226) has mostly replaced traditional duty-free shopping.

Shopping by Neighbourhood

➡ **Circular Quay & The Rocks (p66)** Overpriced souvenirs, tourist-tat, opals and the like.

➡ **Sydney Harbour (p79)** The markets in Kirribilli and Balmain are worth checking out.

➡ **City Centre & Haymarket (p95)** Sydney's shopping mecca, caters for all tastes and budgets.

➡ **Inner West (p114)** Excellent book shops, alternative boutiques and factory outlets.

➡ **Surry Hills & Darlinghurst (p128)** Secondhand boutiques, gay partywear and leather goods.

➡ **Paddington & Centennial Park (p145)** Art, fashion and books.

➡ **Bondi to Coogee (p157)** Surfwear and gear, and Sydney's best mall.

Lonely Planet's Top Choices

Strand Arcade (p95) Fashion retail at its finest.

Queen Victoria Building (p95) Regal surroundings add a sense of gravitas to any splurge.

Westfield Bondi Junction (p157) Huge range of stores and a great food hall.

Westfield Sydney (p95) Huge complex incorporating top restaurants and department stores.

Paddy's Markets (p97) Forget high fashion, head here for bargains and bustle.

Best Markets

Paddington Markets (p145)

Bondi Markets (p157)

Glebe Markets (p115)

Kirribilli Markets (p79)

Surry Hills Markets (p128)

Best for Australiana

RM Williams (p96)

Strand Hatters (p96)

Opal Fields (p66)

Australian Wine Centre (p66)

Best Bookshops

Better Read Than Dead (p115)

Gleebooks (p115)

Best Little Bookshop in Town (p156)

Kinokuniya (p96)

Ariel (p145)

Best for Women's Clothes

Corner Shop (p145)

Poepke (p145)

Capital L (p129)

Leona Edmiston (p146)

Sass & Bide (p146)

Best for Men's Clothes

Blue Spinach (p129)

Herringbone (p147)

Surfection (p157)

Calibre (p146)

Deus Ex Machina (p115)

Best for Vintage Clothing

Grandma Takes a Trip (p128)

Mr Stinky (p129)

Frolic (p116)

Glebe Markets (p115)

C's Flashback (p129)

Best Speciality Shops

Puppet Shop at The Rocks (p67)

Red Eye Records (p96)

Kings Comics (p96)

Hey Presto Magic Studio (p96)

Le Cabinet des Curiosities (p116)

Best for Aboriginal Art

Artery (p129)

Hogarth Galleries (p146)

2 Danks Street (p124)

Original & Authentic Aboriginal Art (p67)

Best for Art

2 Danks Street (p124)

Roslyn Oxley9 Gallery (p146)

NEED TO KNOW

Opening Hours

As a very general rule, shop opening hours are as follows:

➡ 9.30am–6pm Monday–Wednesday, Friday and Saturday

➡ 9.30am–9pm Thursday

➡ 11am–5pm Sunday

Bargaining & Sales

Haggling isn't part of Australia's commercial culture, though you could try at some of the grungier markets around the city, or if you're buying in bulk. Big-store sales usually happen in early January and July.

Warranties

Under local law, all purchases (including secondhand items) have an implied warranty that the goods are of merchantable quality (unless the customer is informed otherwise), are fit for the purpose supplied, and match the sample or description provided. If this is not the case, you are legally entitled to a refund.

Many suppliers (particularly of electrical goods) offer written warranties (guarantees) for fixed terms. Check that they apply worldwide and include service in your home country.

Ray Hughes Gallery (p129)

Iain Dawson Gallery (p146)

Stills Gallery (p146)

Sports & Activities

Who wants to be stuck inside on a beautiful sunny day? Certainly not Sydneysiders. Give them any excuse and they'll be stripping off nonessential clothing and hitting the city's beaches, parks and pools. With looking good such an obvious concern, the city has devised myriad ways to stay built, bronzed and beautiful. Oh, and healthy, too.

Spectator Sports

Sydneysiders like to stay in shape, but not everyone here is a Bondi lifesaver – plenty of people settle for watching rather than participating in the competitive collision of sporting life.

Cycling

Sydney's skinny streets and hectic traffic aren't ideal for two-wheelers, but quite a few adventurous ecowarriors get about on their wheeled steeds. Some roads have designated cycle lanes, but these often run between parked cars and moving traffic (watch for opening doors). If you're just cycling for fun and not commuting, opt for the long cycle paths at North Head (near Manly), Sydney Olympic Park and Centennial Park.

Sailing

An introductory sailing lesson is a brilliant way to get out onto the harbour, though it's not for the budget-conscious. More experienced salts can skipper their own boat.

In-Line Skating & Skateboarding

The beachside promenades at Bondi and Manly are in-line skating hot spots, but Centennial Park is better for serious workouts. You can even skate across Sydney Harbour Bridge. There's a decent skate ramp at the south end of Bondi Beach, and a skate centre at Sydney Olympic Park.

Diving

Sydney's best shore dives are the Gordons Bay Underwater Nature Trail near Coogee, Shark Point at Clovelly and Ship Rock at Cronulla. For boat dives try Coogee's Wedding Cake Island, around the Sydney Heads and off Royal National Park. In Manly you can do a shore dive from Shelly Beach.

Sports & Activities by Neighbourhood

➡ **Circular Quay & The Rocks (p67)** The starting point for several cycling and walking tours.

➡ **Sydney Harbour (p80)** Sail, jet-boat, kayak, swim or take a cruise.

➡ **City Centre & Haymarket (p97)** Walking tours and some great swimming pools.

➡ **Inner West (p116)** Take a punt on the greyhounds or take a dip in Victoria Park.

➡ **Paddington & Centennial Park (p147)** Watch the footy, the cricket or the gee-gees, or circle Centennial Park on a bike, horse or in-line skates.

➡ **Bondi to Coogee (p158)** Dive, snorkel, surf or swim, or kite-board.

➡ **Manly (p165)** Surf, kayak, cycle, snorkel or skate.

Lonely Planet's Top Choices

Let's Go Surfing (p151) Learn to surf at one of the world's most famous beaches.

Sydney Football Stadium (p147) Yell your head off at a rugby league match.

Store Beach (p161) Kayak from Manly to this isolated harbour beach, only accessible from the water.

Centennial Parklands Equestrian Centre (p148) Saddle up for a canter around Centennial Park.

Gordons Bay Underwater Nature Trail (p152) Explore the scenery beneath the waves.

Best Cycling Tours

Bike Buffs (p221)

Bonza Bike Tours (p220)

Manly Bike Tours (p221)

Sydney Architecture Walks (p97)

Best Walking Tours

I'm Free (p97)

Peek Tours (p67)

The Rocks Walking Tours (p67)

Sydney Architecture Walks (p97)

The Rocks Ghost Tours (p67)

Best for Sailing

James Craig (p80)

Sydney by Sail (p80)

Eastsail (p81)

Sydney Flying Squadron (p81)

Best Boat Cruises

Whale Watching Sydney (p80)

Captain Cook Cruises (p80)

Matilda Cruises (p80)

Magistic Cruises (p80)

Sydney Showboats (p80)

Best Swimming Pools

Bondi Icebergs Swimming Club (p151)

Andrew 'Roy' Charlton Pool (p97)

Sydney Olympic Park Aquatic Centre (p108)

North Sydney Olympic Pool (p81)

Cook + Phillip Park (p97)

Best Places for Jogging

The Domain (p86)

Sydney Olympic Park (p108)

Sydney Park (p110)

Jubilee & Bicentennial Parks (p107)

Bondi Beach (p151)

NEED TO KNOW

Sports Seasons

Conveniently, the most popular spectator sports happen in winter, not interrupting the beach schedule too much. The football season (rugby league, rugby union and Aussie Rules) runs from about March to October. Summer sports include cricket, tennis, sailing and surf lifesaving. Soccer is the exception, with a season lasting from August to February.

Transporting Bikes

Bicycles can travel on suburban trains for kids' rates during peak hours, and for free outside peak times. Bikes also ride for free on Sydney's ferries but are banned from buses.

PLAN YOUR TRIP SPORTS & ACTIVITIES

Best Places for Cycling

Sydney Olympic Park (p108)

Centennial Park (p140)

North Head (p161)

Royal National Park (p174)

Best for Kayaking

Natural Wanders (p80)

Manly Kayak Centre (p165)

Sydney Harbour Kayaks (p80)

Audley Boat Shed (p175)

Explore Sydney

Neighbourhoods at a Glance **50**

Circular Quay & The Rocks........**52**
Top Sights 54
Sights....................57
Eating....................62
Drinking & Nightlife.......64
Entertainment 65
Shopping.................66
Sports & Activities........67

Sydney Harbour **68**
Sights....................72
Eating....................78
Drinking & Nightlife.......78
Entertainment 79
Shopping.................79
Sports & Activities........80

City Centre & Haymarket..........**82**
Top Sights 84
Sights....................85
Eating....................90
Drinking & Nightlife.......92
Entertainment 94
Shopping.................95
Sports & Activities........97

Darling Harbour & Pyrmont............**98**
Sights...................100
Eating...................103
Drinking & Nightlife......104
Entertainment 104
Sports & Activities.......104

Inner West **105**
Sights...................107
Eating................... 110
Drinking & Nightlife...... 112
Entertainment 114
Shopping............... 114
Sports & Activities....... 116

Surry Hills & Darlinghurst **117**
Sights...................119
Eating................... 121
Drinking & Nightlife......125
Entertainment 128
Shopping...............128

Kings Cross & Potts Point **130**
Sights...................132
Eating...................132
Drinking & Nightlife......135
Entertainment 137

Paddington & Centennial Park **138**
Sights...................140
Eating...................142
Drinking & Nightlife......143
Entertainment 144
Shopping...............145
Sports & Activities.......147

Bondi to Coogee....**149**
Top Sights 151
Sights...................152
Eating...................155
Drinking & Nightlife......156
Shopping...............157
Sports & Activities.......158

Manly **159**
Sights................... 161
Eating...................163
Drinking & Nightlife......164
Sports & Activities.......165

Day Trips from Sydney **166**
The Blue Mountains 167
Royal National Park......174
Northern Beaches 176

Sleeping...........**179**

SYDNEY'S TOP SIGHTS

Sydney Opera House........54

Sydney Harbour Bridge ...55

Royal Botanic Gardens.....56

Art Gallery of NSW........... 84

Bondi Beach 151

Neighbourhoods at a Glance

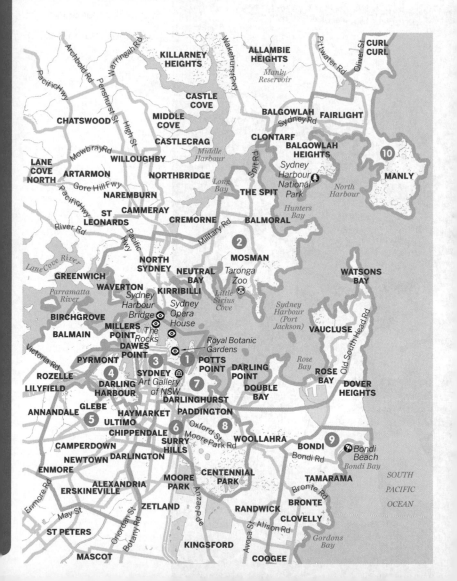

❶ Circular Quay & The Rocks (p52)

The birthplace of both the city and the modern nation, this compact area seamlessly combines the historic with the exuberantly modern. Join the tourist pilgrimage to the Opera House and Harbour Bridge then grab a schooner at a convict-era pub in The Rocks.

❷ Sydney Harbour (p68)

Stretching inland from the heads for 20km until it morphs into the Parramatta River, the harbour has shaped the local psyche for millennia, and today it's the city's sparkling playground. Its inlets, beaches, islands and shorefront parks provide endless swimming, sailing, picnicking and walking opportunities.

❸ City Centre & Haymarket (p82)

Sydney's central business district offers plenty of choices for upmarket shopping, eating and sightseeing, with gracious colonial buildings scattered among the skyscrapers and orderly parks providing breathing space. The breathless jumble of Haymarket and Chinatown provide the yin to the CBD's yang.

❹ Darling Harbour & Pyrmont (p98)

Unashamedly tourist focused, Darling Harbour will do its best to tempt you to its shoreline bars and restaurants with fireworks displays and a sprinkling of glitz. On its western flank, Pyrmont appears to be sinking under the weight of its casino and motorway flyovers.

❺ Inner West (p105)

Quietly bohemian Glebe and more loudly bohemian Newtown are the most well-known of the Inner West's tightly packed suburbs, grouped around the University of Sydney. All the essential hang-outs for students – bookshops, cafes and pubs – are present in abundance.

❻ Surry Hills & Darlinghurst (p117)

Sydney's hippest and gayest neighbourhood is also home to its most interesting dining and bar scene. For the most part, it's more gritty than pretty, and actual sights are thin on the ground, but there's still plenty to do and see here, especially after dark.

❼ Kings Cross & Potts Point (p130)

If Darling Harbour is Sydney dressing up nicely for tourists, the Cross is where it relaxes, scratches itself and belches. In equal parts thrilling and depressing but never boring, this is where you come for late-night blinders or surprisingly pleasant daytime meanders.

❽ Paddington & Centennial Park (p138)

The next band of suburbs to the east is distinctly well-heeled – and in Paddington's case they're probably Manolo Blahniks. Despite taking a hit with the opening of Westfield Bondi Junction just up the road, this is still Sydney's fashion and art heartland.

❾ Bondi to Coogee (p149)

Sydney sheds its suit and tie, ditches the strappy heels and chills out in the Eastern Beaches. Beach after golden-sand beach, alternating with sheer sandstone cliffs, are the classic vistas of this beautiful, laid-back and egalitarian stretch of the city.

❿ Manly (p159)

Sydney's only ferry destination boasting an ocean beach, Manly caps off the harbour with scrappy charm. The surf's good and as the gateway to the Northern Beaches, it makes a popular base for the board-riding brigade.

Circular Quay & The Rocks

CIRCULAR QUAY | THE ROCKS | DAWES POINT | MILLERS POINT

Neighbourhood Top Five

1 Coming face to face with the number-one visual symbol of the city, the **Sydney Opera House** (p54). On a sunny day it's postcard perfect, its curves and points a pinnacle of architectural expression.

2 Strolling the idyllic grounds of the **Royal Botanic Gardens** (p56), with the harbour sparkling below.

3 Being challenged and inspired by edgy offerings at the **Museum of Contemporary Art** (p58).

4 Gazing on the harbour from amid the heavy metal of the **Sydney Harbour Bridge** (p55).

5 Letting the food and view seduce you at **Quay** (p62), or any of the other top harbourside restaurants.

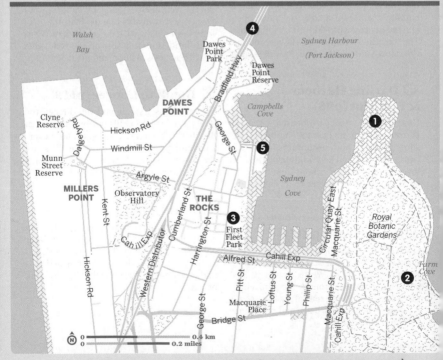

For more detail of this area, see Map p248 ➡

Explore Circular Quay & The Rocks

At some stage you'll almost certainly end up in this neck of the woods – you haven't really been to Sydney if you don't. Set aside the best part of a day to see the sights of this very touristy neighbourhood. Return at night to clink glasses at an upmarket restaurant, to down a schooner in a historic pub or to catch a show. Nowadays Sydney Cove carries the weight of Sydney iconography, with the Harbour Bridge and the Opera House abutting each point of its horseshoe. Sensing photo opportunities, some of Sydney's swankiest hotels and restaurants are also here.

Circular Quay's promenade serves as a backdrop for buskers of mixed merit and locals disgorging from harbour ferries. The Rocks is unrecognisable from the squalid place it once was and is now serves as an 'olde worlde' tourist trap. Over the ridge is Millers Point, a low-key colonial district that makes a calming diversion from the harbourside tourist fray, and Walsh Bay, a redeveloped maritime precinct.

Local Life

➡ **Performing arts** Sydneysiders put aside their aversion to this most touristy part of town to attend performances at the Sydney Opera House (p66) and Walsh Bay theatres (p66).

➡ **Special occasion restaurants** For proposals, zero ending birthdays or that one extravagant night out per year, restaurants such as Quay (p62), Guillaume at Bennelong (p62) and Aria (p62) are popular.

➡ **Parks** You're liable to see locals taking romantic strolls, letting the kids off the leash or shaking out a picnic blanket in the Royal Botanic Gardens (p56) or Observatory Hill (p60).

Getting There & Away

➡ **Train** Circular Quay is one of the City Circle stations.

➡ **Ferry** Circular Quay is Sydney's ferry hub and has services to Double Bay, Watsons Bay, Manly, Taronga Zoo, Kirribilli, North Sydney, Milsons Point, Darling Harbour, Cockatoo Island, Balmain, Sydney Olympic Park and Parramatta, among others.

➡ **Bus** Circular Quay is the major terminus for routes including: 301–303 (Surry Hills); 324 and 325 (Kings Cross–Double Bay–Vaucluse–Watsons Bay); 333 and 389 (Darlinghurst–North Bondi); 373 and 374 (Coogee); 380 (Darlinghurst–Paddington–Bondi–Watsons Bay); 422, 423, 426 and 428 (Newtown); and 470 (Glebe).

Lonely Planet's Top Tip

The best way to avoid the city traffic is to travel here by train or ferry. If you really feel that you must bring the car, come on the weekend, as the Wilson parking building beneath the Opera House charges a set fee of $15 between 6am and 5pm (it's $52 during the week).

✕ Best Places to Eat

➡ Quay (p62)
➡ Guillaume at Bennelong (p62)
➡ Rockpool (p62)
➡ Aria (p62)
➡ Sailors Thai Canteen (p63)

 For reviews, see p62 ➡

☕ Best Places to Drink

➡ Opera Bar (p64)
➡ Hero of Waterloo (p64)
➡ Lord Nelson Brewery Hotel (p64)
➡ Harbour View Hotel (p64)
➡ Argyle (p64)

For reviews, see p64 ➡

◉ Best Heritage Sights

➡ The Rocks Discovery Museum (p58)
➡ Susannah Place (p58)
➡ Government House (p56)
➡ Sydney Observatory (p60)
➡ The Big Dig (p59)

For reviews, see p57 ➡

Gazing upon the Sydney Opera House with virgin eyes is a sure way to send a tingle down your spine. Overcome with admiration, noted architect Louis Kahn said, 'The sun did not know how beautiful its light was until it was reflected off this building.' Gloriously white, curvaceous and pointy, the Opera House perches dramatically at the tip of Bennelong Point, waiting for its close-up. No matter from which angle you point a camera at it, it shamelessly mugs for the camera; it really doesn't have a bad side.

DON'T MISS...

➡ Catching a performance, any performance

➡ Taking a guided tour

PRACTICALITIES

➡ Map p248

➡ ☑9250 7111

➡ www.sydneyoperahouse.com

➡ Bennelong Point

➡ ⒭Circular Quay

Design & Construction

Danish architect Jørn Utzon's competition-winning 1956 design is Australia's most recognisable visual image. It's said to have been inspired by billowing sails, orange segments, palm fronds and Mayan temples, and has been poetically likened to nuns in a rugby scrum, a typewriter stuffed with scallop shells and the sexual congress of turtles. It's not until you get close that you realise that the seemingly solid expanse of white is actually composed of tiles – 1,056,000 self-cleaning cream-coloured Swedish tiles, to be exact.

The Opera House's construction was itself truly operatic – so much so, it was dramatised as *The Eighth Wonder*, performed here by Opera Australia in 1995. The predicted four-year construction started in 1959. After a tumultuous clash of egos, delays, politicking, death and cost blow-outs, Utzon quit in disgust in 1966. The Opera House finally opened in 1973. Utzon and his son Jan were commissioned for renovations in 2004, but Utzon died in 2008 having never seen his finished masterpiece in the flesh.

Performances

Inside, dance, concerts, opera and theatre are staged in the **Concert Hall**, **Opera Theatre**, **Drama Theatre** and **Playhouse**, while more intimate and left-of-centre shows inhabit the **Studio**. The acoustics in the concert hall are superb; the internal aesthetics like the belly of a whale. Most events (2400 of them annually!) sell out quickly, but partial-view tickets are often available on short notice. The free monthly *What's On* brochure lists upcoming events, including info on Kids at the House – a pint-sized entertainment roster of music, drama and dance (including introductory ballet with Australian Ballet dancers).

Tours

The interiors don't live up to the promise of the dazzling exterior, but if you're curious to see inside, one-hour **guided tours** (☑9250 7777; adult/child/family $35/25/90; ☺9am-5pm) depart half-hourly (you'll save $5 if you book online). You can book ahead for tours in various languages, including Auslan sign language, and if you've got limited mobility, Access Tours can be arranged.

Not all tours can visit all theatres because of rehearsals, but you're more likely to see everything if you go early. A highlight is the **Utzon Room**, the only part of the Opera House to have an interior designed by the great man himself. For a more in-depth nosy around, the two-hour early-morning **backstage tour** (tickets $155; tours ☺7am) includes the Green Room and stars' dressing rooms.

TOP SIGHTS
SYDNEY HARBOUR BRIDGE

Whether they're driving over it, climbing up it, jogging across it, shooting fireworks off it or sailing under it, Sydneysiders adore their bridge and swarm around it like ants on ice cream. Dubbed the 'coathanger', it's a spookily big object – moving around town you'll catch sight of it out of the corner of your eye, sometimes in the most surprising of places. Perhaps Sydney poet Kenneth Slessor said it best: 'Day and night, the bridge trembles and echoes like a living thing.'

DON'T MISS...

➡ Sunset from the top of the bridge

➡ The views from the Pylon Lookout

PRACTICALITIES

➡ Map p248

➡ 🚇 Circular Quay

The Structure

At 134m high, 502m long, 49m wide and 53,000 tonnes, the Sydney Harbour Bridge is the largest and heaviest (but not the longest) steel arch in the world. It links the city centre with North Sydney, crossing the harbour at one of its narrowest points.

The two halves of chief engineer JJC Bradfield's mighty arch were built outwards from each shore. In 1932, after nine years of merciless toil by 1400 workers, the two arches were only centimetres apart when 100km/h winds set them swaying. The coathanger hung tough and the arch was finally bolted together. It cost $20 million to build and took until 1988 to pay off. Giving it a new coat of paint takes four years and 80,000 litres.

The bridge is the centrepiece of Sydney's major celebrations, particularly the New Year's Eve fireworks. In 2007, when it reached its 75th birthday, 250,000 people celebrated by walking across the great span.

Get Over It

The best way to experience the bridge is on foot – don't expect much of a view crossing by train or car (driving south there's a toll). Staircases access the bridge from both shores; a footpath runs along its eastern side.

BridgeClimb

Once only painters and daredevils scaled the Harbour Bridge – now anyone can do it (Bruce Springsteen, Bette Midler, Will Smith...). Make your way through the **BridgeClimb** (Map p248; ☎8274 7777; www.bridgeclimb.com; 3 Cumberland St; adult $188-298, child $128-108) departure lounge and the extensive training session, don your headset, an umbilical safety cord and a dandy grey jumpsuit (Elvis would be so proud) and up you go. If you're afraid of heights, the scariest part is crossing over the grates while under the bridge; on the curved span itself the track is wide enough that you never see straight down.

Tours last 2¼ to 3½ hours – a preclimb toilet stop is a smart idea. The priciest climbs are at dawn and **sunset**.

Pylon Lookout

The bridge's hefty pylons may look as though they're shouldering all the weight, but they're largely decorative – right down to their granite facing. There are awesome views from the top of the **Pylon Lookout** (Map p248; ☎9240 1100; www.pylonlookout.com.au; adult/child $11/6.50; ◷10am-5pm), atop the southeast pylon, 200 steps above the bridge's footpath. Inside the pylon there are exhibits explaining how the bridge was built.

TOP SIGHTS
ROYAL BOTANIC GARDENS

These expansive gardens are the inner city's favourite picnic destination, jogging route and snuggling spot for loved-up couples. Bordering Farm Cove, east of the Sydney Opera House, the gardens were established in 1816 and feature plant life from Australia and around the world. They include the site of the colony's first paltry vegetable patch, but their history goes back much further than that; long before the convicts arrived this was an initiation ground for the Cadigal people.

Plants

Highlights include the **rose garden**, the **rainforest walk**, the **succulent garden** and a rare **Wollemi pine** (an ancient tree only discovered in 1994 in a remote pocket of the Blue Mountains.

The **Sydney Tropical Centre** (☑9231 8104; adult/child/family $5.50/3.30/11; ☉10am-4pm) comprises the interconnecting Arc and Pyramid glasshouses – a great place to warm up on a wintry morning. The Arc has a rampant collection of climbers from the world's rainforests; the Pyramid houses Australian species.

Walks & Tours

Free 1½-hour guided walks depart at 10.30am daily from the information booth outside the Garden Shop. From March to November there's also an additional hour-long tour at 1pm on weekdays.

Book ahead for an **Aboriginal Heritage Tour** (☑9231 8134; adult/child $33/17; tours ☉10am Fri), which covers local history, traditional plant uses and bush-food tastings. You can also download self-guided tours from the RBG website.

The park's paths are mostly wheelchair accessible. Estimated walking times on signs are pessimistic (if a sign says something is five minutes away, bank on two). If you're all walked out, take a ride on the **Choochoo Express** (Map p248; www.choochoo.com.au; adult/child $10/5; ☉11am-4pm), a trackless train that departs from Queen Elizabeth II Gate (nearest the Opera House) every half an hour.

Government House

Encased in English-style grounds within the gardens, **Government House** (Map p248; ☑9931 5222; www.hht.net.au; Macquarie St; ☉grounds 10am-4pm, tours 10.30am-3pm Fri-Sun; ⒭Circular Quay) is a Gothic sandstone mansion that served as the home of New South Wales' governors from 1846 to 1996. The governor, who now resides in Admiralty House, still uses it for weekly meetings and hosting visiting heads of state and royalty. Unless there's a bigwig in town, you can tour through the fussy furnishings; look for paintings by Arthur Streeton, Tom Roberts and Russell Drysdale. Disabled access is OK, but it's best to call in advance.

DON'T MISS...

➡ Government House
➡ The rainforest walk
➡ The succulent garden

PRACTICALITIES

➡ Map p248
➡ ☑9231 8111
➡ www.rbgsyd.nsw .gov.au
➡ Mrs Macquaries Rd
➡ ☉7am-sunset
➡ ⒭Circular Quay

◉ SIGHTS

◉ Circular Quay

SYDNEY OPERA HOUSE NOTABLE BUILDING
See p54.

ROYAL BOTANIC GARDENS GARDENS
See p56.

MRS MACQUARIES POINT PARK
(Mrs Macquaries Rd; ℞Circular Quay) Adjoining the Royal Botanic Gardens but officially part of The Domain, Mrs Macquaries Point forms the northeastern tip of Farm Cove and provides beautiful views over the bay to the Opera House and city skyline. It was named in 1810 after Elizabeth, Governor Macquarie's wife, who ordered a seat chiselled into the rock from which she could view the harbour.

Mrs Macquaries Chair, as it's known, remains to this day. Clouds of sulphur-crested cockatoos disturb the peace with their raucous caws during the day, while at night it's a romantic spot for an after-dinner stroll. Open Air Cinema is held here in the summer months.

FREE **CUSTOMS HOUSE** HISTORIC BUILDING
Map p248 (🖉9242 8551; www.sydneycustoms house.com.au; 31 Alfred St; ⊗8am-midnight Mon-Fri, 10am-midnight Sat, 11am-5pm Sun; ℞Circular Quay) Emerging phoenixlike from extensive renovations in 2005, this cavernous harbourside edifice (1885) now houses the three level **Customs House Library** (🖉9242 8555; ⊗10am-7pm Mon-Fri, 11am-4pm

Sat & Sun). There's a great selection of international newspapers and magazines to scan, as well as internet access and interesting temporary exhibitions.

In the lobby, look for the swastikas in the tiling (and the plaque explaining their symbolism), and a charmingly geeky 1:500 model of the inner city under a glass floor. Café Sydney is on the top floor.

JUSTICE & POLICE MUSEUM MUSEUM
Map p248 (🖉9252 1144; www.hht.net.au; cnr Albert & Phillip Sts; adult/child/family $10/5/20; ⊗9.30am-5pm; ℞Circular Quay) In the old Water Police Station (1858), this mildly unnerving museum mimics a late-19th-century police station and court. Focusing on disreputable activities, exhibits include weapons, butt-ugly mugshots, forensic evidence from Sydney's most heinous crimes and at least two stuffed dogs. Wheelchair access to the ground floor only.

MACQUARIE PLACE SQUARE
Map p248 (cnr Loftus & Bridge Sts; ℞Circular Quay) Beneath some shady Moreton Bay fig trees a block or two back from the Quay is this little historic triangle. Look for the actual **cannon and anchor** from the First Fleet flagship (HMS *Sirius*), an ornate but defunct 1857 drinking fountain, a National Trust–classified gentlemen's *pissoir* (closed) and an 1818 **obelisk** erected 'to record that all the public roads leading to the interior of the colony are measured from it'.

The park is overlooked by the imposing 19th-century **Lands Department Building**; the north façade bears statues of Sturt,

CIRCULAR QUAY & THE ROCKS SIGHTS

BENNELONG

Bennelong was born around 1764 into the Wangal tribe, the westerly neighbours of the Cadigal who lived around central Sydney. Captured in 1789, he was brought to Governor Arthur Phillip, who hoped to use Bennelong to understand the local Aborigines' customs and language.

Bennelong took to life with the settlers, developing a taste for alcohol and European food, and learning to speak the language of his new 'masters'. Eventually he escaped, but he returned by 1791 when reassured that he would not be held against his will. He developed a strong friendship with Governor Phillip, who had a brick hut built for him on what is now Bennelong Point.

In 1792 Bennelong went on a 'civilising' trip to England, and returned in 1795 with a changed dress sense and altered behaviour. Described as good natured and 'stoutly made', Bennelong ultimately was no longer accepted by Aboriginal society and never really found happiness with his white friends either. He died a broken, dispossessed man in 1813, probably as a result of his affection for the bottle.

Hume, Leichhardt and other early Australian movers and shakers.

SYDNEY CONSERVATORIUM OF MUSIC HISTORIC BUILDING

Map p248 (☑9351 1222; www.music.usyd.edu.au; Conservatorium Rd; ⓡCircular Quay) The castellated 'Con' was designed by convict architect Francis Greenway as the stables and servants' quarters of Governor Macquarie's new government house. Partly because of the project's extravagance, Macquarie was ousted before the house could be completed. In 1915 the stables were converted into a music conservatorium, which amalgamated with the University of Sydney in 1990.

Subsequent renovations (equally extravagant at $145 million) created five world-class performance venues.

TANK STREAM FOUNTAIN FOUNTAIN

Map p248 (Herald Sq, Alfred St; ⓡCircular Quay) Designed by Stephen Walker, this four-part bronze fountain (1981) near Circular Quay incorporates dozens of sculptures of native Australian animals; play spot-the-echidna. The fountain is dedicated to 'all the children who have played around the Tank Stream', which now runs beneath the city.

SYDNEY WRITERS WALK PATH

Map p248 (ⓡCircular Quay) A series of metal discs cast into the Circular Quay promenade hold ruminations from prominent Australian writers (and the odd literary visitor). The likes of Robert Hughes, Germaine Greer, Peter Carey, Umberto Eco and Clive James wax lyrical on subjects ranging from indigenous rights to the paradoxical nature of glass.

Genres vary from eloquent poems addressing the human condition to a ditty about a meat pie by Barry Humphries.

◉ The Rocks

FREE MUSEUM OF CONTEMPORARY ART GALLERY

Map p248 (MCA; ☑9245 2400; www.mca.com .au; 140 George St; ⊘10am-5pm Fri-Wed, to 9pm Thu; ⓡCircular Quay) A slice of Gotham City on Circular Quay West, the stately art-deco MCA has been raising even the most open-minded Sydney eyebrows since 1991. Constantly changing, often controversial exhibitions from Australia and overseas range

from the incredibly hip to in-your-face, sexually explicit and profoundly disturbing. You'll also find Aboriginal art featured prominently. Quite simply, it's one of Australia's best and most challenging galleries.

At the time of research the MCA was closed for a $53-million redevelopment, grafting on the ultramodern cubic jumble of the new Mordant Family Wing. We're looking forward to taking in the view over Circular Quay from the new indoor-outdoor cafe on the 4th floor.

FREE THE ROCKS DISCOVERY MUSEUM MUSEUM

Map p248 (☑9240 8680; www.rocksdiscovery museum.com; Kendall Lane; ⊘10am-5pm; ⓡCircular Quay) Divided into four chronological displays – Warrane (pre-1788), Colony (1788–1820), Port (1820–1900) and Transformations (1900 to the present) – this excellent museum digs deep into The Rocks' history and leads you on an artefact-rich tour. Sensitive attention is given to The Rocks' original inhabitants, the Cadigal people.

SUSANNAH PLACE MUSEUM MUSEUM

Map p248 (☑9241 1893; www.hht.net.au; 58-64 Gloucester St; adult/child/family $8/4/17; ⊘2-6pm Mon-Fri, 10am-6pm Sat, Sun & school holidays; ⓡCircular Quay) Dating from 1844, the claustrophobic Susannah Pl is a diminutive terrace of tiny houses with a tiny shop selling tiny historical wares. My, haven't we grown? In the backyard, check out how generations of working-class Rocks women cooked and laundered their clothes in a wood-fired copper urn (near the outdoor dunny). Admission is by way of guided tour.

FREE CADMAN'S COTTAGE HISTORIC BUILDING

Map p248 (☑9253 0888; www.npws.nsw.gov .au; 110 George St; ⊘9.30am-4.30pm Mon-Fri, 10am-4.30pm Sat & Sun; ⓡCircular Quay) Built on a now-buried beach for Government Coxswain John Cadman (a boat and crew superintendent) in 1816, Cadman's Cottage is the inner city's oldest house. The Sydney Water Police detained criminals here in the 1840s; it was later converted into a home for retired sea captains. These days the cottage houses the Sydney Harbour National Park Information Centre (p227), which organises tours of the harbour islands.

It has a museum, and a glassed-off area on the lower level revealing a tangle of old drains exposed in an archaeological dig.

WHERE IT ALL BEGAN

After dismissing Botany Bay as a site for the colony, Governor Phillip sailed the First Fleet into what James Cook had named Port Jackson (Warran in the local language) and dropped anchor at a horseshoe bay with an all-important freshwater stream running into it. Phillip astutely christened the bay Sydney Cove after the British Home Secretary, Baron Sydney of Chislehurst, who was responsible for the colonies.

The socio-economic divide of the future city was foreshadowed when the convicts were allocated the rocky land to the west of the stream (known unimaginatively as The Rocks), while the governor and other officials pitched their tents to the east.

Built with convict labour between 1837 and 1844, Circular Quay was originally (and more accurately) called Semi-circular Quay, and acted as the main port of Sydney. In the 1850s it was extended further, covering over the by then festering Tank Stream, which ran through the middle of the cove.

As time went on, whalers and sailors joined the ex-convicts at The Rocks – and inns and brothels sprang up to entertain them. With the settlement filthy and overcrowded, the nouveau riche started building houses on the upper slopes, their sewage flowing to the slums below. Residents sloshed through open sewers, and alleyways festered with disease and drunken lawlessness. Thus began a long, steady decline.

Bubonic plague broke out in 1900, leading to the razing of entire streets, and Harbour Bridge construction in the 1920s wiped out even more. It wasn't until the 1970s that The Rocks' cultural and architectural heritage was finally recognised. Redevelopment saved many old buildings by converting them into tourist-focused businesses. Shops hocking Opera House key rings proliferate, but gritty history is never far below the surface if you know where to look.

ST PATRICK'S CHURCH
CHURCH

Map p248 (②9254 9855; www.stpatschurchhill .org; 20 Grosvenor St; ⊙9am-4.30pm; 🚇Wynyard) This attractive sandstone church (1844) was built on land donated by William Davis, an Irishman transported for his role in the 1798 uprisings. His home (on the site of the chapel-turned-cafe) was arguably the first Catholic chapel in Australia; it was used for clandestine devotions and secretly housed a consecrated host after the colony's only Catholic priest was deported in 1818.

Inside it's incredibly quiet, which makes the brass altar, the stained-glass windows and the colourful statues of St Patrick, St Joan of Arc and St Michael (complete with dragon) seem even more righteous. Guided tours are infrequent but worthwhile; visit the website for details.

FOUNDATION PARK
PARK

Map p248 (Gloucester Walk; 🚇Circular Quay) Thought-provoking Foundation Park is set among the preserved ruins of 1870s houses, built against the cliff face. The oversized furniture by artist Peter Cole evokes the cramped conditions once experienced by working-class Rocks families. It's a great place to pause in the shade and enjoy the views over The Rocks' roofs.

FREE THE BIG DIG
ARCHAEOLOGICAL SITE

Map p248 (www.thebigdig.com.au; 110 Cumberland St; ⊙dusk-dawn; 🚇Circular Quay) Before the outbreak of bubonic plague in the early 20th century and the subsequent slum clearances, this section of The Rocks was a warren of houses connected by tiny lanes. It then spent decades covered by a car park, until 1994 when archaeologists commenced what turned into a 15-year dig, uncovering cobblestones, foundations and little treasures along the way.

Displays bring the ruins to life, including photos of children at play on the very cobblestones on which you're standing.

SUEZ CANAL
STREET

Map p248 (🚇Circular Quay) One of few remaining such lanes, the Suez Canal tapers as it goes downhill until it's less than a metre wide (thus the name, which is also a pun on the word 'sewers'). Constructed in the 1840s, it was notorious as a lurking point for members of the Rocks Push, a street gang that relieved many a drunk of their wallet in the latter part of the 19th century.

Where it intersects Nurses Walk there's a hoist once used for hauling goods to the upper floors.

FREE KEN DONE GALLERY   GALLERY

Map p248 (www.kendone.com.au; 1 Hickson Rd; ⊙10am-5.30pm; ⊠Circular Quay) The cheerful, quasi-childlike work of Sydney artist Ken Done is exhibited inside the lavishly restored Australian Steam Navigation Building. Expect luridly coloured Australian landscapes, Opera House renderings and comic minutiae from Done's days. Help prop up his ailing empire (recently devalued from $61 million to around $8 million) with a visit to his shop just down the road.

CAMPBELL'S STOREHOUSES   HISTORIC BUILDINGS

Map p248 (7 Circular Quay West; ⊠Circular Quay) In 1839, Scottish merchant Robert Campbell started building a private wharf and this gingerbread-style row of 11 storehouses to house his stash of tea, alcohol, sugar and fabric. Construction didn't finish until 1861, and a brick storey was added in 1890. Such storehouses were common around Circular Quay into the early 20th century, but most have been demolished.

These survivors now sustain a string of pricey restaurants.

OVERSEAS PASSENGER TERMINAL   NOTABLE BUILDING

Map p248 (Circular Quay West; ⊠Circular Quay) Multistorey luxury cruise ships weigh anchor at this architecturally dynamic terminal, disgorging hordes of shaky-legged tourists onto Circular Quay West – a slew of ultraflash drinking and dining establishments gives them somewhere to sit down (Quay, p62, being the flashest of them all).

For a killer harbour view, head up to the level-four observation deck in the turret on the northern end.

⊙ Dawes Point

SYDNEY HARBOUR BRIDGE   BRIDGE

See p55.

WALSH BAY   WATERFRONT

Map p248 (www.walshbaysydney.com.au; Hickson Rd; ⊠Wynyard) This section of Dawes Point waterfront was Sydney's busiest before container shipping and the construction of new port facilities at Botany Bay. The last decade has seen the Federation-era wharves here gentrified beyond belief, morphing into luxury hotels, apartments, theatre spaces, power-boat marinas and restaurants.

The self-guided 1.6km **Walsh Bay Heritage Walk** (Map p248) starts at Pier 2 and leads you through 11 stops, with interesting plaques and directions urging you onwards; download a guide from the Walsh Bay website. Pier 4 houses the Wharf Theatre, home to the renowned Sydney Theatre Company, Sydney Dance Company and Bangarra Dance Theatre.

GARRISON CHURCH   CHURCH

Map p248 (☏9247 1268; www.thegarrisonchurch .org.au; 62 Lower Fort St; ⊙9am-5pm; ⊠Circular Quay) Also known as Holy Trinity (1843), this chunky sandstone Anglican church on the western side of the Argyle Cut was the colony's first military church. Below a dark timber ceiling, the hushed interior is spangled with dusty, lank-hanging regimental flags. Australia's first prime minister, Edmund Barton, went to school here (the parish hall doubled as a schoolhouse).

ARGYLE CUT   STREET

Map p248 (Argyle St; ⊠Circular Quay) Convict labourers excavated this canyonlike section of road clear through the sandstone ridge that gave the area its name. The work began in 1843 with hand tools, and was completed (with the aid of dynamite) in 1867. The cut sandstone frames scenery and greenery in a dramatic fashion and makes for a very atmospheric stroll.

⊙ Millers Point

FREE SYDNEY OBSERVATORY   OBSERVATORY

Map p248 (☏9921 3485; www.sydneyobserva tory.com.au; Watson Rd; ⊙10am-5pm; ⊠Circular Quay) Built in the 1850s, Sydney's copper-domed, Italianate observatory squats atop **Observatory Hill**, overlooking Millers Point and the harbour. Inside is a collection of vintage apparatus, including Australia's oldest working telescope (1874). Also on offer are AV displays, an interactive Australian astronomy exhibition including Aboriginal sky stories and modern stargazing, and a virtual reality **3D Theatre** (adult/child/family $8/2/22; ⊙2.30pm & 3.30pm daily, plus 11am & noon Sat & Sun).

Squint at galaxies far, far away during **Night Telescope/3D Theatre sessions** (adult/child/family $18/12/50); bookings

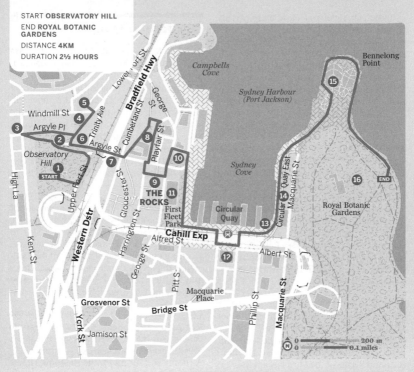

START **OBSERVATORY HILL**
END **ROYAL BOTANIC GARDENS**
DISTANCE **4KM**
DURATION **2½ HOURS**

Neighbourhood Walk
A Rock-Quay Road

Start atop the peaceful knoll of ① **Observatory Hill**. Admire the view, then follow the curvy path down to ② **Argyle Place**, a quiet, English-style village green lined with terraced houses.

Across the road and slightly west, the ③ **Lord Nelson Brewery Hotel** is a contender for the title of Australia's oldest pub. Head back down Argyle Pl and turn left into Lower Fort St. At the corner of Windmill St is the ④ **Hero Of Waterloo**, a rival for the title.

Cross the road to teensy ⑤ **Ferry Lane**. Here you'll find the foundations of Arthur Payne's house; he was the first victim of the 1900 bubonic plague outbreak.

Double back along Lower Fort St to the handsome ⑥ **Garrison Church**. Hook left into Argyle St and head through the ⑦ **Argyle Cut**.

Just past the Cut take the stairs to the left and head along Gloucester Walk to ⑧ **Foundation Park**. Continue along Gloucester Walk, turn right into Atherden

St, then right again, passing Playfair St's terraced houses. Cross Argyle St into Harrington St then jag left into ⑨ **Suez Canal**.

Turn left into George St, Sydney's oldest road (ignore the goofy Harry Potter-ish street numbering). Head down the stairs to the right to ⑩ **Cadman's Cottage**.

Follow Circular Quay past the ⑪ **MCA** and the ferry wharves. Cut underneath the train station to the fabulously renovated ⑫ **Customs House**. Head back to the water to check out the bad buskers and the plaques of the ⑬ **Sydney Writers Walk**. Continue past the ⑭ **Opera Quays** apartment and entertainment complex on Circular Quay East, which is disparagingly referred to by Sydneysiders as 'The Toaster'.

The heaven-sent sails of the ⑮ **Sydney Opera House** are directly in front of you, adjacent to an unmissable perspective of the Sydney Harbour Bridge off to the left. Circumnavigate Bennelong Point, then follow the water's edge to the gates of the ⑯ **Royal Botanic Gardens**.

essential. Or, if you're feeling more earthly, Observatory Hill is great for a picnic. Studded with huge Moreton Bay fig trees, the grassy hilltop buzzes with sweaty hill-climbing joggers, lunchtime CBD escapees and travellers taking time out from The Rocks below. The hill was the site of the colony's first windmill (1796), which ground wheat until someone stole its canvas sails and the structure collapsed.

SH ERVIN GALLERY　　　　GALLERY
Map p248 (☑9258 0173; www.nationaltrust .com.au; Watson Rd, Observatory Hill; adult/child/ under 12 $7/5/free; ☺11am-5pm Tue-Sun; ⓡWynyard) High on the hill inside the old Fort St School (1856), the SH Ervin Gallery exhibits invariably rewarding historical and contemporary Australian art. Annual mainstays include the Salon des Refusés (alternative Archibald Prize entries, see p84) and the Portia Geach Memorial Award. There's a cafe here, too.

ARGYLE PLACE　　　　SQUARE
Map p248 (Argyle St; ⓡCircular Quay) A quiet, English-style village green lined with terraced houses, Argyle Pl offers the sacred appeal of the Garrison Church and the more secular delights of the Lord Nelson Brewery Hotel. Both the Lord Nelson and the Hero of Waterloo hotel, a block north, lay claim to being Sydney's oldest pub. It's said that any Australian has the legal right to graze livestock on the green.

✖ EATING

If you feel like a splurge, this is the place for you. The charismatic back lanes of The Rocks are dotted with little eateries, from 24-hour pancake joints to white-linen palaces. Around the horseshoe from the Harbour Bridge to the Opera House you'll find dozens of upmarket restaurants, all with winning water views. It should come as no surprise that this most touristy of precincts is also the priciest. If at all possible, budget for at least one night where you can throw on your glad rags and let Sydney's showiness seduce you.

✖ Circular Quay

GUILLAUME AT BENNELONG　　　FRENCH $$$
Map p248 (☑9241 1999; www.guillaumeat bennelong.com.au; Sydney Opera House; 2 courses $95; ☺lunch Thu & Fri, dinner Tue-Sat; ⓡCircular Quay) Turn the old 'dinner and a show' cliche into something meaningful under the smallest sail at the Sydney Opera House. Snuggle into a banquette and enjoy the masterful cuisine of acclaimed chef Guillaume Brahimi. His contemporary French fare has fans hollering operatically all over town.

ARIA　　　　MODERN AUSTRALIAN $$$
Map p248 (☑9252 2555; www.ariarestaurant .com; 1 Macquarie St; mains $48; ☺lunch Mon-Fri, dinner daily; ⓡCircular Quay) Aria is a star in Sydney's fine-dining firmament, an award-winning combination of chef Matt Moran's stellar dishes, awesome Opera House views and faultless service. Pre- and after-theatre supper menus are available.

CAFE SYDNEY　　　MODERN AUSTRALIAN $$$
Map p248 (☑9251 8683; www.cafesydney.com; L5, Customs House, 31 Alfred St; mains $34-39; ☺lunch Sun-Fri, dinner Mon-Sat; ⓡCircular Quay) A roomy restaurant on the Customs House roof with harbour views, an outdoor terrace, a glass ceiling, a cocktail bar, friendly staff and Sunday-afternoon jazz. Seafood and wood-grilled dishes prevail.

✖ The Rocks

QUAY　　　　MODERN AUSTRALIAN $$$
Map p248 (☑9251 5600; www.quay.com.au; L3, Overseas Passenger Terminal; set menu lunch/ dinner $125/165; ☺lunch Tue-Fri, dinner daily; ⓡCircular Quay) Quay is shamelessly guilty of breaking the rule that good views make for bad food. Peter Gilmore may be one of Sydney's younger celeb chefs, but Quay's exquisite menu proves he's at the top of his game. And the view? Like dining in a postcard – as long as there's not a cruise ship in the way. Bookings essential.

ROCKPOOL　　　MODERN AUSTRALIAN $$$
Map p248 (☑9252 1888; www.rockpool.com; 107 George St; 2 courses $100; ☺lunch Fri & Sat, dinner Tue-Sat; ⓡCircular Quay) The Neil Perry empire now stretches to seven acclaimed

PEMULWUY'S WAR

Aboriginal resistance to European colonisation was a subject long glossed over in Australian history books, although it began pretty much at first contact. Dutch sailors in the early 17th century had violent run-ins on the Australian west coast, and after Captain Cook came ashore in 1770 and had a rock chucked at him, he wrote of the locals, 'all they seem'd to want was us to be gone'.

Pemulwuy, a member of the Bidjigal group of Dharug speakers from near Botany Bay, very much wanted the British to be gone. He was around 20 years old when Cook visited, and pushing 40 by the time Arthur Phillip and the new arrivals from the First and Second Fleets had begun killing and kidnapping his countrymen and generally acting like they owned the place.

Pemulwuy branded himself as a troublemaker in 1790 by spearing to death Governor Phillip's game shooter. Even though the shooter, John McIntyre, was a convict who reportedly brutalised Aboriginal people, this didn't stop Phillip from threatening a bloody revenge. He sent out the first-ever punitive force against the locals, at first with orders to kill 10 Bidjigals and bring their heads back to Sydney in sacks. Phillip soon calmed down and issued milder orders to capture six for possible hanging.

The mission was an utter flop in any case, and Pemulwuy's 12 years as leader of the struggle against the British began in earnest. At first he limited his guerrilla campaign to small, sporadic raids on farms, stealing livestock and crops; he eventually worked up to leading attacks by groups of more than a hundred men – a huge number by Aboriginal standards of the time.

During his lifetime Pemulwuy survived being shot, as well as having his skull fractured in a rumble with the enormous 'Black Caesar', a bushranger of West Indian descent. He thoroughly cemented his reputation in 1797 in a bloody battle against soldiers and settlers at Parramatta. During the fracas, Pemulwuy took seven pellets of buckshot to the head and body and went down. Bleeding severely and near death, he was captured and placed in hospital. Within weeks he managed to escape, still wearing the leg irons he'd been shackled with.

Pemulwuy's luck ran out in 1802, when he was ambushed and shot dead. It's not entirely clear by whom, but this time there *was* a price on Pemulwuy's head – which was cut off, pickled in alcohol and sent to England (a similar fate befell Yagan, an Aboriginal resistance leader in southwestern Australia, some 30 years later). Pemulwuy's son Tedbury carried on the fight until 1805.

restaurants in three cities, but it was here, in the dying days of the 1980s, that it all began. After two decades the original Rockpool's creations still manage to wow the critics – expect crafty, contemporary cuisine with Asian influences, faultless service and an alluring wine list.

SAILORS THAI CANTEEN   THAI $$

Map p248 (✆9251 2466; www.sailorsthai.com .au; 106 George St; mains $17-29; ⊙lunch & dinner; ⬚Circular Quay) Wedge yourself into a gap between arts-community operators, politicians and media manoeuvrers at Sailors' long communal table and order from the fragrant menu of Thai street-food classics. The balcony tables fill up fast, but fortune might be smiling on you. Downstairs the vibe's more formal and the prices higher.

✖ Dawes Point

FIREFLY   TAPAS $$

Map p248 (✆9241 2031; www.fireflybar.com.au; Pier 7, 17 Hickson Rd; tapas $14-19; ⊙11am-11pm Mon-Sat; ⬚Wynyard) Compact, classy and never snooty, Firefly's outdoor candlelit tables fill with pretheatre patrons having a quick meal before the show (Sydney Theatre is across the road). Come after 8pm when the audience has taken its seats, and tuck into some grilled haloumi, piquillo pepper croquettes and fine wine. Great cocktails, too.

CAFE SOPRA   ITALIAN $$

Map p248 (www.fratellifresh.com.au; 16 Hickson Rd; mains $18-26; ⊙lunch & dinner; ⬚Wynyard) For those who don't want to brave the wilds of Waterloo (p124), there's a branch of the acclaimed Italian eatery and associated Fratelli Fresh providore in Walsh Bay as well.

🍷🍸 DRINKING & NIGHTLIFE

The Rocks has been intoxicated since convict times, with several local pubs dating back to settlement days. The area, particularly along George St, is very touristy, but it's still an interesting place for a brew or two. Circular Quay's eastern shore is lined with mod bars serving pricey drinks, with tables spilling across the promenade.

OPERA BAR
BAR, LIVE MUSIC

Map p248 (www.operabar.com.au; lower concourse, Sydney Opera House; ⊗11.30am-midnight Sun-Thu, to 1am Fri & Sat; ℝCircular Quay) Opera Bar puts all other beer gardens to shame. Right on the harbour with the Opera House on one side and the Harbour Bridge on the other, this perfectly positioned terrace manages a very Sydney marriage of the laid-back and the sophisticated. There's live music from 8.30pm weekdays and 2pm on weekends.

HERO OF WATERLOO
PUB, LIVE MUSIC

Map p248 (✆9252 4553; www.heroofwaterloo .com.au; 81 Lower Fort St; ⊗9.30am-11.30pm Mon-Sat, noon-10pm Sun; ℝCircular Quay) Enter this rough-hewn 1843 sandstone pub to meet some locals, chat up the Irish bar staff and grab an earful of the swing, folk, bluegrass and Celtic bands (Friday to Sunday). Downstairs is an original dungeon where drinkers would sleep off a heavy night before being shanghaied to the high seas via a tunnel leading straight to the harbour.

LORD NELSON BREWERY HOTEL
PUB, BREWERY

Map p248 (✆9251 4044; www.lordnelson.com .au; 19 Kent St; ⊗11am-11pm Mon-Sat, noon-10pm Sun; ℝCircular Quay) Built in 1836 and converted into a pub in 1841, the 'Nello' claims to be Sydney's oldest pub (as do two other pubs). The on-site brewery cooks up robust stouts and ales (try the Old Admiral Ale), and there's decent midrange accommodation upstairs if you've had a few too many.

HARBOUR VIEW HOTEL
PUB

Map p248 (✆9252 4111; www.harbourview.com .au; 18 Lower Fort St; ⊗11am-midnight Mon-Sat, to 10pm Sun; ℝCircular Quay) Built in the 1920s, the curvilicious Harbour View was the main boozer for the Harbour Bridge construction crew. These days it fulfils the same duties for the BridgeClimbers – wave to them from the 2nd-floor balcony as they traverse the lofty girders. The Tooth's KB Lager listed on the tiles out the front is long gone, but there's plenty of Heineken and Boag's on tap.

ARGYLE
BARS, DJ

Map p248 (✆9247 5500; www.theargylerocks .com; 18 Argyle St; ℝCircular Quay) This mammoth conglomeration of five bars is spread through the historic sandstone Argyle Stores buildings, with everything from a cobblestone courtyard to underground cellars resonating with DJs. The decor ranges from rococo couches to white extruded plastic tables, all offset with kooky chandeliers and moody lighting. Great bar food, too.

BLU BAR ON 36
COCKTAIL BAR

Map p248 (✆9250 6000; www.shangri-la.com; L36, 176 Cumberland St; ⊗5pm-midnight Mon-Thu, to 1am Fri & Sat, to 11pm Sun; ℝCircular Quay) The drinks may be pricey, but it's well worth heading up to the top of the Shangri-La hotel for the views, which seem to stretch all the way to New Zealand. The dress code is officially 'smart casual', but err on the side of smart if you can't handle rejection.

AUSTRALIAN HOTEL
PUB

Map p248 (www.australianheritagehotel.com; 100 Cumberland St; ℝCircular Quay) Not only is this pub architecturally notable (c1913), it also boasts a bonza selection of fair dinkum Ocker beer and wine. Keeping with the antipodean theme, the kitchen fires up pizzas topped with kangaroo and saltwater crocodile ($17 to $26).

FORTUNE OF WAR
PUB, LIVE MUSIC

Map p248 (www.fortuneofwar.com.au; 137 George St; ⊗9am-late Mon-Fri, 11am-late Sat, 11am-midnight Sun; ℝCircular Quay) This 1828 drinking den retains much of its original charm and, by the looks of things, some of the original punters, too. There's live music on Friday and Saturday nights from 8pm and on weekend afternoons from 2pm.

☆ ENTERTAINMENT

With the Opera House as its centrepiece, it follows that this neighbourhood is the locus of Sydney's performing-arts scene. Most of the big companies are based here, taking advantage of the area's seven world-class stages. The ratio of theatre luvvies and dance bunnies to the general population is higher in Walsh Bay (home to four major companies and two excellent theatre complexes) than anywhere else in the city. If you're keen to spot famous thespians, there are few better locales.

SYDNEY THEATRE COMPANY   THEATRE

Map p248 (STC; ☎9250 1777; www.sydney theatre.com.au; Pier 4/5, 15 Hickson Rd; tickets free-$90; ☺box office 9am-7pm Mon, to 8.30pm Tue-Fri, 11am-8.30pm Sat, 2hr before show Sun; ☒Wynyard) Established in 1978, the STC is Sydney theatre's top dog and has been an important stepping stone in the careers of many famous Australian actors (including Mel Gibson, Judy Davis, Hugo Weaving, Toni Collette and Miranda Otto). Another alumni, Cate Blanchett, is due to finish her stint as co-artistic director in 2013.

Tours of the company's Wharf and Sydney theatres are held at 10.30am on the first and third Thursdays of the month ($10). Performances are also staged at the Sydney Opera House's Drama Theatre.

OPERA AUSTRALIA   OPERA

Map p248 (☎9318 8200; www.opera-australia .org.au; Sydney Opera House; tickets $85-297; ☒Circular Quay) Opera Australia is the big player in Oz opera, staging over 600 performances a year. The company is based both here and in Melbourne.

BANGARRA DANCE THEATRE   DANCE

Map p248 (☎9251 5333; www.bangarra.com.au; Pier 4/5, 15 Hickson Rd; tickets $33-196; ☒Wynyard) Bangarra is hailed as Australia's finest Aboriginal performance company. Artistic director Stephen Page conjures a fusion of contemporary themes and indigenous traditions, blending Torres Strait Islander dance with Western technique. The company often performs at the Sydney Opera House, as well as interstate and internationally.

SYDNEY DANCE COMPANY   DANCE

Map p248 (SDC; ☎9221 4811; www.sydneydance company.com; Pier 4/5, 15 Hickson Rd; tickets $30-99; ☒Circular Quay) Australia's number one contemporary-dance company has been lubricating the nation's cultural psyche for more than 25 years, staging wildly modern, sexy, sometimes shocking works. SDC dance lessons are just $20! Performances are usually held across the street at Sydney Theatre.

AUSTRALIAN BALLET   DANCE

(☎1300 369 741; www.australianballet.com.au; tickets $33-176) The Melbourne-based Australian Ballet performs a wide repertoire of classic as well as contemporary works. See them twinkle their toes at the Opera House.

SYDNEY SYMPHONY   CLASSICAL MUSIC

(☎02 8215 4600; www.sydneysymphony.com; tickets $35-159) The SSO is blessed with principal conductor and artistic director Vladimir Ashkenazy and plays 140 concerts annually with famous local and international musicians. Catch them at the Sydney Opera House and the City Recital Hall.

AUSTRALIAN CHAMBER ORCHESTRA   CLASSICAL MUSIC

(☎8274 3888; www.aco.com.au; tickets $37-129) Since 1975 the ACO has been making chamber music sexy and adventurous, especially under the tutelage of artistic director and lead violinist Richard Tognetti. Concerts are staged throughout the year at the Opera House and City Recital Hall.

SYDNEY CONSERVATORIUM OF MUSIC   CLASSICAL MUSIC

Map p248 (☎9351 1222; www.music.usyd.edu .au; Conservatorium Rd; tickets free-$30; ☒Circular Quay) This historic venue showcases the talents of its students and their teachers. Choral, jazz, operatic and chamber concerts happen from March to November, along with free lunchtime recitals on Wednesday at 1.10pm.

SYDNEY PHILHARMONIA CHOIRS   CLASSICAL MUSIC

(☎9251 2024; www.sydneyphilharmonia.com.au; tickets $45-90) If you want your world walloped by 350 enthusiastic voices, this is your choir. It also has the 100-voice Symphony Chorus, the 32-voice Chamber Singers and the youth-focused 70-voice Vox. Internationally renowned, the choirs can generally be found at the Opera House, City Recital Hall and St Mary's Cathedral.

BELL SHAKESPEARE THEATRE

(☑1300 305 730; www.bellshakespeare.com.au; tickets $68-79) Australia's Shakespeare specialists stage their Sydney performances in the Opera House's Drama Theatre and Playhouse. Their repertoire deviates from the bard to the likes of Marlowe and Molière.

BASEMENT JAZZ

Map p248 (☑9251 2797; www.thebasement .com.au; 29 Reiby Pl; admission $15-60; ℝCircular Quay) Sydney's premier jazz venue hosts big touring acts and local talent on its intimate stage. A broad musical mandate also sees cabaret, funk, blues, rock and soul bands performing, plus the odd spoken-word gig. Dinner-and-show tickets net you a table by the stage, guaranteeing a better view than the standing-only area by the bar.

OPEN AIR CINEMA CINEMA

(☑1300 366 649; www.stgeorgeopenair.com. au; Mrs Macquaries Rd; tickets $25; ☺box office 6.30pm, screenings 8.30pm Jan & Feb; ℝCircular Quay) Right on the harbour, the outdoor three-storey screen here comes with surround sound, sunsets, skyline and swanky food and wine. Most tickets are purchased in advance, but a limited number of tickets go on sale at the door each night at 6.30pm; check the website for details.

DENDY OPERA QUAYS CINEMA

Map p248 (☑9247 3800; www.dendy.com.au; 2 Circular Quay East; adult/child $17/12; ☺sessions 10am-9pm; ℝCircular Quay) When the harbour glare and squawking seagulls get too much, follow the scent of popcorn into the dark folds of this plush cinema. Screening first-run, independent world films, it's augmented by friendly attendants, a cafe and a bar.

SYDNEY OPERA HOUSE PERFORMANCE VENUE

Map p248 (☑9250 7777; www.sydneyoperahouse. com; Bennelong Point; tickets free-$196; ☺box office 9am-8.30pm Mon-Sat; ℝCircular Quay) The glamorous jewel at the heart of Australian performance, with five main stages: the Concert Hall (capacity 2679), Opera Theatre (1507), Drama Theatre (544), Playhouse (398) and Studio (350 seated, 600 standing). Theatre, comedy, music, dance and ballet are all performed here, but it's the opera that has star billing.

SYDNEY THEATRE PERFORMANCE VENUE

Map p248 (☑9250 1999; www.sydneytheatre .org; 22 Hickson Rd; tickets $30-129; ☺box office 9am-8.30pm Mon-Sat, 3-5.30pm Sun; ℝWynyard) Opened in 2004, this is the most significant theatre built in the city since the Sydney Opera House. The state-of-the-art facility seats 850 and is managed by Sydney Theatre Company. Sydney Dance Company and a host of other troupes also perform here.

WHARF THEATRE PERFORMANCE VENUE

Map p248 (☑9250 1777; www.sydneytheatre .com.au; Pier 4/5, 15 Hickson Rd; tickets $30-90; ℝWynyard) Sydney Theatre Company's own theatre shares a beautiful Edwardian pier building in Walsh Bay with Bangarra Dance Theatre's studios and Sydney Dance Company.

🔒 SHOPPING

Not a place the locals would ever choose for a shopping spree, this 'hood caters mainly to the tastes of wealthy tourists. If you're in the market for some opals, duty-free stuff or tacky souvenirs, this is the place for you. See also Herringbone (p147).

🔒 Circular Quay

AUSTRALIAN WINE CENTRE WINE

Map p248 (☑9247 2755; www.australianwine centre.com; Goldfields House, 1 Alfred St; ℝCircular Quay) This multilingual basement store is packed with quality Australian wine, beer and spirits. Pick up some Hunter Valley semillon or organise a shipment back home. Healthy wallets can access Cuban cigars and a staggering range of prestigious Penfolds Grange wines.

OPAL FIELDS JEWELLERY

Map p248 (☑9247 6800; www.opalfields.com. au; 190 George St; ℝSt James) Billing itself as 'the world's largest opal retailer', this family firm has been turning out jewellery designs incorporating Australia's most famous gemstone for over 30 years. It has another store at 388 George St.

🔒 The Rocks

THE ROCKS MARKET MARKET
Map p248 (www.therocksmarket.com; George St; ⊙10am-4pm Fri-Sun; ⓡCircular Quay) Under a long white canopy, the 150 stalls at the weekend market are a little on the tacky side of the tracks (opals, faux Aboriginal art etc) but are still worth a gander. The Friday 'Foodies Market' is more fulfilling (and filling).

PUPPET SHOP AT THE ROCKS TOYS
Map p248 (⏱9247 9137; www.thepuppetshop. com; 77 George St; ⊙10am-5pm; ⓡCircular Quay) Puppet master Phillip (all the way from the Democratic Republic of Congo) beguiles you with his accent as you 'enter the dazzling caves of wonders'. Dangling from the ceiling of his sandstone cellar are hundreds of incredible handmade wizards, skeletons, soldiers, jesters and spooky Chinese puppets. We'd hate to come here at night…

ORIGINAL & AUTHENTIC ABORIGINAL ART ARTS & CRAFTS
Map p248 (⏱9251 4222; www.authaboriginalart .com au; 79 George St, ⓡCircular Quay) This trustworthy gallery specialises in works from the Central and Western Deserts, Arnhem Land, the Kimberley, Queensland, New South Wales (NSW) and Victoria. There is info available on the artists, and some more unusual stuff for sale, such as painted glass and traditional sand paintings preserved on canvas.

 SPORTS & ACTIVITIES

Circular Quay is the departure point for Sydney Harbour boating activities such as Tribal Warrior (p80), Whale Watching Sydney (p80), Captain Cook Cruises (p80) and Matilda Cruises (p80).

BIKE BUFFS CYCLING
(⏱0414 960 332; www.bikebuffs.com.au; adult/child $95/70; tours ⊙10.30am) Offers four-hour, two-wheeled tours around the harbourside sights (including jaunts over the Harbour Bridge), departing from opposite the Garrison Church (p60). It also hires bikes (per half-day/day/week $35/60/295).

BONZA BIKE TOURS CYCLING
Map p248 (⏱9247 8800; www.bonzabiketours .com; 30 Harrington St; adult/child $99/79; ⓡCircular Quay) These bonza bike boffins run daily four-hour Sydney Classic bike tours – a great introduction to the harbour city, trundling past the Opera House, Hyde Park, Darling Harbour, Chinatown, Sydney Tower and the Royal Botanic Gardens. Other tours tackle the Harbour Bridge, Manly and the city highlights. They also hire bikes (per hour/day $15/40).

PEEK TOURS WALKING TOUR
(⏱0420 244 756; www.peektours.com.au; ⊙10.30am & 2.30pm; ⓡCircular Quay) Gather outside the Customs House (p57) to join a 'free' three-hour walking tour of Circular Quay, the Royal Botanic Gardens, Hyde Park, Macquarie St, Martin Place and The Rocks. OK, so they're not completely free – the guides work them for tips, so you pay what you think is a fair rate.

THE ROCKS WALKING TOURS WALKING TOUR
Map p248 (⏱9247 6678; www.rockswalking tours.com.au; 23 Playfair St; adult/child/family $32/16/80; tours ⊙10.30am, 12.30pm & 2.30pm Mon-Fri, 11.30am & 2pm Sat & Sun; ⓡCircular Quay) Regular 90-minute tours through the historic Rocks, with plenty of not-so-tall tales and interesting minutiae.

THE ROCKS GHOST TOURS WALKING TOUR
(⏱9241 1283; www.ghosttours.com.au; adults $42; tours ⊙6.45pm Apr-Sep, 7.45pm Oct-Mar; ⓡCircular Quay) If you like your spine chilled and your pulse slightly quickened (they're more creepy than properly scary), join one of these two-hour tours, departing Cadman's Cottage nightly. Tours run rain or shine (ponchos provided); bookings essential.

Sydney Harbour

HARBOUR ISLANDS | WATSONS BAY | VAUCLUSE | DOUBLE BAY | DARLING POINT | BALMAIN | NORTH SYDNEY | MOSMAN

Neighbourhood Top Five

❶ Catching a ferry to **Watsons Bay** (p72) and spending an afternoon exploring South Head and lying around Camp Cove before claiming a spot at the pub as the sun sinks over the city.

❷ Gaining a glimpse into the busy world of the Parramatta River (p75) from a ferry's prow.

❸ Sneaking down to secluded **Shark Beach** (p73) for a picnic and a swim.

❹ Exploring the detritus of industry and incarceration on **Cockatoo Island** (p72).

❺ Meeting the native critters at **Taronga Zoo** (p76), the zoo with the awesome view.

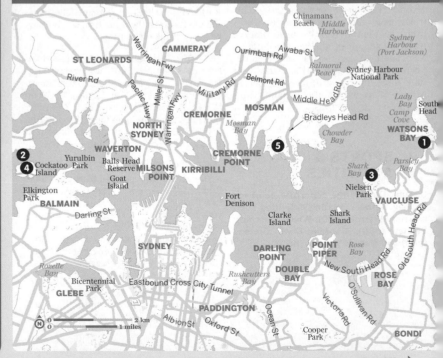

For more detail of this area, see Map p270 ➡

Explore: Sydney Harbour

Sure, it's a stretch to call this large, disparate area a 'neighbourhood', but the harbour is such an integral part of the Sydney experience that we felt it was worth highlighting in this way.

Catch a ferry at Circular Quay for a short hop around the lower North Shore, or allocate half a day to exploring Watsons Bay or heading upriver to Parramatta. Sydney's wealthiest homes are huddled around the harbour in exclusive nooks such as Vaucluse, Point Piper and Darling Point in the Eastern Suburbs and Mosman on the North Shore. Even former working-class bastions such as Balmain, west of the city, are now among the city's most desirable addresses.

Due to its military use, large chunks of the scrub-covered coast have been left much as the First Fleet would have found it. The navy still controls some of the land, but most has been turned over to Sydney Harbour National Park. If you fancy a wilderness walk in the heart of the city, pick a slice to explore and jump on a ferry.

Local Life

➡ **Ferries** There are worse ways of getting to work than cruising on the harbour. For those living close to the water, this is the commute of choice.

➡ **Beaches** Many of the harbour beaches are local treasures, frequented only by those who live in the immediate surrounds.

➡ **Wharves** Dedicated fisherfolk congregate at their favourite spots to try their luck at hooking the big one.

Getting There & Away

➡ **Ferry** Most of the places in this chapter can be reached by ferries from Circular Quay, the major exceptions being Vaucluse and Balmoral.

➡ **Train** Useful stations include Circular Quay, Edgecliff (for Double Bay), Parramatta, Milsons Point, North Sydney and Waverton (for Balls Point).

➡ **Bus** Buses are the only public transport reaching Vaucluse and Balmoral. Useful routes from Circular Quay include 325 (Kings Cross–Double Bay–Rose Bay–Vaucluse–Watsons Bay), 380 (Darlinghurst–Paddington–Bondi–Watsons Bay). The following routes all head from Wynyard through North Sydney and Mosman: 176–180 (for Spit Bridge), 244 (for Obelisk and Cobblers Beach) and 245 (for Balmoral). Bus 229 (for Chinamans Beach) leaves from Milsons Point.

➡ **Parking** A car will come in particularly handy for getting to Vaucluse, Balmoral and Obelisk. Street parking shouldn't be difficult to find, but in busy areas it's often metered.

Lonely Planet's Top Tip

There's no need to shell out on a pricey cruise when you can see exactly the same sights from a ferry. Grab a MyMulti transport ticket (p220), catch the train to Circular Quay and board a ferry to Watsons Bay. Back it up with a river service to Parramatta and you'll have covered more distance than the average cruise. Unless of course you prefer your views accompanied by cocktails, dinner or showgirls...

 Best Places to Eat

➡ Pier (p78)
➡ Bathers' Pavilion (p78)
➡ Ripples (p78)

For reviews, see p78 ➡

 Best Places to Drink

➡ Watsons Bay Hotel (p78)
➡ Golden Sheaf Hotel (p79)
➡ Exchange Hotel (p79)
➡ London Hotel (p79)
➡ Greenwood Hotel (p79)

For reviews, see p78 ➡

Best Beaches

➡ Shark Beach (p73)
➡ Camp Cove (p72)
➡ Balmoral Beach (p78)
➡ Parsley Bay (p73)
➡ Lady Bay (p73)

For reviews, see p72 ➡

SYDNEY HARBOUR

Sydney Harbour

←NORTH

Manly

North Head

South Head

Balmoral Beach

Hunters Bay

Middle Head

Georges Head

Camp Cove

Chowder Head

Taronga Zoo
Even if you've hired a car, the best way to reach this excellent zoo is by ferry. Zip to the top in a cable car then wind your way back down to the wharf.

Taronga Zoo

Little Sirius Cove

Mosman Bay

Manly
Catch a ferry to Manly to explore the outer harbour. Stroll to the beach, drink at the wharf and make sure you're well positioned on your return journey for any photos you missed.

Cremorne Point

Kirribilli
Unless the prime minister and governor-general invite you into their homes for tea, the best views you'll get of Kirribilli House and Admiralty House are from the water. Keep your eyes peeled.

Neutral Bay

Kirribilli House

Kirribilli

Admiralty House

Sydney Harbour Bridge

Luna Park

North Sydney Olympic Pool

Sydney Harbour Bridge
As you pass by the bridge, keep an eye out for the hardy souls trudging along the top on their bridge climb. Head here at sunrise or sunset for golden harbour views.

Top Tip
Don't forget that the harbour continues west of the bridge. Back up a Manly trip with a river ferry service.

Watsons Bay

Imagine Watsons Bay as the isolated fishing village it once was as you pull into its sheltered wharf. Stroll around South Head for views up the harbour and over ocean-battered cliffs.

Fort Denison

Known as Pinchgut, this fortified speck was once a place of fearsome punishment. The bodies of executed convicts were left to hang here as a grisly warning to all; the local Aborigines were horrified.

Ferries

Circular Quay is the hub for state-run Sydney Ferries; nine separate routes leave from here, journeying to 38 different wharves.

Watsons Bay
Vaucluse Bay
Macquarie Lighthouse
Shark Bay

Bradleys Head

Shark Island

Rose Bay
Point Piper

Double Bay

Darling Point

Clark Island

Garden Island

Naval Base

Elizabeth Bay

Fort Denison

Mrs Macquaries Point

Potts Point

Woolloomooloo Finger Wharf

Sydney Opera House

Government House

Farm Cove

Royal Botanic Gardens

Circular Quay

The Rocks

Sydney Opera House

You can clamber all over it and walk around it, but nothing beats the perspective you get as your ferry glides past the Opera House's dazzling sails. Have your camera at the ready.

Circular Quay

Circular Quay has been at the centre of Sydney life since the First Fleet dropped anchor here in 1788. Book your ferry ticket, check the indicator boards for the correct pier and get onboard.

◉ SIGHTS

◉ Harbour Islands

COCKATOO ISLAND   ISLAND
(☎8969 2100; www.cockatooisland.gov.au; tours adult/child $18/14; ⊗tours 11.30am & 1.30pm Sun; 🚢Cockatoo Island) Studded with photogenic industrial relics, convict architecture and art installations, fascinating Cockatoo Island (Wareamah) opened to the public in 2007 and now has regular ferry services, a campground and rental accommodation. Weekly guided tours dig into the island's time as a prison, shipyard and naval base (bookings essential), but information boards and audio tours ($5) make a self-guided wander rewarding.

A spooky tunnel passes clear through the middle of the island and you can also explore the remains of the prison. During WWII most of the old sandstone buildings were stripped of their roofs and converted into bomb shelters. Solitary confinement cells were unearthed here recently after being filled in and forgotten in the 1890s

FORT DENISON   ISLAND, FORTRESS
Map p270 (ferry & tour adult/child $27/17; ⊗tours 12.15pm & 2.30pm daily, plus 10.45am Wed-Sun; 🚢Captain Cook Cruises) Called Mat-te-wan-ye (rocky island) by the Cadigal people, in colonial times the small fortified island off Mrs Macquaries Pt was a sorry site of suffering used to isolate recalcitrant convicts (nicknamed 'Pinchgut' for its meagre rations). Fears of a Russian invasion during the Crimean War in the mid-19th-century led to its fortification. It now has a cafe.

Captain Cook Cruises (p80) runs ferries to the island from Darling Harbour and Circular Quay about seven times a day, but to access the Martello tower you'll need to prebook a tour through the NPWS, based at Cadman's Cottage (p58).

GOAT ISLAND   ISLAND
(adult/child $29/24; 🚢from Cadman's Cottage) Goat Island, west of the Harbour Bridge, has been a shipyard, quarantine station and gunpowder depot in its previous lives. Three-hour heritage tours depart at 10.30am on Sundays from Cadman's Cottage; bookings essential. On the last Sunday of the month the boat departs the island 45 minutes later

(and costs $3 more), allowing extra island time for a picnic lunch (bring your own).

SHARK ISLAND   ISLAND
(ferry adult/child $17/15; 🚢Captain Cook Cruises) Little Shark Island off Rose Bay makes a great picnic getaway, but there's not a lot here except for toilets and drinking water – and at 250m by 100m, you'll soon have explored every inch of it. Captain Cook Cruises runs five ferries per day to the island from Circular Quay (jetty 6) and Darling Harbour (pier 26).

◉ Watsons Bay

The narrow peninsula ending in South Head is one of Sydney's most sublime spots. Approaching from Bondi, as Old South Head Rd leaves the sheer ocean cliffs to descend to Watsons Bay, the view of Sydney Harbour is breathtaking.

WATSONS BAY   NEIGHBOURHOOD
(🚢Watsons Bay) Watsons Bay, east of the city centre and north of Bondi, was once a small fishing village, as evidenced by the tiny heritage cottages that pepper the suburb's narrow streets (and now cost a fortune). While you're here, tradition demands that you sit in the beer garden at Watsons Bay Hotel at sunset and watch the sun fall behind the disembodied Harbour Bridge, jutting up above Bradley's Head.

On the ocean side, **The Gap** is a dramatic cliff-top lookout where proposals and suicides happen with similar frequency.

CAMP COVE   BEACH
(Cliff St; 🚢Watsons Bay) Immediately north of Watsons Bay, this small swimming beach is popular with both families and topless sunbathers. When Governor Phillip realised Botany Bay didn't cut it, he sailed north into Sydney Harbour, dropped anchor and sunk his boots into Camp Cove's gorgeous golden sand on 21 January 1788.

SOUTH HEAD   PARK
(Cliff St; ⊗5am-10pm; 🚢Watsons Bay) At the northern end of Camp Cove, the **South Head Heritage Trail** kicks off, leading into a section of Sydney Harbour National Park. It passes old battlements and a path heading down to Lady Bay, before continuing on to the candy-striped **Hornby**

Lighthouse and the sandstone **Lightkeepers' Cottages** (1858) on South Head itself.

The harbour views and crashing surf on the ocean side make this a very dramatic and beautiful spot indeed.

LADY BAY   BEACH

(Cliff St; ☒Watsons Bay) Also known as Lady Jane, this diminutive gay nudist beach sits at the bottom of a cliff, on top of which (somewhat ironically) is a Royal Australian Navy facility. To get here, follow the cliff-top walking track from (somewhat aptly) Camp Cove. All together now: 'In the navy...'

◉ Vaucluse

Vaucluse is immediately south of Watsons Bay, taking up the middle section of the peninsula that forms South Head. There are no ferries, so it's best reached by New South Head Rd, which is the continuation of William St; bus services are frequent.

VAUCLUSE HOUSE   HISTORIC BUILDING

(www.hht.net.au; Wentworth Rd; adult/child/family $8/4/17; ⊙9.30am-4pm Fri-Sun; ☐325) Vaucluse House is an imposing, turreted specimen of Gothic Australiana set amid 10 hectares of lush gardens. The house was started in 1805 and tinkered with into the 1860s. Decorated with beautiful European period pieces including Bohemian glass, heavy oak 'Jacobethan' furniture and Meissen china, the

---

SYDNEY HARBOUR NATIONAL PARK

Sydney Harbour National Park protects large swaths of bushland around the harbour shoreline, plus several harbour islands. Amid the greenery you'll find walking tracks, scenic lookouts, Aboriginal carvings, beaches and historic sites. The park incorporates South Head and Nielsen Park south of the harbour, but most of it is on the North Shore – including Bradleys Head, Middle Head, Dobroyd Head and North Head. Free brochures, including self-guided tours, are available from the park office in Cadman's Cottage (p58) in The Rocks, which is itself part of the park.

---

house offers visitors a rare glimpse into early (albeit privileged) colonial life in Sydney.

It was occupied from 1827 to 1862 by William Charles Wentworth, his wife Sarah and their children. The son of a convict mother, Wentworth became a barrister and cowrote the first New South Wales colonial constitution, but was outcast from high society because of his democratic leanings. He held the 'outrageous' view that Australian-born colonials were the equals of the English, and that political and legal rights should be extended to emancipists (freed convicts). Wentworth was also an intrepid explorer. In 1831 he was part of the first European expedition to cross the Blue Mountains.

**NIELSEN PARK
& SHARK BEACH**   PARK, BEACH

Map p270 (Vaucluse Rd; ⊙daylight hr; ☐325) If in need of a swim, Will Wentworth would no doubt have strolled down to Shark Beach in Nielsen Park, once part of the then 206-hectare Vaucluse House estate. Despite the beach's ominous name, there's really nothing to worry about – there's a shark net to put paranoid swimmers at ease.

Today the park and Greycliffe House, a beautiful 1851 Gothic sandstone pile (not open to visitors), are surrounded by a section of Sydney Harbour National Park. Visit on a weekday when it's not too busy: just mums, kids, oldies and people taking sickies from work.

PARSLEY BAY   BEACH

(enter near 80a Hopetoun Ave; ☐325) A hidden gem, this little bay has a calm swimming beach, a lawn dotted with sandstone sculptures for picnics and play, and a cute suspension bridge. Keep an eye out for water dragons (native reptiles) as you walk down through the bush.

MACQUARIE LIGHTHOUSE   LIGHTHOUSE

(Old South Head Rd; ☐380) When the original Francis Greenway–designed lighthouse (1818) fell into disrepair and was dismantled, the current lighthouse (1883) was built in front of it as an exact replica. It's a pretty spot, with grassy lawns, heavenly ocean views and a cliff-top trail extending to North Bondi. Before the lighthouse was built, a series of fires were lit along this coast to keeps ships away from the cliffs.

◎ Double Bay

DOUBLE BAY   NEIGHBOURHOOD
(🚇Double Bay) Double Bay (aka 'Double Pay')
maintains a flashy, nouveau-riche rep. The
boutiques here have suffered since Westfield Bondi Junction opened up the hill, but
no one seems too worried. Immediately to
the west, Edgecliff is a nondescript transport hub centred on New South Head Rd,
sheltering the moneyed mansions of Darling Point – one of Sydney's richest nooks.

FREE REDLEAF POOL   BEACH
(536 New South Head Rd; 🚇Double Bay) Not really a pool at all (it's a fenced-off section
of Seven Shillings Beach), family-friendly
Redleaf is the closest swimming spot to the
city – as such, it attracts an urbane cross-
section of inner-eastern locals. A boardwalk runs around the top of the shark net,
and two floating pontoons are sought-after
posing platforms for those who confuse
beaches with catwalks.

◎ Darling Point

LINDESAY   HISTORIC BUILDING
(☎9363 2401; www.nationaltrust.com.au; 1a Car-
thona Ave; tour $8; ⏱tours 10am, 11am & noon
1st Thu of the month; 🚇Darling Point) It's rarely
open but aside from Nicole Kidman inviting you in for tea, this is probably your best
chance to look inside an actual Darling
Point mansion. Built in 1834, it's still got its
Georgian interiors, servants' quarters and
long lawn overlooking the harbour. Lindesay is positioned directly above the Darling
Point ferry stop.

◎ Balmain

Balmain sits on its own peninsula, immediately west of the city centre. There are
frequent ferry services to each of its four
wharves: Balmain East, Balmain (Thames
St), Birchgrove and Balmain West.

BALMAIN   NEIGHBOURHOOD
(🚇Balmain East) Once a tough, working-class
neighbourhood, Balmain now rivals Paddington in Victorian-era desirability – with
the added advantage of being surrounded
by water and city-bound ferries. Darling St
traverses the spine of Balmain's peninsula,
and makes for a decent pub crawl. Balmain's
frangipani-scented streets contain dozens
of historically significant buildings, most of
which are privately owned.

The most notable is the graciously pro-
portioned **Hampton Villa** (12b Grafton St), a
Georgian marine villa (1847). NSW Premier
Sir Henry Parkes, the 'Father of Federation',
lived here from 1888 to 1892. Nearby is the
squat, shingle-roofed **Clontarf Cottage** (4
Wallace St), an impressively restored house
(1844) saved from demolition by protests
in the late 1980s; and the semiderelict **St
Mary's Hall** (7 Adolphus St), built around
1851. Darling St has the **Watch House** (179
Darling St), Sydney's oldest surviving lockup
(1854), **Waterman's Cottage** (12 Darling St),
built in 1841, and **Cathermore** (50 Darling
St), Balmain's first bakery (1841), which
later became the Waterford Arms pub.

ELKINGTON PARK   PARK
(cnr Glassop & White Sts; 🚇Balmain West) If
Balmain's endless photogenia doesn't float
your boat, head to Elkington Park, named
in 1883 after a local politician. At the bottom of the escarpment, the magnificently
restored late-Victorian (1884) timber enclo-
sure at the tidal **Dawn Fraser Baths** (☎9555
1903; www.lpac.nsw.gov.au; adult/child $4.20/$3;
⏱7.15am-6.30pm Oct-Apr) picturesquely protects swimmers from underwater undesirables. Australia's all-conquering 1956–64
Olympian Dawn Fraser sacrificed her youth
here swimming laps.

YURULBIN POINT   PARK
(Louisa Rd; 🚇Birchgrove) On the northern
tip of the Balmain peninsula (technically
Birchgrove), this narrow point stretches
to within 300m of the North Shore. Once
called Long Nose Point, it was a shipyard
until 1971, when it became a public park,
reverting to its indigenous name (meaning
'swift running water') in 1994.

◎ North Sydney

BALLS HEAD RESERVE   PARK
(Balls Head Rd; 🚃Waverton) Scruffy, bushy
Balls Head Reserve not only has great views
of the harbour, the city skyline and the industrial relics on Goat Island, but also a
wiggly waterline and inland paths, ancient
Aboriginal rock paintings and carvings (although they're not easily discernible), and
barbecue facilities.

PARRAMATTA RIVER

Sydney Harbour gets all the attention but a jaunt upriver to the geographical centre of the metropolis is just as interesting. As you pass old industrial sites and gaze into millionaire's back yards, a window opens onto a watery world in the heart of Sydney where school rowing crews get put through their paces, groups of mates glide pasts on yachts, solo kayakers work up a sweat and Mediterranean men fish off the wharves at night.

In geological terms the harbour is actually a drowned river valley, which makes it very hard to distinguish what's harbour and what's river, but as you glide past Cockatoo Island, where the Parramatta and Lane Cove Rivers meet, it's river all the way.

The ferry from Circular Quay to Parramatta takes about 1¼ hours (adult/child $7/3.50), although on some low tides the boats stop at Rydalmere, one wharf earlier, and a bus continues from there. If you feel like making a day of it, Sydney Olympic Park and Parramatta both have a smattering of interesting sights. And if you want to speed up your return trip, both are connected to the train network.

Sydney's reserves of glamour are running dry by the time you get as far west as Parramatta. The second European settlement in Australia, Parramatta was founded by First Fleet convict labour when Sydney Cove proved to be lousy for growing vegies. Originally called Rose Hill (despite the nearest roses being half a world away), the town became known by what is actually a mis-hearing of its Darug Aboriginal name, Burramatta. It roughly translates to 'place of the eels'; the slippery critters are now the mascot of Parramatta's rugby league team. Consumed by Sydney's westward sprawl, Parramatta is a bland commercial centre, with some historic gems nestled among the mostly dreary modern developments.

From the wharf, follow the river west to the knowledgable Parramatta Heritage & Visitor Information Centre (p226) and grab a map of key sights. The centre is a museum in its own right, with temporary exhibits by local artists, as well as a permanent exhibition on Parramatta's history and culture.

Follow Church St to **Bicentennial Square**, the civic centre, containing St John's Cathedral (with towers dating to 1819) and the **Parramatta Town Hall** (1883). The open, paper-dry lawns of **St John's Cemetery** (O'Connell St; ☉sunrise-sunset) are the resting place of many an early settler.

Old Government House (☏9635 8149; www.oldgovernmenthouse.com.au; Parramatta Park; adult/child $9/6; ☉10.30am-4.30pm Tue-Sun), established in 1799, was Parramatta's first farm and housed successive NSW governors until the 1850s. This elegant Georgian Palladian building is now a preciously maintained museum; entry is via hour-long tours around colonially furnished rooms. Phone for details about monthly ghost nights.

Elizabeth Farm (☏9635 9488; www.hht.nsw.gov.au; 70 Alice St; adult/child $8/4; ☉9.30am-4pm Tue-Sun; ☒Rosehill) contains part of Australia's oldest surviving European home (1793), built by renegade pastoralist and rum trader John Macarthur, a ruthless capitalist whose politicking made him immensely wealthy and a thorn in the side of successive governors. It's now a hands-on museum – recline on the reproduction furniture and thumb voyeuristically through Elizabeth Macarthur's letters.

Not far away, surrounded by 200-year-old camphor laurels and English oaks, **Hambledon Cottage** (☏9635 6924; 63 Hassall St; adult/child $4/2; ☉11am-4pm Thu-Sun), built in 1824 for the governess of the Macarthurs' daughter, was later used as weekend lodgings and almost became a car park in the 1980s.

An 1835 colonial bungalow, **Experiment Farm Cottage** (☏9635 5655; www.nsw.nationaltrust.org.au; 9 Ruse St; adult/child $6/5; ☉10.30am-3.30pm Wed-Sun) was built by Governor Phillip in 1791 for emancipist farmer James Ruse as an experiment to see how long it would take him to wean himself from government supplies. Ruse subsequently became Australia's first private farmer; his life is depicted in the musty cellar museum.

Like the Manly Scenic Walkway, it's easy to shut yourself off amid the sandstone and scrub here and imagine how Sydney must have been before European settlement. From Waverton Station turn left and follow Bay Rd, which becomes Balls Head Rd. It's a 10-minute walk.

LUNA PARK AMUSEMENT PARK

Map p270 (☑9922 6644; www.lunaparksydney .com; 1 Olympic Dr; single-ride tickets $10, ride pass $20-40; ☉11am-10pm Fri & Sat, 10am-6pm Sun, 11am-4pm Mon; ☒Milsons Point/Luna Park) Across the Sydney Harbour Bridge from The Rocks is this famous 1935 amusement park with its sinister chip-toothed clown entry. The park has been periodically closed by noise police in recent decades – get in now before it closes again! The Ferris Wheel, the Rotor and the Flying Saucer offer varying degrees of nerve-rack and nausea. You can pay as you go, or buy a height-based unlimited ride pass. Extended hours during school and public holidays.

KIRRIBILLI POINT POINT

Map p270 (☒Kirribilli) The Sydney residences of Australia's governor-general and prime minister are located on Kirribilli Point, east of the Sydney Harbour Bridge. When they're in town, the PM gets some shut-eye in the Gothic Revival–style **Kirribilli House** (Map p270), built in 1854, while the GG bunkers down in **Admiralty House** (Map p270), built in 1846, which is nearer the bridge and is the one everyone dreams of living in (if it came without the job).

Both houses are better spotted from the water than by peering through the lightly fortified gates (they ain't the White House).

Squeezed between the Harbour Bridge and the politicians, the diminutive **Dr Mary Booth Reserve Foreshore Walkway** (Map p270; ☒Milsons Point) offers great views of the Opera House and the city skyline.

MARY MACKILLOP PLACE MUSEUM, CHURCH

Map p270 (☑8912 4878; www.marymackillop place.org.au; 7 Mount St; adult/child/family $8/5/21; ☉10am-4pm; ☒North Sydney) This hushed museum tells the life story of St Mary of the Cross (aka Mary MacKillop), Australia's only Catholic saint, a dedicated and outspoken educator and pioneer who prevailed over conservative hierarchical ideals despite being excommunicated for six months. You'll find St Mary's tomb inside the chapel.

The museum has interesting interactive displays and a kookily whimsical *Nuns on the Run* automaton, proving that the Josephites (the order that MacKillop founded) have a sense of humour.

CREMORNE POINT POINT

Map p270 (☒Cremorne Point) Cremorne Point (technically Robertsons Point; Woolwarra-jurng to the Eora people) is a beaut spot for a picnic on grassy **Cremorne Reserve** (Map p270) or a swim in the free saltwater **MacCallum Pool** (Map p270). The harbour views from here are downright delicious (especially when the New Year's Eve fireworks are erupting).

Ferries chug past, newspaper readers flip pages, and there's a coffee shop in the ferry terminal – pretty darn chilled out.

MAY GIBBS' NUTCOTE MUSEUM

Map p270 (☑9953 4453; www.maygibbs.com.au; 5 Wallaringa Ave; adult/child/family $9/3.50/20; ☉11am-3pm Wed-Sun; ☒Neutral Bay) Spanish Mission–style Nutcote (1925) is the former home of much-loved Australian children's author May Gibbs, who wrote *Snugglepot & Cuddlepie*. It's now restored to its 1930s glory and houses a museum devoted to her life and work. Cheery volunteer guides will show you around, and there are beautiful gardens, a tearoom and a gift shop. It's a five-minute walk from the wharf.

◉ Mosman

🏊 TARONGA ZOO ZOO

Map p270 (☑9969 2777; www.taronga.org.au; Bradleys Head Rd; adult/child $44/22; ☉9am-5pm, last admission 4.30pm; ☒Taronga Zoo) A 12-minute ferry ride from Circular Quay or a short drive from Manly, Taronga Zoo has 75 hectares of bushy harbour hillside chock-full of kangaroos, koalas and similarly hirsute Australians. The zoo's 4000 critters have million-dollar harbour views but seem blissfully unaware of the privilege. The animals are well looked after, with more natural open enclosures than cages.

Highlights include the nocturnal platypus habitat, the Great Southern Oceans section, the Asian elephant display, and seal and bird shows. Animal displays and feedings happen throughout the day; twilight concerts jazz things up in summer.

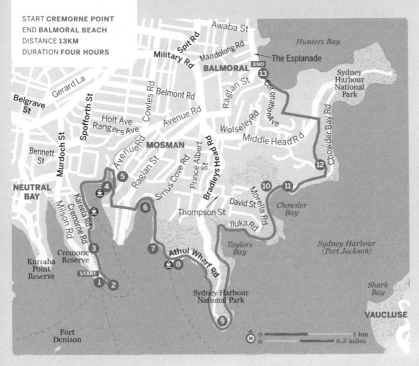

START **CREMORNE POINT**
END **BALMORAL BEACH**
DISTANCE **13KM**
DURATION **FOUR HOURS**

Neighbourhood Walk
North Shore Harbour Hustle

Ride the ferry from Circular Quay to chilled-out ❶ **Cremorne Point**, surrounded by the native shrub of Cremorne Reserve. For views, wander out to ❷ **Robertsons Point** on the tip of the reserve.

Heading north, you'll trundle past the well-tended plots of palms, ferns and philodendrons in ❸ **Lex & Ruby's Garden**, named after the local couple who lovingly tended it for decades; it's now National Trust–protected.

Keep walking around the other side of exclusive ❹ **Mosman Bay**. Check out the historic stone building called the ❺ **Barn**, an early colonial structure that's now a scout hall. Just beyond is the Wharf Store; go up the stairs to Mosman St, following it left to McLeod St.

Turn left at McLeod St, scoot across Musgrave St and take the stairs down to the other side, then cross Raglan St, where more stairs descend to the shore. Wind around ❻ **Little Sirius Cove** and take the stone steps onto a shoreline path, which runs around Taronga Zoo.

Before you reach the zoo, take the stairs down to ❼ **Whiting Beach** (look for the 'No Dogs' sign), a secluded sandy bay. Further along the lush, shady path is the ❽ **Taronga Zoo** entrance and ferry wharf.

Keep following the path into Sydney Harbour National Park, through ❾ **Bradleys Head** and ❿ **Clifton Gardens**, where you'll link up with a track that has amazing views of the heads. Next up is ⓫ **Chowder Bay Naval Base**, with its pedestrian-accessible foreshore.

Wander over to the ⓬ **lookout** on the right, which has a glorious cityscape panorama and views over the battlements that once defended Sydney from threats both real and imagined. Continue down the path as it darts through bushy scrubland.

Follow the track past some magnificently gnarled red gum trees on the right-hand side, then down some steps to ⓭ **Balmoral Beach**.

Tours include **Nura Diya** (☑9978 4782; 90-minute tour adult/child $99/69; ☺9.45am Mon, Wed & Fri), where indigenous guides introduce you to native animals and share Dreaming stories about them, while giving an insight into traditional Aboriginal life. **Roar & Snore** (☑9978 4791; adult/child $275/190) is an overnight family experience that includes a night-time safari, a buffet dinner, breakfast and tents under the stars.

From the wharf, the Sky Safari cable car or a bus will whisk you to the main entrance (for free if you've got a ZooPass), from where you can traverse the zoo downhill back to the ferry. A Zoo Pass (adult/child/family $51/25/143) from Circular Quay includes return ferry rides, the bus or cable-car ride to the top and zoo admission. Parking is scarce – take public transport instead. Disabled access is good, even if arriving by ferry, and wheelchairs are available.

BALMORAL BEACH
BEACH

Map p270 (The Esplanade; ☐245) The beachy enclave of Balmoral faces off with Manly across Middle Harbour, and has some good restaurants and a beaut swimming beach. Split in two by an unfeasibly picturesque rocky outcrop, Balmoral attracts picnicking North Shore families. Swimmers migrate to the shark-netted southern end.

CHINAMANS BEACH
BEACH

(Cyprian St; ☐229) Gorgeous, peaceful and serene, despite its proximity to busy Balmoral. Good for a photogenic swim.

OBELISK
BEACH

Map p270 (Chowder Bay Rd; ☐244) An isolated gay and nudist beach surrounded by bushland in the Middle Head section of Sydney Harbour National Park. It loses the sun quickly in the afternoon (chilly for the nudists).

COBBLERS BEACH
BEACH

Map p270 (Cobblers Beach Rd; ☐244) A nude and secluded beach on the other side of Middle Head from its partner in crime, Obelisk.

✖ EATING

The best harbour restaurants dip their feet in the water, with some offering amazing views of the city.

PIER
SEAFOOD $$$

(☑9327 6561; www.pierrestaurant.com.au; 594 New South Head Rd, Rose Bay; mains $42-45; ☺lunch & dinner; ⬛Rose Bay) Bobbing with the marina yachts on stilts over Rose Bay, Pier serves exhilarating seafood – some critics have suggested that it's the best fish restaurant in the country. Certainly you can be guaranteed a memorable meal, gazing at the harbour from the deck or from inside the glassed-in pavilion. Pier is on New South Rd, the main road between Double Bay and Vaucluse.

BATHERS' PAVILION
FRENCH $$$

Map p270 (☑9969 5050; www.batherspavilion .com.au; 4 The Esplanade, Balmoral Beach; mains restaurant $48, cafe $16-36; ☺lunch & dinner; ☑; ☐245) Spanish Mission–style architecture, harbour views and outstanding food collide at one of Sydney's most enduringly popular restaurants. The seasonal menu focuses on produce from small local providers, with plenty of seafood; there's also a full vegetarian menu. Under the same roof, Bathers' Café opens for breakfast at 7am, serving equally scrumptious fare (including delicious pizza) at more democratic prices.

RIPPLES
FUSION $$

Map p270 (☑9929 7722; www.ripplesmilsons point.com.au; Olympic Dr, Milsons Point; breakfast $12-18, lunch & dinner $29-32; ☺breakfast, lunch & dinner; ⬛Milsons Point/Luna Park) Flanked by the Harbour Bridge, the choppy harbour and Luna Park's insane grin, Ripples does well to compete with the view and come out on top. Expect lots of seafood with subtle Asian and European flavours, along with fish and chips cooked to crispy perfection.

🍷 DRINKING & NIGHTLIFE

WATSONS BAY HOTEL
PUB

(www.watsonsbayhotel.com.au; 1 Military Rd, Watsons Bay; ☺10am-11pm; ⬛Watsons Bay) One of the great pleasures in life is languishing in the rowdy beer garden of the Watsons Bay Hotel, mere metres from the ferry wharf, with a jug of sangria after a day at the beach. Stay to watch the sun go down over the city and grab some seafood if you're hungry – fish and chips or a fiddly platter complete with crabs and cray.

GOLDEN SHEAF HOTEL PUB
(☎9327 5877; www.goldensheaf.com.au; 429 New South Head Rd, Double Bay; ⌖Double Bay) This noble, rambling old brick pub has a shady beer garden, a sports bar with pool tables, a bistro, a cocktail bar, a rooftop terrace and a dance floor. The musical mandate covers DJ-delivered rock, soul, hip hop, samba and house. An impressive memorabilia wall includes autographed photos and albums from the likes of the Beatles and Bowie.

The Golden Sheaf is on the main road passing through Double Bay.

EXCHANGE HOTEL PUB
(☎8755 2555; www.exchangehotel.com.au; cnr Beattie & Mullens Sts, Balmain; ⊗11.30am-midnight Mon-Sat, to 10pm Sun; ⌖Balmain West) The wedge-shaped Exchange (1885) has been lavishly renovated (all charcoal and grey, pressed tin and chandeliers) and now houses an upmarket restaurant. Stake a place on the balcony for a sundowner. From the Balmain West ferry stop, head straight up Elliott St and continue on to Beattie St.

LONDON HOTEL PUB
(☎9555 1377; www.londonhotel.com.au; 234 Darling St, Balmain; ⊗11am-midnight Mon-Sat, noon-10pm Sun; ⌖Balmain) The Harbour Bridge views from the London's long balcony are quintessentially Sydney (about as far from London as you can get). There's a great range of Oz beers on tap, plus a few quality Euro interlopers (Heineken, Hoegaarden), jovial punters and nonstop rugby on the telly. Darling St is Balmain's main drag.

GREENWOOD HOTEL BAR
Map p270 (☎9964 9477; www.greenwoodhotel .com; L1, Greenwood Plaza, 36 Blue St, North Sydney; ⌖North Sydney) The transformation of this slate-roofed sandstone schoolhouse (1878) into a pumping bar has left it largely unchanged. In fact, apart from the Friday night after-work brigade, school is a not-too-distant memory for most of the punters. On Thursdays acoustic musicians strum and DJs spin until 3am; on Friday evenings the decks shift to the courtyard for a laid-back wind down.

☆ ENTERTAINMENT

ENSEMBLE THEATRE THEATRE
Map p270 (☎9929 0644; www.ensemble.com .au; 78 McDougall St, Kirribilli; tickets $54-69; ⌖North Sydney) The long-running Ensemble Theatre presents mainstream theatre by overseas and Australian playwrights (think David Williamson and David Hare), generally with well-known Australian actors.

HAYDEN ORPHEUM PICTURE PALACE CINEMA
Map p270 (☎9908 4344; www.orpheum.com .au; 380 Military Rd, Cremorne; adult/child $19/14; ⊗sessions 11am-8.50pm; ☐244) Return to cinema's golden age at this fab art deco gem (1935). It still has its original Wurlitzer organ, which gets a workout at special events.

STARLIGHT CINEMA CINEMA
Map p270 (☎1300 438 849; www.starlight cinema.com.au; North Sydney Oval, Miller St, North Sydney; adult/child $20/13; ⊗mid-Jan–early Mar; ⌖North Sydney) The lure of big outdoor movie screens is too good for Sydneysiders to pass up on long, hot summer nights.

🛍 SHOPPING

KIRRIBILLI MARKETS MARKET
Map p270 (www.kncsydney.org; Bradfield Park, off South Alfred St, Milsons Point; ⊗7am-3pm 4th Sat of the month; ⌖Milsons Point/Luna Park) A monthly market offering exotic foods and lively harbourside hubbub, selling everything from vintage clothes and real (and faux) antiques to kids' gear and all kinds of jewellery. It also offers a fashion, art and design market on the second Saturday of the month (9am–3pm).

BALMAIN MARKET MARKET
(www.balmainmarket.com.au; 223 Darling St, Balmain; ⊗8.30am-4pm Sat; ⌖Balmain) This small market is set in the shady grounds of St Andrews Congregational Church. Stalls sell arts, crafts, books, clothing, jewellery, plants, and fruit and veg. From the Balmain ferry wharf, head up Thames St to Darling St and turn left.

🏃 SPORTS & ACTIVITIES

JAMES CRAIG
SAILING

Map p254 (☑9298 3888; www.shf.org.au; Wharf 7, Pyrmont; from $199; ⊙10.30am-5pm Sat & Sun every 2nd weekend; 🚢Pyrmont Bay) The *James Craig* is a hulking three-masted iron barque built in England in 1874. Abandoned in Tasmania in the 1930s, she was floated to Sydney and restored in the '70s. Tall-ship tours beyond the Heads on the open-ocean swell take place fortnightly (bookings essential) and include lunch, morning and afternoon tea and a sea shanty or three.

🖋TRIBAL WARRIOR
CULTURAL TOUR

Map p248 (☑9699 3491; www.tribalwarrior.org; Eastern Pontoon, Circular Quay; adult/child $60/40; 🚇Circular Quay) Cruise, learn and experience Aboriginal culture and history on this two-hour boat trip, stopping at Clark Island for a traditional indigenous welcome. You'll also be contributing to a worthwhile community self-sufficiency project. Bookings essential; no cruises Monday.

WHALE WATCHING SYDNEY
CRUISE

Map p248 (☑9583 1199; www.whalewatchingsydney.net; Harbour Master Steps, Circular Quay; adult/child $89/54; 🚇Circular Quay) Humpback and southern right whales habitually shunt up and down the Sydney coastline, sometimes venturing into the harbour. Between May and December, WWS runs three-hour tours (adult/child $85/50) beyond the Heads.

NATURAL WANDERS
KAYAKING

Map p270 (☑0427 225 072; www.kayaksydney.com; Lavender Bay; tours $65-120; 🚢Milsons Point/Luna Park) Offers exhilarating morning tours around the Harbour Bridge, Lavender Bay, Balmain and Birchgrove.

SYDNEY HARBOUR KAYAKS
KAYAKING

(☑9960 4389; www.sydneyharbourkayaks.com.au; 81 Parriwi Rd, Mosman; ⊙9am-5pm Mon-Fri, 7.30am-5pm Sat & Sun; 🚌176-180) Rents kayaks (per hour from $20) and leads half-day ecotours ($99) from near the Spit Bridge, which crosses Middle Harbour.

SYDNEY BY SAIL
SAILING

Map p254 (☑9280 1110; www.sydneybysail.com; 2 Murray St, Darling Harbour; 🚢Pyrmont Bay) Departing daily from outside the Maritime Museum, Sydney by Sail offers cruises (three hours $150) and courses, including a weekend introductory sailing course ($595).

CAPTAIN COOK CRUISES
CRUISE

Map p248 (☑9206 1111; www.captaincook.com.au; Wharf 6, Circular Quay; adult/child $42/24; 🚇Circular Quay) As well as ritzy lunch and dinner cruises, this crew offers the aquatic version of a hop-on/hop-off bus tour, stopping at Watsons Bay, Shark Island, Taronga Zoo, Fort Denison, Circular Quay, Luna Park and Darling Harbour.

MATILDA CRUISES
CRUISE

Map p248 (☑8270 5188; www.matilda.com.au; Wharf 6, Circular Quay; 🚇Circular Quay) Not waltzing but sailing, Matilda offers nine different cruise options on plush catamarans, including daily whale-watching trips between mid-May and October (from $79). Also available are breakfast (from $55), coffee ($49), lunch (from $75), cocktail (from $39) and dinner (from $85) cruises, and a hop-on/hop-off harbour circuit (from $39).

MAGISTIC CRUISES
CRUISE

Map p254 (☑8296 7222; www.magisticcruises.com.au; Wharf 5, King St; 🚢Darling Harbour) The fancy Magistic floaters take you on a range of cruises, ranging from the one-hour sightseeing cruise ($25 to $33) offering all the harbour icons to two-hour lunch (per person $60 to $96) and dinner ($65 to $158) cruises with a seafood buffet. Cruises also depart from Wharf 6 at Circular Quay.

SYDNEY SHOWBOATS
CRUISE

Map p254 (☑8296 7388; www.sydneyshowboats.com.au; Wharf 5, King St; from $100; 🚢Darling Harbour) Settle in for a three-hour, three-course dinner cruise on this paddlewheeler, complete with cabaret singers, showgirls flashing their knickers, and a personal magician for your table. Very, very camp.

HARBOUR JET
BOATING

Map p254 (☑1300 887 373; www.harbourjet.com; Convention Centre Jetty, Darling Harbour; adult/child from $65/45; 🚢Pyrmont Bay) One of several jet-boat operators (Sydney Jet, Oz Jet Boating, Thunder Jet, Jetcruiser – take your pick), these guys run a 35-minute white-knuckle ride with 270-degree spins, fishtails and 75km/h power stops that'll test how long it's been since you had breakfast.

NORTH SYDNEY OLYMPIC POOL   SWIMMING

Map p270 (✆9955 2309; www.northsydney
.nsw.gov.au; Alfred St South; adult/child
$6.70/3.30; ⊙5.30am-9pm Mon-Fri, 7am-7pm
Sat & Sun; 🚊Milsons Point/Luna Park) Next to
Luna Park is this art deco Olympic-sized
outdoor pool, plus a 25m indoor pool, kids'
splash zones, a gym ($18.50 with pool access), a crèche and a cafe, all with unbelievable harbour views.

SYDNEY FLYING SQUADRON   SAILING

Map p270 (✆9955 8350; www.sydneyflying
squadron.com.au; 76 McDougall St, Milsons
Point; 🚊North Sydney) Ferries chug out from
this North Shore yacht club to watch the
18-footers race at close quarters. Cruises
run from 2pm to 4.30pm on Saturday during the yachting season (adult/child/family
$20/12/45).

EASTSAIL   SAILING

(✆9327 1166; www.eastsail.com.au; d'Albora
Marina, New Beach Rd, Rushcutters Bay; 🚊Edge-
cliff) Nobody ever said that yachting was a
cheap sport. Take the two-day Start Yachting course for $575, or arrange a charter.
Rushcutters Bay is just east of Kings Cross.

ROLLERBLADING SYDNEY   SKATING

Map p270 (✆0411 872 022; www.rollerblading
sydney.com.au; Milsons Point train station; per hr
$50; 🚊Milsons Point) An instructor will send
you barrelling across the Harbour Bridge
with lessons, quality in-line skates and protective gear.

SYDNEY BY SEAPLANE   SCENIC FLIGHTS

(✆1300 720 995; www.sydneybyseaplane.com;
15min/30min/45min/1hr flights $175/240/410/
495) Scenic flights over Sydney Harbour
and the Northern Beaches. Fly-and-dine
packages are available for picnics in obscure places. Departs from Rose Bay and
Palm Beach.

City Centre & Haymarket

MACQUARIE STREET, HYDE PARK & THE DOMAIN | CITY CENTRE | HAYMARKET

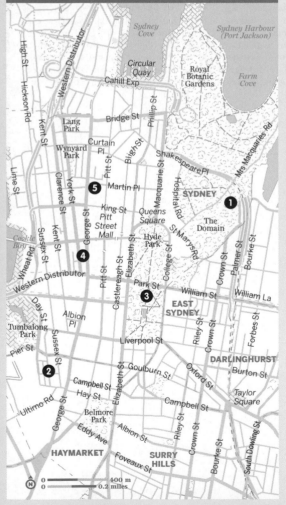

Neighbourhood Top Five

1 Being transported into colonial vistas, Victorian parlours, Buddhist temples, postwar streets, the heart of the outback and the imaginations of generations of artists at the **Art Gallery of NSW** (p84).

2 Shopping and eating your way through the vibrant streets of **Chinatown** (p90).

3 Promenading through the green tunnel at the heart of elegant **Hyde Park** (p85).

4 Enjoying a right royal shopping spree within the grand confines of the **Queen Victoria Building** (p87).

5 Admiring the haughty bastions of commerce lining **Martin Place** (p87).

For more detail of this area, see Map p250 and p255 ➡

Explore: City Centre & Haymarket

Before suburban sprawl started in earnest in the mid-19th century, this area (and The Rocks) was Sydney. Today it's a towering Central Business District (CBD) with skyscrapers shadowing sandstone buildings and churches.

Clinging to the CBD fringes are museums, gracious colonial buildings and leafy retreats. The strip of greenery from Hyde Park through The Domain to the Royal Botanic Gardens counterpoints the clash and throb of Sydney's commerce. Allocate at least a day to explore it properly, and a night to hit some of the ritzy restaurants and hidden bars. Shopaholics might need longer.

Wedged into the Haymarket district, Sydney's Chinatown is a tight nest of restaurants, shops and aroma-filled alleyways, centred on Dixon St. No longer just Chinese, the area is truly pan-Asian. Head here for cheap eats any time of the day or night.

Chinatown now extends towards Central station, an area that's become the epicentre of backpacker mega hostels, with their attendant bars, internet cafes and international buzz. It's not the prettiest part of town, but it is indeed central.

Local Life

➡ **Weekday lunch** On nice days, office workers swarm out of their climate-controlled, strip-lit cells and into the parks. Fitness freaks with showers in their tower jog straight to The Domain to work up a sweat.
➡ **Yum cha** Despite the larger restaurants seating hundreds of dumpling devotees, there always seems to be queues in Chinatown on weekend mornings.
➡ **Pitt Street Mall** Serious suburban shoppers descend on Sydney's retail ground zero on weekends.

Getting There & Away

➡ **Train** The best option for getting here by far, with City Circle stations at Central, Town Hall, Wynyard, St James and Museum. Additionally, the Eastern Suburbs & Illawarra line stops at Martin Place.
➡ **Bus** Numerous routes head to/from The Rocks and Circular Quay. Routes to the North Shore operate from Wynyard Park. Railway Sq is a major bus hub.
➡ **Light rail** City stops include Central, Capitol Square and Paddy's Market, a handy option if you're coming from Glebe or Pyrmont.
➡ **Parking** Street parking is almost nonexistent, but the city council operates a large underground car park on Goulburn St (corner Elizabeth St; per hour/day $8/58, $15 maximum after 6pm).

Lonely Planet's Top Tip

If jetlag or other lifestyle choices leave you with the midnight munchies, Chinatown is the best place in the city to be. Restaurants, even some of the very best ones, stay open late here – we're talking 2am for Chat Thai and East Ocean, 4am for Golden Century, and on Dixon St you can find noodles to slurp at any time of night. Just don't expect service with a smile at 5am.

Best Places to Eat

➡ Sepia (p90)
➡ Tetsuya's (p90)
➡ est. (p91)
➡ Chat Thai (p92)
➡ Mamak (p92)

For reviews, see p90 ➡

Best Places to Drink

➡ Stitch (p92)
➡ Baxter Inn (p92)
➡ Bambini Wine Room (p92)
➡ Grandma's (p93)
➡ Orbit (p93)

For reviews, see p92 ➡

Best Shopping

➡ Strand Arcade (p95)
➡ Queen Victoria Building (p95)
➡ Westfield Sydney (p95)
➡ Paddy's Markets (p97)
➡ David Jones (p96)

For reviews, see p95 ➡

TOP SIGHTS
ART GALLERY OF NSW

With its classical Greek frontage and modern rear end, the Art Gallery of NSW plays a prominent and gregarious role in Sydney society. Blockbuster international touring exhibitions arrive regularly (recent examples include Picasso and the Chinese terracotta warriors) and there's an outstanding permanent collection of Australian art, including a substantial indigenous collection. The gallery also plays host to a lively line-up of lectures, concerts, screenings, celebrity talks and children's activities.

Collection & Layout

As you enter, the galleries to the left are devoted to 20th- and 21st-century **Australian works** (featuring the likes of Brett Whitely, Sidney Nolan, Grace Cossington Smith and James Gleeson), while to the right the central room contains local 19th-century art (Arthur Streeton, Tom Roberts). Either side of this is the **European art collection**, split into 15th to 19th century (Constable, Gainsborough, Rubens), and 19th and 20th century (Degas, Van Gogh, Monet, Rodin).

At the rear of this level is the gallery's excellent **restaurant** (☏9225 1819; www.trippaswhitegroup.com.au; 2-/3-courses $55/70; ☺lunch & high tea daily), and ceramics and religious art from the well-regarded **Asian collection**. The remainder of the Asian collection (Chinese, Korean and Japanese art) is on the first of the lower levels, by the cafe.

Lower level 2 has the constantly changing **Modern** (Picasso, Gormley, Bacon), **Contemporary** (Gilbert & George, Jeff Koons, Sol LeWitt) and **Photography** galleries. Head down again for the **Yiribana Gallery** containing the Aboriginal and Torres Strait Islander collection (Binyinyuwuy, Tom Djawa, Brenda L Croft).

A range of free guided tours is offered on different themes and in various languages; enquire at the desk or check the website.

DON'T MISS...

➡ Yiribana Gallery
➡ *The Balcony 2* (1975), by Brett Whiteley
➡ *Fire's On* (1891), by Arthur Streeton
➡ *Nude in a Rocking Chair* (1956), by Pablo Picasso
➡ *Haft* (2007), by Antony Gormley

PRACTICALITIES

➡ Map p250
➡ ☏1800 679 278
➡ www.artgallery .nsw.gov.au
➡ Art Gallery Rd
➡ admission free
➡ ☺10am-5pm Thu-Tue, to 9pm Wed
➡ ⓡSt James

Art Prizes

The gallery's most famous annual show coincides with the unfailingly controversial Archibald, Wynne and Sulman Prizes (usually in April and May; admission $10).

The $75,000 Archibald Prize for portraiture is the one that garners the most attention, with its lure of celebrity subjects. It's so popular that it's generated three spin-offs: the Salon des Refusés at the SH Ervin Gallery; the highly irreverant Bald Archies; and the Packing Room Prize (judged by the guys who unload the crates, and generally echoing the public's preference for a famous face, realistically drawn).

The $35,000 Wynne Prize for landscape painting or figure sculpture and the $30,000 Sulman Prize for subject or mural painting don't usually cause as much consternation. Neither does the Artexpress exhibition of the year's best school student art, usually held in March and April (admission free).

Gallery Kids

Junior art-lovers can take a free self-guided iPod tour, follow tailored trails and attend free performances (2.30pm Sundays). Tours for Tots are held on certain Tuesdays ($20).

◉ SIGHTS

◉ Macquarie Street, Hyde Park & The Domain

ART GALLERY OF NSW GALLERY
See p84.

HYDE PARK PARK
Map p250 (Elizabeth St; 🚇St James, Museum) It sounds like a cliche, but Hyde Park really is the city's lungs. It's a formal park with manicured gardens, ibises probing the undergrowth (and the rubbish bins), homeless hombres sleeping on benches and a giant chess set attracting nods and whispers from spectators. The tree-formed tunnel running down its spine looks particularly pretty at night, illuminated by fairy lights.

The park's northern end is crowned by the richly symbolic art deco **Archibald Memorial Fountain** (Map p250), featuring Greek mythological figures. At the southern end, the shallow Pool of Remembrance fronts the Anzac Memorial.

FREE ANZAC MEMORIAL MEMORIAL
Map p250 (📞9267 7668; www.rslnsw.com.au; Hyde Park; ⊙9am-5pm; 🚇Museum) This dignified art deco memorial (1934) commemorates the soldiers of the Australia and New Zealand Army Corps (Anzacs) who served in WWI. The interior dome is studded with 120,000 stars – one for each New South Welsh man and woman who served. There's a sobering museum, and the Pool of Remembrance and Rayner Hoff's sculpture *Sacrifice* are particularly poignant.

Pines at the southwestern entry grew from seeds gathered at Gallipoli in Turkey, the site of the Anzacs' most renowned battle.

ST. MARY'S CATHEDRAL CHURCH
Map p250 (📞9220 0400; www.stmaryscath edral.org.au; cnr College St & St Marys Rd; ⊙6.30am-6.30pm; 🚇St James) Built to last, this 106m-long Gothic Revival megalith was begun in 1868, consecrated in 1905 and substantially finished in 1928, but the massive, 75m-high spires weren't added until 2000. The crypt has an impressive terrazzo mosaic floor depicting the Creation, inspired by the Celtic-style illuminations of the *Book of Kells*.

The best time to visit is in the early morning and late afternoon, when the sun streams through the side stained-glass windows (made in Birmingham, England). That's because this cathedral has an unusual north–south orientation rather than the traditional east–west one (facing the rising sun), due to its size and the lie of the land.

HYDE PARK BARRACKS MUSEUM
Map p250 (📞8239 2311; www.hht.net.au; Queens Sq, Macquarie St; adult/child $10/5; ⊙9.30am-5pm; 🚇St James) Convict architect Francis Greenway designed this squarish, decorously Georgian structure (1819) as convict quarters. It later became an immigration depot, a women's asylum and a law court. These days it's a fascinating (if not entirely cheerful) museum, focusing on the barracks' history and the archaeological efforts that helped uncover it.

In 2010 it was one of the Australian convict sites to be inscribed on the UNESCO World Heritage list. Inside you can learn about the offences for which convicts were transported to Australia, some of which seem astoundingly petty today.

ST JAMES' CHURCH CHURCH
Map p250 (📞8227 1300; www.sjks.org.au; 173 King St; ⊙10am-4pm Mon-Fri, 9am-1pm Sat, 7.30am-4pm Sun; 🚇St James) Built from convict bricks, Sydney's oldest church (1819) is another Francis Greenway extravaganza. It was originally designed as a courthouse, but the brief changed: 'Hey Frank, we need an Anglican church!' The cells became the crypt. Check out the dark wood choir loft, the sparkling copper dome, the crypt shop and the cool stained-glass 'Creation Window' from renovations in the 1950s.

LOCAL KNOWLEDGE

WHAT'S IN A NAME?

Details of the original Sydney settlement are still hinted at through place names: Bridge St once spanned the Tank Stream, Sydney's first water supply, which trickled into Sydney Cove (now Circular Quay); crops were planted at Farm Cove to feed the early convicts and marines, the latter of which were housed at the top of Barrack St; Market St was the site of the first produce markets, which later moved south to Haymarket.

Free classical concerts happen at 1.15pm on Wednesdays between March and December. See the website or call for details on daily services.

FREE **PARLIAMENT HOUSE** HISTORIC BUILDING
Map p250 (☑9230 2111; www.parliament.nsw .gov.au; 6 Macquarie St; ☺9am-5pm Mon-Fri; ☒Martin Place) The twin of the Mint, the puce-coloured Parliament House (1816) has been home to the Parliament of New South Wales since 1829, making it the world's oldest continually operating parliament building. And like the Mint, its front section (which now blends into a modern addition on the eastern side) was part of the Rum Hospital.

You need to pass through a metal detector to access the inner sanctum, where you can check out art exhibitions in the lobby and the historical display in the wood-panelled Jubilee Room. On nonsitting days both assembly chambers are open, but when Parliament is sitting, you're restricted to the Public Gallery.

SYDNEY HOSPITAL HISTORIC BUILDING
Map p250 (☑9382 7111; www.sesiahs.health .nsw.gov.au/sydhosp; 8 Macquarie St; ☒Martin Place) Originally the Rum Hospital, Australia's oldest hospital has a grand Victorian sandstone facade and a chequered history. You can't wander around inside, but the central courtyard with its kitsch enamelled fountain studded with submissive swans is open to the public. The weathered-looking Gothic Nightingale Wing (1869) was the site of Australia's first Nightingale School of Nursing.

In provocative recline out the front of the hospital is the pig-ugly bronze statue *Il Porcellino* (1968), a copy of a Florentine statue of a boar. Rubbing its snout is said to bring good luck.

FREE **MINT** HISTORIC BUILDING
Map p250 (☑8239 2288; www.hht.net.au; 10 Macquarie St; ☺9am-5pm Mon-Fri; ☒Martin Place) The stately Mint building (1816) was originally the southern wing of the infamous Rum Hospital, built by two Sydney merchants in return for a monopoly on the rum trade (Sydney's currency in those days). It became a branch of the Royal Mint in 1854, the first outside England.

It's now head office for the Historic Houses Trust, with a small historical collection

and an upstairs cafe. There's not a whole lot to see or do, but it's a worthwhile diversion nonetheless.

STATE LIBRARY OF NSW LIBRARY
Map p250 (☑9273 1414; www.sl.nsw.gov.au; Macquarie St; ☺9am-8pm Mon-Thu, to 5pm Fri, 10am-5pm Sat & Sun; ☒Martin Place) The estimable State Library holds over five million tomes, including James Cook's and Joseph Banks' journals and Captain (later Governor) Bligh's log from the mutinous HMAV *Bounty*. The main reading room is an elegant temple of knowledge clad in milky marble.

Also worth checking out are the temporary exhibitions in the galleries, and the elaborately sculpted bronze doors and grand atrium of the neoclassical Mitchell Wing (1910); note the map of Tasman's journeys in the mosaic floor. Beneath one of the windows on the Macquarie St side of the building is a sculpture of explorer Matthew Flinders with his intrepid cat Trim.

GREAT SYNAGOGUE SYNAGOGUE
Map p250 (☑9267 2477; www.greatsynagogue .org.au; 187a Elizabeth St; tours adult/child $10/5; ☺tours noon Tue & Thu; ☒St James) The heritage-listed Great Synagogue (1878) is the spiritual home of Sydney's oldest Jewish congregation, established in 1831. It's considered the Mother Synagogue of Australia and architecturally is the most important in the southern hemisphere, combining Romanesque, Gothic, Moorish and Byzantine elements. Tours include the AM Rosenblum Museum's artefacts and a video presentation on Jewish beliefs, traditions and history in Australia.

Look out for the starry gold-leaf ceiling (supported by 12 arches representing the tribes of Israel) and the French Gothic wrought-iron gates.

THE DOMAIN PARK
Map p250 (www.rbgsyd.nsw.gov.au; Art Gallery Rd; ☒St James) Administered by the Royal Botanic Gardens, The Domain is a large grassy tract east of Macquarie St, set aside by Governor Phillip in 1788 for public recreation. Phillip's intent rings true: today's lunchtime workers use the space to work up a sweat or eat their lunch. Large-scale public events are also held here, including the Tropfest film festival.

Sculptures dot the park, including a reclining Henry Moore figure and Brett Whiteley's *Almost Once* (1991) – two giant matches, one burnt – rising from the ground near the Art Gallery of NSW.

On the lawn in front of the gallery you can listen to religious zealots, nutters, political extremists, homophobes, hippies and academics express their earnest opinions at the by turns entertaining and enraging **Speakers' Corner** (Map p250; www.speakers corner.org.au; Art Gallery Rd; ⊙2-5pm Sun). Some of them have something interesting to say; most are just plain mad. Either way, it makes for an interesting afternoon. BYO soapbox.

⊙ City Centre

QUEEN VICTORIA BUILDING
NOTABLE BUILDING

Map p250 (QVB; ☑9264 9209; www.qvb.com.au; 455 George St; tours $15; ⊙11am-5pm Sun, 9am-6pm Mon-Wed, Fri & Sat, 9am 9pm Thu, ⊠Town Hall) Unbelievably, this High Victorian masterpiece (1898) was repeatedly slated for demolition before it was restored in the mid-1980s. Occupying an entire city block on the site of the city's first markets, the QVB is a Venetian Romanesque temple to the gods of retail.

Sure, the 200 speciality shops are great, but check out the wrought-iron balconies, the Byzantine copper domes, the stained-glass shopfronts, the mosaic floors, the replica crown jewels, the ballroom, the tinkling baby grand and the hyperkitsch animated Royal Clock (featuring the Battle of Hastings and an hourly beheading of Charles I). Informative 45-minute tours (11.30am Tuesday, Thursday and Saturday) depart from the concierge desk on the ground floor.

Outside there's an imposing statue of Queen Vic herself; nearby is a wishing well featuring a bronze replica of her beloved pooch, Islay (which disconcertingly speaks in the baritone voice of former radio rabble-rouser John Laws).

SYDNEY TOWER EYE
TOWER

Map p250 (☑9333 9222; www.sydneytowereye.com.au; 100 Market St; adult/child $25/20, Skywalk adult/child $65/45; ⊙9am-10.30pm; ⊠St James) The 309m-tall Sydney Tower (built 1970–1981) offers unbeatable 360-degree views from the observation level 250m up. On a clear day you'll see west to the Blue Mountains, south to Botany Bay, east across the harbour to the silvery Pacific and down

onto the city streets. It's high enough to watch rain squalls shift across the suburbs on a stormy day.

The visit starts with the 4D Experience – a short 3D film giving you a bird's-eye view (a parakeet's to be exact) of city, surf, harbour and what lies beneath the water, accompanied by mist sprays and bubbles; it's actually pretty darn cool.

Luke Skywalker aspirations? Don a spiffy 'skysuit' and take the **Skywalk**: shackle yourself to the safety rail and step onto two glass-floored viewing platforms outside Sydney Tower's observation deck, 268m above the street. No place for the weak bowelled...

If you're planning on visiting Sydney Aquarium or Sydney Wildlife World, check out the discounted combined tickets.

MARTIN PLACE
SQUARE

Map p250 (⊠Martin Place) Studded with imposing edifices, long, lean Martin Place was closed to traffic in 1971, forming a terraced pedestrian mall. Once the corporate crowds go home, skateboarders and film crews converge upon the ramps, stairs and fountains.

As iconic in its time as the Opera House, **GPO Sydney** (Map p250; ☑9221 5073; www.gposydney.com; 1 Martin Pl), built in 1874 is a beautiful colonnaded Victorian palazzo that was once Sydney's General Post Office. It has since been gutted, stabbed with office towers and transformed into the Westin Sydney hotel, swanky shops, restaurants and bars. Inspired by Italian Renaissance palaces, architect James Barnet caused a minor fracas by basing the faces carved on the sandstone facade on local identities. Queen Victoria dominates the central white-marble statuary, surrounded by allegorical figures. Under a staircase in the basement there is a small historical display and a pipe housing the dribbling remnants of the Tank Stream.

Built in 1916, the 12-storey **Commonwealth Bank building** (Map p250; 5 Martin Pl) was Australia's first steel-framed 'skyscraper'. Its interiors are largely intact and clock-watching tellers still muse over the inscription on the wall: 'The Noiseless Foot Of Time Steals Swiftly By'. Another **branch** (Map p250; 48 Martin Pl) has taken over the old State Savings Bank building: it's a beaut example of interwar beaux-arts architecture, featuring green-marble Doric columns and an enclosed brass-and-marble teller area.

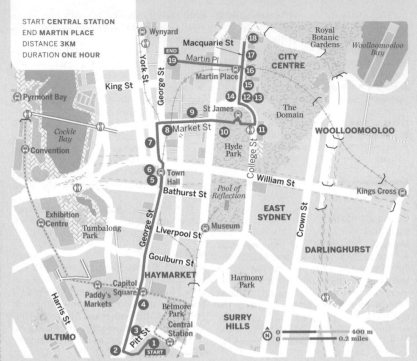

START **CENTRAL STATION**
END **MARTIN PLACE**
DISTANCE **3KM**
DURATION **ONE HOUR**

Neighbourhood Walk
Urban Canyons

Start in the lofty main concourse of **1 Central station**. Take the George St exit, turn left and walk through the small park down to **2 Railway Square**, with its DNA strand towers. Cross Pitt St and head onto George St.

Step off Sydney's main drag into the calming 1845 sandstone **3 Christ Church St Lawrence**. Check the thickness of your moral fibre before George St lures you into a saucy stew of sex clubs and porn shops.

Respite comes in the form of the elaborate Victoriana of the **4 Haymarket library**, **5 St Andrew's Cathedral**, **6 Town Hall** and the **7 Queen Victoria Building**. Walk through the QVB and duck right into Market St. On your right is the extraordinarily extravagant **8 State Theatre**; stop to scan the foyer.

Trundle past the macrospindle of **9 Sydney Tower** and into verdant **10 Hyde Park**. As you cut across, check out the giant chessboard and the splendiferous fountain.

Across College St, skateboarders careen around the sturdily buttressed **11 St Mary's Cathedral**. Curve north from here around the top of Hyde Park under the watchful gaze of **12 Prince Albert**, then angle right into Macquarie St.

Governor Lachlan Macquarie commissioned convicted forger Francis Greenway to design this illustrious strip in the early 19th century. Greenway's **13 Hyde Park Barracks** and **14 St James' Church** guard the south end. In quick succession on the right as you continue north are the **15 Mint**, **16 Sydney Hospital**, **17 Parliament House** and the **18 State Library of NSW**.

Cross the road and head into **19 Martin Place**. Roam through the stately foyers and dodge the skateboarders along this grand pedestrian mall. Channel Seven news is filmed live behind the glass of the Colonial Centre, on the right past Elizabeth St.

Near the George St end of Martin Place you'll find the **Cenotaph**, commemorating Australia's war dead. Abutting Martin Place on George St is the former **Commercial Banking Corporation of Sydney** – an impressive marbled edifice, worth a look if you're passing by.

MUSEUM OF SYDNEY
MUSEUM

Map p250 (MoS; ☑9251 5988; www.hht.net.au; cnr Phillip & Bridge Sts; adult/child $10/5; ⊙9.30am-5pm; ☐Circular Quay) Built on the site of Sydney's first (and infamously pungent) Government House, the MoS is a fragmented, story-telling museum using state-of-the-art installations to explore the city's people, places, cultures and evolution. The history of the indigenous Eora people is highlighted – touching on the millennia of continuous occupation of this place. Be sure to open some of the many stainless-steel and glass drawers (they close themselves).

In the forecourt, check out the disarming *Edge of Trees* sculpture by Janet Laurence and Fiona Foley. There's a cool cafe too.

TOWN HALL
NOTABLE BUILDING

Map p250 (☑9265 9189; www.cityofsydney.nsw.gov.au/sydneytownhall; 483 George St; ⊙8am-6pm Mon-Fri; ☐Town Hall) Mansard roofs, sandstone turrets, wrought-iron trimmings and over-the-top balustrades: the High Victorian wedding-cake exterior of the Town Hall (built 1869–1889) is something to behold. Inside, the elaborate chamber room and the wood-lined concert hall are almost as good (the concert hall has a humongous 8000-pipe organ and hosts free monthly lunchtime concerts).

Unless there's something on, you can explore the halls off the main entrance.

ST ANDREW'S CATHEDRAL
CHURCH

Map p250 (☑9265 1661; www.cathedral.sydney.anglican.asn.au; cnr George & Bathurst Sts; ⊙10am-4pm Mon, Tue, Fri & Sat, 8am-8pm Wed, 10am-6.30pm Thu, 7.30am-8pm Sun; ☐Town Hall) Sporting beautiful stained glass and twin spires inspired by England's York Minster, squat St Andrew's Anglican is the oldest cathedral in Australia (1868). Music is a big deal here: free organ recitals happen on Fridays at 1.10pm and a concert band performs on alternate Wednesdays at 12.30pm.

During school terms 'Young Music' concerts happen at 12.30pm on Mondays and occasional Wednesdays. The accomplished St Andy's choir warbles at various services.

Due to some ugly modifications around the front door, disabled access is good. See the website or call for details of services.

STATE THEATRE
NOTABLE BUILDING

Map p250 (☑136 100; www.statetheatre.com.au; 49 Market St; tours adult/child $23/15; ⊙tours 10am & 1pm Mon-Wed; ☐St James) The utterly ornate State (1929) is Sydney's most ostentatious theatre. Originally built as a movie palace during Hollywood's heyday, it's now a National Trust–classified building, dripping with gilt and velveteen. Live shows (musicals, comedy, middle-of-the-road bands) take the stage, except during the Sydney Film Festival in June.

ST PHILIP'S
CHURCH

Map p250 (☑9247 1071; www.yorkstreetanglican.com; 3 York St; ☐Wynyard) Completed in 1856 by architect Edmund Blacket in High Victorian Gothic style, St Philip's is the latest incarnation of a line descending from Sydney's original Anglican parish church (1793). It's an unobtrusive structure dwarfed by surrounding skyscrapers and is usually kept locked outside Sunday services and special events.

AUSTRALIA SQUARE
NOTABLE BUILDING

Map p250 (☑8247 5200; www.australiasquare.net; 264 George St; ☐Wynyard) Generally acknowledged as Australia's first major office tower, Australia Square (1968) was designed by archi-phenomenon Harry Seidler. His 50-storey design assumes a distinctive cylindrical form, with an open plaza at the base and shops below.

A vibrant Sol LeWitt lobby mural (2004) replaced a rare Le Corbusier tapestry that hung here for decades before the building's owner auctioned it off. Head up to Orbit Bar on the 47th floor – jaw-dropping views for the price of a martini.

GOVERNORS PHILLIP & MACQUARIE TOWERS
NOTABLE BUILDINGS

Map p250 (cnr Phillip, Young & Bent Sts; ☐Circular Quay) Clad in steel, granite and glass, Governor Phillip Tower (1993) is one of Sydney's tallest buildings (254m including antennae). Its distinctive metallic-bladed top has earned it the nickname 'the Milk Crate'. It's propped up on zinc-plated columns for a monumental 10 storeys before the tower proper begins. At 145m, neighbouring Governor Macquarie Tower (1994) is a comparative pipsqueak.

These towers were part of the redevelopment of the site of Governor Phillip's first Government House, which had been semi-derelict for 50 years. At the block's northern end the house's remnant foundations were converted into First Government House Plaza and the Museum of Sydney.

WYNYARD PARK   PARK
Map p250 (York St; ⓡWynyard) Above Wynyard train station is this rare wedge of downtown greenery. Surrounded by skyscrapers and spindly plane trees, it has a certain Manhattan vibe to it. Office workers chew sandwiches, smoke, kick off their heels, read magazines and bitch about the boss.

⊙ Haymarket

CHINATOWN   NEIGHBOURHOOD
Map p255 (www.chinatown.com.au/eng; Dixon St; ⓡTown Hall) With a discordant soundtrack of blaring Canto pop, Dixon St is the heart and soul of Chinatown: a narrow, shady pedestrian mall with a string of restaurants and their urgently attendant spruikers. The ornate dragon gates *(paifang)* at either end are topped with fake bamboo tiles, golden Chinese calligraphy (with English translations), ornamental lions to keep evil spirits at bay and a fair amount of pigeon poo.

This is actually Sydney's third Chinatown: the first was in The Rocks in the late 19th century before it moved to the Darling Harbour end of Market St. Dixon St's Chinatown dates from the 1920s. Look for the fake-bamboo awnings guarded by dragons, dogs and lions, and kooky upturned-wok lighting fixtures.

On Hay St, the surreal **Golden Water Mouth** (Map p255) sculpture drips with gilt and water. Formed from a eucalyptus trunk from Condobolin, the destination of many gold-rush-era Chinese, its feng shui is supposed to promote positive energy and good luck. A little further down Hay St, Paddy's Markets (p97) fills the lower level of a hefty brick building. It started out in the mid-19th century with mainly European traders, but the tightly packed market stalls are more evocative of present-day Vietnam these days.

CENTRAL STATION   NOTABLE BUILDING
Map p255 (Eddy Ave; ⓡCentral station) Sydney's main railway station was built in 1906 on top of an old convent and cemetery (watch

out for ghosts). The 75m Gothic clock tower was added 15 years later. The main sandstone concourse has an impressive vaulted roof and is the terminus for intercity and country trains. It also houses the **Rail Heritage Centre** (Map p255; ☎9379 0111; www.arhsnsw.com.au; admission free; ⊙9am-5.30pm Mon-Fri, to 4pm Sat); check out the stained-glass windows. Suburban trains chug into the outdoor platforms downstairs on the Surry Hills side. As you're pulling into Central from the south, look for the ornate disused **Mortuary Station** (1869) on your left.

✖ EATING

Without harbour views, Sydney's central-city restaurants tend to be discreet, upmarket spots – perfect for secret handshakes over million-dollar deals. Some have beaten geography by perching themselves atop towers. Expect a reverse gradation of prices, starting at the water and lightening considerably as you head inland. Chinatown is Sydney's best bet for a cheap, satisfying meal – especially after midnight. Chinese food dominates, but you'll also find superb Vietnamese, Malaysian, Korean and Thai. You'll also find a tiny Spanish Quarter on Liverpool St just west of George St; Little Korea along Pitt St near Liverpool St; and Thaitown on Campbell St.

✖ City Centre

[TOP CHOICE] SEPIA   JAPANESE, FUSION $$$
Map p250 (☎9283 1990; www.sepiarestaurant.com.au; 201 Sussex St; mains $48, 4-courses $120; ⊙lunch Fri & Sat, dinner Tue-Sat; ⓡTown Hall) There's nothing washed out or brown-tinged about Sepia's food: Martin Benn's picture-perfect creations are presented in glorious technicolour, with each taste worth a thousand words. A Japanese sensibility permeates the boundary-pushing menu, earning this relative newcomer the city's top dining gong in 2012.

TETSUYA'S   FRENCH, JAPANESE $$$
Map p250 (☎9267 2900; www.tetsuyas.com; 529 Kent St; degustation $210; ⊙lunch Sat, dinner Tue-Sat; ⓡTown Hall) Down a clandestine security

driveway, Tetsuya's – rated one of the top restaurants in the world – is for those seeking a culinary journey rather than a simple stuffed belly. Settle in for 12-plus courses of French- and Japanese-inflected food from the creative genius of Japanese-born Tetsuya Wakuda. Book way ahead.

EST.
MODERN AUSTRALIAN $$$

Map p250 (☑9240 3000; www.merivale.com; L1, 252 George St; lunch mains $55-57, 4-course dinner $150, degustation $175; ☺lunch Mon-Fri, dinner Mon-Sat; ☒Wynyard) Pressed-tin ceilings, huge columns, oversized windows and modern furniture make the interior design almost as interesting as the food. Seafood fills around half of the slots on Chef Peter Doyle's menu. At dinner, choose between a four-course 'chef's menu' and a seven-course 'tasting menu'. Sydney dining at its best; thick wallet and fancy threads a must.

CENTRAL BAKING DEPOT
BAKERY $

Map p250 (CBD; www.centralbakingdepot.com.au; 37-39 Erskine St; baked goods $7-9; ☺breakfast & lunch Mon-Sat; ☒Wynyard) Once upon a time the best bakeries were confined to the suburbs, but CBD has brought quality baked goods into the heart of the CBD. Drop by for a savoury snack (pies, sausage rolls, croissants, pizza slices, sandwiches), or a sweet treat with coffee. Seating is limited to a modest scattering of tables and a window bench.

SPICE TEMPLE
CHINESE $$

Map p250 (☑8078 1088; www.rockpool.com; 10 Bligh St; dishes $15-45; ☺lunch Mon-Fri, dinner Mon-Sat; ☒Martin Place) Tucked away in the basement of his Rockpool Bar & Grill, owner/chef Neil Perry runs this darkly atmospheric temple to the cuisine of China's western provinces, especially Sichuan, Yunnan, Hunan, Jiangxi, Guangxi and Xingjiang. Expect plenty of heat and lots of thrills.

ROCKPOOL BAR & GRILL
STEAKHOUSE $$$

Map p250 (☑8078 1900; www.rockpool.com; 66 Hunter St; mains $25-115; ☺lunch Mon-Fri, dinner Mon-Sat; ☒Martin Place) You'll feel like a 1930s Manhattan stockbroker when you dine at this sleek operation in the art deco City Mutual Building. The bar is famous for its dry-aged, full-blood Wagyu burger (make sure you order a side of the hand-cut fat chips), but carnivores will be equally enamoured with the succulent steaks served in the grill.

BISTRODE CBD
BRITISH $$$

Map p250 (☑9240 3000; www.merivale.com; L1, 52 King St; mains $37-40; ☺lunch & dinner Mon-Fri; ☒Wynyard) Bistrode is a celebration of all things carnivorous, with a menu to challenge the lily-livered. And the lily sure ain't gilded – it's more likely dipped in blood and used to garnish the 'lamb's heart and minds' that's on the menu. The food is exceptional: hearty and intricate with plenty of kooky twists.

FELIX
FRENCH $$

Map p250 (☑9240 3000; www.merivale.com; 2 Ash St; mains $28-32; ☺lunch Mon-Fri, dinner Mon-Sat; ☒Wynyard) Waiters bustle about in black ties and long aprons in this *très traditionnel* French bistro, with Parisian subway tiles on the walls and a solid list of tried-and-true classics on the menu. If you feel the urge to work off your coq au vin in *le discothèque* later, the Ivy is upstairs.

ASH ST CELLAR
TAPAS $$

Map p250 (☑9240 3000; www.merivale.com; 1 Ash St; tapas $6-24; ☺8.30am-11pm; ☒Wynyard) Part of the so-hot-right-now Ivy complex, Ash St Cellar is an urbane laneway wine bar that does excellent tapas. Sit outside if it's not too gusty, or inside at communal tables and decide which of the 200-plus wines you'll have with your chorizo and grilled flat bread. Despite the suits sweeping through, the vibe is relaxed and unhurried.

DIN TAI FUNG
CHINESE $

Map p255 (www.dintaifungaustralia.com.au; L1, World Sq, 644 George St; mains $10-15; ☺lunch & dinner daily; ☒Museum) It also does noodles and buns, but it's the dumplings that made this Taiwanese chain famous, delivering an explosion of fabulously flavoursome broth as you bite into their delicate casings. Come early, come hungry, come prepared to share your table. It also has stalls in The Star (p103) and Westfield Sydney (p95).

SYDNEY MADANG
KOREAN $$

Map p250 (☑9264 7010; 371a Pitt St; mains $12-43; ☺lunch & dinner; ☒Museum) Down a teensy Little Korea laneway is this backdoor gem – an authentic barbecue joint that's low on interior charisma but high on quality and quantity. Noisy, cramped and chaotic, yes, but the chilli seafood soup will have you coming back tomorrow.

✖ Haymarket

TOP CHOICE CHAT THAI
THAI $

Map p255 (☑9211 1808; www.chatthai.com
.au; 20 Campbell St; mains $10-19; ◷10am-2am;
⊞Central) Cooler than your average Thai
joint, this Thaitown linchpin is so popular
that a list is posted outside for you to af-
fix your name to should you want a table.
Expat Thais flock here for the dishes that
don't make it onto your average suburban
Thai restaurant menu – particularly the
more unusual sweets.

MAMAK
MALAYSIAN $

Map p255 (www.mamak.com.au; 15 Goulburn
St; mains $6-17; ◷lunch & dinner; ⊞Town Hall)
Get here early (from 5.30pm) if you want
to score a table without queuing, because
this eat-and-run Malaysian joint is one of
the most popular cheapies in the city. The
satays are cooked over charcoal and are
particularly delicious when accompanied
by a flaky golden roti. No bookings and
BYO alcohol.

EAST OCEAN
CHINESE $$

Map p255 (☑9212 4198; www.eastocean.com
.au; 421 Sussex St; dishes $9-29; ◷10am-2am;
☎; ⊞Central) Insanely popular on weekends
for its yum cha (over 100 kinds), this mas-
sive Chinese restaurant can seat hundreds
of hungry folk – mostly discerning Asian
diners. A few trolleys trundle around, but
mostly it's a case of ticking your selelctions
on cards provided. Aside from dim sum, the
seafood is also excellent.

GOLDEN CENTURY
CHINESE, SEAFOOD $$

Map p255 (☑9212 3901; www.goldencentury
.com.au; 393-399 Sussex St; mains $13-32; ◷noon-
4am; ⊞Town Hall) The fish tank at this frenetic
Cantonese place forms a window-wall to the
street, full of a whole lot of nervous fish,
crabs, lobsters and abalone. Splash out on
the whole lobster cooked in ginger and shal-
lots: tank–net–kitchen–you.

MARIGOLD RESTAURANT
CHINESE $$

Map p255 (☑9281 3388; www.marigold.com.au;
L5, 683 George St; yum cha $15-25, banquet $30-
48; ◷10am-3pm & 5.30pm-midnight; ⊞Central)
This vast yum cha palace has more mir-
rors, crimson and gold than seems plausi-
ble. Spread over two levels (800 seats!), it's
a constant whirl of trolley dollies in silk
dresses and waiters in bowties delivering
dumplings, steamed pork buns, chicken
feet and all the other usual suspects.
Kitsch in the best possible way. Expect to
queue on weekends.

DRINKING & NIGHTLIFE

**The city centre has long been known
for upmarket, after-work booze rooms,
none of which you would describe as
cosy locals. Some are worth checking
out for their views, cocktails, sassy
decor or historical interest; most are
what you might call 'drycleaners' –
good places to pick up suits. However,
the recent change of liquor-licensing
laws has seen speakeasy-style places
springing up in the most unlikely back
alleys and basements, and even the
coolest of cats are drinking in the city
these days. Except on Sundays, when
the wells run dry.**

TOP CHOICE STITCH
BAR

Map p250 (www.stitchbar.com; 61 York St; ◷4pm-
midnight Mon & Tue, 4pm-2am Wed & Sat, noon-
2am Thu & Fri; ⊞Wynyard) The finest exemplar
of Sydney's penchant for fake speakeasys,
Stitch is accessed via swinging doors at the
rear of what looks like a tailor's workshop.
Hidden beneath is a surprisingly large but
perpetually crowded space, decorated with
sewing patterns and wooden Singer cases.
A charming maître d' manages the inevita-
ble wait for a booth seat with considerable
skill; the food is excellent too.

TOP CHOICE BAXTER INN
BAR

Map p250 (www.thebaxterinn.com; 156 Clarence
St; ◷4pm-1am Mon-Sat; ⊞Town Hall) Yes, it re-
ally is down that dark lane and through that
unmarked door (it's easier to find if there's
a queue; otherwise look for the bouncer
lurking nearby). Whisky's the poison at
this particular speakeasy. Despite the bow-
ties and comedy hipster moustaches, the
friendly barmen really know their stuff and
can help you select from the huge list.

BAMBINI WINE ROOM
WINE BAR

Map p250 (☑9283 7098; www.bambinitrust
.com.au; 185 Elizabeth St; ◷3-10pm Mon-Fri, 5.30-
11pm Sat; ⊞St James) Don't worry, this bar
doesn't sell wine to *bambinis* – it's a very

grown-up, European affair. The tiny dark-wood-panelled room is the sort of place where you'd expect to see Oscar Wilde holding court in the corner. It has an extensive wine list, slick table service, free almonds and breadsticks, and disembodied postmodern cornices dangling from above.

GRANDMA'S
COCKTAIL BAR

Map p250 (www.grandmasbarsydney.com; basement, 275 Clarence St; ⊗3pm-midnight Mon-Thu, noon-1am Fri, 5pm-1am Sat; ℝTown Hall) Billing itself as a 'retrosexual haven of cosmopolitan kitsch and faded granny glamour', Grandma's hits the mark. A stag's head greets you on the stairs and ushers you into a tiny subterranean world of parrot wallpaper and tiki cocktails. Someone's suprisingly cool granny must be very proud.

ORBIT
COCKTAIL BAR

Map p250 (☏9247 9777; www.summitrestaurant.com.au; L47, Australia Square, 264 George St; ⊗10am-late Mon-Fri, 5pm-late Sat & Sun; ℝWynyard) Shoot up to this murderously cool revolving *Goldfinger*-esque bar, offering killer cocktails and views to die for. Sink into an Eero Saarinen tulip chair and sip a kung fu mojito while all of Sydney is paraded before you.

GOOD GOD SMALL CLUB
CLUB, LIVE MUSIC

Map p250 (www.goodgodgoodgod.com; 55 Liverpool St; front bar free, club free-$20; ⊗5pm-1am Wed, 5pm-2am Thu, 5pm-5am Fri, 6pm-5am Sat; ℝTown Hall) In a defunct underground taverna near Chinatown, Good God's rear dancetaria hosts everything from live indie bands to Jamaican reggae, '50s soul, rockabilly and tropical house music. Its success lies in the focus on great music rather than glamorous surrounds.

ESTABLISHMENT
BAR

Map p250 (☏9240 3100; www.merivale.com; ground level, 252 George St; ⊗11am-late Mon-Fri, 6pm-late Sat; ℝWynyard) Establishment's cashed-up crush proves that the art of swilling cocktails after a hard city day is not lost. Sit at the majestic marble bar, in the swish courtyard or be absorbed by a leather lounge as stockbrokers scribble their phone numbers on the backs of coasters for flirty city chicks.

IVY
BAR, CLUB

Map p250 (☏9254 8100; www.merivale.com; L1, 330 George St; admission free-$20; ⊗11am-late Mon-Fri, 5pm-late Sat; ℝWynyard) Hidden down a laneway off George St, the Ivy is a supersexy complex featuring bars, restaurants, discreet lounges...even a swimming pool. It's also Sydney's most hyped venue; expect lengthy queues of suburban kids teetering on infeasibly high heels, waiting to shed $20 for the privilege of entry on a Saturday night.

MARBLE BAR
BAR, LIVE MUSIC

Map p250 (☏9265 2000; www.marblebarsydney.com.au; basement, Hilton Hotel, 488 George St; ⊗4pm-midnight Sun-Thu, 3pm-2am Fri & Sat; ℝTown Hall) Built for a staggering £32,000 in 1893 as part of the Adams Hotel on Pitt St, this incredibly ornate underground bar is one of the best places in town for putting on the ritz (even if this is the Hilton). When the Adams was demolished in 1968, every marble slab, wood carving and bronze capital was dismantled, restored, then reassembled here.

Musos play anything from jazz to funk from Wednesday to Saturday.

GRASSHOPPER
BAR

Map p250 (www.thegrasshopper.com.au; 1 Temperance Lane; ⊗noon-late Mon-Fri, 5.30pm-late Sat; ℝSt James) The first of many grungy laneway bars to open in the inner city couldn't have chosen a more darkly ironic location than Temperance Lane. The heart of the operation is the cool downstairs bar; hop upstairs for food.

SPICE CELLAR
BAR, CLUB

Map p250 (www.thespicecellar.com.au; 58 Elizabeth St; club free-$25; ⊗bar 4pm-midnight Wed Fri, club 10pm-late Fri & Sat; ℝMartin Place) Saunter down to this stylish underground bunker for cocktails in the lounge bar, accompanied by live jazz on Thursdays. On weekends the attached club has one of Sydney's hottest little dance floors, which despite its size attracts the occasional turntable legend to its decks.

SLIP INN & CHINESE LAUNDRY
BAR, CLUB

Map p250 (☏8295 9999; www.merivale.com; 111 Sussex St; club $15-25; ⊗10am-midnight Mon-Thu, to 2am Fri, 5pm-2am Sat; ℝWynyard) Slip in to this warren of moody rooms on the edge of Darling Harbour and bump hips with the kids. There are bars, pool tables, a beer garden, dance floors, pizza and Thai. On Friday nights the bass cranks up at the attached Chinese Laundry nightclub; on

Saturdays there's a roster of international and local electro, house and techno DJs.

TANK STREAM BAR BAR

Map p250 (☑9240 3100; www.merivale.com; 1 Tankstream Way; ◷4pm-midnight Mon-Thu, noon-midnight Fri; ⊠Wynyard) After work suits head to this watering hole above Sydney's original water supply. The Tank Stream runs thick with bottled beer, wine and cocktails, with high stools and flashes of steel enhancing the original warehouse interior.

REDOAK BOUTIQUE BEER CAFE BEER HALL

Map p250 (☑9262 3303; www.redoak.com.au; 201 Clarence St; ◷11am-late Mon-Sat; ⊠Wynyard) With over 20 handmade beers available, this place should keep you off the streets for a while. Pull up a stool among the international crew and work your way through the much-awarded list. If things start to slip away from you, slow your descent with a meal (mains $22 to $29; tasting boards matched with four beer samples $20).

BAVARIAN BIER CAFÉ BEER HALL

Map p250 (☑8297 4111; www.bavarianbiercafe.com; 24 York St; ◷11am-midnight; ⊠Wynyard) Stepping in the door here you'll feel as though you've put your head inside an enormous chandelier – sparkling racks of steins dangle above the central bar, waiting to be filled with litres of Löwenbräu. Soak it all up with some bratwurst, sauerkraut and a schnitzel at long *bierhalle* tables. Also at Manly Wharf.

CRYSTAL BAR BAR, BURLESQUE

Map p250 (☑9229 7799; www.gposydney.com; Lower Level, 1 Martin Pl; ◷5pm-late Wed-Fri, 8pm-late Sat; ⊠Martin Place) Down in the bowels of the GPO building, Crystal Bar is a lavish, clandestine booze room with smooth-stylin' DJs and 'Crystal Boudoir' – a sassy French knickers-and-high-kicks cabaret show every Saturday night ($30). Who would have thought camp cabaret would appeal to 22-year-olds? Don't you dare dress down.

ARTHOUSE HOTEL BAR, DJ

Map p250 (☑9284 1200; www.thearthousehotel.com.au; 275 Pitt St; ◷11am-11pm Mon-Thu, 11am-1am Fri, 5pm-1am Sat; ⊠Town Hall) It's easy to lose your way in this sumptuous, multistorey heritage site (1836), which was once the School of Arts. After-work punters seem to know their way around the various bars – follow someone good-looking.

ZETA BAR

Map p250 (☑9265 6070; www.zetabar.com.au; L4, Hilton Hotel, 488 George St; Sat $20; ◷5pm-2am Mon-Fri, to 3.30am Sat; ⊠St James) Ride the Hilton escalators up to Zeta, which captivates a chic young city crew with its white vinyl lounges, discreet curtained booths (exactly what was Snoop Dogg smoking in there?) and enormous gas inferno. Here you can sip grilled-fruit cocktails and eyeball the QVB dome from the terrace.

 ENTERTAINMENT

☆ City Centre

TOP CHOICE **CITY RECITAL HALL** PERFORMANCE VENUE

Map p250 (☑8256 2222; www.cityrecitalhall.com; 2 Angel Pl; tickets $20-92; ◷box office 9am-5pm Mon-Fri; ⊠Martin Place) Based on the classic configuration of the 19th-century European concert hall, this custom-built 1200-seat venue boasts near-perfect acoustics. Catch top-flight companies such as Musica Viva, the Australian Brandenburg Orchestra and the Australian Chamber Orchestra here.

TOP CHOICE **STATE THEATRE** PERFORMANCE VENUE

Map p250 (☑136 100; www.statetheatre.com.au; 49 Market St; tickets $60-235; ◷box office 9am-5pm Mon-Fri; ⊠St James) The beautiful 2000-seat State Theatre is a lavish, gilt-ridden, chandelier-dangling palace. It hosts the Sydney Film Festival, concerts, comedy, opera, musicals and the odd celebrity chef.

TOP CHOICE **METRO THEATRE** PERFORMANCE VENUE

Map p250 (☑9550 3666; www.metrotheatre.com.au; 624 George St; tickets $29-100; ⊠Town Hall) Easily Sydney's best venue to catch local and alternative international acts (the Maccabees, Public Enemy, Ladyhawke) in well-ventilated, easy-seeing comfort. Other offerings include comedy, cabaret and dance parties.

EVENT CINEMAS GEORGE ST CINEMA

Map p250 (☑9273 7300; www.eventcinemas
.com.au; 505 George St; adult/child $19/14;
☉9.30am-midnight; ⑭Town Hall) An orgy of
popcorn-fuelled mainstream entertainment, this monster movie palace has 18
screens and plenty of eateries and teen-
centric distractions. All tickets are $11 on
tight-arse Tuesday.

MUSICA VIVA AUSTRALIA CLASSICAL MUSIC

(☑8394 6666; www.mva.org.au; tickets $30-86)
Musica Viva is the largest stager of ensemble music in the world, providing some 2500
concerts around Australia in a number of
musical styles (including chamber music,
a cappella, experimental and jazz). Sydney
concerts are normally held at the City Recital Hall.

**AUSTRALIAN BRANDENBURG
ORCHESTRA** CLASSICAL MUSIC

(☑9328 7581; www.brandenburg.com.au; tickets
$28-167) The ABO is a distinguished part of
Australia's artistic landscape, playing ba-
roque and classical music on period-perfect
instruments. Leading international guest
artists appear frequently. Performances are
usually held at the City Recital Hall.

PINCHGUT OPERA OPERA

(www.pinchgutopera.com.au) This small player
stages one intimate, oft-overlooked chamber opera every December at the City Recital Hall.

☆ **Haymarket**

**SYDNEY ENTERTAINMENT
CENTRE** PERFORMANCE VENUE

Map p255 (☑9320 4200; www.sydentcent.com
.au; 35 Harbour St; tickets $89-130; ⑭Central)
A big 12,000-seat concrete box between
Chinatown and Darling Harbour, purpose-
built for superstar extravaganzas (Radio-
head, the Black Keys, the Wiggles).

CAPITOL THEATRE PERFORMANCE VENUE

Map p255 (☑9320 5000; www.capitoltheatre
.com.au; 13 Campbell St; tickets $59-199; ☉box
office 9am-5pm Mon-Fri; ⑭Central) Lavishly
restored, this large city theatre is home to
long-running musicals (*The Lion King, A
Chorus Line*) and the occasional big name
concert (Diana Ross, Chris Isaak).

 **SHOPPING**

Sydneysiders head to the city when
they've got something special to buy or
some serious retail therapy is required.
The city centre's upmarket stores –
centred around Pitt St Mall, Market St
and George St – offer plenty of choice
for gifts and treats. Shopping is one
of Chinatown's big drawcards, with
countless bargains of the 'Made in
China/Taiwan/Korea' variety. The insane
buzz of Paddy's Markets is half the fun.

🛍 **City Centre**

TOP
CHOICE **STRAND ARCADE** SHOPPING CENTRE

Map p250 (www.strandarcade.com.au; 412 George
St; ☉9am-5.30pm Mon-Wed & Fri, 9am 8pm
Thu, 9am-4pm Sat, 11am-4pm Sun; ⑭St James)
Constructed in 1891, the Strand rivals the
QVB in the ornateness stakes. Three floors
of designer fashions, Australiana and old-
world coffee shops will make your short cut
through here considerably longer.

Top Australian designers commune
and collude on the upper levels: low-cut,
butt-hugger jeans from **Bettina Llano**
(Map p250; www.bettinaliano.com.au), devil-
ishly daring gear from **Wayne Cooper** (Map
p250; www.waynecooper.com.au), fishnets and
flounce from **Alannah Hill** (Map p250; www
.alannahhill.com.au), plus Corner Shop (p145),
Dinosaur Designs (p146), Leona Edmiston
(p146), Love+Hatred (p96), Sass & Bide
(p146) and Strand Hatters (p96).

TOP
CHOICE **QUEEN VICTORIA
BUILDING** SHOPPING CENTRE

Map p250 (QVB; ☑9264 9209; www.qvb.com.au;
455 George St; ☉11am-5pm Sun, 9am-6pm Mon-
Wed, Fri & Sat, 9am-9pm Thu; ⑭Town Hall) The
magnificent QVB takes up a whole block
and boasts nearly 200 shops on five levels.
It's a High Victorian masterpiece – without
doubt Sydney's most beautiful shopping
centre. Tenants of note include Herringbone (p147), Opal Fields (p66) and Victoria's Basement (p116).

TOP
CHOICE **WESTFIELD SYDNEY** MALL

Map p250 (www.westfield.com.au/sydney; cnr Pitt
St Mall & Market St) The city's newest shopping
mall is a bafflingly large complex gobbling
up Sydney Tower and a fair chunk of Pitt

St Mall. It's upped the glamour by ensnaring some of the city's top restaurants into spaces adjacent to the excellent food court. Shops include branches of Calibre (p146), Jurlique (opposite), Leona Edmiston (p146), Oxford (p116), RM Williams (right), Sass & Bide (p146) and Zimmermann (p145).

DAVID JONES — DEPARTMENT STORE

Map p250 (⌨9266 5544; www.davidjones .com.au; 86-108 Castlereagh St; ☺9.30am-7pm Sat-Wed, to 9pm Thu & Fri; ☒St James) In two enormous city buildings, DJs is Sydney's premier department store. The Castlereagh St store has women's and children's clothing; Market St has menswear, electrical goods and a high-brow food court. Neither has enough huge photos of supermodel Miranda Kerr... David Jones also takes up a sizeable chunk of Westfield Bondi Junction (p157).

MYER — DEPARTMENT STORE

Map p250 (⌨9238 9111; www.myer.com.au; 436 George St; ☺9am-7pm Fri-Wed, to 9pm Thu; ☒St James) At seven storeys, Myer (formerly Grace Bros) is one of Sydney's largest stores and a prime venue for after-Christmas sales. It's marginally less swanky than David Jones (the difference between Jennifer Hawkins and Miranda Kerr), but you'll still find plenty of high-quality goods and some slick cafes. There's another branch at Westfield Bondi Junction.

RED EYE RECORDS — MUSIC

Map p255 (⌨9262 9755; www.redeye.com.au; 370 Pitt St; ☺9am-6pm Mon-Fri, to 9pm Thu, to 5pm Sat; ☒Museum) Entering this red-walled rock refuge is like waking up inside a huge, hungover eyeball. The shelves are stocked with a rampaging collection of classic, rare and collectable records, CDs, crass rock T-shirts, books, posters and music DVDs. New music is at the **York St branch** (Map p250; 143 York St; ☒Town Hall).

KINOKUNIYA — BOOKS

Map p250 (⌨9262 7996; www.kinokuniya.com; L2, The Galeries, 500 George St; ☺10am-7pm Fri-Wed, to 9pm Thu; ☒Town Hall) This outpost of the Japanese chain is the largest bookstore in Sydney, with over 300,000 titles. The comics section is a magnet for geeky teens – the imported Chinese, Japanese and European magazine section isn't. There's a cool little cafe here, too.

DYMOCKS — BOOKS

Map p250 (⌨9235 0155; www.dymocks.com.au; 424 George St; ☺9am-6pm Mon-Wed & Fri, 9am-8pm Thu, 9.30am-5.30pm Sat, 10.30am-5pm Sun; ☒St James) Heavy on the bestsellers, this mammoth, mainstream bookstore has more than 250,000 titles spread over three floors (including a helluva lot of Lonely Planet guides). Stationery and a cafe, too.

STRAND HATTERS — ACCESSORIES

Map p250 (⌨9231 6884; www.strandhatters .com.au; Strand Arcade, 412 George St; ☺9am-5.30pm Mon-Wed & Fri, 9am-8pm Thu, 9.30am-4.30pm Sat, 11am-4pm Sun; ☒Town Hall) Got a cold or wet head, or a serious case of the *Crocodile Dundees*? Strand Hatters will cover your crown with a classically Australian Akubra bush hat (made from rabbit felt). Staff will block and steam hats to customer requirements (crocodile-teeth hatbands cost extra).

RM WILLIAMS — CLOTHING, ACCESSORIES

Map p250 (⌨9262 2228; www.rmwilliams.com .au; 389 George St; ☒Wynyard) Urban cowboys and country folk can't get enough of this hard-wearing outback gear. It's the kind of stuff politicians don when they want to seem 'fair dinkum' about something. Prime-ministerial favourites include Driza-Bone oilskin jackets, Akubra hats, moleskin jeans and leather work boots. There's another branch in The Rocks.

KINGS COMICS — COMICS

Map p250 (www.kingscomics.com; 310 Pitt St; ☺9am-6pm Sat-Wed, to 8pm Thu & Fri; ☒Town Hall) Like a tractor beam for geeks (and we use that term with all due respect), Kings drags them in with its collection of comics, manga, graphic novels, toys, collectibles and, we're sorry to say, apparel.

HEY PRESTO MAGIC STUDIO — MAGIC

Map p250 (www.heyprestomagic.com.au; 84 Pitt St; ☺10am-5pm Mon-Wed & Fri, to 8pm Thu, to 4pm Sat; ☒Wynyard) If you've ever wanted to pull a rabbit out of a hat, here's where you'll find the hat. Beautiful assistants not provided.

LOVE+HATRED — JEWELLERY

Map p250 (⌨9233 3441; www.loveandhatred .com.au; L1, Strand Arcade, 412 George St; ☺noon-4pm Sun, 10am-5.30pm Mon-Wed & Fri, 10am-8pm Thu, 10am-4.30pm Sat; ☒St James) This plush, sensual, wood-panelled store is aglow with custom-made jewellery by Sydney designer Giovanni D'Ercole. Sapphire rings, natural pearls and rose-gold pieces manifest an unostentatious, mystic blend of Celtic, art nouveau and contemporary styles.

JURLIQUE
BEAUTY

Map p250 (☎9235 0928; www.jurlique.com.au; 420 George St; ◉St James) An international success story, this plant-based skincare range from South Australia is a decadent treat. There's other branches in Westfield Sydney (p95), Westfield Bondi Junction (p157) and in Bondi if your skin is a little parched postsurf.

CHIFLEY PLAZA
SHOPPING CENTRE

Map p250 (www.chifleyplaza.com.au; 2 Chifley Sq; ◉9.30am-6pm Mon-Fri, to 4pm Sat; ◉Martin Place) Overseas luxury brands compete with branches of Leona Edmiston (p146), Herringbone (p147), Oxford (p116) and RM Williams (opposite) at the base of this office tower.

🛏 Haymarket

🏆 PADDY'S MARKETS
MARKET

Map p255 (www.paddysmarkets.com.au; 9-13 Hay St; ◉9am-5pm Wed-Sun; ◉Central) Cavernous, 1000-stall Paddy's is the Sydney equivalent of Istanbul's Grand Bazaar, but swap the hookahs and carpets for mobile-phone covers, Eminem T-shirts and cheap sneakers. Pick up a VB singlet for Uncle Bruce or wander the aisles in capitalist awe.

MARKET CITY
SHOPPING CENTRE

Map p255 (☎9288 8900; www.marketcity.com.au; 9-13 Hay St; ◉10am-7pm; ◉Central) This large shopping centre above Paddy's Markets includes a big food court, heaps of fashion outlet stores (cheap Converse anyone?), Chinese cinemas and video-game parlours.

🏃 SPORTS & ACTIVITIES

COOK + PHILLIP PARK
SWIMMING

Map p250 (☎9326 0444; www.cookandphillip.org.au; 4 College St; adult/child $6.40/4.80; ◉6am-10pm Mon-Fri, 7am-8pm Sat & Sun; ◉St James) This Olympic-sized indoor pool has a hydrotherapy area and a gym ($18 including pool use), plus massage, pilates, a basketball court, yoga, swimming lessons and a wave pool to cool off the kids.

ANDREW 'BOY' CHARLTON POOL
SWIMMING

(☎9358 6686; www.abcpool.org; 1c Mrs Macquaries Rd; adult/child $5.80/4.40; ◉6am-7pm mid-Sep–Apr; ◉441) Sydney's best saltwater pool – smack bang next to the harbour – is a magnet for water-loving gays, straights, mums and fashionistas. Serious lap swimmers rule the pool, so maintain your lane if you're not so serious. Wheelchair accessible; five-star change rooms.

FREE I'M FREE
WALKING TOUR

Map p250 (www.imfree.com.au; ◉10.30am & 2.30pm; ◉Town Hall) Departing twice daily from the square off George St between the Town Hall and St Andrew's Cathedral (no bookings taken – just show up), these highly rated three-hour tours are nominally free but are run by enthusiastic young guides for tips. The route takes in The Rocks, Circular Quay, Martin Place, Pitt St and Hyde Park.

SYDNEY ARCHITECTURE WALKS
TOUR

Map p250 (☎0403 888 390; www.sydneyarchitecture.org; adult/concession walk $35/25, cycle $120/110; ◉Circular Quay) These bright young archi-buffs run a five-hour cycling tour and four themed two-hour walking tours (art, place and landscape; the city; Utzon and the Sydney Opera House; and harbouredge architecture). The tours depart from the Museum of Sydney, rain or shine; call for bookings and departure times.

Darling Harbour & Pyrmont

DARLING HARBOUR | PYRMONT

Neighbourhood Top Five

❶ Escaping the hustle and bustle of the city within the tranquil paths of the **Chinese Garden of Friendship** (p100). The lush greenery and tinkling waters provide cool respite on a hot day.

❷ Facing your fears in the underwater tunnels of **Sydney Aquarium's** (p100) shark tanks.

❸ Meeting the stars of the Australian bush in the heart of the city at **Wild Life Sydney** (p100).

❹ Being eyed up by pelicans while gorging on fish and chips at **Sydney Fish Market** (p101).

❺ Exploring the innards of the historic ships and submarine at the **Australian National Maritime Museum** (p100).

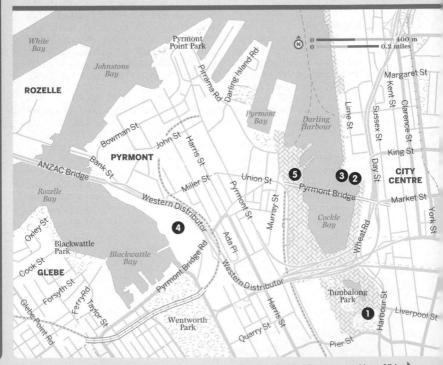

For more detail of this area, see Map p254 ➡

Explore: Darling Harbour & Pyrmont

Dotted between the flyovers and fountains of Sydney's purpose-built tourist hub (opened for the bicentennial in 1988) are some of the city's highest-profile paid attractions. Every other inch of this former dockland is given over to bars and restaurants. Come during the day to visit the big-ticket tourist traps or just to stroll about. It's also busy at night. Firework displays occur with alarming frequency; most Saturday nights go off with a bang.

The state government has parts of Darling Harbour in its sights for a makeover. Depending on when you visit, you might find a work in progress.

West of Darling Harbour, in Pyrmont proper, The Star casino complex has just had its own expensive do over, yet it remains like such establishments the world over: big and soulless beneath a thin veneer of glamour. If you're after a slice of real Sydney life you won't find it here, but it's still worth allocating an hour for a walkabout.

Local Life

➡ **Sydney Fish Market** Sydneysiders head to this market (p101) to stock up for dinner parties or to indulge in fish and chips by the water's edge.

➡ **Tumbalong Park playground** The inner city's best playground is always busy.

➡ **Harris St** The closest thing to a local shopping strip; pick up fancy deli goods from the branch of Simon Johnson at number 181.

Getting There & Away

➡ **Train** The eastern edge of Darling Harbour is within walking distance of Town Hall station. For King St Wharf, Wynyard station is closer.

➡ **Light Rail** If you're heading to Pyrmont from Central or Glebe, light rail is your best option. Convenient stops include Exhibition, Convention, Pyrmont Bay, The Star and Fish Market.

➡ **Ferry** Balmain services chug from Circular Quay to Darling Harbour and Pyrmont Bay. Parramatta River services also stop at Darling Harbour.

➡ **Bus** Bus 443 heads from Circular Quay to the Maritime Museum via George and Harris Sts.

➡ **Parking** Try Harbourside car park, under the Novotel (enter 100 Murray St; per hour/day $9/28).

Lonely Planet's Top Tip

Sydney Aquarium, Madame Tussauds, Wild Life Sydney, Sydney Tower Eye and Manly Oceanworld are all owned by the same people. You'll save a pretty penny on admission by purchasing a combo ticket, available in almost every permutation of attractions.

✗ Best Places to Eat

➡ Zaaffran (p103)

➡ Kazbah (p103)

➡ Adriano Zumbo (p103)

➡ Cafe Morso (p103)

➡ Sydney Fish Market (p101)

For reviews, see p103 ➡

🍷 Best Places to Drink

➡ Home (p104)

➡ Flying Fish (p104)

➡ Loft (p104)

➡ Cargo Bar (p104)

➡ Pontoon (p104)

For reviews, see p104 ➡

👁 Best Attractions

➡ Chinese Garden of Friendship (p100)

➡ Sydney Aquarium (p100)

➡ Wild Life Sydney (p100)

➡ Australian National Maritime Museum (p100)

➡ Madame Tussauds (p100)

For reviews, see p100 ➡

DARLING HARBOUR & PYRMONT

◉ SIGHTS

◉ Darling Harbour

CHINESE GARDEN OF FRIENDSHIP
GARDENS

Map p254 (☑9240 8888; www.chinesegarden.com.au; Harbour St; adult/child/family $6/3/15, audioguide $4; ◎9.30am-5.30pm; ☒Town Hall) Built according to Taoist principles, the Chinese Garden of Friendship is an oasis of tranquillity. Designed by architects from Guangzhou (Sydney's sister city) for Australia's bicentenary in 1988, the garden interweaves pavilions, waterfalls, lakes, paths and lush plant life. It's too serene for words (so shut up and be still).

SYDNEY AQUARIUM
AQUARIUM

Map p254 (☑8251 7800; www.sydneyaquarium.com.au; 1-5 Wheat Rd; adult/child $35/20; ◎9am-8pm; ☒Town Hall) This place brings in more paying visitors than any other attraction in Australia – even with its hefty admission charges. Highlights include clownfish (howdy Nemo), platypuses, an intimidating array of sharks, massive rays and swoon-worthy corals. Residents of the penguin enclosure have lawless amounts of fun.

The aquarium's two dugongs were rescued when washed up on Queensland beaches, and attempts to return them to the wild failed; they're some of only a handful of these large marine mammals in captivity worldwide.

Needless to say, kids love this place. Arrive early to beat the crowds. Booking online will save you a few dollars.

WILD LIFE SYDNEY
ZOO

Map p254 (☑9333 9288; www.wildlifesydney.com.au; 1-5 Wheat Rd; adult/child $35/20; ◎9am-6pm Apr-Nov, to 8pm Dec-Mar; ☒Town Hall) Complementing its sister and neighbour Sydney Aquarium, this large complex houses an impressive collection of Australian native reptiles, butterflies, spiders, snakes and mammals. The nocturnal section is particularly good, bringing out the extrovert in the quolls, potoroos, echidnas and possums, but the kids may be more interested in holding snakes and posing with koalas.

You'll save around $20 on a combined ticket with the Aquarium and there are often excellent deals if you book online.

AUSTRALIAN NATIONAL MARITIME MUSEUM
MUSEUM

Map p254 (☑9298 3777; www.anmm.gov.au; 2 Murray St; adult/child $7/3.50; ◎9.30am-5pm; ☒Pyrmont Bay) Beneath an Utzon-like roof (a low-rent Opera House?), the Maritime Museum sails through Australia's inextricable relationship with the sea. Exhibitions range from Aboriginal canoes to surf culture to the navy. There are free tours every day and kids' activities on Sundays.

The 'big ticket' (adult/child $25/10) includes the cost of touring the vessels moored outside, including the submarine HMAS *Onslow*, the destroyer HMAS *Vampire* and an 1874 square rigger, the *James Craig*. Normally a replica of James Cook's *Endeavour* also drops anchor.

Outside, the austere 100m-long **Welcome Wall** (2 Murray St) honours Sydney's migrants, allowing families to inscribe names and register their history on the database.

MADAME TUSSAUDS
MUSEUM

Map p254 (www.madametussauds.com/sydney; Aquarium Pier; adult/child $35/20; ◎9am-8pm; ☒Town Hall) In this celebrity-obsessed age, it's hardly surprising that Madame Tussauds' hyper-realistic waxwork dummies are just as popular now as when the eponymous madame lugged her macabre haul of French revolution death masks to London in 1803. I mean, where else do mere mortals get to strike a pose with Hugh Jackman and cosy up to Kylie?

TUMBALONG PARK
PARK

Map p254 (☒Town Hall) Flanked by the new Darling Walk development, this grassy circle on Darling Harbour's southern rump is set up for family fun. Sunbakers and frisbee-throwers occupy the lawns; tourists dunk their feet in fountains on hot summer afternoons. There's also an excellent children's playground with a rubber floor (in case the kids don't bounce) and a 21m flying fox.

COCKLE BAY WHARF
NOTABLE BUILDING

Map p254 (www.cocklebaywharf.com; ☒Town Hall) The first vaguely tasteful development in Darling Harbour, Cockle Bay Wharf occupies the harbour's cityside frontage as far as Pyrmont Bridge. Its sharp, contemporary angles are softened by the use of timber and whimsical sculptures (we particularly like the jaunty dancing storks).

CHINESE SYDNEY

Chinese immigrants started to come to Australia around 1840, when convict transportation ceased and labouring jobs became freely available. Initially they were considered a solution to labour shortages, but as gold-rush fever took hold, racial intolerance grew. The tireless Chinese were seen as threats, and state entry restrictions were enforced from the early 19th century into much of the 20th century.

In 1861 the New South Wales Government enacted the 'White Australia Policy', aimed at reducing the influx of Chinese. This included a ban on naturalisation, work-permit restrictions and acts such as the 1861 *Chinese Immigration Regulation & Restriction Act*. As a result, the Chinese population remained low (many also returned to China after the gold rush ended). The White Australia Policy wasn't totally dismantled until 1973.

Sydney's Chinese community eventually gravitated to Dixon St near Darling Harbour, an area once known for opium and gambling but now better known for tasty and great-value food. Today people of Chinese extraction make up 7.9% of Sydney's population, with well over half of these born in Australia.

Housing upmarket restaurants and bars, Cockle Bay helped yank Darling Harbour out of the financial mire in the 1990s. Sydney's megaclub Home set a new standard for stylish clubbing and bucked the colonial trend by spawning an offshoot in London.

KING STREET WHARF
NOTABLE BUILDINGS

Map p254 (www.ksw.com.au; Lime St; ⓇWynyard) Cockle Bay Wharf in ultramodern metal drag, the $800-million King St Wharf continues the Darling Harbour precinct north beyond Pyrmont Bridge. All the plush apartments are sold and the office space leased out, but you can still get a sniff of the high life at the waterfront bars and restaurants.

HARBOURSIDE
SHOPPING CENTRE

Map p254 (www.harbourside.com.au; Darling Dr; ☺10am-9pm; ⓇConvention) The first major Darling Harbour development, Harbourside shopping centre is like that nightclub guy still wearing a pirate shirt and an unreconstructed mullet; its 1980s stylings are no match for the chic constructions loitering on the other side of the harbour. Their tagline insists that 'Harbourside is Happening', but we're not convinced.

SYDNEY CONVENTION & EXHIBITION CENTRE
NOTABLE BUILDINGS

Map p254 (☎9282 5000; www.scec.com.au; Darling Dr; ⓇConvention) No, you're not in Texas. They like to do things big in Sydney too: this behemoth on Darling Harbour's western edge, for example. It was designed by Aussie architect Philip Cox, who also did the Sydney Aquarium and the Maritime Museum (unsurprisingly he's been quoted

as saying, 'Sydney is unimaginable without Darling Harbour').

The Exhibition Centre on the south end has steel masts from which the roof dangles; the Convention Centre is the rounder bit nearer the harbour. At the time of writing, the state government was planning to modify or replace these buildings with, you guessed it, something bigger. In any case they're likely to be closed for three years from late 2013.

DARLING WALK
NOTABLE BUILDING

Map p254 (Harbour St; ⓇTown Hall) The $560-million environmentally conscious Darling Walk development is Darling Harbour's newest block of restaurants and offices, all wrapped up in a curvy glass shell.

⊙ Pyrmont

SYDNEY FISH MARKET
MARKET

Map p254 (☎9004 1100; www.sydneyfishmarket.com.au; Bank St; ☺7am-4pm; ⓇFish Market) This piscatorial precinct on Blackwattle Bay shifts over 15 million kilograms of seafood annually, and has restaurants, a deli, a wine centre and an oyster bar. Chefs, locals and overfed seagulls haggle over mud crabs, Balmain bugs, lobsters and slabs of salmon. Check out the early-morning auctions on a behind-the-scenes **tour** (☎9004 1143; adult/child $20/10; ☺6.40am Mon, Thu & Fri), or sign up for a cooking class.

ANZAC BRIDGE
BRIDGE

Map p254 (Western Distributor) Completed in 1996, Sydney's other eye-catching bridge

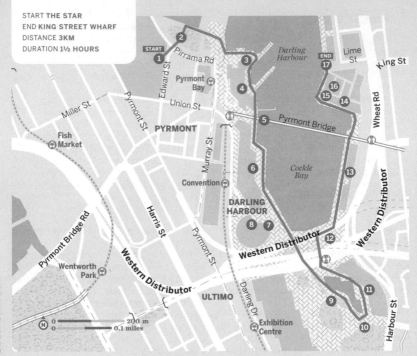

START **THE STAR**
END **KING STREET WHARF**
DISTANCE **3KM**
DURATION **1½ HOURS**

Neighbourhood Walk
A Darling Harbour Dawdle

Catch the light rail to **①** **The Star** and try to negotiate your way out of the casino complex without haemorrhaging money or piling on pounds at Adriano Zumbo's luscious patisserie. Cross over to **②** **Pyrmont Bay Park** and turn right when you reach the water. As you enter Darling Harbour you'll pass the **③** **Welcome Wall**, celebrating immigration to Australia, and the little lighthouse, moored ships and submarine that form part of the **④** **Australian National Maritime Museum**.

Cross under the 1902 **⑤** **Pyrmont Bridge** (the world's first electric swing bridge doncha know) and zoom through the **⑥** **Harbourside shopping centre**. Check out the cool **⑦** **sunken spiral fountain** in front of the **⑧** **Sydney Convention Centre** (if it hasn't been bowled down already). Can you reach the centre and keep your feet dry?

Duck under the freeway and continue through the hectic playgrounds of

⑨ **Tumbalong Park** to the **⑩** **Chinese Garden of Friendship**, arguably the most tranquil spot in the city (we'd argue if it wasn't so tranquil). Soak up the Zen over tea and cake in the teahouse.

Boomerang back past glassy **⑪** **Darling Walk** and the giant **⑫** **IMAX Cinema** and trace the waterline past the restaurants and bars of **⑬** **Cockle Bay Wharf**; keep an eye out for the frolicking storks. After scooting under Pyrmont Bridge again you'll pass Darling Harbour's big attractions in quick succession: **⑭** **Sydney Aquarium**, **⑮** **Madame Tussauds** and **⑯** **Wild Life Sydney**. Listen out for the squawks of the native birds in the giant netted aviary.

Continuing along the waterline, **⑰** **King Street Wharf** is lined with still more restaurants and bars. Reward your walking efforts with a beer and a bite here or backtrack to any of the numerous establishments that took your fancy along the way.

spans Johnstons Bay, connecting Pyrmont and Rozelle. It's the longest cable bridge in Australia (345m), and affords some magic views as you truck into the city from the west. The two main towers are shaped like needle eyes, with the road as the thread.

The Anzac theme is reinforced by an Australian flag atop the eastern tower, a New Zealand flag on the western, and two big soldier statues – one Australian and one New Zealander. For a sea-level perspective, take the pathway between Blackwattle Bay and Bicentennial Park.

THE STAR   CASINO
Map p254 (⏩9777 9000; www.star.com.au; 80 Pyrmont St; ⏲24hr; ⏏The Star) After a name change and a $961-million renovation, The Star reopened in late 2011 amid much hype and hoopla. The complex includes high-profile restaurants, bars, a nightclub, an excellent food court, a light rail station and the kind of high-end label stores that will ensure that in the unlikely event that you do happen to strike it big, a large proportion of your winnings will remain within the building.

✖ EATING

Rows of restaurants line Darling Harbour, many of them pairing their sea views with seafood. Most are pricey tourist-driven affairs that are good but not outstanding. Since reopening The Star has sought to assert itself as Sydney's fine-dining mecca, luring many a gifted restaurateur. There are some truly excellent restaurants here, but we're not sure the atmosphere justifies the prices. Boathouse on Blackwattle Bay (p110), across the water from Pyrmont, is seafood nirvana.

✖ Darling Harbour

ZAAFFRAN   INDIAN $$
Map p254 (⏩9211 8900; www.zaaffran.com.au; L2, Harbourside; mains $19-30; ⏲lunch & dinner; ✚; ⏏Convention) In a city with a gazillion cheap Indian joints, Zaaffran is a stand-out. Authentic and innovative curries by chef Vikrant Kapoor (of Singapore's Raffles fame) are served up with awesome

views across Darling Harbour's sparkle and sheen. Book a balcony seat and launch yourself into the tiger prawn coconut curry. Good vegetarian selection, too.

KAZBAH   NORTH AFRICAN $$
Map p254 (⏩9555 7067; www.kazbah.com.au; The Promenade, Harbourside; breakfast $15-22, lunch $21-26, dinner $31-38; ⏲breakfast, lunch & dinner; ⏏Convention) Rock the Kazbah for beautifully presented, tasty dishes from the Maghrib and Middle East. The breakfasts are legendary, whether you opt for the exotic (sweet couscous, breakfast tagine) or the tried and true (eggs benedict, pancakes), and the tagines are exceptional at any time of day. The original restaurant in Balmain is that suburb's best eatery.

✖ Pyrmont

ADRIANO ZUMBO   PATISSERIE $
Map p254 (www.adrianozumbo.com; ground floor, The Star, 80 Pyrmont St; sweets $2.50-10; ⏲11am-9pm Sun, to 11pm Mon-Sat; ⏏The Star) The man who introduced Sydney to the macaron has indulged his Willy Wonka fantasies in this concept store, with everything artfully displayed amid pastel colours and pink neon. The macarons (or zumbarons, as they're known here), tarts, pastries and cakes are as astonishing to look at as they are to eat. Take away or sit down at the dessert train. There are also branches in Manly (p163) and Balmain.

CAFE MORSO   CAFE $$
Map p254 (⏩9692 0111; www.cafemorso.com.au; Jones Bay Wharf; breakfast $11-20, lunch $22-32; ⏲breakfast & lunch; ⏏The Star) The most popular eatery along Jones Bay Wharf, Morso lures black-clad, laptop-focused business bods and yacht skippers. Sassy breakfasts morph into Mod Oz lunches.

CAFÉ COURT   FOOD COURT $
Map p254 (www.star.com.au; ground floor, The Star, 80 Pyrmont St; mains $10-15; ⏲11am-11pm; ⏏The Star) The Star has done a great job of filling its ground-floor food court with some of the best operators of their kind, such as **Din Tai Fung** (Map p254; mains $10-15) for dumplings, **Messina** (Map p254; www.gelatomessina.com; 2 scoops $5; ⏏The Star) for gelato and Adriano Zumbo for sweet delights.

DRINKING & NIGHTLIFE

Darling Harbour's bright lights herald a slew of glitzy bars that get more clublike as the night progresses. More brash than classy, they attract a buttoned-up, high-heeled, boozy crowd – young accountants on their nights off and private-school kids making their first forays into the city's nightlife.

HOME
CLUB, LIVE MUSIC

Map p254 (☑9266 0600; www.homesydney .com; 1 Wheat Rd, Cockle Bay Wharf; admission free-$55; ☺club Fri & Sat; ☒Town Hall) Welcome to the pleasuredome: a three-level, 2100-capacity timber and glass 'prow' that's home to a dance floor, countless bars, outdoor balconies, and sonics that make other clubs sound like transistor radios. Catch top-name international DJs, plus live bands amping it up at Tokio Hotel downstairs from Tuesday to Saturday.

FLYING FISH
COCKTAIL BAR

Map p254 (☑9518 6677; www.flyingfish.com.au; Jones Bay Wharf; ☺noon-5pm Sun, 6-10.30pm Mon-Sat; ☒The Star) Beyond the architects and investment groups along Jones Bay Wharf is this romantic restaurant-bar. The city lights work their magic all too easily here, aided by an indulgent cocktail list (from $18). Aside from all that romance stuff, it has the coolest toilets in town – the clear-glass stalls frost over when you close the door.

LOFT
BAR

Map p254 (☑9299 4770; www.theloftsydney .com; 3 Lime St, King St Wharf; ☺4pm-1am Mon-Thu, noon-3am Fri & Sat, noon-1am Sun; ☒Wynyard) The Loft is far from lofty – it's more like an open-plan office space – but the walls fold back and disappear, sweeping your eye out across Darling Harbour and beyond. Interior design is Moroccan chic and service is snappy. Book for high tea at high noon on Saturday and Sunday. Live music on Fridays.

CARGO BAR
BAR

Map p254 (☑9262 1777; www.cargobar.com .au; 52 The Promenade, King St Wharf; ☺11am-late; ☒Wynyard) This pioneering Darling Harbour bar still lures beautiful boys, babes and backpackers, who get wall-to-wall boozy after 11pm. Before the drinkers descend, savour the harbour views, tasty pizzas and salads. DJs and live bands fire things up.

PONTOON
BAR, DJ

Map p254 (☑9267 7099; www.pontoonbar.com; The Promenade North, Cockle Bay Wharf; ☺11am-midnight Sun-Wed, to 3am Thu-Sat; ☒Town Hall) Perennially busy Pontoon offers water breezes, cool tunes and high-tech sound and screens. The crowd is less appealing – rugby necks, back-slapping office bully boys and deep-cleavaged 50-somethings – but it's still a reliable place for a beer and DJs from Thursday to Sunday.

ENTERTAINMENT

IMAX CINEMA
CINEMA

Map p254 (☑9281 3300; www.imax.com.au; 31 Wheat Rd; adult/child from $21/16; ☺sessions 10am-8.15pm; ☒Town Hall) It's big bucks for a 45-minute movie, but everything about IMAX is big, and this is reputedly the biggest IMAX in the world. The eight-storey screen shimmers with kid-friendly documentaries (sharks, Mars, haunted castles etc) as well as blockbuster features, many in 3D. Size matters.

LYRIC THEATRE
PERFORMING ARTS

Map p254 (☑9657 8500; www.star.com.au; The Star; tickets $40-140; ☒The Star) This 2000-seat theatre within the casino stages big-name musicals and the occasional concert.

🏃 SPORTS & ACTIVITIES

Darling Harbour and Pyrmont are departure points for many harbour-based activities. The following are based here: James Craig, Sydney by Sail, Magistic Cruises, Sydney Showboats, Harbour Jet (all on p80).

DARLING HARBOUR ROAD TRAIN
TOUR

(☑0408 290 515; adult/child $4.50/3.50; ☺10am-5pm) This people mover 'train' tootles around Darling Harbour (signal the driver to jump on board). It's good for the kids or for resting your legs.

Inner West

ULTIMO | CHIPPENDALE | GLEBE | CAMPERDOWN | DARLINGTON | NEWTOWN | ALEXANDRIA | ENMORE | ERSKINEVILLE | ANNANDALE

Neighbourhood Top Five

❶ Grazing your way around the farmers' market, scoffing at conceptual art, being mystified by an avant-garde performance or sitting down to a high-octane Italian meal within the capacious **Carriageworks** (p108) complex.

❷ Gawking at ancient booty in Sydney University's fascinating **Nicholson Museum** (p107).

❸ Challenging your cultural stereotypes and expanding your mind at **White Rabbit** (p107).

❹ Catching a gig at the **Vanguard** (p113) or any of the Inner West's other live-music hot spots.

❺ Getting down with the brown at **Campos** (p111), king of the coffee-bean scene.

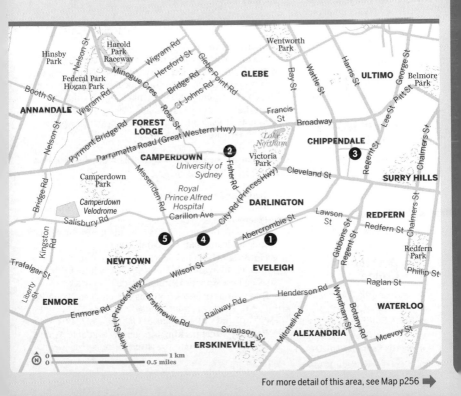

For more detail of this area, see Map p256 ➡

Lonely Planet's Top Tip

Tucked between Central station, Surry Hills and Sydney University, the tiny suburb of Chippendale is one to watch. The White Rabbit gallery (opposite) is an early herald of what is likely to become one of Sydney's coolest neighbourhoods, particularly once the Jean Nouvel/Sir Norman Foster–driven Central Park complex of sustainable plant-covered towers and terraces starts to take shape. Meanwhile Frank Gehry is working on a dramatic crumpled-looking building just across Broadway. Watch this space.

✖ Best Places to Eat

➡ Eveleigh Farmers' Market (p111)

➡ Boathouse on Blackwattle Bay (p110)

➡ Bloodwood (p111)

➡ Deus Cafe (p110)

➡ Luxe (p111)

For reviews, see p110 ➡

● Best Places to Drink

➡ Bank Hotel (p113)

➡ Courthouse Hotel (p113)

➡ Hive (p114)

➡ Jester Seeds (p113)

➡ Corridor (p113)

For reviews, see p112 ➡

✖ Best for Coffee

➡ Campos (p111)

➡ Deus Cafe (p110)

➡ Black Star Pastry (p111)

➡ Luxe (p111)

➡ Mecca Espresso (p110)

For reviews, see p110 ➡

INNER WEST

Explore: Inner West

The Inner West is a sociological stew of students, goths, urban hippies, artists, Mediterranean immigrants and sexual subculturists. At its heart is Sydney University, a bastion of old-world architecture that dominates the tiny suburbs of Camperdown, Darlington and Chippendale.

Between the university and Rozelle Bay, Glebe is home to an Aboriginal community, students, lesbians and New Agers and cool bookstores. The First Fleet's chaplain was granted 160 hectares of church land here (technically a 'glebe'). Mansions sprouted in 1826, but after 1855 the church leased its remaining land for cheap housing, which degenerated into slums. In the mid-1970s Gough Whitlam's federal government bought the whole estate and rejuvenated the area for low-income families.

Where stoners and home renovators collide, Newtown shadows sinuous King St, lined with funky boutiques, bookshops, yoga studios, cafes and Thai restaurants. It's definitely climbing the social rungs, but Newtown is still free-thinking and bolshy.

Erskineville is similar but more upmarket, with an endearing village vibe and an outcrop of pubs and cafes.

Local Life

➡ **Camperdown Park** When the sun shines, the Newtown tribes descend with their picnic rugs. Even the goths brave the the risk of absorbing vitamin D, unpacking their baskets in the adjacent cemetery.

➡ **Pubs** The centre of Inner Western social life, whether for watching the footy, grabbing a cheap meal, checking out a band, catching up with mates or hooking up.

➡ **Markets** Yummy mummies stock up on organic whatnots at Eveleigh (p111), while hippy chicks peruse preloved frocks at Glebe (p115).

Getting There & Away

➡ **Train** Newtown is well served by trains, with four stations (Macdonaldtown, Newtown, Erskineville and St Peters) on three train lines (Inner West, South and Bankstown). Redfern station is handy for Darlington, Chippendale and parts of Camperdown.

➡ **Light Rail** Glebe has two light rail stops (Glebe and Jubilee Park); walk uphill and you'll reach Glebe Point Rd. The best stop for Ultimo is Paddy's Market.

➡ **Bus** Dozens of buses from the city ply Glebe Point Rd (370, 431–433), Parramatta Rd (413, 436–440, 461, 480–483, M10) and City Rd/King St (352, 370, 422–428, M30).

➡ **Parking** Street parking is generally available. Watch out for the maze of one-way streets around Newtown.

◉ SIGHTS

◉ Ultimo

POWERHOUSE MUSEUM MUSEUM
Map p256 (☎9217 0111; www.powerhousemu
seum.com; 500 Harris St; adult/child $12/6;
☺9.30am-5pm; ☒Paddy's Markets) A short
walk from Darling Harbour, Sydney's most
kid-focused museum whirs away inside the
former power station for Sydney's defunct
tram network. Interactive demonstrations
wow school groups with the low-down on
how lightning strikes, magnets grab and engines growl. Look out for the Strasburg Clock
replica on level three and the mad scientist
experimentation stuff on level one.

Grab a map of the museum once you're inside, and a free copy of the *Daily Telegraph*
on your way out. Good disabled access

◉ Chippendale

FREE WHITE RABBIT GALLERY
Map p256 (www.whiterabbitcollection.org; 30 Balfour St; ☺10am-6pm Thu-Sun; ☒Redfern) If you're
an art lover or a bit of a Mad Hatter, this par
ticular rabbit hole will leave you grinning
like a Cheshire Cat. There are so many works
in this private collection of cutting-edge, contemporary Chinese art, that only a fraction
can be displayed at one time.

Who knew that the People's Republic was
turning out work that was so edgy, funny,
sexy or idiosyncratic?

◉ Glebe

SZE YUP TEMPLE TEMPLE
(☎9660 6465; 2 Edward St; ☺10am-5pm; ☒Ju-
bilee Park) This humble backstreet temple
was opened in 1898 by immigrants from
the Sze Yup area of China. It's dedicated to
3rd-century folk hero Kwan Ti, whose em-
broidered, green-robed image, flanked by
two guards, takes centre stage on the altar.
Known for his loyalty, physical prowess and
masculinity, he is looked to by supplicants
as a wise judge, guide and protector.

At Chinese New Year it's a hectic place:
kids' laughter in the forecourt is offset by
solemn offerings of incense and fruit at the
altar. Respectful visitors are welcome (take
your shoes off before entering).

JUBILEE & BICENTENNIAL PARKS PARKS
(Glebe Point Rd; ☒Jubilee Park) These two rolling, grassy parks merge together to offer
some tasty views across Rozelle Bay and
of both the Anzac and Harbour Bridges.
Massive fig and palm trees dot the lawns.
A path leads from here along the shoreline
to Blackwattle Bay, passing the Victorian
Italianate **Bellevue Cottage** (1896) and a
park built around the templelike ruins of
an industrial incinerator.

◉ Camperdown

UNIVERSITY OF SYDNEY UNIVERSITY
Map p256 (☎9351 2222; www.usyd.edu.au; Parramatta Rd; ☒422-440) Australia's oldest
tertiary territory (1850) has over 45,000
students and even boasts its own postcode.
You don't need to have a PhD to grab a free
campus map and wander around. Flanked
by two grand halls that wouldn't be out of
place in Harry Potter's beloved Hogwarts,
the **Quadrangle** has a Gothic Revival design that tips its mortarboard towards the
stately colleges of Oxford.

Also here is the arresting Nicholson Museum and the small **University Art Gallery**
(Map p256; ☺10am-4.30pm Mon-Fri, noon-4pm
1st Sat of month). Nearby, the **Macleay Museum** (Map p256; ☺10am-4.30pm Mon-Fri,
noon-4pm 1st Sat of month) has a musty dead
smell (old dons or the historic collection of
taxidermied Australian fauna?).

FREE NICHOLSON MUSEUM MUSEUM
Map p256 (☎9351 2812; www.usyd.edu.au;
University of Sydney; ☺10am-4.30pm Mon-Fri,
noon-4pm 1st Sat of month; ☒422-440) Within
the University of Sydney's quadrangle, this
museum is a must-see for ancient-history
geeks. Inside is an amazing accumulation
of Greek, Roman, Cypriot, Egyptian and
Near Eastern antiquities, including Padi-
ashaikhet the mummy. It was founded in
1860 by orphan-made-good Sir Charles Nicholson, a key figure in the establishment
of both the University of Sydney and the
Australian Museum.

VICTORIA PARK PARK
Map p256 (cnr Parramatta & City Rds; ☒422-440)
The green gateway to the Inner West and
the University of Sydney, Victoria Park is a
9-hectare grassy wedge revolving around
pondlike **Lake Northam** and Victoria Park

Pool (p116). In February 75,000 people descend on the park for the Mardi Gras Fair Day: dog shows, live performances and the 'Miss Fair Day' drag competition (no, it doesn't involve cars).

⊙ Darlington

FREE CARRIAGEWORKS   ARTS CENTRE
Map p256 (☑8571 9111; www.performancespace.com.au; 245 Wilson St; ⊗10am-6pm; ⏛Redfern) Built between 1880 and 1889, this intriguing group of huge Victorian-era workshops was part of the Eveleigh Railyards. The rail workers chugged out in 1988 and in 2007 the artists pranced in. It's now home to various avant-garde arts and performance

projects, and there's usually something interesting to check out.

One of Sydney's top contemporary galleries, **Anna Schwartz Gallery** (Map p256; www.annaschwartzgallery.com; ⊗10am-6pm Wed-Fri, 1-5pm Sat), is here, alongside Performance Space (p114), the Eveleigh Farmers' Market (p111) and Artisans' Market (p115).

⊙ Newtown

CAMPERDOWN CEMETERY   CEMETERY
Map p256 (☑9557 2043; www.ststephens.org.au; 189 Church St; tours $10; ⊗sunrise-sunset, tours 11.30am 1st Sun of the month Feb-Dec; ⏛Newtown) Take a self-guided tour beyond the monstrous 1848 fig tree into this

---

WORTH A DETOUR

SYDNEY OLYMPIC PARK

More than just Olympic nostalgia, the 640-hectare Sydney Olympic Park, 14km west of the city centre, is a sprawling sustainable world unto itself. Each year 850 million litres of water are captured in the park's water features, reducing its demand on city water by half, and banks of solar panels generate much of the site's electricity. In the post-Olympic years the surrounding land has been transformed into nature reserves, 35km of cycleways and residential enclaves.

The train deposits you at the heart of the complex, near the **visitor centre** (☑9714 7888; www.sydneyolympicpark.com.au; 1 Showground Rd; ⊗9am-5pm; ⏛Olympic Park). Drop in for maps and information on tours and events. Ferry is another option, though the wharf is at the far northern tip of the complex, next to the **Newington Nature Reserve**. From here it's a 3.5km walk (about 45 minutes) to the visitor centre, or you can catch bus 526 (16 minutes, departs every 30 minutes).

The best way to explore is by bike. **Bike Hire @ Sydney Olympic Park** (☑9746 1572; www.bikehiresydneyolympicpark.com.au; Bicentennial Dr, Bicentennial Park; mountain bike per 1/2/4/8/24hr $15/20/30/40/50; ⊗8.30am-5.30pm) operates daily from Bicentennial Park (1.6km from the visitor centre) and on weekends and school holidays from **Blaxland Riverside Park** (1.5km west along the river from the ferry wharf), renting mountain bikes, kid's bikes and tandems.

The Olympic venues are near the train station, including the **Aquatic Centre** (☑9752 3666; www.aquaticcentre.com.au; Olympic Blvd; adult/child $7/6; ⊗5am-9pm Mon-Fri, 6am-7pm Sat & Sun; ⏛Olympic Park). **ANZ Stadium** (☑8765 2300; www.anzstadium.com.au; Olympic Blvd; tours $29/19; ⊗tours 11am, 1pm & 3pm; ⏛Olympic Park), the main Olympic arena, is an imposing oval bedpan with a colourful sculpture of native feathers spiralling over its main entrance. Apart from the regular venue tour, daredevils can take a walk along the gantry, 45m above the pitch (adult/child $49/19, 2pm daily). In the shadow of the stadium is **Games Memories**, an outdoor multimedia installation consisting of 480 decorated poles, and the silver flying saucer that burst into Olympic flame, which has been converted into a **fountain**.

East of the showgrounds, the arresting **Brickpit Ring Walk** (Australia Ave; ⊗sunrise-sunset) is a brightly coloured circular walkway supported 18m above an abandoned brickworks on what looks like metal chopsticks. Three billion bricks were made here between 1911 and 1988. Built into the loop are multimedia exhibits about the brick workers and their amphibious replacements, including the endangered green and golden bell frog.

START **ERSKINEVILLE STATION**
END **KING ST**
DISTANCE **1½ KM**
DURATION **ONE HOUR**

Neighbourhood Walk
Social-History Stroll

Exiting **① Erskineville train station**, turn left and cruise through Erskineville Village. On your left you'll pass the lavishly tiled **② Rose of Australia** pub, and on your right the defunct **③ South Sydney City Council Chambers** (South Sydney merged with the City of Sydney in 2004) and the art deco **④ Erskineville Hotel**.

Cinematic déjà vu! You may recognise the **⑤ Imperial Hotel** on the Union St corner as the spot from which the bus departed in *The Adventures of Priscilla, Queen of the Desert*. In June 1931 this unassuming side street also was the setting for the 'Battle of Union St', one of several Great Depression eviction clashes. Hundreds of people gathered and jeered as police brutally evicted residents who had barricaded themselves inside a house.

Another socialist landmark, **⑥ Green Bans Park**, just before the railway bridge on Erskineville Rd, owes its existence to the construction workers' green bans of the

1980s and '90s. Ceramic tiles tell the story of the 1992 union ban that led to this land being retained as a community park. Similar green bans saved Woolloomooloo's Finger Wharf and parts of The Rocks.

Cross the bridge and truck up to King St, Newtown. Across the road is a prominent **⑦ Martin Luther King mural**. Cut down Mary St to the narrowest slice of **⑧ Camperdown Memorial Rest Park**, Newtown's green meeting place.

Turn right on Lennox St then left into Church St; the evocatively ramshackle **⑨ Camperdown Cemetery** is on your left. Grab a self-guided tour pamphlet from the box near the gate and go exploring.

Leaving the cemetery go straight ahead on Victoria St then turn right into Hordern St (check out the mix of grungy and restored terraces), before hanging left onto **⑩ King Street**, Newtown's pulsing thoroughfare. Above shop level the largely extant facades tie the streetscape to its past.

dark, eerily unkempt cemetery next to St Stephens Church. Famous Australians buried here between 1849 and 1942 include Eliza Donnithorne, the inspiration for Miss Havisham in Dickens' *Great Expectations*. Book guided tours via the website.

◉ Alexandria

SYDNEY PARK
PARK

(Sydney Park Rd; ⊠St Peters) Full of dog walkers, kite flyers and stragglers from last night's party, 40-hectare Sydney Park is a great place to chill out. From the bald hilltop the city rises like a volcanic island from a sea of suburbia, while to the south there are views over the airport to Botany Bay. Much of the land has been reclaimed from swamps, clay pits and brickworks.

✗ EATING

Newtown's King St is among the city's most diverse eat streets, with Thai restaurants sitting alongside Vietnamese, Macedonian, Lebanese and Mexican. And when it comes to coffee culture, all roads point to the Inner West.

✗ Ultimo

📷 MECCA ESPRESSO
CAFE $

Map p256 (www.meccaespresso.com.au; 646 Harris St; mains $7-11; ⊙breakfast & lunch Mon-Sat; ⊠Central) Mecca has devotees cramming its industrial interior – more for the transcendent coffee than the food, it's fair to say, but there are tasty cooked breakfasts, paninis, and 'roast on a roll'.

SYDNEY KOPITIAM
MALAYSIAN $$

Map p256 (📞9282 9883; 592 Harris St; mains $10-15; ⊙lunch daily, dinner Tue-Sun; ⊠Paddy's Market) Kopitiam (meaning 'coffee shop') isn't going to win design awards (low ceiling, daggy tiled floor, plastic furniture and Malaysian Airlines tourism posters), but the great-value, authentic Malaysian soups, stir-fries and curries are spectacular.

✗ Glebe

BOATHOUSE ON BLACKWATTLE BAY
SEAFOOD $$$

(📞9518 9011; www.boathouse.net.au; end of Ferry Rd; mains $41-48; ⊙lunch Thu-Sun, dinner Tue-Sun; ⊠Glebe) The best restaurant in Glebe, and one of the best seafood restaurants in Sydney. Offerings range from oysters so fresh you'd think you shucked them yourself to a snapper pie that'll go straight to the top of your favourite-dish list. Amazing Anzac Bridge views; reservations essential.

SAPPHO BOOKS, CAFE & WINE BAR
CAFE $

Map p256 (📞9552 4498; www.sapphobooks.com.au; 51 Glebe Point Rd; mains $6-18; ⊙8.30am-6.30pm Sun-Tue, to 11pm Wed-Sat; ⊠Glebe) Sequestered in the back of a raggedy bookshop, Sappho is a beaut bohemian garden cafe, its walls scrawled with generations of graffiti. The coffee's excellent, the staff's good-lookin' and the food is a healthy selection of salads, panini and light breakfasts. Wine and tapas kick in after 6pm.

YUGA
CAFE $$

Map p256 (📞9692 8604; www.yugaflora.com.au; 172 St Johns Rd; mains $12-18; ⊙7am-4pm; ⊠Glebe) What a sweet-smelling combo: a florist *and* a cafe that's stylish, reasonably priced and friendly. Sophisticated and serene Yuga serves Aussie breakfasts morphing into Japanese- and Italian-flavoured lunches.

✗ Camperdown

DEUS CAFE
CAFE $$

Map p256 (📞9519 3669; 98-104 Parramatta Rd; breakfast & lunch $8-17, dinner $18-25; ⊙breakfast & lunch daily, dinner Wed-Sun; ⊠436-440) Strewn with vintage motorcycles and kooky two-wheelin' art, Deus Cafe is an extension of an eccentric motorbike shop on frenzied Parramatta Rd. Start the day with a classic: a Triumph Bonneville T100 or a ham-and-cheese croissant with a high-revving coffee. Hearty mains (burgers, steak sandwiches, pasta) kick in as the day progresses.

WORTH A DETOUR

LEICHHARDT

The main drag of predominantly Italian Leichhardt (affectionately referred to as Dykeheart by the local lesbians) is famous for its Italian restaurants and improbable piazza. The **Italian Forum** (www.theitalianforum.com.au; 23 Norton St; ⊘10am-10pm; 🚊Petersham) has copped its fair share of criticism, and yes, it's totally Disney-goes-to-Rome, but it is a reliable place for a strong coffee, some pasta or a pair of expensive sunglasses. Immaculate waiters without a hair out of place deliver your gelato or macchiato as the kids play Caligula. Remember to say 'ciao' as often as possible.

The culinary highlight of Leichhardt, **Grappa** (☑9560 6090; www.grappa.com.au; 267-277 Norton St; mains $20-40; ⊘lunch Tue-Fri & Sun, dinner Tue-Sun; 🚊Lilyfield) has an open kitchen and snazzy bar – it's the setting for rich, succulent dishes (such as baked snapper in a rock-salt crust) and bounteous wood-fired pizzas. If it's warm, sit outside on the terrace, sip chianti and think of Tuscany. Ahhh, Tuscany...

✕ Darlington

EVELEIGH FARMERS' MARKET   MARKET $
Map p256 (www.eveleighmarket.com.au; Carriageworks, 243 Wilson St; ⊘8am 1pm Sat, 🚊Redfern) Over 70 regular stallholders sell their goodies at Sydney's best farmers' market, held in a heritage-listed railway workshop. Food and coffee stands do a brisk business; celebrity chef Kylie Kwong can often be spotted cooking up a storm.

✕ Newtown

🍴BLOODWOOD   INTERNATIONAL $$
Map p256 (www.bloodwoodnewtown.com; 416 King St; dishes $7-32; ⊘lunch Fri-Sun, dinner Wed-Mon; 🚊Newtown) Relax over a few drinks and a progression of small plates (we love those polenta chips!) in the front bar, or make your way to the rear to enjoy soundly conceived and expertly cooked dishes from across the globe. The decor is industrial-chic and the vibe is alternative – very Newtown. It doesn't take bookings.

LUXE   CAFE $
Map p256 (194 Missenden Rd; breakfast $6-11, lunch $10-16; ⊘breakfast & lunch; 🚊Macdonaldtown) Campos next door might be the pinnacle of caffeine culture but if you want to sit down, read the paper and eat something more substantial, Luxe is the dux. The menu is limited (a couple of cooked brekky options; pasta or fish for lunch) but the counter of this industrial-chic bakery-cafe is chocka with chunky sandwiches, moist cakes and delicate tarts.

🍴VARGABAR ESPRESSO   CAFE $
Map p256 (☑9517 1932; www.vargabarnewtown.com.au; 10 Wilson St; mains $10-16; ⊘7am-6pm Mon-Fri, 8am-5.30 Sat & Sun; 🛜; 🚊Newtown) A diminutive dark-pink cafe with an electric-blue coffee machine, Varga trades on big breakfasts and generates too many hard decisions for 8am. The pesto fried eggs or the breakfast burrito? Both?

BLACK STAR PASTRY   BAKERY $
Map p256 (www.blackstarpastry.com.au; 277 Australia St; items $6-10; ⊘7am-5pm; 🚊Newtown) Wise people follow the Star to pay homage to excellent coffee, a large selection of sweet things and a few very good savoury things (gourmet pies and the like). There are only a couple of little tables; it's more a snack-and-run or picnic-in-the-park kind of place.

CAMPOS   CAFE $
Map p256 (☑9516 3361; www.camposcoffee.com, 193 Missenden Rd; items $4; ⊘7am-4pm Mon-Sat; 🚊Macdonaldtown) Trying to squeeze into crowded Campos, king of Sydney's bean scene, can be a challenge. Bean fiends come from miles around – hat-wearing students, broadsheet literati, window-seat daydreamers and doctors on a break from the hospital – all gagging for a shot of 'Campos Superior' blend.

THANH BINH   VIETNAMESE $$
Map p256 (☑9557 1175; www.thanhbinh.com.au; 111 King St; mains $14-24; ⊘lunch Wed-Sun, dinner daily; 🚊Macdonaldtown) If you're used to Vietnamese restaurants where everything is prerolled and ready to be shovelled straight into your mouth, you haven't really had Vietnamese food. At Thanh Binh playing with your food is part of the fun.

Load up your prawn cracker, soak your rice paper, pluck your herbs and launch into a wrapping, rolling, dipping and feasting frenzy.

GUZMAN Y GOMEZ
MEXICAN **$**

Map p256 (📞9517 1533; www.guzmanygomez.com; 175 King St; mains $7.50-11; ⏱11am-11pm; 🚆Macdonaldtown) A spicy alternative for fast-food aficionados, this zippy blue-and-yellow diner uses fresh local produce to whip up authentic Mexican tacos, burritos and quesadillas. Everything's marinated and grilled daily. Look out for other branches around Sydney.

KINGFISH BISTRO
SEAFOOD **$$**

Map p256 (www.kingfishbistro.com.au; 503 King St; mains $27-32; ⏱lunch Sun, dinner Tue-Sat; 🚆St Peters) Is it possible to have a good seafood meal with a white-linen ambience without breaking the bank? Most Sydney-siders will assure you it isn't, but Kingfish would beg to differ. It's a family affair, with mum chatting with the customers while son turns out the likes of bream, barramundi and swordfish for less than $30 a main.

BEACH BURRITO COMPANY
MEXICAN **$**

Map p256 (www.beachburritocompany.com; 1a Bedford St; mains $10-19; ⏱11am-late; 🚆Newtown) Painted skateboards, movie stills and a shrine of skulls provide the ambience at this exceedingly popular Mexican joint. Grab a seat at one of the long tables and get stuck in to a cheap, tasty and filling fajita, chimichanga, quesadilla, *taquito* or burrito.

THAI POTHONG
THAI **$$**

Map p256 (📞9550 6277; www.thaipothong.com; 294 King St; mains $15-30; ⏱lunch & dinner; 🚆Newtown) This place has won a bowlful of 'Best Thai Restaurant in Sydney' awards. The menu is predictable and the usual crowd of golden Buddhas festoons the walls, but the mood is oddly romantic. Pull up a window seat and watch the Newtowners pass by.

✕ Enmore

COW & THE MOON
ICE CREAM **$**

Map p256 (www.cowandthemoon.com.au; 181 Enmore Rd; 2 scoops $4.50; ⏱8am-10.30pm Sun-Tue, 8am-midnight Wed-Sat; 🚆Newtown) Forget the diet and slink into this cool corner cafe, where an array of creamy gelato, sinful truffles and colourful macarons beckon seductively. If the staff are flummoxed (as they were when we last visited), amuse yourself looking at the old postcards and board games set into the tables.

✕ Erskineville

MAGGIE'S
THAI **$$**

Map p256 (📞9516 5270; 75 Erskineville Rd; mains $13-26; ⏱lunch Wed-Fri, dinner daily; 🚗; 🚆Erskineville) More intimate than King St's vast Thai palaces, Maggie's has a dining room strung with fairy lights and an open-sided kitchen painted in zingy lime green. The Thai greatest hits on the menu are supplemented by seasonal specials chalked up on the wall.

🍷 DRINKING & NIGHTLIFE

Devotees of the comfortable, atmospheric local pub rejoice! The Inner West has plenty of pubs in varying degrees of gentrification, ranging from 'not at all' to 'within an inch of its life'. A thirsty student population sustains a barrage of bars and live-music venues, while a sizeable lesbian and gay community also makes its presence felt.

🍷 Glebe

FRIEND IN HAND HOTEL
PUB

Map p256 (📞9660 2326; www.friendinhand.com.au; 58 Cowper St; ⏱10am-10pm Sun, 8am-midnight Mon-Sat; 🚆Glebe) At heart Friend in Hand is still a working-class pub with a resident loud-mouth cockatoo and a cast of grizzly old-timers and local larrikins propping up the bar. But then there's all the other stuff: life drawing, poetry readings, crab racing, comedy nights. Strewth Beryl, bet you weren't expecting that.

A.B. HOTEL
PUB

Map p256 (📞9660 1417; www.abhotel.com.au; 225 Glebe Point Rd; ⏱10am-midnight Mon-Sat, to 10pm Sun; 🛜; 🚆Glebe) An old fave with a $5-million facelift, the former Ancient Briton is looking good, particularly the

Pacific Penthouse, with live fish swimming around inside the bar. Heavy drapes and portraits of Lenin adorn the walls and there's a cute courtyard.

🍷 Annandale

ANNANDALE HOTEL   LIVE MUSIC

Map p256 (📞9550 1078; www.annandalehotel .com; 17 Parramatta Rd; admission free-$28; 🚌436-440) At the forefront of Sydney's live-music scene, the Annandale coughs up alt-rock, metal, punk and electronica. Punters traverse the sticky carpet between sets by local kids on a stage that's held the likes of the Dandy Warhols and the Yeah Yeah Yeahs. Yum cha lunches on weekends.

EMPIRE HOTEL   LIVE MUSIC

(📞9557 1701; www.empirehotelannandale.com .au; 103a Parramatta Rd; admission free-$20; 🚌; 🚉Stanmore) The Empire's well-managed 300-capacity bar gets down 'n' dirty with some of Sydney's best blues and roots bands, along with a smattering of folk rock, pop, soul and jazz acts.

🍸 Newtown

🏆TOP CHOICE BANK HOTEL   PUB, DJ

Map p256 (📞8568 1900; www.bankhotel.com .au; 324 King St; ⏰10am-late; 🚉Newtown) There's been bags of cash splashed about the Bank, but it still attracts a kooky mix of lesbians (especially for Lady L on Wednesdays), students, sports fans, gay guys and just about everyone else – they just don't wear their ugh boots to the pub anymore. The portfolio includes a rooftop terrace, cocktail bar, Thai restaurant and DJs.

COURTHOUSE HOTEL   PUB

Map p256 (📞9519 8273; 202 Australia St; ⏰10am-midnight Mon-Sat, to 10pm Sun; 🚉Newtown) What a brilliant pub! A block back from the King St fray, the 150-year-old Courthouse is the kind of place where everyone from pool-playing goth lesbians to magistrates can have a beer and feel right at home. How ironic – the complete absence of social judgement in a pub called the Courthouse. Beer specials, decent house red and good pub grub, too.

JESTER SEEDS   COCKTAIL BAR

Map p256 (www.jesterseeds.com; 127 King St; ⏰4pm-midnight Tue-Sat, to 10pm Sun; 🚉Macdonaldtown) Jester Seeds is very Newtown. By that we mean a bit gloomy, a little grungy and very hip, with the requisite mismatched furniture, graffiti, obtuse name, astroturf 'garden' and a classic but credible soundtrack. And the cocktails are great.

CORRIDOR   COCKTAIL BAR

Map p256 (www.corridorbar.com.au; 153a King St; ⏰3pm-midnight Tue-Fri, 1pm-midnight Sat, 1-10pm Sun; 🚉Macdonaldtown) The name exaggerates this bar's skinniness, but not by much. Downstairs the bartenders serve old-fashioned cocktails and a good range of wine, while upstairs there's interesting art (for sale) and a tiny deck.

VANGUARD   LIVE MUSIC

Map p256 (📞9557 7992; www.thevanguard.com .au; 42 King St; dinner & show $51-82, general admission $16-32; 🚉Macdonaldtown) Intimate 1920s-themed Vanguard stages live music most nights (including some well-known names), as well as burlesque, comedy and classic-movie screenings. Most seats are reserved for dinner-and-show diners.

SANDRINGHAM HOTEL   LIVE MUSIC

Map p256 (📞9557 1254; www.sando.com.au; 387 King St; admission free-$35; 🚌; 🚉Newtown) Minimal (or no) cash will score you a live-music fix (everything from acoustic acts to goth metal) at the Sando, where, according to local band The Whitlams, God drops by.

ZANZIBAR   BAR

Map p256 (📞9519 1511; www.zanzibarnewtown .com.au; 323 King St; ⏰10am-5am Mon-Sat, to midnight Sun; 🚉Newtown) Eastern opulence continues all the way to the roof at this late-night Newtown bar with a winged art deco facade. Catch the sunset from the rooftop, settle into a cushioned couch or shoot pool in the funky downstairs bar. Beaut bar food; $8 cocktails until 10pm.

MARLBOROUGH HOTEL   PUB

Map p256 (📞9519 1222; www.marlboroughhotel .com.au; 145 King St; ⏰10am-late Mon-Sat, noon-late Sun; 🚉Macdonaldtown) The Marly has a front sports bar with live bands on weekends, a shady beer garden, a cellar nightclub and a large cocktail floor with a cool wraparound terrace.

INNER WEST DRINKING & NIGHTLIFE

♀ Enmore

SLY FOX PUB
Map p256 (☑9557 1016; www.theslyfox.com
.au; 199 Enmore Rd; ⊘10am-late; ⊠Newtown)
This blue-collar pub hosts Sydney's biggest
weekly lesbian night on Wednesdays, when
drag kings pack their crotches and hit the
stage – gay men don't have a monopoly on
gender illusion in this town. Cheap cocktails ($6!) every night from 6pm to 9pm.

♀ Erskineville

IMPERIAL HOTEL GAY, CLUB
Map p256 (www.theimperialhotel.com.au; 35 Erskineville Rd; front bar free, cellar club before/after
10pm free/$10, cabaret bar Fri/Sat $10/15; ⊘3pm-
late; ⊠Erskineville) The art deco Imperial is legendary as the setting for *The Adventures of
Priscilla, Queen of the Desert*. The front bar
is a lively place for pool-shooting and cruising, with the action shifting to the cellar club
late on a Saturday night. But it's in the cabaret bar that the legacy of Priscilla survives.

🍸 HIVE BAR
Map p256 (☑9519 9911; www.thehivebar.com.au;
93 Erskineville Rd; ⊘11.30am-midnight Mon-Fri,
9am-midnight Sat, to 10pm Sun; ⊠Erskineville) In
increasingly groovy Erskineville village, this
breezy little corner bar lures the neighbourhood's hipsters with excellent food, cocktails,
DJs spinning funk and soul, crazy murals
and a quiet bolthole upstairs. Order a plate
and share it over a glass of vino.

ROSE OF AUSTRALIA PUB
Map p256 (☑9565 1441; www.roseofaustralia
.com.au; 1 Swanson St; ⊘10am-11pm; ⊠Erskine-
ville) The aubergine and umber renovations
to this gorgeous old corner pub haven't
dented the tiled front bar's charm one iota.
Locals of all persuasions hang out here,
catching some afternoon rays at the streetside tables, a footy game on the big screens
or a meal upstairs. Live bands Fridays.

☆ ENTERTAINMENT

NEW THEATRE THEATRE
Map p256 (☑1300 13 11 88; www.newtheatre
.org.au; 542 King St; adult/concession $30/25;
⊠St Peters) Australia's oldest continuously

performing theatre (since 1932), Newtown's
eclectic New Theatre produces toothy new
dramas as well as more established pieces.

SEYMOUR CENTRE PERFORMING ARTS
Map p256 (☑9351 7940; www.seymourcentre
.com.au; cnr City Rd & Cleveland St; tickets $16-
65; ⊘box office 9am-6pm Mon-Fri, 11am-3pm Sat;
⊠Redfern) Behind a glass curtain wall on an
insanely busy intersection, this Sydney Uni-
affiliated theatre (actually, four theatres)
shows an eclectic selection of plays, cabaret,
comedy and musicals.

ENMORE THEATRE PERFORMING ARTS
Map p256 (☑9550 3666; www.enmoretheatre
.com.au; 130 Enmore Rd; tickets $18-79; ⊘box
office 9am-6pm Mon-Fri, 10am-2pm Sat; ⊠New-
town) Originally a vaudeville playhouse, the
elegantly wasted, 2500-capacity Enmore
now hosts such acts as Queens of the Stone
Age, Wilco and PJ Harvey, plus theatre
and comedy. There's a cafe, wooden floors,
lounge areas and balconies.

PERFORMANCE SPACE PERFORMING ARTS
Map p256 (☑8571 9111; www.performancespace
.com.au; Carriageworks, 245 Wilson St; tickets
adult/concession $30/20; ⊠Redfern) This edgy
artists' hub stages performances of new
dance, acrobatic and multimedia works –
basically anything that can be lumped under the broad umbrella of 'the Arts'.

DENDY NEWTOWN CINEMA
Map p256 (☑9550 5699; www.dendy.com.au; 261
King St; adult/child $17/12; ⊠Newtown) Follow
the buttery scent of popcorn into the dark
folds of this plush cinema, screening first-
run, independent world films.

SHOPPING

**Newtown and Glebe are hot spots for
anything punky, alternative, socialist,
greenie, intellectual or noir. King St,
Newtown, has interesting boutiques,
secondhand stores and (along with Glebe
Point Rd) the city's best bookstores.
New homewares stores strike the fear
of gentrification into the hearts of long-
term locals. There are also branches of
Holy Kitsch! (p128), Berkelouw Books and
C's Flashback (p129). The semi-industrial
area of Alexandria, east of Erskineville, is
known for its factory-outlet shops.**

🏛 Glebe

GLEEBOOKS   BOOKS
Map p256 (☑9660 2333; www.gleebooks.com
.au; 49 Glebe Point Rd; ☉9am-7pm Sun-Wed, to
9pm Thu-Sat; 🚊Glebe) Generally regarded
to be Sydney's best bookshop. The aisles
are packed with politics, arts and general
fiction, and staff really know their stuff.
Check its calendar for author talks and
book launches. Children's and secondhand
books are at their **other store** (Map p256;
☑9552 2526; 191 Glebe Point Rd; ☉11am-7pm).

GLEBE MARKETS   MARKET
Map p256 (www.glebemarkets.com.au; Glebe Public School, cnr Glebe Point Rd & Derby Pl; ☉10am-
4pm Sat; 🚊Glebe) The best of the west;
Sydney's dreadlocked, shoeless, inner-city
contingent beats an aimless course to this
crowded hippy-ish market.

BROADWAY SHOPPING
CENTRE   SHOPPING CENTRE
Map p256 (www.broadway.com.au; cnr Broadway
& Bay St; ☉10am-7pm Fri-Wed, to 9pm Thu; 🚹;
🚌422-440) Inside the rejuvenated Grace
Bros building (check out the cool old globes
above the facade), this centre has dozens of
shops, a food court, a cinema complex and
two supermarkets.

🏛 Camperdown

DEUS EX MACHINA   CLOTHING, ACCESSORIES
Map p256 (☑8594 2800; http://au.deuscustoms
.com; 98-104 Parramatta Rd; ☉9am-5pm; 🚌436-
440) Translating to 'God is in the machine',
this kooky showroom is crammed with
classic and custom-made motorcycles and
surfboards. A hybrid workshop, cafe and
offbeat boutique, it stocks men's and wom-
en's threads, including Deus-branded jeans,
tees and shorts.

🏛 Darlington

EVELEIGH ARTISANS' MARKET   MARKET
Map p256 (www.eveleighmarket.com.au; Carriageworks, 243 Wilson St; ☉10am-3pm 1st Sun of the
month; 🚊Redfern) A monthly forum for contemporary artisans and designers in various fields to sell their treasures directly to
the public.

🏛 Newtown

🏆 BETTER READ THAN DEAD   BOOKS
Map p256 (☑9557 8700; www.betterread.com
.au; 265 King St; ☉9.30am-9pm; 🚊Newtown)
This just might be our favourite Sydney bookshop, and not just because of
the pithy name and the great selection
of Lonely Planet titles. Nobody seems
to mind if you waste hours perusing the
beautifully presented aisles, stacked with
high-, middle- and deliciously low-brow
reading materials.

BERKELOUW BOOKS   BOOKS
Map p256 (☑9557 1777; 6-8 O'Connell St;
☉10am-9pm; 🚊Newtown) Six generations of
Berkelouws have specialised in secondhand
books and printed rarities since setting up
shop in Holland in 1812, but its contemporary stores are just as good for new releases
and coffee sipping.

GOULD'S BOOK ARCADE   BOOKS
Map p256 (☑9519 8947; www.gouldsbooks.com;
32 King St; ☉10am-10pm; 🚊Macdonaldtown)
Possibly the world's scariest secondhand
bookstore, the floor-to-ceiling racks and
stacks threaten to bury you under a tonne
of Stalinist analysis. All manner of musty
out-of-print books are stocked, with the
owner's leftie leanings displayed along one
very large wall. Cassettes, records and video tapes, too (VHS and Beta!).

FASTER PUSSYCAT   CLOTHING, ACCESSORIES
Map p256 (☑9519 1744; www.fasterpussycaton-
line.com; 431a King St; ☉11am-6pm; 🚊Newtown)
Inspired by 'trash pop culture, hot rods
and rock and roll', this cool cat coughs up
clothing and accessories for all genders and
ages (including baby punkwear) in several
shades of Newtown black.

NEWTOWN OLD WARES   ANTIQUES
Map p256 (☑9519 6705; 439 King St; ☉10am-
5pm Tue-Sun; 🚊Newtown) Yearning for a
vintage Cilla Black poster, a safari suit
or a Blaxploitation lamp? This funky antiques store covers the cool and the kitsch
from 'deco to disco': old transistor radios,
TVs, telephones, jukeboxes, barstools, vinyl
couches...perfect for pottering about.

BEEHIVE GALLERY
HANDICRAFTS

Map p256 (☎9550 2515; www.beehivegallery
.com.au; 441 King St; ☺11am-5pm Tue, Wed & Fri-
Sun, to 7pm Thu; ☐Newtown) If it's homemade,
it has a home in this store, which stocks
quality fashion, jewellery, and arts and
crafts from around 100 artisans. The walls
are peppered with interesting pictures of
Sydney scenes – good souvenirs.

FROLIC
CLOTHING, ACCESSORIES

Map p256 (☎9519 9895; 461 King St; ☺11am-6pm
Wed-Mon, to 3.30pm Tue; ☐Newtown) Funky
tees, sunnies, hats, vintage dresses – Frolic
specialises in 1950s to 1980s secondhand
men's and women's clothes, and also stocks
several local brands. Masquerade as a local
with a Newtown Jets T-shirt.

QUICK BROWN FOX
CLOTHING, ACCESSORIES

Map p256 (☎9519 6622; www.quickbrownfox
.com.au; 231 King St; ☐Newtown) No lazy dogs
here – just plenty of fast-looking, tanned
vixens snapping up funky vintage fashions that veer from 'hello, boys!' cuteness
to indecent-exposure sexiness. Catchy patterns and fabrics, chic boots and bags.

EGG RECORDS
MUSIC

Map p256 (☎9550 6056; www.eggrecordsonline
.com; 3 Wilson St; ☺10am-6.30pm Mon-Sat, 11am-
5pm Sun; ☐Newtown) There's something a bit
too cool about this secondhand and new
music store, but it's the perfect place to, say,
complete your collection of 1980s David
Bowie 12" singles, or pick up a Cramps T-
shirt or a Gene Simmons figurine.

LE CABINET DES CURIOSITIES
CLOTHING, MUSIC

Map p256 (www.curiosities.com.au; 97 Enmore
Rd; ☺11am-6pm Tue, Wed & Fri-Sun, to 8pm Thu;
☐Newtown) Enter, if you dare, into a dark
world of black metal, goth, paganism and
the occult, and depart, if you're able, laden
with chunky jewellery, skull-encrusted
platform boots, scarlet and black corsets
and a copy of *Gothic Beauty* magazine.

🏠 Alexandria

VICTORIA'S BASEMENT
HOMEWARES

Map p256 (☎9557 1954; www.victoriasbasement
.com.au; cnr Euston Rd & Harley St; ☺10am-5pm;

☐370) This huge warehouse (on the 1st floor,
not in the basement) is packed to overflow-
ing with high-quality kitchen and tableware
at bargain-basement prices (wedding and
house-warming gifts aplenty). Despite a ban
on shopping-tour buses it's always frantic
on weekends. Full-price branch in the QVB
(p95).

OXFORD
CLOTHING, ACCESSORIES

Map p256 (☎9318 1718; www.oxfordshop.com
.au; 141-143 McEvoy St; ☺9am-5pm; ☐Green
Square) A bargain outlet for a big local
brand, Oxford stocks reasonably priced but
stylish mens- and womenswear, including
well-tailored shirts, suits and ties. For its
latest range head to the stores in **Paddington** (Map p264; ☎9380 9666; 264 Oxford St;
☐380), Chifley Plaza, Westfield Sydney or
Westfield Bondi Junction.

🏃 SPORTS & ACTIVITIES

WENTWORTH PARK
SPECTATOR SPORT

Map p256 (☎9552 1799; www.wentworthpark-
sport.com.au; Wentworth Park Rd; ☺Fri & Sat eve-
nings; ☐Wentworth Park) Wentworth Park is
Australia's premier greyhound-racing complex, where the fast, skinny mutts salivate
after tin hares twice weekly. Dog races have
been happening here since 1932, and there's
a lovely old-fashioned vibe about the place.
Bars and bistro on site.

VICTORIA PARK POOL
SWIMMING

Map p256 (☎9518 4800; www.cityofsydney.nsw
.gov.au; cnr Parramatta & City Rds; adult/child
$5.20/3.30; ☺6am-7pm; ☐431-440) This 50m
heated outdoor pool in Victoria Park serves
as Newtown and Glebe's beach. There's also
a gym ($15 with pool access), a crèche, a
cafe and a swim shop.

INNER CITY CYCLES
BYCYLE RENTAL

Map p256 (☎9660 6605; www.innercitycycles
.com.au; 151 Glebe Point Rd; hire per day/week
$33/88; ☺9.30am-6pm Mon-Wed & Fri, 9.30am-
8pm Thu, 9.00am-4pm Sat, 11am-3pm Sun;
☐Glebe) Hire bikes and performs repairs.

Surry Hills & Darlinghurst

SURRY HILLS | DARLINGHURST

Neighbourhood Top Five

❶ Eating your way around Sydney's gastronomic heartland – starting with the slow-cooked meat at **Porteño** (p121) and then returning again and again to sample the variety of tastes the neighbourhood has to offer.

❷ Grabbing a cocktail at **Pocket** (p126) and then exploring Darlinghurst's thriving small bar scene.

❸ Examining the sobering displays and video testimonies at the **Sydney Jewish Museum** (p119).

❹ Soaking up the atmosphere of Oxford St, Sydney's gay strip – at its best around Mardi Gras.

❺ Perking up at **Single Origin Roasters** (p122) or any of Surry Hills' numerous temples to the coffee bean.

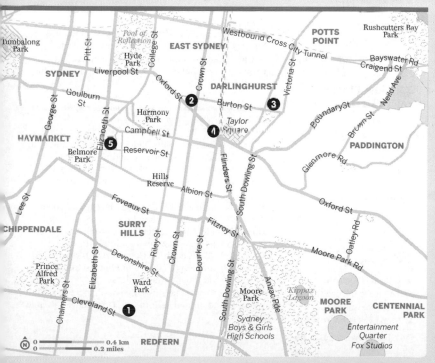

For more detail of this area see Map p260 ➡

Lonely Planet's Top Tip

Many of the neighbourhood's hippest eateries – Bar H (p121), Billy Kwong (p122), Bodega (p122), House (p121), Longrain (p121), Porteño (p121) and Spice I Am (p122), among them – don't take bookings. This is great for travellers: if they took bookings, chances are you wouldn't get a table. To avoid a lengthy wait, turn up early (around 6pm). You'll need to have your whole party present to secure a table. Otherwise put your name on the list and wait at a nearby bar until called.

 Best Places to Eat

➡ Porteño (p121)

➡ Universal (p124)

➡ Longrain (p121)

➡ Bar H (p121)

➡ House (p121)

For reviews, see p121 ➡

 **Best Places to Drink**

➡ Pocket (p126)

➡ Hinky Dinks (p126)

➡ Shady Pines Saloon (p126)

➡ Beresford Hotel (p125)

➡ Cricketers Arms Hotel (p126)

For reviews, see p125 ➡

 Best Gay Venues

➡ Oxford Hotel (p127)

➡ Palms On Oxford (p127)

➡ Midnight Shift (p127)

➡ Stonewall Hotel (p127)

For reviews, see p125 ➡

Explore: Surry Hills & Darlinghurst

Surry Hills bears absolutely no resemblance to the beautiful hills of Surrey, England, from which it takes its name. And these days it also bears little resemblance to the tightly knit, working-class community so evocatively documented in Ruth Park's classic Depression-era novels. The rows of Victorian terrace houses remain, but now they're home to a mishmash of inner city hipsters, yuppies and gay guys, many of whom rarely venture beyond the excellent local pubs and eateries.

The warehouses lining Surry Hills' moody lower canyons, near Central station, are the remnants of the local rag trade and print industry. They now contain coffee shops, art galleries, interior-design outlets and apartments.

Abutting the lower end of Oxford St (Sydney's sequinned mile), Darlinghurst is synonymous with the gay community – it's home to most of the city's gay venues and the Mardi Gras parade. Downhill from here, Darlinghurst morphs into East Sydney, with what remains of a tiny Italian enclave centred on Stanley St.

Local Life

➡ **Brunch** The neighbourhood's cafes are popular at the best of times, but come the weekend, they heave.

➡ **Sunday sessions** Squeezing the last drop of drinking time out of a weekend is a cherished tradition in these parts. Pubs with beer gardens fill up on sunny Sunday afternoons and stay busy into the evening.

➡ **Eat streets** Restaurants cluster on Surry Hills' Crown St, Darlinghurst's Victoria St and East Sydney's Stanley St.

Getting There & Away

➡ **Train** A train station is seldom more than a kilometre away. Exit at Museum for East Sydney and the blocks around Oxford St; Central for the rest of Surry Hills; and Kings Cross for the northern and eastern reaches of Darlinghurst.

➡ **Bus** Numerous buses traverse Cleveland, Crown, Albion, Oxford, Liverpool and Flinders Sts. Useful routes include 339 (The Rocks to Clovelly via Albion and Flinders), 355 (Newtown to Bondi Junction via Cleveland), 372 (Central to Coogee via Elizabeth and Cleveland) and 373/377 (Circular Quay to Coogee/Maroubra via Oxford and Flinders).

➡ **Car** Street parking is usually possible, but it's often metered and limited in duration. Don't leave valuables visible.

⊙ SIGHTS

⊙ Surry Hills

FREE **BRETT WHITELEY STUDIO** GALLERY
Map p260 (✆9225 1881; www.brettwhiteley.org; 2 Raper St; ⊙10am-4pm Fri, Sat & Sun; ⊠Central) Whiteley (1939–1992) lived fast and without restraint, and when he let fly on the canvas, people took notice. His hard-to-find studio (look for the signs on Devonshire St) has been preserved as a gallery for some of his best work. At the door is a miniature of his famous sculpture *Almost Once*, which you can see in all its glory in The Domain.

FREE **OBJECT GALLERY** GALLERY
Map p260 (✆9361 4511; www.object.com.au; 415 Bourke St; ⊙11am-5pm Tue-Fri, 10am-5pm Sat; ⊠Central) Inside the cylindrical former St Margaret's Hospital chapel (a 1958 Modernist classic by architect Ken Woolley), nonprofit Object presents innovative exhibitions of new craft and design from Australia and overseas. Furniture, fashion, textiles and glass festoon three levels.

⊙ Darlinghurst

SYDNEY JEWISH MUSEUM MUSEUM
Map p260 (✆9360 7999; www.sydneyjewishmus eum.com.au; 148 Darlinghurst Rd; adult/child/ family $10/6/22; ⊙10am-4pm Sun-Thu, to 2pm Fri; ⊠Kings Cross) Created as a memorial to the Holocaust, the Sydney Jewish Museum examines Australian Jewish history, culture and tradition from the time of the First Fleet (which included 16 known Jews) to the present day, along with the history of Judaism in general. Video testimony and touch-screen computers are used to good effect. The sobering Holocaust section includes a moving Children's Memorial.

Allow at least two hours to take it all in. Free 45-minute tours leave at noon on Monday, Wednesday, Friday and Sunday.

AUSTRALIAN MUSEUM MUSEUM
Map p260 (✆9320 6000; www.amonline.net .au; 6 College St; adult/child/family $12/6/30; ⊙9.30am-5pm; ⊠Museum) This natural-history museum, established just 40 years after the First Fleet dropped anchor, strives to shrug off its museum-that-should-be-in-a-museum feel. Hence dusty taxidermy has been interspersed with video projections and a terrarium with live snakes, while dinosaur skeletons cosy up to life-size re-creations.

There are also interesting displays on extinct megafauna (giant wombats – simultaneously cuddly and terrifying), and a sad 'where are they now' exhibit featuring stuffed remains and video footage of recently extinct species.

Yet it's the most old-fashioned section that is arguably the most interesting – the large collection of crystals and precious stones. The hall of skeletons has an intriguingly bizarre tableau of a skeletal man riding a horse, and another sitting in a comfy chair next to his underfed pets. Also worthwhile is the Indigenous Australians section, covering Aboriginal history and spirituality, from Dreamtime stories to videos of the Freedom Rides of the 1960s.

FREE **NATIONAL ART SCHOOL** HISTORIC BUILDINGS, GALLERY
Map p260 (✆9337 8744; www.nas.edu.au; Forbes St; ⊙10am-4pm Mon-Sat; ⊠Kings Cross) From 1841 to 1912 these sandstone buildings were Darlinghurst Gaol: writer Henry Lawson was incarcerated here several times for debt (he called the place 'Starvinghurst'). If today's art students think they've got it tough, they should spare a thought for the 732 prisoners who were crammed in here, or the 76 who were hanged.

The circular central building was the chapel. A tiny former morgue near the Burton St exit has creepy skull-and-crossbone carvings. There's also an excellent on-site gallery showcasing students' work.

GREEN PARK PARK
Map p260 (cnr Victoria & Burton Sts; ⊠Kings Cross) Once the residence of Alexander Green, hangman of Darlinghurst Gaol, Green Park is a cheery space during the day, but as the many syringe-disposal bins attest, it's best avoided nocturnally. At the top of the slope, the inverted pink triangular prism backed by black pillars is the Gay & Lesbian Holocaust Memorial.

It was founded by the late Dr Kitty Fischer, who as a young Jewish girl in Auschwitz was kept alive by food smuggled to her by a gay inmate forced to wear the pink triangle. In a lower corner of the park is the Victor Chang Memorial – before he was murdered in 1991, he was a famed heart surgeon who worked at neighbouring St Vincent's Hospital.

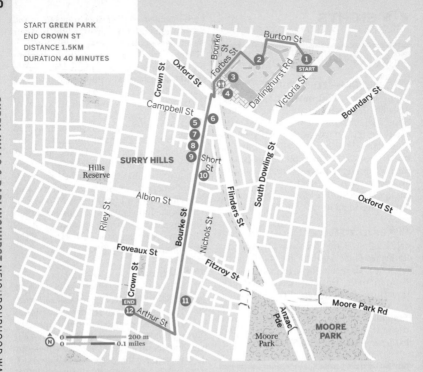

START **GREEN PARK**
END **CROWN ST**
DISTANCE **1.5KM**
DURATION **40 MINUTES**

Neighbourhood Walk
'Hurst to Hills Hike

1 Green Park sits at the start of the Victoria St restaurant strip, flanked by the Sydney Jewish Museum, St Vincent's Hospital and Sacred Heart Hospice. Both the hospital and the hospice found themselves at the front line of the AIDS epidemic when it hit in the 1980s.

Head west on Burton St, following the sandstone walls of the **2 National Art School** – formerly Darlinghurst Gaol. As you enter, look for the creepy morgue on your right. Turn right at the circular chapel, exit onto Forbes St and head left past the stolid **3 Darlinghurst Courthouse** and enter **4 Taylor Square**, the heart of Sydney's main gay strip, Oxford St.

Cross over to the Surry Hills side. Before you head up Bourke St, note the art deco **5 Belgenny apartment building** and the **6 antique red post box**.

The first block of Bourke St boasts reminders of the neighbourhood's once-prominent Greek community. **7 Christopher's Cake Shop** has been selling Greek sweets since 1955. A few doors down is **8 St Sophia and Three Daughters Greek Orthodox Church**.

Shuffle along Bourke St to the old **9 St Margaret's Hospital** site, now housing the Object Gallery. Pricey apartments and restaurants stand in stark contrast to the sandstone **10 Wesleyan Chapel** (1847) across the road, where the Edward Eager Lodge assists the Hills' many homeless.

Continuing along Bourke St you'll pass some interesting houses, including a sandstone Georgian block with a deep verandah and some hefty Victorian terraces, gentrified and otherwise. Just after number 454, tiny **11 Fred Miller Park** commemorates a very Surry Hills character. Miller (1926–1992) was a plumber turned Labor politician who, despite being married with children, was a staunch supporter of gay rights.

Hook right into Arthur St, which spits you out onto **12 Crown Street**, Surry Hills' main cafe, bar and hipster strip.

TAYLOR SQUARE
SQUARE

Map p260 (cnr Oxford & Bourke Sts; ⊠Museum)
You know it's been a rough night if you wake up in Taylor Sq – a vaguely defined paved area straddling Oxford St, and also the hub of Darlinghurst's gay nightlife. The stern Greek Revival Darlinghurst Courthouse (1842) watches the goings-on, no doubt disapprovingly.

Near the courthouse is a heritage-listed Edwardian underground toilet (closed), while on the Surry Hills side a sporadic fountain shoots enemas at unsuspecting passers-by. Continuing the theme are sculpted, metre-high suppositories, housing an outdoor gallery of sorts.

ST JOHN'S CHURCH
CHURCH

Map p260 (✆9360 6844; www.stjohnsanglican.org.au; 120 Darlinghurst Rd; ⊙10am-2.30pm Mon, Tue & Thu-Sat; ⊠Kings Cross) Grab a pamphlet inside this lovely sandstone church (1850) for an interesting 10-minute, self-guided tour. It makes for a hushed escape from the urban jangle of Darlinghurst Rd and the car wash next door. The Anglican congregation runs the Rough Edges Community Centre, working with the area's many homeless.

✖ EATING

Scruffy Surry Hills' transformation into Sydney's foodie nirvana was sudden, roughly commencing with the 1999 opening of the Eastern Distributor, which made peaceful tree-lined backstreets out of Crown and Bourke Sts (once the main routes to the airport). Some would suggest that rising rents mark the start of a decline, but many of the city's top-rated restaurants still reside here. For a cheap vegetarian meal, try the Indian eateries along Cleveland St. Stanley St has a few Italian places, while Victoria St offers a heady blend of ethnic cuisines.

✖ Surry Hills

PORTEÑO
ARGENTINIAN $$

Map p260 (✆8399 1440; www.porteno.com.au; 358 Cleveland St; sharing plates $12-44; ⊙dinner Mon-Sat; ⊠Central) The hip lads who made their mark with Bodega (p122) have stepped up their robust homage to the foods of South America, and they've taken loads of fans along for the ride. Bring a huge appetite and a posse; you can only book for five or more. Don't miss the magnificent eight-hour wood-fired suckling pig.

LONGRAIN
THAI $$$

Map p260 (✆9280 2888; www.longrain.com; 85 Commonwealth St; lunch $27-48, dinner $31-44; ⊙lunch Fri, dinner daily; ⊠Central) Inside a century-old, wedge-shaped printing-press building, diners slurp Longrain's signature modern Thai specialities, such as pork and prawn-filled eggnet or caramelised pork hock with chilli vinegar. Sip a Thai-inflected cocktail at the bar afterwards.

BAR H
CHINESE $$

Map p260 (✆9280 1980; www.barhsurryhills.com; 80 Campbell St; dishes $10-36; ⊙dinner Tue-Sun; ⊠Museum) The pork buns and wontons served at this sexy, shiny, black-walled corner eater are a revelation. Larger dishes – pork belly, steamed fish and roast duck – are just as good.

HOUSE
THAI $

Map p260 (✆9280 0364; www.housethai.com.au; 202 Elizabeth St; mains $10-18; ⊙11.30am-late; ⊠Central) On a sticky Sydney night, House's lantern-strung courtyard really feels like Southeast Asia, not least because of the constant traffic passing and the chicken embryo on the menu. Specialising in the street food of the Issan region of northeast Thailand, the food is deliciously authentic. Serves aren't large and when they say spicy, believe them.

MARQUE
MODERN AUSTRALIAN $$$

Map p260 (✆9332 2225; www.marquerestaurant.com.au; 355 Crown St; 5/8 courses $95/150; ⊙lunch Fri, dinner Mon-Sat; ⊠Central) It's Mark Best's delicious, inventive, beautifully presented food that has won Marque various best-restaurant gongs in recent years; it's certainly not the somewhat stuffy ambience or insipid decor. There's an excellent-value, three-course set lunch on Fridays ($45).

LE MONDE
CAFE $

Map p260 (www.lemondecafe.com.au; 83 Foveaux St; mains $9-16; ⊙breakfast & lunch Mon-Sat; ⊠Central) Some of Sydney's best breakfasts are served among the demure dark wooden walls of this small streetside cafe. Top-notch coffee and a terrific selection of tea will gear you up to face the world.

SINGLE ORIGIN ROASTERS CAFE $

Map p260 (☑9211 0665; www.singleorigin .au; 60-64 Reservoir St; mains $11-16; ☺6.30am-4pm Mon-Fri; ℞Central) These impassioned, bouncing-off-the-walls caffeine fiends love to chat about the fair-trade or environmental credentials of their beans. The menu's full of cutely described yummies such as the 'salad of weeds, waxies and scratchies' and the 'fish finger sarnie innit'. Unshaven graphic artists roll cigarettes at the little outdoor tables in the bricky Chicago-esque hollows of deepest Surry Hills.

BENTLEY RESTAURANT & BAR MODERN AUSTRALIAN $$$

Map p260 (☑9332 2344; www.thebentley.com.au; 320 Crown St; mains $33-40; ☺lunch & dinnner Tue-Sat; ℞Museum) The reincarnation of this old corner pub as an upmarket restaurant hasn't thrown the bar out with the bathwater. You can still just drop by to sample from the extensive wine list, or settle in for the beautifully presented food at the highly regarded restaurant. Portions are small but inventiveness is high.

FOURATEFIVE CAFE $$

Map p260 (www.fouratefive.com; 485 Crown St; breakfast $9-17, lunch $12-18; ☺breakfast & lunch; ℞Central) Band posters and kooky art fill the walls of this excellent postgrunge cafe where the vibe is chilled and the food is a crowd-pleasing mix of fancy sandwiches (including the ingredient du jour, pulled pork), salads and burgers. The tables on the street fill up quickly.

BOURKE STREET BAKERY CAFE $

Map p260 (☑9669 1011; www.bourkestreetbak ery.com.au; 633 Bourke St; items $4-10; ☺breakfast & lunch; ℞355) Queuing outside teensy Bourke St Bakery is an essential Surry Hills experience. It sells a mean selection of pastries, cakes, croissants and tarts, all baked with that rare combo of deliciousness, dedication and delight. If you're hungover, the coffee here will right your rudder. There are a few tables inside but on a fine day you're better off on the street.

BANGBANG CAFE $

Map p260 (113 Reservoir St; mains $9-20; ☺breakfast & lunch; ℞Central) If anyone knows the value of a restorative breakfast it's a DJ; this stylish little cafe is run by one (the headphones mural is the giveaway). At lunchtime, bangbang shoots out pulled-pork

sandwiches and cooked meals. Settle into a shiny silver saddle seat and enjoy.

BISTRODE MODERN AUSTRALIAN $$$

Map p260 (☑9380 7333; www.bistrode.com; 478 Bourke St; mains $34-39; ☺lunch Fri, dinner Tue-Sat; ℞Central) Once awfully offally, Bistrode moved to a less blood-splattered menu when husband Jeremy Strode opened Bistrode CBD and wife Jane Strode took the helm here. More Asian flavours have crept into the British-influenced dishes, and the food remains as excellent as ever.

BOOK KITCHEN CAFE $$

Map p260 (☑0420 239 469; www.thebookkitch en.com.au; 255 Devonshire St; breakfast $10-23, lunch $17-21, dinner $29-34; ☺breakfast & lunch daily, dinner Fri & Sat; ℞355) Nobody's cooking the books here. They're all too busy preparing inventive meals or delivering them with a smile to your table. Grab a table on the sunny footpath or inside the brick warehouse, where foodie books line the walls, waiting to be sold raw. At lunchtime $25 buys you a main, wine and coffee.

BODEGA TAPAS $$

Map p260 (☑9212 7766; www.bodegatapas.com; 216 Commonwealth St; tapas $8-28; ☺lunch Thu & Fri, dinner Mon-Sat; ℞Central) The coolest progeny of Sydney's recent tapas explosion, Bodega has a casual vibe, good-lookin' staff and a funky matador mural. Tapas dishes vary widely in size and price, from spiced pumpkin and feta empanadas to hefty slabs of seared salmon with tahini and pickled cucumber. Wash 'em down with Hispanic wine, sherry, port or beer and plenty of Mediterranean gusto.

BILLY KWONG CHINESE $$

Map p260 (☑9332 3300; www.kyliekwong.org; 3/355 Crown St; mains $22-48; ☺dinner Mon-Sat; ☑; ℞Central) There's something wonderfully egalitarian about top restaurants where queuing is required – perfect for travellers who don't have the luxury of booking weeks ahead. Chef Kylie Kwong cooks up a modern Chinese menu from the best organic, sustainable and fair-trade ingredients.

SPICE I AM THAI $

Map p260 (☑9280 0928; www.spiceiam.com; 90 Wentworth Ave; mains $8-18; ☺lunch & dinner Tue-Sun; ℞Central) Once the preserve of expat Thais, this little red-hot chilli pepper now has queues out the door. No wonder, as everything we've tried from the 70-plus dishes on the menu is superfragrant and superspicy. It's been so successful that they've opened the upmarket **Spice I Am – The Restaurant** (Map p260; 9280 0928; www.spiceiam.com; 296-300 Victoria St; mains $28-38; lunch Thu-Sun, dinner daily; ; Kings Cross) in Darlinghurst.

TOKO
JAPANESE $$

Map p260 (9357 6100; www.toko.com.au; 490 Crown St; dishes $13-29; lunch Tue-Fri, dinner Mon-Sat; Central) Toko dishes up superb modern Japanese *otsumami* (tapas) such as soft-shell crab, eggplant with miso and meaty options from the *robata* (charcoal grill). Settle into a communal table, make a selection from the extensive wine and sake list, and expect to spend around $30 on food – more if you're a sashimi junkie.

RED LANTERN
VIETNAMESE $$

Map p260 (9698 4355; www.redlantern.com.au; 545 Crown St; mains $28-43; lunch Tue-Fri, dinner daily; ; Central) At the Cleveland St end of the gourmet mile-and-a-bit that is Crown St, this atmospheric eatery is run by television presenters Luke Nguyen (*Luke Nguyen's Vietnam*), Mark Jensen (*Ready Steady Cook*) and sister/wife Pauline Nguyen (author of the excellent *Secrets of the Red Lantern* cookbook-cum-autobiography). It serves modern takes on classic Vietnamese dishes, and is deservedly popular.

EL CAPO
LATIN AMERICAN $$

Map p260 (www.elcapo.com.au; 52 Waterloo St; mains $25; lunch Fri & Sat, dinner Mon-Sat; Central) 'Latin street gang chic' may be a questionable design brief but El Capo's hombres regularly blow heads off with their spicy Latin American street food. Grab a stool made of bank notes, sit amid the murals of guns and cars, and order a 'prison dinner tray' (set meal $15, Monday to Wednesday only).

FALCONER
CAFE $$

Map p260 (www.thefalconer.com.au; 31 Oxford St; breakfast $9-15, lunch $10-20, dinner $18-28; breakfast & lunch daily, dinner Tue-Sat; Museum) Retaining the old wooden counter and scooped booth seats of its lost-in-time European predecessor, the lads at the Falconer have added crackly vinyl records to the mix and brought a welcome slice of boho cool to the scrappy end of Oxford St. Expect

Mediterranean takes on breakfast classics and souped up comfort food (pasta, risotto, fish and chips, etc).

FORMAGGI OCELLO
CAFE $

Map p260 (9357 7878; www.ocello.com.au; Shop 16, 425 Bourke St; mains $8-13; 10am-6.30pm; Central) Like lactose? Then Formaggi Ocello is for you. Display even the slightest hint of dairy devotion and you'll have the staff at your elbow. Cheeses are mostly Italian, Spanish and French, with some top Aussie selections, too. Check out the humongous cheese wheels in the ageing room. Also serving soups, salads, focaccias, panini, wine and coffee.

MESSINA
ICE CREAM $

Map p260 (www.gelatomessina.com; 241 Victoria St; 2 scoops $5; noon-11pm; Kings Cross) Join the queues of people who look like they never eat ice cream at the counter of Sydney's best gelato shop. Clearly even the beautiful people can't resist quirky flavours, such as figs in Marsala and salted caramel. The attached cake shop serves sweets masquerading as burgers and toadstools.

NORFOLK ON CLEVELAND
MEXICAN $

Map p260 (www.thenorfolk.co; 305 Cleveland St; mains $8-17; noon-10pm; Central) There are plenty of reasons to visit this old pub – the cosy beer garden, $20 sangria jugs, the interesting crowd – but it's the cheap and tasty Mexican food that lures us to the wrong side of Cleveland St, particularly the ever-changing line-up of soft-shell tacos ($5.50 each or $20 for four).

PIZZA BIRRA
ITALIAN $$

Map p260 (9332 2510; www.pizzabirra.com.au; 500 Crown St; mains $20-25; lunch Thu-Sun, dinner daily; Central) Bentwood chairs clatter across the polished-concrete floor; friends laugh, clink glasses and unwind; waiters spin and smile. Pizza Birra is stylish enough to be cool, and familiar enough to be comfortable. Try the Capricciosa pizza – tomato, mozzarella, rocket, prosciutto and parmesan – washed down with a cold Peroni.

EL LOCO
MEXICAN $

Map p260 (9211 4945; www.merivale.com.au; 64 Foveaux St; mains $10-15; lunch & dinner; Central) As much as we lament the passing of live rock at the Excelsior Hotel, we have to admit that the hip Mexican cantina that's taken over the band room is pretty

WORTH A DETOUR

WATERLOO

In recent years Waterloo's Danks St has emerged as a shopping and eating enclave, with some beaut cafes and galleries perfect for losing a few hours in. If the wonderful **Danks Street Depot** (☑9698 2201; www.danksstreetdepot.com.au; 2 Danks St; mains $10-20; ☺9am-4pm Sun-Fri, 8.30am-4.30pm Sat; ☑M20, 355) cafe isn't enough to tempt you, the 11 commercial galleries that inhabit the rest of the converted warehouse at **2 Danks Street** (www.2danksstreet.com.au; 2 Danks St; ☺11am-6pm Tue-Sat; ☑M20, 355) should do the trick. Displays cover a broad range of contemporary arts, including photography, sculpture, painting, jewellery and Aboriginal and Pacific art.

Across the road, in-the-know gastronomes pour into **Cafe Sopra** (☑9699 3174; www.fratellifresh.com.au; 7 Danks St; mains $18-26; ☺breakfast Sat, lunch daily; ☑M20, 355), well secluded above gourmet providore Fratelli Fresh. The lengthy blackboard menu is very seasonal, using the best fresh and imported produce from downstairs; the osso bucco, ragu gnocchi and antipasto platters are show stealers. Expect lengthy queues, especially on weekends; it doesn't take bookings.

A 10-minute walk further into Waterloo will lead you to the off-the-beaten-track **Darren Knight Gallery** (☑9699 5353; www.darrenknightgallery.com; 840 Elizabeth St; ☺11am-6pm Tue-Sat; ☑Green Square), which showcases established and up-and-coming artists from Australia and New Zealand – including Ricky Swallow, whose work hangs in New York's MoMA and the National Gallery of Australia. From Danks St, head south on Young St, turn right onto Powell, then left onto Elizabeth.

darn cool. The food's tasty and inventive and at $5 per taco, fantastic value.

CAFFE SICILIA ITALIAN $
Map p260 (☑9699 8787; www.caffesicilia.com.au; 628 Crown St; breakfast $8-15, lunch $8-18, dinner $20-30; ☺breakfast, lunch & dinner; ☑Central) We're sure it's not intentional but this traditional Italian eatery may as well be a theme park for extravagant Italianness. It's great fun watching the cocksure waiters swaggering around in their white shirts and black ties, delivering steaming plates of pasta to the little marble tables. The sweets here are sublime.

✕ Darlinghurst

UNIVERSAL FUSION $$
Map p260 (☑9331 0709; www.universalrestaurant.com; courtyard, 248 Palmer St; dishes $27-31; ☺lunch Fri, dinner Mon-Sat; ☑Museum) Simple decor and dramatic lighting set the scene for food which is certainly dramatic but anything but simple. Celebrity chef Christine Manfield's latest venture tours the cuisines of the known universe and creates something out of this world. Dishes are designed to be shared; three per head is recommended but we found two plus dessert ample. The smutty-sounding cocktails shouldn't be missed.

DUKE MODERN AUSTRALIAN $$
Map p260 (☑9332 3180; www.dukebistro.com.au; level 1, 63 Flinders St; dishes $10-26; ☺dinner Tue-Sat; ☑373, 377) Head upstairs from the dingily atmospheric Flinders pub to this restaurant where the eccentricity starts with the decor (forest-green walls, floral couches, boar's head), continues with the service (flirtacious, funny, efficient) and peaks with the food (shared plates of meaty food at its most adventurous). The menu's minimal descriptions help to lure boring eaters out of their comfort zones.

A TAVOLA ITALIAN $$
Map p260 (☑9331 7871; www.atavola.com.au; 348 Victoria St; mains $24-38; ☺lunch Fri, dinner Mon-Sat; ☑Kings Cross) At this classy pasta joint, the menu only has a handful of dishes to choose from, but you can be confident that they will all be fantastic. Don't be afraid to bump elbows with your co-diners at the long communal table – chances are they'll be too absorbed by the taste synapses firing inside their brains to notice.

FISH FACE SEAFOOD $$$
Map p260 (☑9332 4803; www.fishfaceaustralia.com.au; 132 Darlinghurst Rd; mains $35-40; ☺lunch Sun, dinner Tue-Sun; ☑Kings Cross) It's not near the water and it looks like an old deep-fry takeaway, but this tiled, triangular, sardine-sized eatery is among the best

fish restaurants in Sydney. The kitchen consumes most of the room – stools and benches are an afterthought.

BILLS
CAFE $$

Map p260 (☎9360 9631; www.bills.com.au; 433 Liverpool St; mains $14-26; ☺breakfast & lunch; ☒Kings Cross) Sydney adores Bill Granger (aka Mr Scrambled Egg) and his original sunny eatery with its newspaper-strewn communal table. Dishes such as sweetcorn fritters served with roast tomato, spinach and bacon are equally adorable. Can't get a seat? Head for bills in **Surry Hills** (Map p260; ☎9360 4762; 359 Crown St; ☺7am-10pm; ☒Central) or **Woollahra** (Map p264; ☎9328 7997; www.bills.com.au; 118 Queen St; mains $14-26; ☺breakfast & lunch; ☒389).

13B
CAFE $

Map p260 (13b Burton St; breakfast $10-18, lunch $5-11, dinner $15-19; ☺breakfast, lunch & dinner; ☒Museum) Equal parts cafe and cocktail bar, 13b is a glammed-up space with dark walls and lots of mirrors. We prefer its breakfast incarnation: avocado mash, truffled eggs and heart-jolting coffee. At lunchtime it shifts into mini-burger and sandwich territory, while night-time is tipple-time, with platters and pasta to soak it up.

DON DON
JAPANESE $

Map p260 (☎9331 3544; 80 Oxford St; mains $10-14; ☺lunch & dinner Mon-Fri; ☒Museum) For years we've thumbed our way through diminutive Don Don's photo menu, discovering consistently delicious dishes. Expect everything from *katsudon* (rice with deep-fried chicken, beef or pork, egg and condiments) to sashimi, mostly served with rice, miso and Japanese pickles on the side. Be prepared to queue.

TEN BUCK ALLEY
CAFE $

Map p260 (☎9356 3000; 185a Bourke St; mains $7-14; ☺breakfast & lunch Mon-Sat; ℙ; ☒Kings Cross) The name pays homage to the back laneway, once a notorious hang-out for transsexual prostitutes. This tiny cafe continues the alley's bang-for-your-buck tradition, only with delicious food and even better coffee.

FORBES & BURTON
CAFE $$

Map p260 (☎9356 8788; www.forbesandburton. com.au; 252 Forbes St; mains $12-24; ☺breakfast & lunch; ☏; ☒Kings Cross) Tune in beyond the weekend chatter in this sandstone room and you'll hear satisfied sighs emanating from the regulars. During the week, some take up advantage of the free wi-fi to set up office, drinking copious amounts of coffee as rent. The menu ranges from beaut all-day breakfasts (great bacon-and-egg rolls) through to more adventurous lunches.

PABLO'S VICE
CAFE $

Map p260 (3/257 Crown St; mains $8-15; ☺7.30am-4pm Mon-Sat; ☒Museum) A tiny triangular kitchen half-buried below street level with two tables bolted to the wall outside. Big enough for the best coffee in Darlinghurst? You betcha! Grab a seat and unkempt staff will serve you a croissant, salad, wrap, sandwich or all-day breakfast.

DRINKING & NIGHTLIFE

Sydney's main hipster haven, Surry Hills has long been known for its grungy live-music pubs, but recently many have been converted into chic bar-restaurants. Meanwhile Darlinghurst's famed Oxford St gay strip has been swamped by trashy bogan clubs. But dry your eyes: these neighbourhoods still contain some of Sydney's best drinking spots. You just have to look harder to find them. The 'small bar' phenomenon has taken off here, with many of Sydney's best lurking down the most unlikely lanes.

Surry Hills

BERESFORD HOTEL
PUB, LIVE MUSIC

Map p260 (☎9357 1111; www.theberesford .com.au; 354 Bourke St; ☺noon-1am; ☒Central) The once-grungy Beresford (circa 1870) has turned into a superslick architectural tractor beam designed to lure the beautiful people. And it works! The crowd will make you feel either inadequate or right at home, depending on how the mirror is treating you. There's a vast new beer garden, and upstairs is a schmick live-music/club space.

CRICKETERS ARMS HOTEL
PUB

Map p260 (☎9331 3301; 106 Fitzroy St; ☒339) The Cricketers, with its cruisy, cosy vibe, is a favourite haunt of arts students, turntable fans and locals of all persuasions. It's ace for a beer any time, and there are open fires for when you need warming up.

THE WINERY
WINE BAR

Map p260 (www.thewinerysurryhills.com.au; 285a Crown St; ⊘noon-midnight; ⓡMuseum) Set back from the road in the shady grounds of a historic water reservoir, this wine bar serves dozens of wines by the glass to the swankier sector of Surry Hills. Sit for a while and you'll notice all kinds of kitsch touches lurking in the greenery: garden gnomes, upside-down parrots, iron koalas.

TIO'S CERVECERIA
BAR

Map p260 (4-14 Foster St; ⊘4pm-midnight Mon-Sat, 2-10pm Sun; ⓡMuseum) Tio likes tequila. Heaps of different types. And wrestling, Catholic kitsch and Day of the Dead paraphernalia. Surry Hills skaters, beard-wearers and babydoll babes love him right back.

HOTEL HOLLYWOOD
PUB

Map p260 (⊘9281 2765; 2 Foster St; ⊘11am-midnight Mon-Wed, 11am-3am Thu & Fri, 6pm-3am Sat; ⓡMuseum) An inner-city art deco gem, the Hollywood hasn't buffed itself up to a superficial sheen. A mixed crowd of Surry Hillbillies gets down to serious beer business in the pub that time forgot.

SHAKESPEARE HOTEL
PUB

Map p260 (⊘9319 6883; 200 Devonshire St; ⓡCentral) A classic Sydney pub (1879) with art nouveau tiled walls, skuzzy carpet, the horses on the TV and $12.50 bar meals. Not a hint of glitz or interior design. Perfect!

VENUE 505
LIVE MUSIC

Map p260 (www.venue505.com; 280 Cleveland St; cover varies; ⊘from 7.30pm Mon-Sat; ⓡCentral) Focusing on jazz, roots, reggae, funk, gypsy and Latin music, this small, relaxed venue is artist-run and thoughtfully programmed. The space features comfortable couches and murals by a local artist.

🍸 Darlinghurst

TOP CHOICE POCKET
BAR

Map p260 (www.pocketsydney.com.au; 13 Burton St; ⊘4pm-midnight; ⓡMuseum) Sink into the corner Pocket's comfy leather couches, order a drink from one of the cheery wait-staff and chat about the day's adventures

accompanied by a decade-defying indie soundtrack. Pop-art murals and exposed brickwork add to the comfortably underground ambience.

TOP CHOICE HINKY DINKS
COCKTAIL BAR

Map p260 (www.hinkydinks.com.au; 185 Darlinghurst Rd; ⊘5pm-midnight Mon-Sat; ⓡKings Cross) Everything's just hunky dory in this little cocktail bar styled after a 1950s milkshake parlour. Try the Hinky Fizz, an alcohol-soaked strawberry sorbet served in a waxed paper sundae cup.

TOP CHOICE SHADY PINES SALOON
BAR

Map p260 (www.shadypinessaloon.com; shop 4, 256 Crown St; ⊘4pm-midnight; ⓡMuseum) With no sign or street number on the door and an entry from a shady back lane (look for the white door before Bikram Yoga on Foley St), this subterranean honky-tonk bar caters to the urban boho. Sip whisky and rye with the good ole hipster boys amid Western memorabilia and taxidermy.

VICTORIA ROOM
COCKTAIL BAR

Map p260 (⊘9357 4488; www.thevictoriaroom.com; Level 1, 235 Victoria St; ⊘6pm-midnight Tue-Thu, 5pm-2am Fri, noon-2am Sat, noon-midnight Sun; ⓡKings Cross) Plush chesterfields, art nouveau wallpaper, dark-wood panelling and bamboo screens – the Victoria Room is the spoilt love child of a 1920s Bombay gin palace and a Hong Kong opium den. Don your white linen suit and panama and order a Raspberry Debonair at the bar.

OXFORD ART FACTORY
BAR, LIVE MUSIC

Map p260 (www.oxfordartfactory.com; 38-46 Oxford St; cover charge & opening hours vary; ⓡMuseum) Indie kids party against an arty backdrop at this two-room multipurpose venue modelled on Warhol's NYC creative base. There's a gallery, bar and performance space that often hosts international acts and DJs. Check the website for what's on.

EAU-DE-VIE
COCKTAIL BAR

Map p260 (www.eaudevie.com.au; 229 Darlinghurst Rd; ⊘6pm-1am; ⓡKings Cross) Take the door marked 'restrooms' at the back of the Kirketon Hotel's Art Lounge (itself a ritzy bar, with baroque-style gilt couches and regular live music) and enter this sophisticated black-walled speakeasy, where a team of dedicated shirt-and-tie-wearing mixologists concoct the sort of beverages that win best-cocktail gongs.

OXFORD HOTEL   GAY

Map p260 (☑8324 5200; www.theoxfordhotel .com.au; 134 Oxford St; ☺10am-late; ☛; ☒Museum) Over the course of 30 years and numerous facelifts the main bar at the Oxford has remained the locus of beer-swilling gay blokedom. On weekends the Bar Underground basement miniclub spins pop and indie. Upstairs, the Supper Club and Polo Lounge play host to an eclectic program of cabaret, DJs and private functions.

GREEN PARK HOTEL   PUB

Map p260 (☑9380 5311; www.greenparkhotel .com.au; 360 Victoria St; ☺10am-2am Mon-Sat, noon-midnight Sun; ☒Kings Cross) The everrockin' Green Park has pool tables, rolledarm leather couches, a beer garden with funky Dr Seuss-inspired lighting and a huge tiled central bar teeming with travellers, gay guys and pierced locals.

DARLO BAR   PUB, DJ

Map p260 (☑9331 3672; www.darlobar.com .au; 306 Liverpool St; ☺10am-midnight MonSat, noon-midnight Sun; ☒Kings Cross) The Darlo's triangular retro room is a magnet for thirsty urban bohemians, fluoro-clad ditch diggers and architects with a book or a hankering for pinball or pool. Pool comp on Tuesday night; trivia on Wednesday. It's quiet during the day, but fires up with DJs on Friday and Saturday nights.

BEAUCHAMP HOTEL   PUB

Map p260 (☑9331 2575; www.thebeauchamp .com.au; 265 Oxford St; ☺noon-2am Mon-Thu, to 3am Fri & Sat, to midnight Sun; ☒Kings Cross) The design lords have transformed this old corner pub into something very hip indeed. On weekends it gets packed – and incredibly noisy – with stylish Eastern Suburbs 20-somethings. There's a cool terrace upstairs and the Velvet cocktail lounge in the basement. It's pronounced *Beech*-um.

RUBY RABBIT   COCKTAIL BAR

Map p260 (www.rubyrabbit.com.au; 231 Oxford St; ☒Kings Cross) There's a ground-floor eatery and a 1st-floor nightclub but it's the topfloor cocktail bar that's really worth checking out. Sydney's most over-the-top space is best described as *Alice in Wonderland* drops acid with Liberace in the Palace of Versailles: shiny teal surfaces, rococo

couches, mirrors and large portraits of duck-headed royals.

FREE PALMS ON OXFORD   GAY, CLUB

Map p260 (☑9357 4166; 124 Oxford St; ☺8pm-1am Thu & Sun, to 3am Fri & Sat; ☒Museum) No one admits to coming here, but the lengthy queues prove them liars. In this underground dance bar, the heyday of Stock Aitken Waterman never ended. It may be uncool, but if you don't scream when Kylie hits the turntables you'll be the only one.

MIDNIGHT SHIFT   GAY, CLUB

Map p260 (☑9358 3848; www.themidnightshift .com.au; 85 Oxford St; admission free-$10; ☺noon-2am Mon & Tue, to 4am Wed, Thu & Sun, to 6am Fri & Sun; ☒Museum) The grand dame of the Oxford St gay scene, the Shift boasts two quite distinct venues. Downstairs the video bar attracts an unpretentious mix of blokes, twinks and bears, and has a musical mandate ranging from Top 40 to camp classics. Upstairs is a serious tits-to-the-wind club (open from 10pm Fridays and Saturdays), with grinding beats (and teeth) and lavish drag productions.

STONEWALL HOTEL   GAY

Map p260 (☑9360 1963; www.stonewallhotel .com; 175 Oxford St; ☺noon-6am Mon-Fri, 9am-6am Sat & Sun; ☒Museum) Nicknamed 'Stonehenge' by those who think it's archaic, Stonewall has three levels of bars and dance floors, attracting a younger crowd. Hosted by drag queens such as Penny Tration and Tora Hymen, cabaret, karaoke and games nights spice things up – Wednesday's Malebox is an inventive way to bag yourself a boy.

ARQ   GAY, CLUB

Map p260 (☑9380 8700; www.arqsydney.com .au; 16 Flinders St; admission free-$25; ☺9pm-late Thu-Sun; ☒Museum) If Noah had to fill his Arq with groovy gay clubbers, he'd head here with a big net and some tranquillisers. This flash megaclub has a cocktail bar, a recovery room and two dance floors with hienergy house, drag shows and a hyperactive smoke machine. Look out for the notorious Fomo foam party.

EXCHANGE HOTEL   BAR, CLUB

Map p260 (☑9331 2956; www.exchangehotel.biz; 34-44 Oxford St; admission free-$25; ☺10am-late Mon-Thu, 9am-6am Fri-Sun; ☒Museum) There's a whole mess of venues here, mashed together under one roof. Q Bar pumps out house, funk and punk; Spectrum is an alt-indie club with live bands; 34B does burlesque; and sweaty, sexy Phoenix is home to wild-eyed clubbers, gay and straight. Sandwiched in between, the Vegas and Nevada lounges offer the chance of a cooling beverage and a nice sit down.

⭐ ENTERTAINMENT

BELVOIR ST THEATRE
THEATRE

Map p260 (☎9699 3444; www.belvoir.com.au; 25 Belvoir St; tickets $42-62; ⓡCentral) In a quiet corner of Surry Hills, this intimate venue hosts the often-experimental and consistently excellent Company B. Shows sometimes feature big stars, such as Geoffrey Rush.

SBW STABLES THEATRE
THEATRE

Map p260 (☎9361 3817; www.griffintheatre.com .au; 10 Nimrod St; tickets $15-49; ⓡKing Cross) In the 19th century this place was knee-high in horse dung; now it's home to the Griffin Theatre Company, dedicated to nurturing new Australian writers. It's also where many actors started out – Cate Blanchett and David Wenham both trod the boards here. Rush tickets ($15) are available on the day of certain performances.

GAELIC CLUB
LIVE MUSIC

Map p260 (☎9211 1687; www.thegaelic.com; 64 Devonshire St; tickets free-$50; ⓡCentral) Whether it's the latest darlings of the British music press or some local sonic assailants made good, concerts at the Gaelic bridge the gap between the pub scene and the larger theatres.

GOVINDA'S
CINEMA

Map p260 (☎9380 5155; www.govindas.com .au; 112 Darlinghurst Rd; dinner & movie $30, movie only $14; ⓒsessions 7-9.15pm Tue-Thu, 4.30-9.45pm Fri-Sun; ⓡKings Cross) The Hare Krishna Govinda's is an all-you-can-gobble vegetarian smorgasbord, including admission to the movie room upstairs. Expect blockbusters, art-house classics, incense in the air and cushions on the floor.

SHOPPING

🔒 Surry Hills

SURRY HILLS MARKETS
MARKET

Map p260 (www.shnc.org/markets; Shannon Reserve, Crown St; ⓒ7am-4pm 1st Sat of the month; ⓡCentral) There's a chipper community vibe at this monthly market, with mainly locals renting stalls to sell/recycle their old stuff: clothes, CDs, books and sundry junk. Bargains aplenty; if only it were more frequent!

SYDNEY ANTIQUE CENTRE
ANTIQUES

Map p260 (☎9361 3244; www.sydantcent.com .au; 531 South Dowling St; ⓒ10am-6pm; 🚌339) Sydney's oldest antique centre has 50-plus dealers specialising in porcelain, silver, glass, collectables and furniture. Items range from sports memorabilia to grandfather clocks and art deco jewellery. Pick up a 19th-century alabaster mannequin and drag it around the cafe and bookshop.

HOLY KITSCH!
GIFTS

Map p260 (www.holykitsch.com.au; 321 Crown St; ⓒ11am-6.30pm; ⓡCentral) When you've a hole that only Day of the Dead and Mexican wrestling paraphenalia can fill, come here. There's another branch in Newtown.

WHEELS & DOLLBABY
CLOTHING

Map p260 (☎9361 3286; www.wheelsanddollbaby .com; 259 Crown St; ⓒ10am-6pm Mon-Wed, Fri & Sat, to 8pm Thu, noon-5pm Sun; ⓡMuseum) 'Clothes to Snare a Millionaire' is the name of the game here, and what a wicked, wicked game it is: lace, leather and leopard print; studs, suspenders and satin. Tight wrapped and trussed up; it won't just be the millionaires who'll be looking your way. Male rockers will have to settle for T-shirts.

GRANDMA TAKES A TRIP
CLOTHING, ACCESSORIES

Map p260 (☎9356 3322; www.grandmatakesa trip.com; 263 Crown St; ⓒ10am-6pm Sat-Wed, to 8pm Thu; ⓡCentral) We don't know where Granny's gone, but she sure left a crazy wardrobe behind. And so did Grandpa. Sourced mostly in the UK and overseas, this is mint-condition vintage, plus retro swimwear and the odd flouncy negligee.

MR STINKY · CLOTHING

Map p260 (☏9310 7005; www.mrstinky.com.au; 482 Cleveland St; ⏰noon-6pm Tue-Sat; 🚌372) The mildly chaotic Stinkmeister deals in groovy vintage gear for dudes and babes, including Hawaiian shirts, Vegas '74 casino-crawler pants and psychedelic muumuus. The range is wide, the prices reasonable and the staff helpful (and with no discernible odour). It also does costume hire; handy for the crazier Sydney parties.

RAY HUGHES GALLERY · ART

Map p260 (☏9698 3200; www.rayhughesgallery .com; 270 Devonshire St; ⏰10am-6pm Tue-Sat; 🚊Central) Beyond the corrugated-iron cows and enormous wooden fish, old-time art dealer Ray Hughes displays the work of the contemporary Australian, New Zealand and Chinese artists he represents. His bohemian warehouse gallery is worth a look whether you're in the art market or not.

🏠 Darlinghurst

ARTERY · ART

Map p260 (☏9380 8234; www.artery.com.au; 221 Darlinghurst Rd; ⏰10am-6pm Mon-Fri, 11am-4pm Sat & Sun; 🚊Kings Cross) Step into a world of mesmerising dots and swirls at this small gallery devoted to Aboriginal art. Artery's motto is 'ethical, contemporary, affordable', and while large canvases by more established artists cost in the thousands, small, unstretched canvases start at around $35.

BOOKSHOP DARLINGHURST · BOOKS

Map p260 (☏9331 1103; www.thebookshop .com.au; 207 Oxford St; ⏰10am-10pm; 🚊Kings Cross) This outstanding bookshop specialises in gay and lesbian tomes, with everything from queer crime and lesbian fiction to glossy pictorials and porn. A diverting browse, to say the least (hmm...which would look better on my coffee table: the *Big Book of Breasts* or the *Big Penis Book*?).

HOUSE OF PRISCILLA · CLOTHING, ACCESSORIES

Map p260 (☏9286 3023; www.houseofpriscilla .com.au; Level 1, 47 Oxford St; ⏰10am-6pm Mon-Wed, Fri & Sat, to 8pm Thu; 🚊Museum) Not only is Priscilla the queen of the desert, she also has her own boutique – not bad for a cinematic bus. Run by some of the city's leading drag artistes, Priscilla is the place for feathered angel wings and boas, naughty nurse outfits, Beyoncé wigs, kinky thigh-high boots and sequinned frocks to fit front-row forwards. Very camp women also welcome.

SAX FETISH · CLOTHING, ACCESSORIES

Map p260 (☏9331 6105; www.saxfetish.com; 110a Oxford St; ⏰11am-7pm; 🚊Museum) No, it's not a bar for jazz obsessives, but rather a sexy, dark-hearted shop selling high-quality leather and rubber gear. All genders are catered for, and the 'accessories' range goes a little further than your standard belts and handbags (cufflinks and ties take on a whole new meaning here).

BLUE SPINACH · CLOTHING, ACCESSORIES

Map p260 (☏9331 3904; www.bluespinach.com .au; 348 Liverpool St; ⏰10am-6pm Mon-Sat, 11am-4pm Sun; 🚊Kings Cross) High-end consignment clothing for penny-pinching label lovers of all genders. If you can make it beyond the shocking blue facade (shocking doesn't really do it justice), you'll find Paul Smith and Gucci at (relatively) bargain prices.

CAPITAL L · CLOTHING, ACCESSORIES

Map p260 (☏9361 0111; www.capital-l.com; 333 South Dowling St; ⏰noon-6pm Sun-Wed, 11am-8pm Thu; 🚊Kings Cross) Owner Louise stocks 26 funky up-and-coming designers to complement those already in the limelight. Hip sales staff break from tradition and actually help you find and try on clothes by emerging local talents such as Jessie Hill and Tighttigers.

C'S FLASHBACK · CLOTHING, ACCESSORIES

Map p260 (☏9331 7833; 316 Crown St; ⏰10am-6pm Fri-Wed, 11am-9pm Thu; 🚊Museum) Looking for a secondhand Hawaiian shirt, some beat-up cowboy boots or a little sequinned 1940s hat like the Queen wears? We're not sure exactly what C was on, but her flashback men's and women's threads are pretty trippy. There's another branch in **Newtown** (Map p256; ☏9565 4343; 180 King St).

Kings Cross & Potts Point

POTTS POINT | ELIZABETH BAY | WOOLLOOMOOLOO | KINGS CROSS

Neighbourhood Top Five

1 Soaking up the sights, sounds and smells of Darlinghurst Rd (p133), Sydney's seediest strip.

2 Ducking into Llankelly Place (p134) for a coffee or a cocktail.

3 Admiring the Georgian grace of **Elizabeth Bay House** (p132).

4 Harbour-gazing and celebrity-spotting at **Wool-loomooloo Finger Wharf** (p132).

5 Kick-starting a night out you'll never forget (or won't remember) at the **Kings Cross Hotel** (p135).

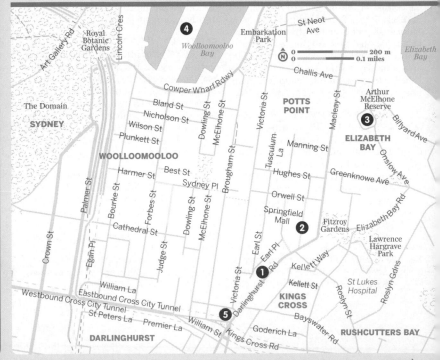

For more detail of this area, see Map p259 ➡

Explore: Kings Cross & Potts Point

The beginning of Sydney's Eastern Suburbs, the city-fringe suburbs of Woolloomooloo, Kings Cross, Potts Point and Elizabeth Bay are a world unto themselves.

Kings Cross is a bizarre, densely populated dichotomy: strip joints, tacky tourist shops and backpacker hostels bang heads with classy restaurants, funky bars and gorgeous guesthouses as 'the Cross' pumps 24/7. A weird cross-section of society is drawn to the lights: buskers, beggars, tourists, prostitutes, pimps, groomed metrosexuals, horny businessmen and underfed artists roam the streets on equal footing. Sometimes the razzle-dazzle has a sideshow appeal; sometimes walking up Darlinghurst Rd promotes boring. Either way, it's never boring.

Down McElhone Stairs from the Cross, Woolloomooloo has also cleaned up its act. Harry's Cafe de Wheels and the drunken sailors are still here, but things are less pugilistic than in the past.

Gracious, tree-lined Potts Point and Elizabeth Bay seem worlds away. Well-preserved Victorian, Edwardian and art deco houses and flats flank picturesque avenues.

Local Life

➡ **Cafes & Bars** Mainstays include Piccolo Bar and the Old Fitzroy but once you get off the Darlinghurst Rd strip, most of the cafes and bars are well patronised by locals.

➡ **Parks** Residents of the apartment blocks of Potts Point and Elizabeth Bay can be seen spreading out towels in tiny Arthur McElhone Reserve or walking their pampered pooches in Embarkation Park.

➡ **Potts Point Boys** The subculture of well-heeled, well-groomed, gym-buffed gay men who frequent the local cafes and all of the big dance parties.

Getting There & Away

➡ **Train** Everywhere is within walking distance of Kings Cross station, although the western fringe of Woolloomooloo is closer to St James.

➡ **Bus** Route 311 hooks through Kings Cross, Potts Point, Elizabeth Bay and Woolloomooloo on its way from Railway Sq to the bottom of town. Routes 324 and 325 pass through Kings Cross (Bayswater Rd) en route between Circular Quay and Watsons Bay.

➡ **Car** The city council operates a 24-hour car park at 9a Elizabeth Bay Rd in Kings Cross (entry via Ward Ave; per hour/day $6/30, more on weekends). Street parking is possible, but often metered and limited in duration. Clearways are ruthlessly enforced. Don't leave valuables visible.

Lonely Planet's Top Tip

Where exactly is Kings Cross? Although technically it's just the intersection of William and Victoria Sts, in reality it's more of a mindset than an exact geographical place. What most people call Kings Cross falls within the suburb of Potts Point; businesses tend to use a Potts Point address if they want to sound classy and Kings Cross if they want to emphasise their party cred. Either way, you'll know Kings Cross when you see it.

KINGS CROSS & POTTS POINT

✖ Best Places to Eat

➡ Otto Ristorante (p135)
➡ Aki's (p135)
➡ Uliveto (p134)
➡ Zinc (p134)
➡ Ms G's (p134)

For reviews, see p132 ➡

🍷 Best Places to Drink

➡ Old Fitzroy Hotel (p137)
➡ Waterbar (p137)
➡ Tilbury (p137)
➡ Gazebo Wine Garden (p137)
➡ Sugarmill (p136)

For reviews, see p135 ➡

☆ Best Places to Party

➡ Kings Cross Hotel (p135)
➡ Sugarmill (p136)
➡ World Bar (p136)
➡ Soho (p136)
➡ Tilbury (p137)

For reviews, see p135

◉ SIGHTS

◉ Potts Point

FITZROY GARDENS PARK

Map p259 (cnr Macleay St & Darlinghurst Rd; 🚇Kings Cross) It's testimony to the 'cleaning up' of the Cross that this once-dodgy park is now a reasonably safe place to hang out (probably helped by the austere police station in the corner). It still feels seedy, though: malnourished seagulls compete for scraps with pigeons who look like Keith Richards, while groaning, bearded homeless guys compile cigarettes from discarded butts.

Known locally as the 'elephant douche', the dandelion-esque **El Alamein Fountain** (Map p259; Macleay St, Fitzroy Gardens; 🚇Kings Cross), built 1961, sends waves of chlorinated spray across the open space. An organic food market sets up here on Saturday mornings, while on Sundays a little flea market takes its place.

MCELHONE STAIRS LANDMARK

Map p259 (Victoria St; 🚇Kings Cross) These stone stairs were built in 1870 to connect spiffy Potts Point with the Woolloomooloo slums below. The steep steps run past an apartment block: residents sip tea on their balconies and stare bemusedly at the fitness freaks punishing themselves on the 113-stair uphill climb.

◉ Elizabeth Bay

ELIZABETH BAY HOUSE HISTORIC BUILDING

Map p259 (📞9356 3022; www.hht.net.au; 7 Onslow Ave; adult/child/family $8/4/17; ⊗9.30am-4pm Fri-Sun; 🚇Kings Cross) Completed in 1839 for Colonial Secretary Alexander Macleay, this elegant neoclassical mansion by architect John Verge was one of the finest houses to be built in the colony (and still is one of the finest). Its grounds – a sort of botanical garden for Macleay, who collected plants from around the world – once extended from the harbour all the way up the hill to Kings Cross.

Ugly 20th-century apartments now surround the house, but the exquisite oval salon and stairwell are timeless architectural delights.

◉ Woolloomooloo

WOOLLOOMOOLOO FINGER WHARF NOTABLE BUILDING

Map p259 (Cowper Wharf Rd; 🚇Kings Cross) A former dock, this beautiful Edwardian wharf faced oblivion for decades before a 2½ year demolition-workers' green ban on the site in the late 1980s saved it. It was spruced up in the late 1990s and has emerged as one of Sydney's most exclusive eating, drinking, sleeping and marina addresses.

It's still a public wharf, so feel free to explore the innards, past industrial conveyorbelt relics, the five-star hotel BLUE (p187) and its designery Water Bar. Along the way the wharf's history is etched into glass walls. You might even squeeze in some starspotting – songbird Delta Goodrem and everyman-megastar Russell Crowe have both had plush pads here.

FREE ARTSPACE GALLERY

Map p259 (📞9356 0555; www.artspace.org.au; 43-51 Cowper Wharf Rd; ⊗11am-5pm Tue-Sun; 🚇Kings Cross) Artspace is spacey: its eternal quest is to fill the void with vigorous, engaging Australian and international contemporary art. Things here are decidedly avant-garde – expect lots of conceptual pieces, audio-visual installations and new-media masterpieces. It's an admirable attempt to liven things up in Sydney's art scene, experimenting with sometimes-disturbing concepts. Excellent disabled access.

HARRY'S CAFE DE WHEELS LANDMARK

Map p259 (📞9347 3074; www.harryscafedewheels. com.au; Cowper Wharf Rd; pies $3-4; ⊗9am-1am Sun, 8.30am-3am Mon-Sat; 🚌311) Sure, it's a humble pie cart, but Harry's is a tourist attraction nonetheless. Open since 1938 (except for a few years when founder Harry 'Tiger' Edwards was on active service), Harry's has served everyone from Pamela Anderson to Frank Sinatra and Colonel Sanders.

You can't leave without trying a Tiger: a hot meat pie with sloppy peas, mashed potato, gravy and tomato sauce.

EATING

With the exception of the phalanx of upmarket restaurants on Woolloomooloo's Finger Wharf, these 'burbs don't

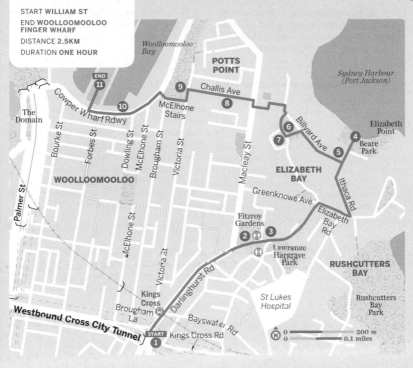

START **WILLIAM ST**
END **WOOLLOOMOOLOO FINGER WHARF**
DISTANCE **2.5KM**
DURATION **ONE HOUR**

Neighbourhood Walk
A Risqué Ramble

Start under the giant Coca-Cola sign at the William St overpass: the 'Top of the Cross'. It's this intersection, where the streets named after two kings cross, that gives this part of Potts Point its name (OK, so one's a queen but Monarchs Cross doesn't have the same ring). Behind you is Ken Unsworth's much derided ❶ **Stones Against the Sky** sculpture. Locals call it 'Shits On Sticks', which is maybe why it's changed colour from brown to grey.

Take a deep breath and follow Darlinghurst Rd into the dark heart of the Cross. If you don't want to make eye contact with any strip-club touts, dealers or hookers, scan the ground for a series of inscriptions offering titbits of local history. Continue to the spindly ❷ **El Alamein Fountain**.

Cut past the distinctive round ❸ **Gazebo tower**, turn left into Elizabeth Bay Rd and follow it downhill then sharply right at a roundabout. Turn left at Ithaca Rd and head down to ❹ **Elizabeth Bay** itself, where there's a tiny park by the water.

Backtrack slightly and turn right into Billyard Ave, where you'll pass by the high walls of ❺ **Boomerang**, one of Australia's most expensive private houses. Take the stairs on the left leading up to genteel ❻ **Arthur McElhone Reserve**. Beyond this little park is stately ❼ **Elizabeth Bay House**.

Turn right (downhill) and take the stairs just before 17 Billyard Ave. At the top turn right into Macleay St and then left into caffeinated Challis Ave, where you'll pass an impressive row of ❽ **colonnaded mansions**. At the bottom is ❾ **Embarkation Park**, with photogenic views over Woolloomooloo and the city.

Head down McElhone Stairs to Woolloomooloo, where ❿ **Harry's Cafe de Wheels** has been a Sydney institution since 1938. Refuel with a pie or continue onto ⓫ **Woolloomooloo Finger Wharf** for a classier finale.

have any harbourside razzle-dazzle. Instead you'll find a buzzy set of small bistros and cafes with heaps of charisma. Tiny Llankelly Place has a clutch of hip microcafes.

✕ Kings Cross

ULIVETO
CAFE $

Map p259 (☎9357 7331; www.ulivetocafe.com.au; 33 Bayswater Rd; mains $10-19; ⊙breakfast & lunch; ☒Kings Cross) Beautiful all-day eggy breakfasts, scrummy muffins, fresh juices and top-notch coffee are the staples of this chilled-out cafe, set in a tree-lined plaza. The people-watching's not bad either. Check your foam; this place is known for its 'latte art'.

ROOM 10
CAFE $

Map p259 (10 Llankelly Pl; mains $8-12; ⊙breakfast & lunch; ☒Kings Cross) If you're wearing a flat cap, sprouting a beard and obsessed by coffee, chances are you'll recognise this tiny room as your spiritual home in the Cross. The food's limited to sandwiches, salads and such – tasty and uncomplicated.

HUGO'S BAR PIZZA
ITALIAN $$

Map p259 (☎9332 1227; www.hugos.com.au; 33 Bayswater Rd; mains $24-36; ⊙dinner Tue-Sun; ☒Kings Cross) This indoor-outdoor neighbourhood nook has long been seducing pizza fans with its delicious discs and homestyle Italian fare; try the puttanesca pizza. The marble-fronted bar and sunken velvet lounge spell luxury, but the menu won't break the bank. If you feel like a drink, head to Hugo's Lounge Bar upstairs.

LL WINE & DINE
ASIAN $$

Map p259 (☎9356 8393; www.llwineanddine.com.au; 42 Llankelly Pl; mains $29-33; ⊙lunch Thu-Sun, dinner Tue-Sun; ☒Kings Cross) The progression from cock tales to cocktails at this former porn shop and illegal gambling den has been dramatic, and the result is much more savoury (in both senses of the word). LL may borrow its double consonant from Welsh, but it's the flavours of China, Japan and Southeast Asia that dominate. The weekend yum cha is excellent.

WILBUR'S PLACE
CAFE $$

Map p259 (www.wilbursplace.com; 36 Llankelly Pl; breakfast $6-12, lunch $12-14, dinner $19; ⊙8am-9.30pm Tue-Sat, to 4pm Sun; ☒Kings Cross) With limited bench seating inside and a few tables on the lane, tiny Wilbur's is an informal spot for a quick bite on what's become the Cross' coolest cafe strip. Expect simple, straightforward food: *croque monsieur*, sandwiches and, after 5pm, bistro fare.

PICCOLO BAR
CAFE $

Map p259 (www.piccolobar.com.au; 6 Roslyn St; mains $9-15; ⊙6am-2am; ☎; ☒Kings Cross) A surviving slice of the old bohemian Cross, this tiny cafe hasn't changed much in nearly 60 years. The walls are covered in movie-star memorabilia, the battered jukebox plays Marianne Faithfull and Paolo Conti, and Vittorio Bianchi still serves up strong coffee, omelettes and abrasive charm as he's done for over 30 years.

GUZMAN Y GOMEZ
MEXICAN $

Map p259 (www.guzmanygomez.com; cnr Bayswater Rd & Pennys La; mains $7.50-11; ⊙11am-10pm Sun-Thu, to 4am Fri & Sat; ☒Kings Cross) A branch of the Newtown *taqueria* (p112), offering quality takeaways for sloshy stomachs.

✕ Potts Point

ZINC
CAFE $$

Map p259 (☎9358 6777; www.cafezinc.com.au; 77 Macleay St; breakfast $8.50-14, lunch $8.50-19, dinner $25-27; ⊙breakfast & lunch daily, dinner Tue-Sat; ☒; ☒Kings Cross) Zinc was built on breakfasts, and the kitchen continues to create too many hard decisions for 7am. It doesn't get much easier choosing between the tasty sandwiches and salads offered at lunchtime or the range of bistro dinners. The good-looking staff are full of smiles.

MS G'S
ASIAN $$

Map p259 (☎9240 3000; www.merivale.com; 155 Victoria St; mains $16-29; ⊙lunch Fri & Sun, dinner daily) Offering a cheeky, irreverent take on Asian cooking (hence the name – geddit?), Ms G's is nothing if not an experience. It can be loud, frantic and painfully hip, but the adventurous combinations of Vietnamese, Thai, Korean, Chinese, Taiwanese and European flavours have certainly got Sydney talking.

FRATELLI PARADISO
ITALIAN $$

Map p259 (☎9357 1744; www.fratelliparadiso.com; 12-16 Challis Ave; mains $22-31; ⊙7am-11pm Mon-Sat, to 6pm Sun; ☒Kings Cross) This underlit trattoria has them queuing at the door (especially on weekends). The intimate room showcases seasonal Italian dishes cooked with Mediterranean zing: lots of busy black-clad waiters, lots of Italian chatter, lots of oversized sunglasses – somehow Rome doesn't seem so far away... No bookings.

CAFE SOPRA
ITALIAN $$
Map p259 (www.fratellifresh.com.au; 81 Macleay St; mains $18-28; ☺lunch & dinner daily; ℝKings Cross) Attached to the mighty impressive Fratelli Fresh provedore, Sopra serves no-fuss, perfectly prepared Italian food in a bustling atmosphere. The huge menu changes seasonally, but some favourites (eg the fabulous *rigatoni alla bolognese*) are constants.

JIMMY LIK'S
SOUTHEAST ASIAN $$
Map p259 (☎8354 1400; www.jimmyliks.com; 188 Victoria St; mains $22-38; ☺6-11pm; ℝKings Cross) The menu at this hip, low ceilinged food nook draws inspiration from Southeast Asian street food. Dishes such as crispy-skin duck with tamarind and orange are bold, balanced and invariably delicious. There's usually a wait for a seat at the long communal table – grab a stool and a cocktail at the attached bar.

CAFE DOV
CAFE $$
Map p259 (☎9368 0600; www.cafedov.com.au; 130 Victoria St; breakfast $11-18, lunch $13-24, dinner $19-29; ☺breakfast & lunch daily, dinner Tue-Sat; ℝKings Cross) Opening onto the leafiest part of Victoria St, L-shaped Dov will tempt you into lingering all morning over your newspaper and caffeine. If they sleep through breakfast, locals, backpackers, style mongers and film-makers squish in for lunch and dinner.

LA BUVETTE & SPRING ESPRESSO
CAFE $$
Map p259 (☎9358 5113; 35 Challis Ave; mains $12-16; ☺breakfast & lunch daily, dinner Tue-Sun; ℝKings Cross) This elbow-to-elbow pair of linked microcafes are always crammed with the beautiful, the famous and the guppies (gay urban professionals), all clad in designer sunglasses and yabbering into hands-free mobile phones. The salmon breakfast hits the spot every time.

✖ Woolloomooloo

OTTO RISTORANTE
ITALIAN $$$
Map p259 (☎9368 7488; www.ottoristorante .com.au; Woolloomooloo Finger Wharf; mains

$38-44; ☺lunch & dinner; ℝKings Cross) Forget the glamorous waterfront location and the A-list crowd – Otto will be remembered for single-handedly dragging Sydney's Italian cooking into the new century with dishes such as *strozzapreti con gamberi* (artisan pasta with fresh Yamba prawns, tomato, chilli and black olives). Bookings essential.

AKI'S
INDIAN $$
Map p259 (☎9332 4600; www.akisindian.com .au; 1/6 Cowper Wharf Rd; mains $21-36; ☺lunch Sun-Fri, dinner daily; ☎✏; ℝKings Cross) The first cab off the rank as you walk onto Woolloomooloo's wharf is Aki's. And you need walk no further: this is beautifully presented, intuitively constructed high-Indian cuisine, supplemented by a six-page wine list showcasing local and international drops by the glass or bottle. The Kerala chilli beef is a simmering sensation.

TOBY'S ESTATE
CAFE $
Map p259 (☎9358 1196; www.tobysestate.com .au; 129 Cathedral St; meals $9-15; ☺breakfast & lunch; ℝSt James) Coffee is undoubtedly the main event at this cool little charcoal-coloured roaster, but it's also a great place for a quick baguette, a lamb salad or a wedge of cake. And the caffeine? Strong, perfectly brewed and usually fair trade.

🍷 DRINKING & NIGHTLIFE

Sydney's premier party precinct, this neighbourhood has stacks of bars ranging from snug locals to superslick posing palaces to raucous booze barns. Kings Cross is the destination of choice for suburban party kids, glamming it up for a night on the tiles. On Friday and Saturday nights the streets can resemble a war zone; it's best to keep your wits about you and enough sobriety to avoid trouble if it looms.

🍸 Kings Cross

TOP CHOICE **KINGS CROSS HOTEL** PUB, LIVE MUSIC
Map p259 (www.kingscrosshotel.com.au; 244-248 William St; ☺noon-3am Sun-Thu, to 6am Fri & Sat; ℝKings Cross) With five floors above ground

and one below, this grand old pub is a hive of boozy entertainment which positively swarms on weekends. Best of all is FBi Social, an alternative radio station–led takeover of the 2nd floor, bringing with it an edgy roster of live music. The roof bar has DJs on weekends and awesome city views.

SUGARMILL BAR
Map p259 (www.sugarmill.com.au; 33 Darlinghurst Rd; ⊙10am-5am; ®Kings Cross) For a bloated, late-night, Kings Cross bar, Sugarmill is actually pretty cool. Columns and high pressed-tin ceilings hint at its bankery past, while the band posters plastered everywhere do their best to dispel any lingering capitalist vibes. Cheapskates feast on cheap steaks daily, while on Friday nights a hip dude with a guitar duels with TV sports.

WORLD BAR BAR, CLUB
Map p259 (☑9357 7700; www.theworldbar.com; 24 Bayswater Rd; admission free-$15; ⊙2pm-late; ®Kings Cross) World Bar (a reformed bordello) is an unpretentious grungy club with three floors to lure the backpackers

and cheap drinks to loosen things up. DJs play indie, hip hop, power pop and house nightly. Propaganda (indie classics, new and used) on Thursday is a sure-fire head start to your weekend. Live bands on Friday.

KIT & KABOODLE CLUB
Map p259 (www.kitkaboodle.com.au; 33 Darlinghurst Rd; admission free-$10; ⊙8pm-late Thu-Sun) The club above Sugarmill comes into its own on a Sunday night, when hospitality workers take advantage of the cheap drinks to kick-start their belated weekend.

🍷 Potts Point

SOHO BAR, CLUB
Map p259 (www.sohobar.com.au; 171 Victoria St; ⊙10am-midnight Mon-Wed, 10am-4am Thu, 10am-6am Fri, 9am-6am Sat, 9am-4am Sun; ®Kings Cross) The beautiful art deco Piccadilly Hotel is a dark, sexy establishment with smooth leather lounges that have felt the weight of Keanu Reeves', Nicole Kidman's and Ewan McGregor's celebrity booties. It's rumoured

---

LOCAL KNOWLEDGE

KINGS CROSS CONFIDENTIAL

Mandy Sayer, author of several books set in Kings Cross, on 'the only place in Australia that never sleeps'.

The Soho of Sydney
Every great city has a racy, raffish, artistic village: Paris has Montmartre, New York has The Village, London has Soho, and Sydney has Kings Cross. As an aspiring writer growing up in the area, I discovered my first and most enduring muse: the pulsing vivid neon signs; the buskers and prostitutes; the strip clubs; the many artists, actors and musicians who shared crumbling terrace houses. It also had a history of crime and corruption, dating back to the razor gangs that roamed the back lanes in the early 20th century.

Every Outsider Is an Insider
Today, the terraces are no longer crumbling but Kings Cross is still known predominantly for its nightlife. The village embraces all sorts of residents, from the loose posse of homeless people on Darlinghurst Rd, to authors and film-makers, to dealers and pimps, to lawyers and doctors, to ex–prime ministers. It's a superlative place for people-watching, which is why I still live here.

Insider Tips
A stroll along Macleay St will reveal some of the most stunning art deco architecture in Australia, while a walk down Victoria St, below a leafy cathedral of trees, showcases some of the colony's first Victorian houses; and at the end of the street is one of the most breathtaking panoramas of Sydney Harbour. Some venues I'd recommend: Piccolo Bar (p134), a tiny bohemian cafe dating back to the early 1950s; the outdoor restaurants and bars along Kellett St, strung with magical fairy lights; the Old Fitzroy (opposite), for an old fashioned English pub experience; LL Wine & Dine (p134), for fine Asian dining and great service; Hinky Dinks (p126), for luscious cocktails and 1950s ambience.

to be where Kylie met Michael Hutchence. Downstairs, the club pumps out electro, house and dub from Thursday to Saturday.

BOOTLEG   BAR
Map p259 (www.bootlegbar.com.au; 175 Victoria St; ⊙4pm-11pm Sun, Tue & Wed, to 1am Thu-Sat; ⊠Kings Cross) If you're looking for a quieter, more sophisticated alternative to the Darlinghurst Rd melee (or just a chance to catch your breath), slink into a booth at this bar-cum-Italian eatery and order a wine from the list. The decor's an odd mix of industrial and Chicago lounge bar, but it works.

JIMMY LIK'S   COCKTAIL BAR
Map p259 (☑8354 1400; www.jimmyliks.com; 186-188 Victoria St; ⊙5pm-midnight; ⊠Kings Cross) Understated, slim and subtle, Jimmy's is very cool, with benches almost as long as the Southeast Asian–influenced cocktail list (try a Mekong Mary with chilli vodka and *nam jim*).

Elizabeth Bay

GAZEBO WINE GARDEN   WINE BAR
Map p259 (☑9357 5333; www.gazebowinegarden.com.au; 2 Elizabeth Bay Rd; ⊙3pm-midnight Mon-Thu, noon-midnight Fri-Sun; ⊠Kings Cross) A hip wine bar in skanky old Fitzroy Gardens? Who would have believed it 10 years ago? This place has groovy decor (wrought-iron gates, bespoke benches, eclectic couches) and a hi-tech vino storage system that shoots gas into open bottles (meaning that 55 sometimes-obscure wines are available by the glass to join the 300 by the bottle).

Woolloomooloo

TOP CHOICE OLD FITZROY HOTEL   PUB
Map p259 (☑9356 3848; www.oldfitzroy.com.au; 129 Dowling St; ⊙11am-midnight Mon-Sat,

3-10pm Sun; ⊠Kings Cross) Islington meets Melbourne in the back streets of Woolloomooloo: this totally unpretentious theatre pub is also a decent old-fashioned boozer in its own right. There are airy streetside tables, and a grungy upstairs area with a pool table and scruffy lounges.

WATERBAR   BAR
Map p259 (☑8356 2553; www.waterbaratblue.com; Woolloomooloo Finger Wharf; ⊙5-10pm Sun & Mon, to midnight Tue-Sat; ⊠Kings Cross) After a few martinis in the heart of Woolloomooloo's Finger Wharf, time becomes meaningless and escape pointless. This lofty romantic space sucks you in to its pink-love world of candles, corners, deep lounges and ottomans as big as beds. Great for business (if you really must), but better for lurve.

TILBURY   PUB
Map p259 (☑9368 1955; www.tilburyhotel.com.au; 12-18 Nicholson St; ⊠Kings Cross) Once the dank domain of burly sailors and salty ne'er-do-wells, the Tilbury now sparkles on Sydney's social scene. Yuppies, yachties, suits, gays and straights alike populate the light, bright interiors. The bistro, bar and beer garden are packed on weekends (especially on Sunday afternoon); DJs play soul, funk and rare-groove Thursday to Sunday. And sailors can still get a beer!

ENTERTAINMENT

OLD FITZROY THEATRE   THEATRE
Map p259 (☑9356 3848; www.oldfitzroy.com.au; 129 Dowling St; tickets $21-33; ⊠Kings Cross) Is it a pub? A theatre? A bistro? Actually, it's all three. Grassroots company the Tamarama Rock Surfers has premiered dozens of new Australian plays here.

Paddington & Centennial Park

PADDINGTON | WOOLLAHRA | CENTENNIAL PARK & MOORE PARK

Neighbourhood Top Five

1 Engaging in a seriously fashionable shopping spree, window or otherwise, in Paddington's boutiques; **Paddington Markets** (p145) is a good place to start.

2 Exploring the vast open space within the gated grounds of **Centennial Park** (p140).

3 Screaming yourself hoarse at a Roosters game at **Sydney Football Stadium** (p147).

4 Hopping between galleries, both commercial and altruistic, including the **Australian Centre for Photography** (p140).

5 Spreading out a picnic under the stars at **Moonlight Cinema** (p144).

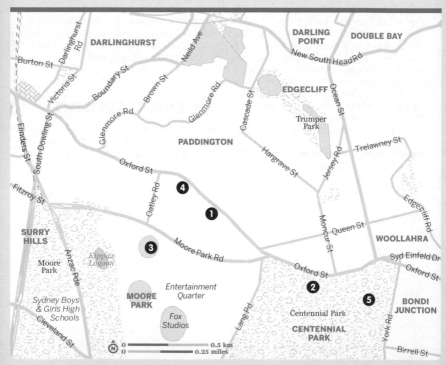

For more detail of this area, see Map p264 ➡

Explore: Paddington & Centennial Park

Paddington, also known as 'Paddo', is an elegant, expensive area of beautifully restored terrace houses and steep leafy streets where fashionable folks drift between designer shops, chic restaurants, art galleries and bookshops. Built over an ancient walking track used by the Cadigal people, the suburb's pulsing artery is Oxford St, extending from nearby Darlinghurst. The best time to visit is on Saturday, when the markets are at their most effervescent.

Rugged bushland until the 1860s, Paddington was built for aspiring Victorian artisans, but following the lemminglike rush to quarter-acre blocks in the outer suburbs after WWII, it became Australia's worst slum. A renewed passion for Victorian architecture (and the realisation that the outer suburbs were unspeakably boring) led to Paddington's resurgence in the 1960s. By the 1990s real estate here was beyond all but the lucky and loaded.

In contrast to Paddington, monocultural Woollahra was never a slum. This is upper-crust Sydney at its finest: leafy streets, mansions, wall-to-wall BMWs and expensive antique shops. Maybe this is your bag; maybe it isn't – either way, an afternoon here is socially enlightening.

South of Oxford St, the Centennial Parklands cut a giant green swath, enclosing a cluster of sports venues.

Local Life

→ **Sports** The cheering, swearing hordes come out in force to support the local lads at the Sydney Football Stadium and Sydney Cricket Ground.

→ **Five Ways** This five-way intersection north of Oxford St is the real heart of the neighbourhood.

→ **Fitness** Sit in Centennial Park for long enough and it will seem like half the neighbourhood has passed by in one big jogging/cycling/in-line skating blur.

Getting There & Away

→ **Bus** Buses are the main public transport mode in these parts. Major routes include 355 (Bondi Junction to Newtown via Lang Rd), 373 (Circular Quay to Coogee via Moore Park), 378 (Railway Sq to Bronte via Oxford St), 380 (Circular Quay to Watsons Bay via Oxford St and Bondi) and 389 (Circular Quay to North Bondi via Glenmore Rd, Moncur and Queen Sts).

→ **Train** Walk downhill from Kings Cross or Edgecliff station to Rushcutters Bay and the Paddington and Woollahra lowlands; or from Bondi Junction station to the eastern reaches of Centennial Park.

→ **Car** Street parking is usually possible, although it's usually metered and limited in duration.

Lonely Planet's Top Tip

The street numbers on Oxford St reset themselves with each new suburb. Oxford St Darlinghurst becomes Oxford St Paddington east of Barcom St, which becomes Oxford St Woollahra at Jersey Rd. This can be extremely confusing; if you're looking for the Arts Hotel at 21 Oxford St, for instance, make sure you're in Paddington or you may end up ringing the bell of a private house in Bondi Junction or a gay newspaper in Darlinghurst.

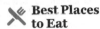

Best Places to Eat

→ Four In Hand (p142)
→ Bistro Moncur (p143)
→ Neild Avenue (p143)

For reviews, see p142 →

Best Places to Drink

→ Wine Library (p143)
→ 10 William Street (p143)
→ Light Brigade Hotel (p144)
→ Royal Hotel (p143)
→ Paddington Inn (p143)

For reviews, see p143 →

Best Shopping

→ Paddington Markets (p145)
→ Ariel (p145)
→ Corner Shop (p145)
→ Andrew McDonald (p145)
→ The Art of Dr Seuss (p147)

For reviews, see p145 →

◉ SIGHTS

◉ Paddington

FREE VICTORIA
BARRACKS
HISTORIC BUILDINGS

Map p264 (✆8335 5170; Oxford St; ⊙tours 10am Thu; ☐380) A manicured malarial vision from the peak of the British Empire (built 1841 to 1848), these Georgian buildings have been called the finest of their kind in the colonies. Tours take in a flag-raising ceremony, a marching band (weather permitting) and the paraphernalia-packed war museum. Good disabled access.

FREE AUSTRALIAN CENTRE FOR
PHOTOGRAPHY
GALLERY

Map p264 (✆9332 0555; www.acp.org.au; 257 Oxford St; ⊙noon-7pm Tue-Fri, 10am-6pm Sat & Sun; ☐380) The nonprofit ACP exhibits the photographic gems of renowned Sydney and international photographers. It's particularly passionate about photomedia, video and digital-imaging works, its displays extending into a multiexhibition space next door.

PADDINGTON RESERVOIR
GARDENS
PARK

Map p264 (cnr Oxford St & Oatley Rd; ☐380) Opened to much architectural acclaim in 2008, this impressive park makes use of Paddington's long-abandoned 1866 water reservoir, incorporating the brick arches and surviving chamber into an interesting green space featuring a sunken garden, pond, boardwalk and lawns.

They've even preserved some of the graffiti dating from the many years when it was boarded up and abandoned to feral cats and stealthy spray-can artists.

FREE SHERMAN CONTEMPORARY
ART FOUNDATION
GALLERY

Map p264 (✆9331 1112; www.sherman-scaf .org.au; 16 Goodhope St; ⊙11am-5pm Wed-Sat; ☐389) After 21 years as a cutting-edge commercial gallery, Sherman Galleries celebrated its coming-of-age by reopening as a not-for-profit gallery. The focus is on temporary exhibitions of work by influential and innovative artists from Australia, the Asia-Pacific region and the Middle East.

FREE NEILD AVENUE MAZE
PARK

Map p264 (Neild Ave; ☒Kings Cross) This tiny maze of thigh-high hedges hides behind a gargantuan plane tree on a Paddington back street, squished into a cranny between a gallery and someone's back fence. It mightn't take you forever to find your way through, but it'll add a smile to your day.

RUSHCUTTERS BAY
PARK

Map p264 (New South Head Rd; ☒Edgecliff) Surrounded by enormous Moreton Bay fig trees, luxury yachts and pampered pooches, this unpretentious waterfront park is a beaut spot for a quiet stroll or jog. In December the world's greatest yachties prepare for the gruelling Sydney to Hobart race here. Rushcutters Bay Park Tennis Courts are also on hand.

JUNIPER HALL
HISTORIC BUILDING

Map p264 (248 Oxford St; ☐380) Paddington's oldest home (1824), this restored Georgian mansion was built by Robert Cooper with profits from his gin business (he named it after the essential gin-making ingredient). It's owned by the National Trust but it's usually tenanted as a commercial property.

◉ Woollahra

QUEEN STREET
STREET

Map p264 (Queen St; ☐389) Despite its status as the premier antique-shopping strip in Australia (the first shop opened in 1957), tree-lined Queen St retains a village vibe, with pricey boutiques, delis, summer chestnuts hanging heavy on the bough and kids who say, 'Hey, nice Ferrari!'. There was once a famous annual street fair here, until noise-phobic residents shut it down in the early 1980s.

◉ Centennial Park & Moore Park

CENTENNIAL PARK
PARK

Map p264 (✆9339 6699; www.centennialpark lands.com.au; Oxford St; ⊙vehicles sunrise-sunset; ☒Bondi Junction) Scratched out of the sand in 1888 in grand Victorian style, Sydney's biggest park is a rambling 189-hectare expanse full of horse riders, joggers, cyclists and in-line skaters. During

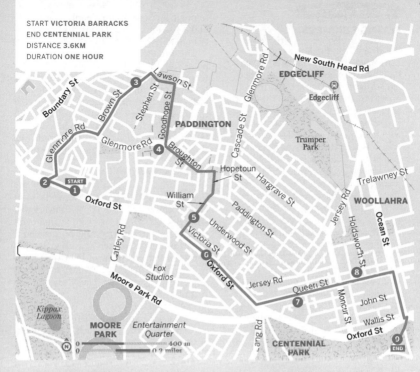

START **VICTORIA BARRACKS**
END **CENTENNIAL PARK**
DISTANCE **3.6KM**
DURATION **ONE HOUR**

Neighbourhood Walk
Fashionable Footsteps

This walk should take around an hour, not including Centennial Park, extended shopping frenzies or getting lost in the Neild Avenue maze.

The old ❶ **Victoria Barracks** are still an active army base, so unless you join the tour you'll have to ogle the impressive Georgian sandstone structures from the guarded gates. Cross Oxford St, turn left and head down to ❷ **Glenmore Rd** where temptation comes in the form of sassy boutiques.

Turn right into Glenmore Rd, follow its curves for several blocks then jag downhill on Brown St to the cute ❸ **Neild Avenue maze**. Turn right into Lawson St, then second right into Goodhope St and continue to ❹ **Five Ways** – a roundabout at the confluence of five roads. Oxford St may be the main drag, but the quirky cafes, galleries, shops and pub here make it the hip heart of Paddington.

From Five Ways, head uphill along Broughton St, turn right into Hopetoun St and follow it around to the bottom of ❺ **William Street**. This photogenic side street has sprouted a strip of classy boutiques.

Turn left onto ❻ **Oxford St**, Sydney's fashionista freeway. Local and international designers fill the shopfronts, selling swanky threads for ladies and lads. Cafes, pubs and homeware stores join the competition to prise the credit card from your wallet.

At the eastern end of the strip hang left into Queen Street, the beginning of upmarket Woollahra. Boutiques give way to antique stores and providores as you head downhill. ❼ **Simon Johnson** at number 55 sometimes has tastings – drop in for a nibble. At number 132, ❽ **Victor Churchill** may look like another boutique but its actually a butcher's – the flashest butcher's you'll ever see.

Turn right into Ocean St and head back up to Oxford St. Cross the road and enter the leafy folds of ❾ **Centennial Park**.

LOCAL KNOWLEDGE

FLYING FOXINESS

If you cast an eye to the Sydney sky at sunset, you'll see a cloud of bats. You'll find them throughout the city, particularly in Centennial Park, where they arrive in a great black cloud. The silent, spectral swoop of fruitbats on the wing might make you want to cower behind a crucifix, but there's really nothing to fear – they'd rather suck on a Moreton Bay fig than your jugular. The only damage they're likely to inflict is on the paintwork of your car (their droppings are incredibly corrosive).

These bats are grey-headed flying foxes (*Pteropus ploiocephalus*), and they're an important part of Sydney's ecology, spreading seeds and pollinating flowers as they feed. Unlike other bats, flying foxes don't live in caves, don't use echolocation and can't see particularly well in the dark. Neither do they fly in a jerky manner like their smaller cousins, but rather use their metre-wide wingspan to glide around gracefully, much like birds do.

For more information on these critters, check out www.sydneybats .org.au.

summer Moonlight Cinema (p144) attracts the crowds.

Among the wide formal avenues, ponds and statues is the domed **Federation Pavilion** (Map p264) – the spot where Australia was officially proclaimed a nation (on 1 January 1901) – surrounded by the various state flags. If you're feeling peckish, **Centennial Parklands Dining** (Map p264; www.cpdining .com.au; Grand Drive; breakfast $13-17, lunch $18-29, kiosk snacks $6-10; ⊙breakfast & lunch) near the centre of the park encompasses a cafe, wine bar and kiosk. At the southern edge of the park is Royal Randwick Racecourse (p148), while on its eastern edge it joins Queens Park and continues for another 26 hectares.

MOORE PARK   PARK

Map p264 (☑9339 6699; www.centennialpark lands.com.au; Anzac Pde; ℞Central) Part of the broader Centennial Parklands (a huge green swath that cuts from Surry Hills to Bondi) Moore Park covers 115 hectares south of Paddington. With sports fields,

tennis courts, an 18-hole public golf course and a site for visiting circuses, there's plenty here to keep you off the streets.

The broader precinct also includes the homes of the Sydney Swans Aussie rules team, the Sydney City Roosters rugby league team and the Sydney Mardi Gras party – the historic Sydney Cricket Ground (p147), the Sydney Football Stadium (p147) and the Hordern Pavilion (p145), respectively; try not to get them confused! The Entertainment Quarter spices up the mix.

ENTERTAINMENT QUARTER   NEIGHBOURHOOD

Map p264 (☑8117 6700; www.entertainment quarter.com.au; 122 Lang Rd; ⊙10am-midnight; ☐372-374, 391-397) If we were feeling cynical, we might say that the purpose-built Entertainment Quarter is a vacuous, self-perpetuating specimen of lightweight global commercialism, but we'll try to restrain ourselves. Instead, we'll just say that its palm-lined avenues, cinemas, ice rink and weekend markets are a good distraction for the kids. Fox Studios (where *The Matrix* and two *Star Wars* prequels were filmed) is next door.

EATING

This conservative enclave has traditionally offered good eating that shies away from the aggressively modern tendencies of its neighbours – reliable places where the just-so steak paired with the perfect wine is done to perfection and the service is well-mannered to match. Lately a few rogue operators have moved in, shaking things up with their hip ways and trendy food.

Paddington

FOUR IN HAND   MODERN AUSTRALIAN **$$$**

Map p264 (☑9362 1999; www.fourinhand.com .au; 105 Sutherland St; mains $38; ⊙lunch & dinner Tue-Sun; ℞Edgecliff) You can't go far in Paddington without tripping over a beautiful old pub with amazing food. This is the best of them, famous for its slow-cooked and nose-to-tail meat dishes, although it also offers fabulously fresh seafood dishes and a delectable array of desserts. The bar

menu (mains $20 to $23) is a more affordable option.

NEILD AVENUE — MEDITERRANEAN $$$
Map p264 (www.idrb.com; 10 Neild Ave; mains
$35-42; ⊘lunch Fri-Sun, dinner daily; ▣Edge-
cliff) Known for its coal-grilled meats,
unusual grains, no-bookings policy and
lengthy waits for tables, this uberhip,
warehouse-filling restaurant is Sydney at
its look-at-me best. Despite its 'dude food'
repute, most of the clientele seem to have
teetered straight out of *Sex & the City* central casting. The food's excellent and the
vibe beyond buzzy.

SONOMA — CAFE $
Map p264 (www.sonoma.com.au; 241 Glenmore Rd;
mains $10-16; ⊘7am-4pm; ▣389) 'Artisan sour-
dough' is the speciality of this mini chain of
bakery cafes, and the toast with ricotta and
the sourdough sandwiches are suitably impressive. The popular Paddington branch offers a tasty $7 'coffee and pastry' deal. There
are also branches in Glebe and Bondi.

✗ Woollahra

BISTRO MONCUR — FRENCH $$
Map p264 (☑9327 9713; www.bistromoncur.com
.au; 116 Queen St; mains $30-43; ⊘lunch Tue-Sun,
dinner daily; ▣389) Minimoguls and lunch-
eon ladies while away long afternoons beneath Bistro Moncur's vaulted ceilings and
monochromatic mural. Chef Damien Pigno-
let's menu changes seasonally but signature
dishes such as French onion souffle gratin
and grilled sirloin Cafe de Paris delight din
ers year-round. The wine list will make you
want to take up mogulling, too.

CHISWICK RESTAURANT — MODERN AUSTRALIAN $$
Map p264 (☑8388 8688; www.chiswickrestau
rant.com.au; 65 Ocean St; mains $28-30; ⊘lunch
& dinner Tue-Sun; ▣Edgecliff) It's Chiswick
Gardens that's the star of the show here,
more so even than celebrity chef Matt
Moran. The garden wraps around the dining room and dictates the menu, which
couldn't be more fresh and seasonal. Which
isn't to say that the vegetables have taken
over completely: meat from the Moran family farm and local seafood feature prominently too.

🍷🍸 DRINKING & NIGHTLIFE

Some cool Darlinghurst-style bars spill over into Paddington, but generally this area is a little more refined – and a lot less interesting. Any pretension dissolves when the sports fans spew out of the nearby Sydney Cricket Ground and Sydney Football Stadium and into Paddo's pubs.

🍸 Paddington

10 WILLIAM STREET — WINE BAR
Map p264 (10 William St; ⊘6-11pm Mon-Sat;
▣380) The Italian boys behind Potts Point's
Fratelli Paradiso (p134) are behind this *mi-
nuscolo* slice of dolce vita on the fashion
strip. Expect excellent imported wines and
equally impressive food.

ROYAL HOTEL — PUB
Map p264 (www.royalhotel.com.au; 237 Glenmore Rd; ▣389) One of the points on the
five-pointed junction star, this fine pub is
spread over three floors. At the top, the Elephant Bar has views over the city skyline.

PADDINGTON INN — PUB
Map p264 (☑9380 5913; www.paddingtoninn
.com.au; 338 Oxford St; ▣380) The Paddo
seems to get a new look every few years,
perhaps in keeping with its prime fashion-
strip position. Eager locals elbow around
the pool table and get stuck into $10 week-
day lunches and $10 Sunday jugs.

🍸 Woollahra

WINE LIBRARY — WINE BAR
Map p264 (18 Oxford St, Woollahra; ⊘11.30am-
11.30pm Mon-Fri, 10am-11.30pm Sat, 10am-10pm
Sun; ▣380) With an impressive range of
wines by the glass and a stylish but casual feel, this little bar is a sophisticated pit
stop for battle-hardened shoppers. When
it's time to eat you can choose from the
Mediterranean-inclined bar menu or consider sauntering around the corner to **Buzo**
(Map p264; www.buzorestaurant.com.au; 3 Jersey
Rd; mains $26-35; ⊘dinner Mon-Sat), a much-
loved local trattoria run by the same team.

LIGHT BRIGADE HOTEL PUB

Map p264 (☑9357 0888; www.lightbrigade.com
.au; 2a Oxford St, Woollahra; ⊙11am-midnight
Mon-Sat, to 10pm Sun; ☑380) Charge into this
curvy art deco pub for its relaxed ground-
floor sports bar with a good-value menu
($10 weekday lunch), pool table and lots of
black tiles and angular stainless steel. Upstairs beyond a huge clock face is chic Italian restaurant and cocktail bar **La Scala on
Jersey** (Map p264; ☑9357 0815; www.lascalaon
jersey.com.au; mains $27-39; ⊙dinner Mon-Sat).

LORD DUDLEY HOTEL PUB

Map p264 (☑9327 5399; www.lorddudley.com
.au; 236 Jersey Rd; ⊙11am-11pm Mon-Wed, 11am-
midnight Thu-Sat, noon-10pm Sun; ☑Edgecliff)
Packed with poncy, scarf-wearing MG
drivers and block-shouldered rugby union
types, the Lord Dudley is as close to an English pub as Sydney gets. Dark woody walls
and quality beers by the pint. 'I say, Giles
old bean... May I have another Pimm's?'

WOOLLAHRA HOTEL PUB, LIVE MUSIC

Map p264 (☑9327 9777; www.woollahrahotel
.com.au; 116 Queen St; ⊙noon-midnight Mon-Sat,
noon-10pm Sun; ☑389) It's a bit suity most of
the time, but this sports pub is worth checking out for the free jazz, salsa, soul and
funk bands on Sundays (6pm to 9pm) and
Thursdays (7pm to 11pm), and the DJs from
Thursday to Sunday night.

☆ ENTERTAINMENT

☆ Paddington

CHAUVEL CINEMA CINEMA

Map p264 (☑9361 5398; www.chauvelcinema
.net.au; cnr Oxford St & Oatley Rd; adult/child
$19/11; ⊙sessions 10am-9.30pm; ☑380) The
revamped Chauvel Cinema, located inside
the historic Paddington Town Hall, strives
to offer distinct and alternative cinema
experiences and to foster Sydney's film
culture. It also plays host to various quirky
film festivals.

PALACE VERONA CINEMA

Map p264 (☑9360 6099; www.palacecinemas
.com.au; 17 Oxford St; adult/child $19/14; ⊙ses-
sions 10am-9.30pm; ☑380) This urbane
cinema has a cool cafe and bar, useful for

NIDA

The former stomping ground of Mel
Gibson, Cate Blanchett and Geoffrey
Rush, the stage of the **National Institute of Dramatic Art** (☑02 9697 7600;
www.nida.edu.au; 215 Anzac Pde, Randwick;
tickets $15-60; ☑M50) is the place to see
future stars of the stage and screen on
the way up. Student and graduate plays
happen throughout the year in four
intimate performance spaces.

discussing the artistic merits of the non-
blockbuster flick you've just seen.

☆ Centennial Park & Moore Park

SYDNEY COMEDY STORE COMEDY

Map p264 (☑9357 1419; www.comedystore.com
.au; Suttor Ave; tickets $10-35; ⊙from 7pm Tue-
Sat; ☑372-374, 391-397) This purpose-built
comedy hall lures big-time Australian and
overseas stand-ups and nurtures new talent
with open-mic and New Comics nights. US,
Irish and Edinburgh Festival performers
have 'em rolling in the aisles on a regular
basis. Bookings advisable.

MOONLIGHT CINEMA CINEMA

Map p264 (☑1300 551 908; www.moonlight.com.
au; Belvedere Amphitheatre, cnr Loch & Broome
Aves; adult/child $18/14; ⊙screenings sunset Dec-
Mar; ☑Bondi Junction) Take a picnic and join
the bats under the stars in magnificent Centennial Park; enter via Woollahra Gate on
Oxford St. A mix of new-release blockbuster,
art house and classics is programmed.

**HOYTS ENTERTAINMENT
QUARTER** CINEMA

Map p264 (☑9332 1300; www.hoyts.com.au;
Bent St; adult/child $19/14; ⊙sessions 10.30am-
9.20pm; ☑339) This hefty movie complex
has more than a dozen cinemas, including an IMAX screen and La Premiere,
the cinematic equivalent of a first-class
cabin, with waiter service, lounge chairs,
bar access and popcorn included ($35).
Art-house films and ethnic film festivals
screen in **Cinema Paris** (Map p264), just
down Bent St.

HORDERN PAVILION   PERFORMANCE VENUE
Map p264 (☎9921 5333; www.playbillvenues
.com; 1 Driver Ave; tickets $46-110; ☐372-374,
391-397) Holding over 5000 heaving music
fans, the historic white and grey Hordern
(1924) hosts plenty of big-name rock gigs
(Coldplay, Nine Inch Nails, The Presets)
and, along with neighbouring halls, the
massive Mardi Gras Party. If these walls
could talk...

🛍 SHOPPING

**As well as three of Sydney's premier
shopping strips – Oxford St and
William St in Paddington (fashion and
homewares) and Queen St in Woollahra
(antiques and fashion) – this area also
secretes dozens of commercial art
galleries in its back streets.**

🛍 Paddington

PADDINGTON MARKETS   MARKET
Map p264 (☎9331 2923; www.paddingtonmar
kets.com.au; 395 Oxford St; ☉10am-4pm Sat;
☐380) A cultural experience, these quirky,
long-running markets turn Saturdays in
Paddington into pandemonium. Originat-
ing in the 1970s, Paddington Markets were
a beacon for larrikin artists and artisans,
punks, skinheads, patchouli-scented hippies and fledgling fashion designers. It's a
tad more mainstream now, but still worth
checking out for its new and vintage clothing, creative crafts, jewellery, food, palm
reading and holistic treatments.

ARIEL   BOOKS
Map p264 (☎9332 4581; www.arielbooks.com
.au; 42 Oxford St; ☉9am-midnight; ☐380) Fur-
tive artists, architects and students roam
Ariel's aisles late into the night. 'Undercul-
ture' is the thrust here – glossy art, film,
fashion and design books, along with kids'
books, travel guides and a queer-lit section.

CORNER SHOP   CLOTHING
Map p264 (☎9380 9828; www.thecornershop
.com.au; 43 William St; ☐380) This treasure
trove of a boutique is stocked with unique
and original foreign goodies like stylish
jeans, cosy turtlenecks and wispy things
that go 'slink' in the night. There's a healthy

mix of casual and high end, with some jewellery for good measure.

ANDREW MCDONALD   SHOES
Map p264 (☎9358 6793; www.andrewmcdonald.
com.au; 58 William St; ☉10am-6pm Mon-Sat;
☐380) Sydney's best in custom footwear
for men and women can be had at this
small Paddington workshop. Choose your
materials, colours and even styles (or they
can replicate a desired design) and expect
exquisite, long-wearing and perfectly fitted
shoes. Great for those with 'difficult' feet, or
just anyone who wants something unique.

BERKELOUW BOOKS   BOOKS
Map p264 (☎9360 3200; www.berkelouw.com
.au; 19 Oxford St; ☉9am-10pm; ☐380) Expect-
ing the dank aroma of secondhand books?
Forget it! Follow your nose up to the cafe,
then browse through three floors of preloved
tomes, new releases, antique maps and Australia's largest collection of rare books. The
Berkelouws have specialised in secondhand
books and printed rarities over six generations since setting up shop in Holland in 1812.
There's another branch in Newtown (p115).

POEPKE   CLOTHING
Map p264 (www.poepke.com; 47 William St;
☉10am-6pm Mon-Sat, noon-5pm Sun; ☐380)
One of Paddington's more interesting
boutiques, stocking a range of Australian
(Rittenhouse, Tru$t Fun!) and Internation-
al designers (Dries Van Noten, Nom*D).

ZIMMERMANN   CLOTHING
Map p264 (www.zimmermannwear.com; 2-16
Glenmore Rd; ☉10am-6pm Fri-Wed, to 8pm Thu;
☐380) Chic and cheeky women's street
clothes and swimwear from sisters Nicky
and Simone Zimmermann. There are other
stores in the Sydney and Bondi Junction
Westfields.

MECCA COSMETICA   BEAUTY
Map p264 (☎9361 4488; www.meccacosmetica
.com.au; 126 Oxford St; ☉10am-6pm Fri-Wed,
to 8pm Thu; ☐380) Aptly named, this is the
make-up mecca for beauty devotees. As
well as its own brand, Mecca Cosmetica
stocks cult cosmetics from Nars, Kevyn
Aucoin, Stila and Serge Lutens, as well as
some well-selected scents. Test the divine
blood orange lotion, pick an inky dark nail
polish and get a quick makeover if it's not
too busy.

DINOSAUR DESIGNS   JEWELLERY, HOMEWARES
Map p264 (☑9361 3776; www.dinosaurdesigns
.com.au; 339 Oxford St; ☺9.30am-5.30pm Mon-Sat, 11am-4pm Sun; ☐380) If the Flintstones opened a jewellery store, this is what it would look like: oversized, richly coloured, translucent resin bangles and baubles sit among technicoloured vases and bowls, and chunky sterling-silver rings and necklaces.

LEONA EDMISTON   CLOTHING, ACCESSORIES
Map p264 (☑9331 7033; www.leonaedmiston
.com; 88 William St; ☐380) Leona Edmiston knows frocks – from little and black to whimsically floral or all-out sexy. Her exuberantly feminine, flirtatious and fun designs are cut from the best cotton, silk and jersey fabrics in colours that range from luscious, sophisticated reds to pinstripes and polka dots. Also at Westfield Bondi Junction, Westfield Sydney, Chifley Plaza and the Strand Arcade.

SASS & BIDE   CLOTHING, ACCESSORIES
Map p264 (☑9360 3900; www.sassandbide
.com; 132 Oxford St; ☺10am-6pm Fri-Wed, to 8pm Thu; ☐380) Brisbane's Heidi Middleton and Sarah-Jane Clarke got their start with a stall on London's Portobello Rd before heading to Sydney in 1999 and creating the label that has made them international fashion stars. Come here for sassy low-cut women's jeans, body-hugging jackets and mini dresses.

CALIBRE   CLOTHING, ACCESSORIES
Map p264 (☑9380 5993; www.calibreclothing
.com.au; 398 Oxford St; ☐380) Hip, high-calibre Calibre fills the wardrobes of Sydney's power players with schmick suits and shirts in seasonal fabrics and colours. You'll also find them in Westfield Bondi Junction and Sydney.

**SCANLAN &
THEODORE**   CLOTHING, ACCESSORIES
Map p264 (☑9380 9388; www.scanlantheodore
.com.au; 122 Oxford St; ☐380) Scanlan & Theodore excels at beautifully made and finely silhouetted women's outfits for evening or the office. Plenty of sophisticated patterns and colours complement fabrics you just can't help but fondle.

EASTON PEARSON   CLOTHING
Map p264 (www.eastonpearson.com; 30 Glenmore Rd; ☺10am-6pm Mon-Fri, 11am-5pm Sat & Sun; ☐380) Brisbane designers who popularised ethno-chic in Australia and are particularly beloved by women of a slightly fuller figure.

WILLOW   CLOTHING
Map p264 (www.willowltd.com.au; 3a Glenmore Rd; ☐380) Local designer Kit Willow has made it big around the globe with the sleek silhouettes of her womenswear.

HOGARTH GALLERIES   ART
Map p264 (☑9360 6839; www.aboriginalartdirec
tory.com; 7 Walker Lane; ☺10am-5pm Tue-Sat; ☐380) A cultural beacon in an obscure Paddington laneway, Hogarth has supported and promoted Aboriginal art since 1972. Honouring established artists and sourcing up-and-comers, Hogarth exhibits contemporary dot paintings, basketry, framed prints, fabrics, spears and didgeridoos. From Oxford St take Shadforth St, turn right onto Walker Lane, then right again to enter from the side lane.

IAIN DAWSON GALLERY   ART
Map p264 (☑9358 4337; www.iaindawson.com; 443 Oxford St; ☺10am-6pm Tue-Sat; ☐380) This hip new gallery specialises in emerging Australian artists (Hugh Ford, Miranda Skoczek) in their first years of professional artistry. Sculptors, photographers, painters and screen printers – buy 'em now before they make it big!

STILLS GALLERY   ART
Map p264 (☑9331 7775; www.stillsgallery.com
.au; 36 Gosbell St; ☺11am-6pm Tue-Sat; ☐Kings Cross) Have a gander at some cutting-edge photography at this spacey backstreet gallery. It represents a swag of internationally recognised photographers, including William Yang, Anne Noble and Sandy Edwards.

ROSLYN OXLEY9 GALLERY   ART
Map p264 (☑9331 1919; www.roslynoxley9
.com.au; 8 Soudan Lane; ☺10am-6pm Tue-Sat; ☐Edgecliff) For 30 years this high-powered commercial gallery has showcased innovative contemporary work, representing artists such as Tracey Moffatt, David Noonan and Bill Henson. It's great for a nosy even if you're not looking to buy.

🛍 Woollahra

THE ART OF DR SEUSS — ART

Map p264 (www.tvhgallery.com.au; 8 Oxford St; ⊙10.30am-5.30pm Fri-Wed, to 8pm Thu; 🚌380) You'd have to be the Grinch not to be charmed by this, the only Dr Seuss gallery outside the US. Pick up a limited-edition print of Horton, the Lorax or Foona-Lagoona Baboona and pretend it's for the kid in your life.

COLLETTE DINNIGAN — CLOTHING

Map p264 (✆9363 2698; www.collettedinnigan .com; 104 Queen St; 🚌389) Hollywood's Aussie gals head here whenever they need a new slinky beaded, sequinned or lacy number for a red carpet (Nicole or Naomi might be in the next change room). The queen of Aussie couture delivers fabulously feminine frocks with exquisite trimming.

HERRINGBONE — CLOTHING, ACCESSORIES

Map p264 (✆9327 6470; www.herringbone.com; 102 Queen St; ⊙10am-6pm Mon-Sat, 11am-5pm Sun; 🚌389) Combining Australian design with Italian woven fabrics, Herringbone produces something surprisingly English-looking – beautiful men's and women's shirts with crisp collars and bright colours. When the stock market went south in 2008, suit sales took a king hit, but the 'Bone boys have somehow endured.

LESLEY MCKAY'S BOOKSHOP — BOOKS

Map p264 (✆9328 2733; www.lesleymckay.com .au; 118 Queen St; ⊙9am-6pm Fri-Wed, to 8pm Thu; 🚌389) This independent bookseller stocks an excellent range of fiction, biography and history titles. There's an especially good selection of children's books, too, and the knowledgable staff won't let you down.

KIDSTUFF — TOYS

Map p264 (✆9363 2838; www.kidstuff.com.au; 126a Queen St; ⊙9am-5.30pm Mon-Sat, to 5pm Sun; 🚌389) This small, vaguely hippie shop is filled with educational, traditional, low-tech toys and games. Aiming to engage and expand kids' minds, well-known brands mix with costumes, musical instruments, soft toys, dolls' houses and magnetic fridge letters.

🛍 Centennial Park & Moore Park

EQ VILLAGE MARKETS — MARKET

Map p264 (www.entertainmentquarter.com.au; Showring, Bent St; ⊙10am-3.30pm Wed, Sat & Sun; 🚌372-374, 391-397) The Entertainment Quarter's Wednesday and Saturday markets have loads of regional produce, including delicious cheese and yoghurt, while the craft-based Sunday market features clothing, accessories, toys and homewares, along with hot-food stalls.

🏃 SPORTS & ACTIVITIES

SYDNEY FOOTBALL STADIUM — SPECTATOR SPORT

Map p264 (Allianz Stadium; www.allianzstadium. com.au; Moore Park Rd) It's now officially named after an insurance company but these naming rights change periodically, so we'll stick with the untainted-by-sponsorship moniker for this elegant 45,500-capacity stadium. It's home to local heroes, the **Sydney Roosters** (www.sydneyroosters.com.au) rugby league team, the NSW **Waratahs** (www.waratahs.com. au) rugby union team and the **Sydney FC** (www.sydneyfc.com) A-league football (soccer) team.

All of these teams have passionate fans (possibly the most vocal are the crazies in the Roosters' 'chook pen'), so a home game can be a lot of fun. Book through Ticketek.

SYDNEY CRICKET GROUND — SPECTATOR SPORT

Map p264 (SCG; ✆9360 6601; www.sydneycricket ground.com.au; Driver Ave; 🚌372-374, 391-397) During the cricket season (October to March), the stately old SCG is the venue for sparsely attended interstate cricket matches (featuring the NSW Blues), and sell-out five-day international test, one-day and 20/20 limited-over matches. As the cricket season ends the Australian rules football season starts and the stadium becomes a barracking blur of red-and-white-clad fans of the home team, the **Sydney Swans** (www .sydneyswans.com.au).

SCG TOUR EXPERIENCE   TOUR
(📞1300 724 737; www.sydneycricketground.
com.au; Driver Ave; tours adult/child/family
$25/17/65; ⊙tours 10am, noon & 2pm Mon-Fri,
10pm Sat) Run up the players' race from the
dressing rooms in your own sporting fan-
tasy during this behind-the-scenes guided
tour of the facilities at the SCG.

CENTENNIAL PARKLANDS
EQUESTRIAN CENTRE   HORSE RIDING
Map p264 (📞9332 2809; www.cpequestrian.com
.au; 114-120 Lang Rd; escorted park ride from $80;
🚌372-374, 391-397) Take a one-hour, 3.6km
horse ride around tree-lined Centennial
Park, Sydney's favourite urban green space.
Several stables within the centre conduct
park rides, including **Centennial Stables**
(Map p264; 📞9360 5650; www.centennialstables.
com.au), **Eastside Riding Academy** (Map
p264; 📞9360 7521; www.eastsideriding.com.au)
and **Moore Park Stables** (Map p264; 📞9360
8747; www.mooreparkstables.com.au). Equine
familiarity not required.

CENTENNIAL PARK CYCLES   BICYCLE RENTAL
Map p264 (📞0401 357 419; www.cyclehire.com
.au; Grand Dr; ⊙9am-5pm) Hires mountain
bikes and hybrids (per hour/day $15/50),
road bikes ($20/70), kids' bikes ($10/45),
tandems ($25/75) and pedal cars (per hour
$30-$40).

SKATER HQ   SKATING, BICYCLE RENTAL
Map p264 (📞9368 0945; www.skaterhq.com.au;
Bent St; ⊙10am-7pm Sun-Fri, to 9pm Sat; 🚌372-
374 & 391-397) Handy to Centennial Park,
these guys can fix you up with top-of-the-
range in-line-skate and skateboard hire
($20 per hour with safety gear), or give you
a lesson in how to ride 'em ($60 per hour).
They also hire bikes (per hour/day $15/25).

ROYAL RANDWICK
RACECOURSE   HORSE RACING
(📞9663 8400; www.ajc.org.au; Alison Rd; admission $15-20; 🚌372-4) Royal Randwick
attracts some glam fillies, plus the usual parade of 'colourful' racing identities and connections. Gates open at 11am on race days,
and the last race is around 5pm. The big
event on the calendar is the **Sydney Carnival** (www.ajc.org.au; Royal Randwick Racecourse
& Rosehill Gardens; ⊙Mar-Apr; 🚌393); check
the online calendar for regular racing days.
Dance-kids head here for the **Future Music
Festival** (www.futureentertainment.com.au) in
late February.

Bondi to Coogee

BONDI | TAMARAMA | BRONTE | CLOVELLY | COOGEE

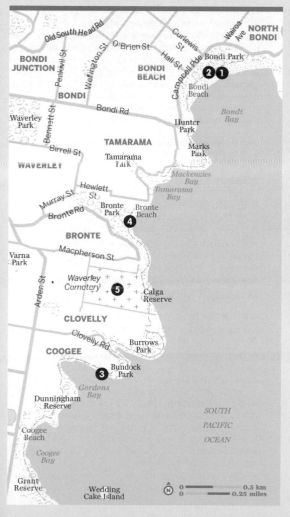

Neighbourhood Top Five

1 Whiling away the day on the golden sands of **Bondi Beach** (p151), periodically cooling off in the surf and cruising the promenade.

2 Revelling in the spectacular coastal scenery of the Bondi to Coogee walk (p153).

3 Coming face to face with the scaly locals on the **Gordons Bay Underwater Nature Trail** (p152).

4 Grilling up a storm (only figuratively, hopefully) at a **Bronte** (p152) beachside barbecue.

5 Waving at the winter parade of whales from the cliffs of **Waverley Cemetery** (p152).

For more detail of this area, see Map p266 and p267 ➡

Lonely Planet's Top Tip

Bondi Junction, situated 2.5km from Bondi Beach and 6km from Circular Quay, is the transport hub for the Eastern Beaches. The Eastern Suburbs train line terminates beneath the main bus station, right next to the Westfield shopping complex. If you've got a My-Multi pass and you're near a station, catch the train and head upstairs to connect by bus to the beach. It's much quicker than catching the bus from the city.

 ### Best Places to Eat

➡ Icebergs Dining Room (p155)

➡ Three Blue Ducks (p156)

➡ Clodeli (p156)

➡ Harry's Espresso Bar (p155)

➡ North Bondi Italian Food (p155)

For reviews, see p155 ➡

Best Places to Drink

➡ North Bondi RSL (p156)

➡ Icebergs Bar (p157)

➡ Corner House (p156)

➡ Clovelly Hotel (p157)

➡ Beach Road Hotel (p157)

For reviews, see p156 ➡

Best Places to Swim

➡ Bondi Beach (p151)

➡ Bronte Beach (p152)

➡ Mahon Pool (p155)

➡ Clovelly Beach (p152)

➡ Coogee Beach (p152)

For reviews, see p152 ➡

Explore: Bondi to Coogee

Improbably good-looking arcs of sand framed by jagged cliffs, the Eastern Beaches are a big part of the Sydney experience. Most famous of all is the broad sweep of Bondi Beach, where the distracting scenery and constant procession of beautiful bods never fail to take your mind off whatever it was you were just thinking about... This is where Sydney comes to see and be seen, preferably wearing as little as possible (it's not an affirming place for those with body-image issues).

The unique flavour of Bondi has been greatly influenced by the Jewish, British and Kiwi immigrants who populated it before it became hip. Housing prices on Bondi's strangely treeless slopes have skyrocketed, but the beach remains a priceless constant.

South of Bondi, Bronte is a steep-sided beach 'burb, its bowl-shaped park strewn with picnic tables and barbecues. Further south is the concrete-fringed, safe swimming inlet of Clovelly, a great place to dust off your snorkel. Next stop heading south is Coogee, an Aboriginal word for rotting seaweed... But don't let that deter you: the beach is wide and handsome, and beery backpackers fill the takeaways and pubs.

Local Life

➡ **Beaches** People move to these suburbs to be near the beaches, so don't think they're just for tourists.

➡ **Brunch** On weekends brunchsters descend on the cafes from near and far. Once you step back from Bondi's Campbell Pde, Sydneysiders are in the majority.

➡ **Clovelly Hotel** A proper neighbourhood pub; most of the punters stroll here from the surrounding streets.

Getting There & Away

➡ **Train** The Eastern Suburbs line heads to Bondi Junction, which is 2.5km from Bondi Beach, 3km from Bronte Beach and 4km from Coogee Beach.

➡ **Bus** For Bondi take bus 333 (express) or 380 via Oxford St, or 389 via Woollahra; all depart from Circular Quay. For Bronte take bus 378 from Railway Sq via Oxford St. For Clovelly take bus 339 from The Rocks via Central and Surry Hills. For Coogee take bus 373 from Circular Quay via Oxford St or bus 372 from Railway Sq via Surry Hills. Various routes start at the Bondi Junction interchange, including 381 and 382 to Bondi Beach, 361 to Tamarama, 360 to Clovelly, and 313, 314 and 353 to Coogee.

➡ **Car** Parking is difficult, especially on weekends – be prepared to park, pay and walk.

TOP SIGHTS
BONDI BEACH

Definitively Sydney, Bondi is one of the world's great beaches: ocean and land collide, the Pacific arrives in great foaming swells and all people are equal, as democratic as sand. It's the closest ocean beach to the city centre (8km away), has consistently good (though crowded) waves, and is great for a rough-and-tumble swim (the average water temperature is a considerate 21°C). If the sea's angry or you have small children in tow, try the saltwater sea baths at either end of the beach. Ice-cream vendors strut the sand in summer.

DON'T MISS...

➡ Bodysurfing between the flags

➡ Bondi Pavilion

➡ A beachside barbecue

➡ Learning to surf

PRACTICALITIES

➡ Map p266

➡ Campbell Pde

➡ ▣380

Surf's Up

The two surf clubs – Bondi and North Bondi – patrol the beach between sets of red-and-yellow flags, positioned to avoid the worst rips and holes. Thousands are rescued from the surf each year (enough to make a TV show about it), so don't become a statistic: swim between the flags. Surfers carve up sandbar breaks at either end of the beach.

Bondi Pavilion

Built in the Mediterranean Georgian Revival style in 1929, **Bondi Pavilion** (Map p266; ☑8362 3400; www.waverley.nsw.gov.au; Queen Elizabeth Dr; ◷9.30am-5.30pm; ▣380) is more a cultural centre than changing shed, although it does have changing rooms, showers and lockers. **Bondi Openair Cinema** (Map p266, ☑Moshtix 1300 438 849, www.bondiopenair.com .au; tickets $22) takes place on the lawn in the summer months, with live bands providing prescreening entertainment. 'The Pav' is also home to a gelato shop, art exhibitions and a plethora of courses and live performances.

Outdoor Facilities

Prefer wheels to fins? There's a **skate ramp** (Map p266) at the beach's southern end. If posing in your budgie smugglers (Speedos) isn't having enough impact, there's an outdoor **workout area** (Map p266) near the North Bondi Surf Club. Coincidentally (or perhaps not), this is the part of the beach where the gay guys hang out. At the beach's northern end there's a grassy spot with coin-operated barbecues. Booze is banned on the beach.

Surf Lessons

North Bondi is a great beach for learning to surf. **Let's Go Surfing** (Map p266; ☑9365 1800; www.letsgosurfing.com.au; 128 Ramsgate Ave), based down the far northern end of the beach, caters to practically everyone, with classes for grommets aged seven to 16 (1½ hours $49), adults (two hours $99, women-only classes available) and private tuition (1½ hours $175). And if you just want to hire gear to hit the waves, it does that too (board and wetsuit one hour/two hours/day/week $25/30/50/150).

Bondi Icebergs

With supreme views of Bondi Beach, **Icebergs** (Map p266; ☑9130 4804; www.icebergs.com .au; 1 Notts Ave; adult/child $5.50/3.50; ◷6.30am-6.30pm Fri-Wed; ▣380) is a Sydney institution. Only hardened winter-swimming fanatics can become fully fledged members, but anyone can pay for a casual entry. Otherwise soak up the views from the Crabbe Hole cafe (p155) or the very swanky Icebergs (p155) restaurant and bar.

◉ SIGHTS

◉ Bondi

BONDI BEACH BEACH
See p151.

**ABORIGINAL ROCK
ENGRAVINGS** ARCHAEOLOGICAL SITE
Map p266 (Bondi Golf Club, 5 Military Rd; 🚌380)
On the cliff-top fairways of Bondi Golf Club, a short walk north from Bondi Beach, you'll find Eora Aboriginal rock engravings (look for the fenced areas about 20m southeast of the enormous chimney, and watch out for flying golf balls). It seems inappropriate by today's standards, but the original carvings were regrooved by Waverley Council in the 1960s to help preserve them. Some of the images are hard to distinguish, though you should be able to make out the marine life and the figure of a man.

BEN BUCKLER POINT LOOKOUT
Map p266 (Ramsgate Ave; 🚌380) Forming the northern tip of the Bondi horseshoe, this point offers wonderful views of the entire beach. The 235-tonne, car-sized rock near the beach's northern tip was spat out of the sea during a storm in 1912. The lookout is at the end of Ramsgate Ave, or you can follow the trail which runs along the rocks from the beach.

◉ Tamarama

TAMARAMA BEACH BEACH
Map p266 (Pacific Ave; 🚌361) Surrounded by high cliffs, Tamarama has a deep tongue of sand with just 80m of shoreline. Diminutive, yes, but ever-present rips make Tamarama the most dangerous patrolled beach in New South Wales; it's often closed to swimmers.

When it earned its nickname 'Glamarama' in the '80s, Tamarama was probably Sydney's gayest beach. Reflecting increasing acceptance, the gay guys have migrated en masse to North Bondi, leaving the huge waves here to the surfers. It's hard to picture now, but between 1887 and 1911 a roller coaster looped out over the water as part of an amusement park.

◉ Bronte

BRONTE BEACH BEACH
(Bronte Rd; 🚌378) A winning family-oriented beach hemmed in by sandstone cliffs and a grassy park, Bronte lays claims to the title of the oldest surf lifesaving club in the world (1903). Contrary to popular belief, the beach is named after Lord Nelson, who doubled as the Duke of Bronte (a place in Sicily), and not the famous literary sorority. There's a kiosk and a changing room attached to the surf club, and outdoor seating near the coin-operated barbecues.

WAVERLEY CEMETERY CEMETERY
Map p267 (www1.waverley.nsw.gov.au/cemetery; St Thomas St; ⊘7am-sunset; 🚌378) Many Sydneysiders would die for these views... and that's the only way they're going to get them. Blanketing the cliff tops between Bronte and Coogee, the white marble gravestones here are dazzling in the sunlight. Eighty-thousand people have been interred here since 1877, including writer Henry Lawson and cricketer Victor Trumper. It's an engrossing (and strangely uncreepy) place to explore, and maybe spot a whale offshore during winter.

◉ Clovelly

CLOVELLY BEACH BEACH
Map p267 (Clovelly Rd; 🚌339) It might seem odd, but this concrete-edged ocean channel is a great place to swim, sunbathe and snorkel. It's safe for the kids, and despite the swell surging into the inlet, underwater visibility is great. A beloved friendly grouper fish lived here for many years until he was speared by a tourist. Bring your goggles, but don't go killing anything...

On the other side of the car park is the entrance to the **Gordons Bay Underwater Nature Trail** (Map p267; www.gordonsbay scubadivingclub.com; Clovelly Road), a 500m underwater chain guiding divers past reefs, sand flats and kelp forests.

◉ Coogee

COOGEE BEACH BEACH
Map p267 (Arden St; 🚌372-373) Bondi without the glitz and the posers, Coogee (locals

START **BONDI BEACH**
END **COOGEE BEACH**
DISTANCE **6KM**
DURATION **TWO TO THREE HOURS**

Neighbourhood Walk
Bondi to Coogee

Arguably Sydney's most famous, most popular and best walk, this coastal path shouldn't be missed. Both ends are well connected to bus routes, as are most points in between should you feel too hot and bothered to continue – although a cooling dip at any of the beaches en route should cure that (pack your swimmers). There's little shade on this track, so make sure you dive into a tub of sunscreen before setting out.

Starting at ❶ **Bondi Beach**, take the stairs up the south end to Notts Ave, passing above the glistening ❷ **Icebergs** pool complex. Step onto the cliff-top trail at the end of Notts Ave.

Walking south, the blustery sandstone cliffs and grinding Pacific Ocean couldn't be more spectacular (watch for dolphins, whales and surfers). Small but perfectly formed ❸ **Tamarama** has a deep reach of sand, totally disproportionate to its width.

Descend from the cliff tops onto ❹ **Bronte Beach** and take a dip or hit a beachy cafe for a coffee, a chunky lunch or a quick snack. Cross the sand and pick up the path on the other side.

Some famous Australians are among the subterranean denizens of the amazing cliff edge ❺ **Waverley Cemetery**. On a clear day this is a prime vantage point for whale watchers.

Duck into the sunbaked Clovelly Bowling Club for a beer or a game of bowls, then breeze past the cockatoos and canoodling lovers in ❻ **Burrows Park** to sheltered ❼ **Clovelly Beach**, a fave with families.

Follow the footpath up through the car park, along Cliffbrook Pde, then down the steps to the upturned dinghies lining ❽ **Gordons Bay**, one of Sydney's best shore-dive spots.

The trail continues past ❾ **Dolphin Point** then lands you smack-bang on glorious ❿ **Coogee Beach**. Swagger into the Coogee Bay Hotel and toast your efforts with a cold lager.

pronounce the double *o* as in the word 'took') has a deep sweep of sand, historic ocean baths and plenty of green space for barbecues and frisbee hurling. Between World Wars, Coogee had an English-style pier, with a 1400-seat theatre and a 600-seat ballroom...until the surf took it.

Offshore, compromising the surf here a little, is craggy Wedding Cake Island, immortalised in a surf-guitar instrumental by Midnight Oil.

At Coogee Beach's northern end below Dolphin Point, **Giles Baths** (Map p267) is what's known as a 'bogey hole' – a semiformal rock pool open to the surging surf. At the beach's southern end, **Ross Jones Memorial Pool** (Map p267) has sand-castle-like concrete turrets.

MCIVERS BATHS
BEACH

Map p267 (Beach St; ☐372-373) Perched against the cliffs south of Coogee Beach is the women-only McIvers Baths. Well screened from passers-by, this spot has been popular for women's bathing since before 1876. Its strictly women-only policy has made it popular with an unlikely mixture of nuns, Muslim women and lesbians. Small children of either gender are permitted.

DOLPHIN POINT
PARK

Map p267 (Baden St; ☐372-373) This grassy tract at Coogee Beach's northern end has superb ocean views and the sea-salty Giles Baths ocean pool. A sobering shrine commemorates the 2002 Bali bombings. Coogee was hit hard by the tragedy, with 20 of the 89 Australians killed coming from hereabouts.

Formerly known as Dunningham Park, its name was changed to honour the six members of the Coogee Dolphins rugby league team who died in the blast.

LOCAL KNOWLEDGE

EASTERN SUBURBS

David Mills, editor of local newspaper, the *Wentworth Courier*, shares his love for his patch.

Why Go Anywhere Else?
When the people of Sydney's south, west or north shore criticise snooty eastern suburbs types for never venturing out of the patch, they don't realise that what they think is a cruel put-down is in fact a badge of honour. The fact is, the hardened eastern suburbanite doesn't go west of the city because there's no need. The best beaches, restaurants, watering holes and outdoor areas: they're all in the east.

Bondi & the Beaches
For me Bondi is distilled in four essential experiences. One: breakfast at the Bondi Trattoria, which pulls a local crowd despite its prominence on the Campbell Pde tourist trap. Two: the Bondi to Bronte walk, invigorating at all times of the year, but especially during whale-watching season or the annual Sculptures by the Sea exhibition. Three: a drink upstairs at **Ravesi's** (Map p266; www.ravesis.com.au; cnr Campbell Pde & Hall St; ⊙10am-1am Mon-Sat, to midnight Sun) to watch the local hipsters at play. And four: the beach itself.

But the east offers so much more than Bondi. Try the Hermitage Walk from Rose Bay to Vaucluse, one of Sydney's most underrated attractions, or spend a few hours at Parsley Bay (p73), a place I like to think of as the picnic spot from central casting.

For Food?
Surry Hills is where Sydney goes for dinner, and a simple rule of thumb is to stick to the restaurants with one word titles: Porteño (p121); Bodega (p122) and Bentley (p122).

And for a Drink?
The Golden Sheaf (p79) at Double Bay, or a Sunday-afternoon session at the Beresford (p125) in Darlinghurst. Spend a few hours with the locals in these places and that reluctance to leave the east starts making a lot of sense.

MAROUBRA

The last major beach before you hit Botany Bay, 'the Bra' is Bondi's match in the waves department, but its suburban location provides immunity from Bondi's more pretentious trappings. The notorious Bra Boys gang (documented in the movie *Bra Boys* by Sunny Abberton) remains entrenched in the community psyche, but don't let it keep you out of the surf. Hidden within the cliffs, 500m north of the beach, **Mahon Pool** (Marine Pde; 376-377) is an idyllic rock pool where the surf crashes over the edges at high tide. It's quite possibly Sydney's most beautiful bogey hole.

EATING

The Eastern Beaches restaurants are as eclectic and unpredictable as the surf. Bondi offers everything from chin-up, tits-out glamour to funky surfie cafes, while Bronte is a top spot for brunch (spot migrating whales over your flat white). For the Ritz of food halls, check out Westfield Bondi Junction – and while you're there, stock up on snags for chucking on the coast's well-maintained coin-operated beachside barbecues. If that all sounds like too much hassle, snaffle some fish and chips on the sand.

Bondi

ICEBERGS DINING ROOM ITALIAN $$$

Map p266 (9365 9000; www.idrb.com; 1 Notts Ave; mains $36-54; lunch & dinner Tue-Sun; 380) Poised above the famous Icebergs swimming pool, Icebergs' views sweep across the Bondi Beach arc to the sea. Jacketed, bow-tied waiters deliver fresh seafood and steaks cooked with élan.

HARRY'S ESPRESSO BAR CAFE $

Map p266 (136 Wairoa Ave; mains $7-14; breakfast & lunch; 380) Harry's game is coffee and he's winning down this end of the beach. For breakfast, try a 'smashed croissant' – a croissant that's been squashed and then slathered with ricotta, blueberries, almonds and mint. Everything comes with a side order of graffiti art.

NORTH BONDI ITALIAN FOOD ITALIAN $$

Map p266 (www.idrb.com; 118-120 Ramsgate Ave; mains $18-34; lunch Fri-Sun, dinner daily; 380) As noisy as it is fashionable, this terrific trattoria in the North Bondi RSL building has a casual vibe, simple but *molto delizioso* food and a democratic no-booking policy. Come early to snaffle a table overlooking the beach.

POMPEI'S ITALIAN $$

Map p266 (9365 1233; www.pompeis.com.au; 126-130 Roscoe St; mains $19-33; lunch Fri-Sun, dinner Tue-Sun; 380) The pizza here is among the best in Sydney, but it's the northern Italian dishes whipped up by explosive expat George Pompei that are really special. Try the handmade ravioli stuffed with spinach, ricotta and nutmeg, and leave some space for a scoop of white peach gelato.

CRABBE HOLE CAFE $

Map p266 (Lower Level, 1 Notts Ave; mains $10-12; 7am-5pm; 380) Tucked within the Icebergs pool complex (there's no need to pay admission if you're only eating), this crab-sized nook is the kind of place locals would prefer wasn't in this book. Toasted sandwiches, muesli and banana bread star on the small but perfectly formed menu; coffees are automatic double shots unless you wimp out. The views are blissful.

EARTH FOOD STORE CAFE, DELI $

Map p266 (9365 5098; www.earthfoodstore.com.au; 81 Gould St; mains $4-16; 6.30am-5.30pm; 380) An organic cafe, deli and naturopath under one roof, this eatery serves up a healthy range of salads, quiches, sushi, panini and tennis-ball-sized felafel balls, plus takeaway nuts, herbs, spices, teas, fruit and veg. We're so glad they don't serve any of that awful Martian food; we hear the food miles are astronomical. Counter seating is limited.

BONDI TRATTORIA ITALIAN $$

Map p266 (9365 4303; www.bonditrattoria.com.au; 34 Campbell Pde; breakfast $9-21, lunch $16-24, dinner $19-35; 8am-late; 380) For a Bondi brunch, you can't go past the trusty 'Trat', as it's known in these parts. Tables spill out onto Campbell Pde for those hungry for beach views, while inside there's a trad trat feel: wooden tables and the obligatory Tuscan mural and black-and-white photography. As the day progresses, pizza, pasta and risotto dominate the menu.

WORTH A DETOUR

CRONULLA

Cronulla is a beachy surf suburb south of Botany Bay, its long surf beach stretching beyond the dunes to the Botany Bay refineries. It can be an edgy place (captured brilliantly in the '70s teen cult novel *Puberty Blues*), with dingy fish-and-chip shops, insomnious teens and a ragged sense of impending 'something', which in 2005 erupted into racial violence. That said the beach is beautiful, with a pleasant promenade, and it's easy to reach by train from Bondi Junction.

Spread out along the street facing the beach, **Northies** (www.northies.com.au; cnr Kingsway & Elouera Rd) is the main drinking hole, offering a lively roster of sports, DJs, bands and quiz nights.

On the main shopping strip, look for the **Best Little Bookshop in Town** (www .bestlittlebookshopintown.com.au; 136 Cronulla St); it lives up to its name with passionate, knowledgable staff and an excellent selection of new and secondhand books.

SABBABA
ISRAELI $

Map p266 (☑9365 7500; www.sabbaba.com.au; 82 Hall St; mains $9-17; ☺11am-10pm; ☑; ☑389) There are more boardshorts than black coats on view at this Middle Eastern joint in Bondi's main Hassidic strip. Falafels served in pitta are a bargain, and there's a sticky-sweet array of baklava to finish off with. There are branches in Westfield Sydney and Newtown.

THE SHOP
CAFE, BAR $

Map p266 (www.theshopbondi.com; 78 Curlewis St; mains $9-15; ☺6am-10pm; ☑389) Operating as both a cafe and a wine bar (with a name that reflects neither), this tiny space serves cooked breakfasts, pastries, sandwiches, salads and a tapas menu from 4pm. It's a bit self-consciously cool, squiggly graffiti and all, but the food and coffee are excellent.

✖ Bronte

TOP CHOICE THREE BLUE DUCKS
CAFE $$

Map p267 (www.threeblueducks.com; 143 Macpherson St; breakfast $12-19, lunch $18-26, dinner shared plates $17; ☺breakfast & lunch Tue-Sun, dinner Thu-Sat; ☑378) These ducks are a fair waddle from the water but that doesn't stop queues forming outside the graffiti-covered walls for weekend breakfasts. The adventurous owners have a strong commitment to using local, organic and fair-trade food whenever possible.

✖ Clovelly

CLODELI
CAFE, DELI $

Map p267 (☑9664 1885; www.clodeli.com; 210 Clovelly Rd; mains $11-15; ☺breakfast & lunch;

☑339) Everyone in Clovelly, regardless of age or gender, seems to be pushing a pram – the footpath out the front of Clodeli is a preschool parking lot. Inside it's all about big breakfasts and takeaway deli delights – and if you ask for a strong coffee, the hyper-efficient staff won't hold back. The massive mezze platter makes a terrific shared lunch.

🍷 DRINKING & NIGHTLIFE

If you're a backpacker from anywhere cold and northern hemispheric, it makes sense that you'd want to cram as much beery beach time into your Sydney holiday as possible. You'll find plenty of company in the backpacker haunts along the coast, plus a few slick credit-card-maxing cocktail joints as well.

🍷 Bondi

NORTH BONDI RSL
BAR

Map p266 (☑9130 3152; www.northbondirsl .com.au; 120 Ramsgate Ave; ☺noon-midnight Mon-Thu, 10am-midnight Fri-Sun; ☑380, 389) This Returned & Services League bar ain't fancy, but with views no one can afford and drinks that everyone can, who cares? Bring ID, as nonmembers need to prove that they live at least 5km away. There are live bands most Saturdays, trivia on Tuesdays and cheap steaks on Wednesdays.

CORNER HOUSE
BAR

Map p266 (www.thecornerhouse.com.au; 281 Bondi Rd; ☺5pm-midnight Mon-Fri, 3pm-midnight

Sat, 3-10pm Sun; ☐380) Three spaces – the Kitchen (wine bar), Dining Room (restaurant) and Living Room (bar) – make this a happy house, especially once you hit the cocktails.

ICEBERGS BAR
BAR

Map p266 (✆9365 9000; www.idrb.com; 1 Notts Ave; ☉noon-midnight Tue-Sat, to 10pm Sun; ☐380) Most folks come here to eat next door, but the ooh-la-la Icebergs bar is a brilliant place for a drink. The hanging chairs, colourful sofas and ritzy cocktails are fab, but the view looking north across Bondi Beach is the absolute killer. Dress sexy and make sure your bank account is up to the strain.

BEACH ROAD HOTEL
PUB, DJ

Map p266 (✆9130 7247; www.beachroadbondi .com.au; 71 Beach Rd, ☉10am-1am Mon-Sat, to 10pm Sun; ☐389) Weekends at this big boxy pub are a boisterous multilevel alcoholiday, with Bondi types (bronzed, buff and brooding) and woozy out-of-towners playing pool, drinking beer and digging live bands and DJs.

Clovelly

CLOVELLY HOTEL
PUB, DJ

Map p267 (✆9665 1214; www.clovellyhotel.com .au; 381 Clovelly Rd; ☉10am-midnight Mon-Fri, 8am-midnight Sat, 8am-10pm Sun; ☐339) A recently renovated megalith on the hill above Clovelly Beach, this pub has a shady terrace and water views – perfect for post-beach Sunday-afternoon bevvies and the sleepy sounds of acoustic twangers. Singer-songwriters strum their stuff on Thursdays and DJs crank it up on weekends.

Coogee

AQUARIUM
BAR, DJ

Map p267 (✆9664 2900; www.beachpalace hotel.com.au; 169 Dolphin St; ☉4pm-midnight Fri, noon-midnight Sat & Sun; ☐372-374) On the top floor of the historic Beach Palace Hotel (1887), a massive booze barn at the northern end of Coogee Beach, Aquarium is a good place to be on a Sunday afternoon. The views from the terrace are awesome; DJs and live acoustic acts provide the theme tunes.

COOGEE BAY HOTEL
PUB, CLUB

Map p267 (✆9665 0000; www.coogeebayhotel .com.au; cnr Coogee Bay Rd & Arden St; ☉9am-3am Mon-Thu, to 5am Fri & Sat, to midnight Sun; ☐372-374) This rambling, rowdy complex still packs in the backpackers for live music, open-mic nights, comedy and big-screen sports in the beaut beer garden, sports bar and Selina's nightclub. Sit on a stool in the window overlooking the beach and sip on a cold one.

 # SHOPPING

Surf shops are the mainstay of the beach shopping scene. Up in Bondi Junction, serious shoppers from all over the city flock to Westfield, the mall-to-end-all-malls.

WESTFIELD BONDI JUNCTION
MALL

(✆9947 8000; www.westfield.com.au; 500 Oxford St; ☉9.30am-6pm Fri-Wed, to 9pm Thu; ☒Bondi Junction) Vast. That's the only word to describe Australia's flashest shopping mall. Expect to get lost; the space-time continuum does funny things as you explore the 438 stores set over six levels. It's even worse in the underground car park.

Local fashion outlets include branches of Calibre (p146), Oxford (p116), Sass & Bide (p146), Zimmermann (p145) and Leona Edmiston (p146), alongside the big internationals such as Hugo Boss, Armani and G Star. Australia's two big department stores – Myer (p96) and David Jones (p96) – do battle here, along with Jurlique (p97), Mecca Cosmetica (p145) and RM WIlliams (p96). Plus there are cinemas, bars, supermarkets, food courts...

SURFECTION
CLOTHING, ACCESSORIES

Map p266 (www.surfection.com; 31 Hall St; ☐380) Selling boardies, bikinis, sunnies, shoes, watches, tees...even luggage – Bondi's coolest surf store has just everything the stylish surfer's heart might desire (except for spray-in hair bleacher; you'll still need to take your paper bag to a discreet chemist for that). Old boards hang from the ceiling, while new boards fill up the racks (JS, Al Merrick, Channel Islands, Takayama).

BONDI MARKETS
MARKETS

Map p266 (✆9315 8988; www.bondimarkets .com.au; Bondi Beach Public School, Campbell

Pde; ⊙9am-1pm Sat, 10am-4pm Sun; ☐380)
The kids are at the beach on Sunday while
their school fills up with Bondi characters
rummaging through tie-dyed secondhand
clothes, books, beads, earrings, aroma-
therapy oils, candles, old records and more.
There's a farmers' market on Saturdays.

GERTRUDE & ALICE   BOOKS
Map p266 (☑9130 5155; www.gertrudeandalice
.com.au; 46 Hall St; ⊙7.30am-10pm; ☐380) This
shambolic secondhand bookshop and cafe
is so un-Bondi: there's not a model or a surfer in sight. Locals, students and academics
hang out reading, drinking coffee and acting like Americans in Paris. Join them for
some lentil stew and theological discourse
around communal tables.

RIP CURL   CLOTHING, ACCESSORIES
Map p266 (☑9130 2660; www.ripcurl.com; 82
Campbell Pde; ⊙9am-6pm; ☐380) The quin-
tessential Aussie surf shop, Rip Curl began
down south in Victoria, but drops in perfectly overlooking the Bondi shore breaks.
Beyond huge posters of burly surfer dudes
and beach babes, you'll find bikinis, watches, thongs, boardshorts, wetsuits, sunglasses, hats, T-shirts and (surprise!) surfboards.

KEMENYS   WINE
(☑13 88 81; www.kemenys.com.au; 137-147 Bondi
Rd; ⊙8am-9pm; ☐380) A short walk up (and
then a wobble down) the hill from Bondi
Beach, Kemenys occupies a large soft spot
in the hearts, minds and livers of all Bondi
locals. Proffering the best local and imported wines, ales and spirits to the surf
set since 1960, it's staunchly resisted being
taken over by the big chains. Respect.

🏃 SPORTS & ACTIVITIES

WYLIES BATHS   SWIMMING
Map p267 (☑9665 2838; www.wylies.com.au;
Neptune St; adult/child $4.50/1; ⊙7am-7pm
Oct-Mar, to 5pm Apr-Sep; ☐373-374) On the
rocky coast, south of Coogee Beach, this

WORTH A DETOUR

KITEBOARDING
Sydney Harbour's too busy and the
ocean's too rough, but Botany Bay is
just right for strapping yourself into
a parachute and going surfing! Brush
up your aqua-aeronautic skills with a
Kitepower (☑9529 6894; www.kite
power.com.au; 302 The Grand Pde, Sans
Souci; 2hr $200; ⊙9am-5.30pm Mon-Sat,
10am-2pm Sun; ☐303) lesson.

superb seawater pool (1907) is more target-
ed to swimmers than general beachgoers.
After your swim, take a yoga class ($15), en-
joy a massage or have a coffee at the kiosk,
which has magnificent ocean views.

DIVE CENTRE BONDI   DIVING
(☑9369 3855; www.divebondi.com.au; 198 Bondi
Rd; ⊙9am-6pm Mon-Fri, 7.30am-6pm Sat & Sun;
☐380) This Professional Association of Diving Instructors (PADI) five-star centre offers
weekly learn-to-dive courses (three days
$425), plus various more advanced boat and
shore dives around Sydney.

CLOVELLY BOWLING CLUB   BOWLING
Map p267 (☑9665 1507; www.clovellybowling
club.com.au; cnr Ocean & Boundary Sts; ⊙3.30-
6.30pm Mon-Thu, noon-6.30pm Fri-Sun; ☐360)
A sunbaked square of cliff-top grass, this
lawn-bowls club offers sensational ocean
views and something of a hipster scene on
weekends. Drop in for a thirst-quenching
lager as you traverse the Bondi to Coogee walk. If you want to bowl, it'll cost you
$12 (be sure to book). Free coaching for
beginners.

BONDI GOLF CLUB   GOLF
Map p266 (☑9130 3170; www.bondigolf.com.au;
5 Military Rd; 9/18 holes $22/27; ⊙7.30am-5pm
Mon-Fri, 11.30am-5pm Sat & Sun; ☐380) It's not
much of a course (nine holes, par 28) but the
views are awesome and hazards can include
Aboriginal rock engravings and the Pacific
Ocean. Try not to hit any passing surfers or
whales. Club hire $20.

Manly

MANLY | BALGOWLAH HEIGHTS | CLONTARF | WARRINGAH

Neighbourhood Top Five

1 Splashing about on long, lovely **Manly Beach** (p161), Sydney's second-most famous stretch of golden sand. Fully embrace the local lifestyle by learning to surf.

2 Hopping between headlands and beaches along the beautiful Manly Scenic Walkway (p162).

3 Exploring the wild, rugged surrounds of the **North Head** (p161) section of Sydney Harbour National Park.

4 Hiring a kayak and paddling to isolated, bush-lined **Store Beach** (p161).

5 Delving into the sad and spooky history of **Q Station** (p161) on a guided tour.

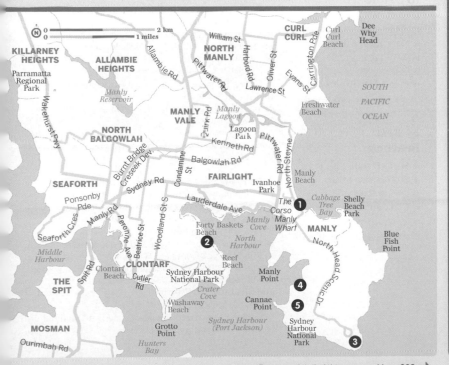

For more detail of this area see Map p268 ➡

Lonely Planet's Top Tip

If you don't have a spare four hours to traverse North Head on foot, hire a bike. Otherwise, rent a kayak and paddle between the secluded bays facing the harbour. Beautiful little Store Beach can only be reached from the water.

Best Places to Eat

➡ Pilu at Freshwater (p164)

➡ Barefoot Coffee Traders/ Adriano Zumbo (p163)

➡ Pilu Kiosk (p164)

➡ Belgrave Cartel (p163)

➡ Hugos Manly (p164)

For reviews, see p163 ➡

☕ Best Places to Drink

➡ Manly Wharf Hotel (p164)

➡ Hotel Steyne (p165)

➡ Bavarian Bier Café (p165)

➡ Hugos Manly (p164)

For reviews, see p164 ➡

◉ Best Beaches

➡ Manly Beach (p161)

➡ Store Beach (p161)

➡ Freshwater (p163)

➡ Curl Curl (p163)

➡ Manly Cove (p161)

For reviews, see p161 ➡

Explore: Manly

Laid-back Manly clings to a narrow isthmus between ocean and harbour beaches abutting North Head, Sydney Harbour's northern gatepost. With its shaggy surfers, dusty labourers and relaxed locals, it makes for a refreshing change from the stuffier harbour suburbs nearby.

Manly's unusual name comes from Governor Phillip's description of the physique of the native people he met here; his Excellency was clearly indulging in an early example of the very Sydney habit of body-scrutinising.

The Corso connects Manly's ocean and harbour beaches; here surf shops, burger joints, juice bars, pubs and lousy coffee houses are plentiful. The refurbished Manly Wharf has classier pubs and restaurants, and there's a much better set of cafes scattered around the back streets.

In summer, allocate a day to walking and splashing about. In winter, it's worth heading over for a quick visit, if only for Sydney's best ferry journey. Don't bother staying after dark – there are better eateries and bars elsewhere.

Local Life

➡ **Surfing** A fair proportion of Manly residents live to surf, squeezing in a few hours riding the swell before or after work. The beach's three surf lifesaving clubs are hubs of community life.

➡ **Manly-Warringah Sea Eagles** The local rugby league team are neighbourhood heroes, having won the premiership twice in the last decade. Home games are played further north at Brookvale, but Manly's pubs are lively places to watch matches.

➡ **Cafes** They may not be as self-consciously hip as they are in Surry Hills and Newtown, but Manly has its own dedicated band of baristas bringing quality coffee to those in the know.

Getting There & Away

➡ **Ferry** Frequent ferry services head directly from Circular Quay to Manly, making this by far the best (and most scenic) way to get to Manly. Regular Sydney Ferries take 30 minutes for the journey while fast ferries take just 18 minutes.

➡ **Bus** PrePay express bus E70 takes 37 minutes to get to Manly Wharf from near Wynyard Station, while regular bus 171 takes about an hour. From Manly Wharf, useful routes include 132 and 171 (Balgowlah Heights and Clontarf), 135 (North Head), 139 (Freshwater and Curl Curl) and 140, 143 and 144 (Spit Bridge).

➡ **Parking** Street parking is restricted and metered in central Manly and near the beach.

◉ SIGHTS

◉ Manly

MANLY BEACH
BEACH

Map p268 (🚢Manly) Manly Beach stretches for nearly two golden kilometres, lined by Norfolk Island pines and scrappy mid-rise apartment blocks. The southern end of the beach, nearest The Corso, is known as South Steyne, with North Steyne in the centre and Queenscliff at the northern end; each has its own surf lifesaving club.

NORTH HEAD
OUTDOORS

(North Head Scenic Dr; 🚌135) About 3km south of Manly, spectacular, chunky North Head offers dramatic cliffs, lookouts and sweeping views of the ocean, the harbour and the city; hire a bike and go exploring. A 9km, four-hour walking loop is outlined in the Manly Scenic Walkway brochure, available from the visitor centre. Also here is the Q Station.

North Head is believed to have been used as a ceremonial site by the native Camaraigal people. These days, most of the headland is part of Sydney Harbour National Park.

FREE Q STATION
HISTORIC BUILDING

(📞9466 1500; www.qstation.com.au; 1 North Head Scenic Dr; ⊙museum 10am-2pm Mon-Thu, 10am-2pm & 5-8pm Fri, 10am-8pm Sat, 10am-4pm Sun; 🚌135) The eerie-but-elegant Manly Quarantine Station was used to isolate newly arrived epidemic-disease carriers between 1828 and 1972 in an attempt to limit the spread of cholera, smallpox and bubonic plague. It was then used until 1984 to house illegal immigrants. These days the 'Q Station' has been reborn as a tourist destination, with a museum, B&B accommodation, a ritzy restaurant and a whole swag of tour options.

The 2½-hour **Adult Ghost Tour** (Wed-Fri & Sun $44, Sat $52; ⊙8pm Wed-Sun) rattles some skeletons; the two-hour **Family Ghosty** (adult/child $34/26; ⊙7pm Fri & Sat) tour softens some of the horrors. The two-hour **Quarantine Station Story Tour** (adult/child/concession $35/25/29; ⊙3pm Sat & Sun) highlights the personal stories of those who worked and waited here, while the 45-minute **Wharf Wander** (Mon-Fri adult/child $15/12, Sat & Sun $18/14; ⊙11am daily, plus 1pm Sat & Sun) is a truncated version for those short on time. Bookings are required for all tours.

STORE BEACH
BEACH

(⊙dawn-dusk) A hidden jewel on North Head, magical Store Beach can only be reached by kayak or boat. It's a fairy-penguin breeding ground, so access is prohibited from dusk, when the birds waddle in.

MANLY COVE
BEACH

Map p268 (🚢Manly) Split in two by Manly Wharf, this sheltered enclave has shark nets and calm water, making it a popular choice for families with toddlers. Despite the busy location, the clear waters have plenty of appeal.

FAIRY BOWER BEACH
BEACH

(Bower Lane; 🚌135) Indulge your mermaid fantasies (the more seemly ones at least) in this pretty triangular ocean pool set into the rocky shoreline. The life-size sea nymphs of Helen Leete's bronze sculpture *Oceanides* (1997) stand on the edge, washed by the surf. Fairy Bower is best reached by the promenade heading around Manly Beach's south headland.

OCEANWORLD
AQUARIUM

Map p268 (📞8251 7877; www.oceanworld.com.au; West Esplanade; adult/child/family $20/10/48; ⊙10am-5.30pm, last admission 4.45pm; 🚢Manly) This ain't the place to come if you're on your way to Manly Beach for a surf. Inside this daggy-looking 1980s building are underwater glass tubes through which you become alarmingly intimate with 3m sharks. Reckon they're not hungry? **Shark Dive Xtreme** (📞8251 7878; introductory/certified dives $270/195) takes you into their world... Crocodiles and large turtles also put in an appearance.

On weekends and school holidays, kids aged five to 13 can snorkel around a tropical reef ($75 including entry).

FREE MANLY ART GALLERY & MUSEUM
GALLERY, MUSEUM

Map p268 (📞9976 1420; www.manly.nsw.gov.au; West Esplanade; ⊙10am-5pm Tue-Sun; 🚢Manly) A short stroll from Manly Wharf is this passionately managed community gallery, maintaining a local focus with exhibits of surfcraft, camp swimwear and beachy bits-and-pieces. There's also a ceramics gallery, and lots of old Manly photos to peer at.

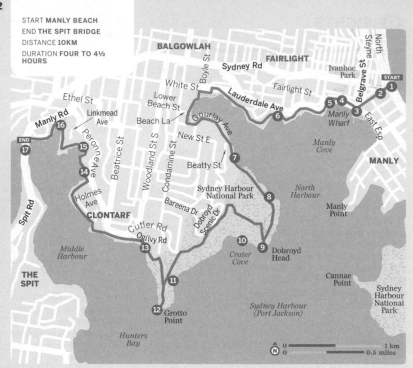

START **MANLY BEACH**
END **THE SPIT BRIDGE**
DISTANCE **10KM**
DURATION **FOUR TO 4½ HOURS**

Neighbourhood Walk
Manly Scenic Walkway

This epic walk traces the coast west from Manly past million-dollar harbour-view properties and then through a rugged 2½ km section of Sydney Harbour National Park that remains much as it was when the First Fleet sailed in. There aren't any eateries en route, so fortify yourself in Manly beforehand or stock up for a picnic. Make sure you carry plenty of water, slop on some sunscreen, slap on a hat and wear sturdy shoes.

Check the surf at **1 Manly Beach** then cruise down **2 The Corso** to the **3 visitor information centre** where you can pick up a walk brochure with a detailed map.

Head down to **4 Manly Cove** and pick up the path near **5 Oceanworld**. After 700m you'll reach **6 Fairlight Beach**, where you can scan the view through the heads. Yachts tug at their moorings as you trace the North Harbour inlet and after 2km you'll come to **7 Forty Baskets Beach**. Kookaburras cackle as you enter the national park and approach **8 Reef Beach**.

The track becomes steep, sandy and rocky further into the park – keep an eye out for wildflowers, spiders in bottlebrush trees and fat goannas sunning themselves. The views from **9 Dobroyd Head** are unforgettable. Check out the deserted 1930s sea shacks at the base of **10 Crater Cove** cliff, and **11 Aboriginal rock carvings** on an unsigned ledge left of the track before the turnoff to **12 Grotto Point Lighthouse**.

Becalmed **13 Castle Rock Beach** is at the western end of the national park. From here the path winds around the rear of houses to **14 Clontarf Beach**. **15 Sandy Bay** follows and then **16 Fisher Bay** before you reach **17 Spit Bridge**. From the southern end of the bridge you can either bus it back to Manly (buses 140, 143 or 144) or into the city (176 to 180).

THE CORSO
STREET

Map p268 (🚢Manly) The quickest route from the Manly ferry terminal to Manly's ocean beach is along The Corso, a part-pedestrian mall lined with surf shops, pubs and sushi bars. Kids splash around in the fountains and spaced-out surfies shuffle back to the ferry after a hard day carving up the swell.

If you need some surfboard wax, you're in the right place, but don't expect to see much Sydney bling here – the mood is suburban and relaxed.

⊙ Balgowlah Heights

REEF BEACH
BEACH

(Beatty St, Balgowlah Heights; 🚌171) Despite what you might have heard, this little cove on Manly Scenic Walkway is neither nude nor full of dudes; the Manly Council put pay to that in 1993. Now it's often deserted.

FORTY BASKETS BEACH
BEACH

(Beatty St, Begowlah Heights; 🚌171) On the Manly Scenic Walkway, just before heading into the Begowlah Heights section of Sydney Harbour National Park. The picnic area is cut off at high tide.

⊙ Clontarf

WASHAWAY BEACH
BEACH

(Cutler Rd, Clontarf; 🚌171) Rugged and beautiful, Washaway is a secluded little spot within Sydney Harbour National Park, near Grotto Point on the Manly Scenic Walkway.

CLONTARF BEACH
BEACH

(Sandy Bay Rd, Clontarf; 🚌132) A low-lapping elbow of sand facing the Spit Bridge that's popular with families, with grassy picnic areas.

⊙ Warringah

FRESHWATER
BEACH

(Moore Rd; 🚌139) This discreet sandy bay just north of Manly has a cool ocean pool and plenty of teenagers. Good for learner surfers.

CURL CURL
BEACH

(Carrington Pde; 🚌139) Attracting a mix of family groups and experienced surfers, Curl Curl is a larger beach north of Freshwater with rocky saltwater pools at each end, a swampy lagoon and curly waves.

WORTH A DETOUR

LANE COVE NATIONAL PARK

This 601-hectare **park** (www.environ ment.nsw.gov.au; Lady Game Dr; per car $7; ⊙9am-6pm; 🚉North Ryde), surrounded by North Shore suburbia, is a great place to stretch out on some mid-sized bushwalks. It's home to dozens of critters, including some endangered owls and toads. If you visit in spring, the water dragons will be getting horny and the native orchids and lilies will be flowering. There's a boat shed on Lane Cove River that rents out row boats and kayaks, but swimming isn't a good idea. You can also cycle and camp, and some sections are wheelchair accessible

✖ EATING

Sandy Manly has dozens of fairly average eateries with a couple of starlets in their midst. Local surf-hippies guarantee a sprinkling of organic and vegetarian options, too.

✖ Manly

BAREFOOT COFFEE TRADERS
CAFE $

Map p268 (📞0412 328 810; www.barefootcoffee. com.au; 18a Whistler St; items $3-6; ⊙breakfast & lunch; 🚢Manly) Run by surfer lads serving fair-trade organic coffee from a bathroom-sized shop, Barefoot heralds a new wave of Manly cool. Food is limited but the Belgian chocolate waffles go magically well with macchiato. Opposite the wharf, there's a second **cafe** (Map p268; 40 East Esplanade; ⊙breakfast & lunch), which works symbiotically with its neighbour **Adriano Zumbo** (Map p268; cnr East Esplanade & Wentworth St, Manly; ⊙7am-7pm Mon-Fri, 8am-5.30pm Sat & Sun); grab some sublime patisserie and devour it over a coffee.

BELGRAVE CARTEL
CAFE $

Map p268 (6 Belgrave St; mains $5-13; ⊙breakfast & lunch daily, dinner Thu; 🚢Manly) Little Cartel may be grungy but it's nowhere as sinister as it sounds; the only drug being peddled here is pure, unadulterated caffeine. 'Mismatched everything' seems to be the design brief and the food is restricted to the likes of paninis and toasted sandwiches (called

ROSE SEIDLER HOUSE

Iconic Sydney architect Harry Seidler designed this modest 50-sq-metre house (1950) for his mother and father, Rose and Max. **Rose Seidler House** (☑9989 8020; www.hht.nsw. gov.au; 71 Clissold Rd; adult/child/family $8/4/17; ⊙10am-5pm Sun; ☐575) is a modernist gem, with free-flowing open spaces, retro colour schemes and hip furnishings. Every year the Historic Houses Trust holds a Fifties Fair (usually in August) on the grounds. The house is around 22km northwest of Manly and a fair hike from Wahroonga train station (approximately 40 minutes; around 3km) – the bus gets closer but you're better off with your own wheels.

jaffles in these parts), but it's certainly tasty and served with a smile.

HUGOS MANLY
ITALIAN $$

Map p268 (☑8116 8555; www.hugos.com.au; Manly Wharf; pizzas $20-28, mains $32-38; ⊙lunch & dinner; ☑Manly) Occupying an altogether more glamorous location than its Kings Cross parent, Hugos Manly serves the same acclaimed pizzas but tops them with harbour views. A dedicated crew concocts cocktails, or just slide in for a cold beer.

CHAT THAI
THAI $

Map p268 (☑9976 2939; www.chatthai.com. au; Manly Wharf; mains $10-19; ⊙lunch & dinner; ☑Manly) Set inside Manly Wharf, this branch of the Thaitown favourite (p92) misses out on the harbour views but delivers on flavour.

PURE WHOLEFOODS
VEGETARIAN $

Map p268 (☑8966 9377; www.purewholefoods. com.au; 10 Darley Rd; mains $10-15; ⊙breakfast & lunch; ☑; ☑Manly) This wholefood minimart has a great little street cafe serving organic vegetarian goodies, including flavoursome flans, salads, nori rolls, cakes, cookies, wraps, burgers and smoothies. Vegan, sugar-free, gluten-free and dairy-free purists are also catered for.

BENBRY BURGERS
BURGERS $

Map p268 (www.benbryburgers.com.au; 5 Sydney Rd; burgers $8-14; ⊙lunch & dinner; ☑Manly) A popular takeaway assembling juicy burgers for beach bums and backpackers.

✗ Warringah

PILU AT FRESHWATER
ITALIAN $$$

(☑9938 3331; www.piluatfreshwater.com.au; Moore Rd; mains $42-45; ⊙lunch Tue-Sun, dinner Tue-Sat; ☐139) Housed within a heritage-listed beach house overlooking the ocean, this multi-award-winning Sardinian restaurant serves specialities such as oven-roasted suckling pig and traditional flatbread. Your best bet is to plump for the tasting menu ($115) and thereby eliminate any possible order envy. Freshwater is just north of Manly.

PILU KIOSK
CAFE $

(www.piluatfreshwater.com.au; Moore Rd; breakfast $6-9, lunch $11-13; ⊙7am-3pm; ☐139) It may be attached to the pricy Pilu restaurant, but this beach cafe is an altogether more relaxed affair. Boardshorts and thongs (flip-flops) are the norm – if you're wearing a shirt, that's a bonus. The coffee is great and the suckling-pig paninis are legendary.

🍷 DRINKING & NIGHTLIFE

Manly has a sandy party scene revolving around The Corso and Manly Wharf.

MANLY WHARF HOTEL
PUB

Map p268 (☑9977 1266; www.manlywharfhotel. com.au; Manly Wharf; ⊙11.30am-midnight Mon-Sat, 11am-10pm Sun; ☑Manly) Harking back to 1950s design (all feature walls are bamboo and stone), the Manly Wharf Hotel is perfect for sunny afternoon beers. Tuck away a few schooners after a hard day in the surf, then pour yourself onto the ferry. Sports games draw a crowd and DJs liven up Sunday afternoons. Great pub food, too, with specials throughout the week.

HOTEL STEYNE
PUB

Map p268 (☑9977 4977; www.steynehotel.com.au; 75 The Corso; ☺9am-3am Mon-Sat, 9am-midnight Sun; ☺Manly) Boasting numerous bars over two levels, this landmark pub accommodates everyone from sporty bogans to clubby kids to families. The internal courtyard isn't flash (people still smoke here!), but the rooftop bar more than makes up for it with wicked views over the beach. Live bands and DJs entertain.

BAVARIAN BIER CAFÉ
BEER HALL

Map p268 (www.bavarianbiercafe.com; Manly Wharf; ☺11am-midnight Mon-Fri, 9am-midnight Sat & Sun; ☺Manly) Transplanted from York St (p94) to the beach, the Bavarian offers 10 brews on taps and 10 more imported beers by the bottle.

🏃 SPORTS & ACTIVITIES

MANLY SURF SCHOOL
SURFING

Map p268 (☑9977 6977; www.manlysurfschool.com; North Steyne Surf Club; adult/child $60/50; ☺Manly) Offers two-hour surf lessons year-round at Manly, Collaroy, Dee Why or Palm Beach. Also runs surf safaris up to the Northern Beaches, including two lessons, lunch, gear and city pick-ups ($100).

MANLY KAYAK CENTRE
KAYAKING

Map p268 (☑1300 529 257; www.manlykayakcentre.com.au; West Esplanade; 1/2/8hr from $20/35/70; ☺9am-6pm Dec-Feb, reduced hours Mar-Nov; ☺Manly) As long as you can swim, you can hire a kayak or paddle board from this stand near Oceanworld (with a second stand near Manly Wharf Hotel). You'll be provided with a life jacket, paddling instruction and tips on secluded beaches to visit. Three-hour kayak tours cost $89.

🌿 MANLY BIKE TOURS
CYCLING

Map p268 (☑8005 7368; www.manlybiketours.com.au; 54 West Promenade; hire per hr/day from $14/28; ☺9am-6pm; ☺Manly) Hires bikes and runs daily two-hour bike tours around Manly (10.30am, $89, bookings essential).

DIVE CENTRE MANLY
DIVING

Map p268 (☑9977 4355; www.divesydney.com.au; 10 Belgrave St; ☺9am-6pm; ☺Manly) One of the largest dive shops in Sydney, offering shore and boat dives. A three-day learn-to-dive PADI adventure costs $395. Hire snorkelling/dive gear for $25/70 per day.

🌿 ECOTREASURES
TOUR, SNORKELLING

(☑0415 121 648; www.ecotreasures.com.au) Small group tours include *Manly Snorkel Walk & Talk* (90 minutes, adult/child $45/30) and longer excursions to the Northern Beaches and Ku-ring-gai Chase National Park, including Aboriginal Heritage Tours lead by indigenous guides.

PRO DIVE
DIVING

(☑9977 5966; www.prodivesydneymanly.com; 169 Pittwater Rd; ☺9am-7pm; ☺151) This outfit offers everything from introductory Discover Scuba dives (from $147) to three-day open-water courses (from $297).

DRIPPING WET
SURFING

Map p268 (☑9977 3549; 95 North Steyne; ☺9am-6pm; ☺Manly) This beachside surf shop hires out surfboards (per hour/day/week, $15/50/150), bodyboards (per hour/day/week, $5/20/60) and wetsuits (same as bodyboards).

BASE
SURFING

Map p268 (☑9976 0591; 46 North Steyne Rd; hire per hr $15; ☺9am-6pm; ☺Manly) Sells, hires and repairs boards.

SKATER HQ
SKATING

Map p268 (☑8667 7892; www.skaterhq.com.au; 49 North Steyne; ☺9am-6pm; ☺Manly) The Manly branch of Skater HQ (p148), offers the same deals as its Entertainment Quarter sibling.

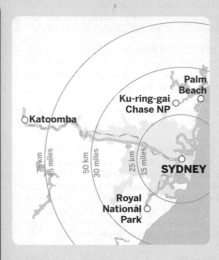

Day Trips from Sydney

The Blue Mountains p167

For more than a century, the Blue Mountains has lured Sydneysiders up from the sweltering plains with promises of cool-climate relief, naughty fireside weekends, astounding scenery and brilliant bushwalks.

Royal National Park p174

A prime stretch of wilderness at the city's doorstep, encompassing secluded beaches, vertiginous cliffs, scrub, heath, rainforest, swamp wallabies, lyrebirds and raucous flocks of yellow-tailed black cockatoos.

Northern Beaches p176

It requires a little effort to reach them (no trains run here and buses seem to take forever), but the Northern Beaches are some of Sydney's very best suburbs. Especially if you're a *Home & Away* fan.

The Blue Mountains

Explore

Forming part of the Great Dividing Range, the Blue Mountains begin 60km inland from Sydney and rise to more than 1200m above sea level. Plenty of people trundle up the Great Western Hwy for the day, just to gawp at a classic Australian vista of sheer rock walls and eucalyptus-shrouded valleys.

Katoomba's Echo Point, with the dramatic Three Sisters rock formation, is the main port of call for day-trippers. If you've got more time, make like a Sydneysider and ensconce yourself in a B&B for a couple of days. Leafy Leura is your best bet for romance, while Blackheath is a good base for hikers; both are better choices than built up Katoomba, although the latter has excellent hostels. All are connected to Sydney's train network.

The Best...

➔ **Sight** Sublime Point (p167)
➔ **Place to Eat** Silk's Brasserie (p172)
➔ **Place to Drink** Leura Garage (p172)

Top Tip

Be prepared for a climatic shift as you assail the Blue Mountains – swelter in Coogee, shiver in Katoomba. Autumn fogs create an eerie atmosphere, and in winter it sometimes snows.

Getting There & Away

➔ **Car** Head west on Parramatta Rd to Strathfield and take the tolled M4. West of Penrith, the motorway becomes the Great Western Hwy. An alternative route is Bells Line of Road.

➔ **Train** The Blue Mountains line departs Central station approximately hourly for Glenbrook, Faulconbridge, Wentworth Falls, Leura and Katoomba (adult/child $8.20/4.10, two hours). Roughly every second train continues on to Blackheath, Mt Victoria, Zig Zag and Lithgow.

➔ **Bus** The hop-on/hop-off services of **Blue Mountains Bus** (☑4751 1077; www.

bmbc.com.au) cover the major towns and sights. Dozens of tour buses head to the mountains from Sydney.

Need to Know

➔ **Area Code** 02
➔ **Location** Sixty kilometres west of central Sydney
➔ **Tourist Office** (☑1300 653 408; www.visitbluemountains.com.au; Echo Point, Katoomba; ◷9am-5pm)

 SIGHTS

SUBLIME POINT — LOOKOUT

(Sublime Point Rd) Sublime Point is a sharp triangular outcrop south of Leura that narrows to a dramatic lookout with sheer cliffs on each side. We prefer it to Katoomba's more famous Echo Point, mainly because it's quieter. On sunny days cloud shadows dance across the vast blue valley below.

ECHO POINT — LOOKOUT

(☑1300 653 408; Echo Point Rd, Katoomba; parking per hour $4.40; ◷visitor centre 9am-5pm)

HARTLEY HISTORIC SITE

In the 1830s, the Victoria Pass route (through Mt Victoria) from Sydney to inland NSW made the journey from the coast a helluva lot easier. However, travellers soon faced a new risk – being bailed up by bushrangers. To counter the problem, a police post was established at **Hartley**, 11km northwest of Mt Victoria, the village flourishing until the railway bypassed it in 1887. Now deserted, this tiny, sandstone ghost town still has a curious crop of historic buildings.

The **NPWS Information Centre** (☑6355 2117; www.environment.nsw.gov.au; ◷10am-4.20pm Sat-Thu) is in the old Farmer's Inn (1845), near St Bernards Church (1848). You can wander around the village of Hartley for free, or take a guided tour of the 1837 **Greek Revival Courthouse** (per person $6.60, minimum four people; ◷hourly 10am-3pm).

THE BELLS LINE OF ROAD

The Great Western Hwy barrels straight through the Blue Mountains, but the spectacular 90km **Bells Line of Road** is far more rewarding. Named after Archibald Bell Jr, the 19-year-old who discovered the route in 1823, the road was constructed by convicts in 1841, navigating a pass between Richmond and Lithgow. It's far quieter than the highway and offers bountiful views from the mountains' eastern slopes.

Between Bilpin and Bell, **Blue Mountains Botanic Gardens, Mount Tomah** (☑4567 2154; www.rbgsyd.nsw.gov.au; Bells Line of Road; ◷10am-4pm) is the cool-climate sibling of Sydney's Royal Botanic Gardens. Native plants cuddle up to exotic species, including magnificent rhododendron displays. There's a cafe here, and many areas are wheelchair accessible; a people mover circles on the hour.

Gorgeous **Mt Wilson** (www.mtwilson.com.au) is 8km north of Bells Line of Road. Like Katoomba, this town was settled by Anglophiles, but unlike Katoomba, with its guesthouses and cool cafes, Mt Wilson is all hedgerows, Northern Hemisphere trees and mansions with big gates and driveways. When we last visited, Baz Luhrmann was shooting *The Great Gatsby* within its leafy surrounds. About 1km from the village is the **Cathedral of Ferns**, a wet rainforest remnant with tree ferns, where native doves explode from the foliage – an almost unbearably serene 10-minute stroll.

Reaching from north of Bells Line of Road to the Hunter Valley, **Wollemi National Park** (☑4787 8877; www.environment.nsw.gov.au/nationalparks) is the state's largest forested wilderness area (nearly 5000 sq km). Access is limited and the park's centre is so isolated that a particular species of tree, the utterly rare Wollemi pine (see www.wollemipine.com) wasn't discovered until 1994. But don't expect to find any yourself – their location remains strictly under wraps. An equally secret site is a huge gallery of ancient Aboriginal rock art, uncovered in 2003.

Echo Point's clifftop viewing platform is the busiest spot in the Blue Mountains thanks to the views it offers of the area's most essential sight: a rocky trio called the **Three Sisters**. The story goes that the sisters were turned to stone by a sorcerer to protect them from the unwanted advances of three young men, but the sorcerer died before he could turn them back into humans.

Warning: Echo Point draws vast, serenity-spoiling tourist gaggles, their idling buses farting fumes into the mountain air – arrive early or late to avoid them.

SCENIC WORLD CABLE CAR

(☑4782 2699; www.scenicworld.com.au; cnr Violet St & Cliff Dr, Katoomba; railway & cableway adult/child/family $21/10/52, skyway $16/8/40, combo $28/14/70; ◷9am-5pm) If you can stomach the megaplex vibe, ride what's billed as the steepest railway in the world down the 52-degree incline to the Jamison Valley floor. From here you can wander a 2.5km forest boardwalk or hike the track to the **Ruined Castle** rock formation (12km, six hours return), then

catch the Scenic Cableway, an enclosed, wheelchair-accessible cable car, back up the slope.

There's also a cable car called the Scenic Skyway (adult/child $16/8), which floats out across Katoomba Falls gorge. Its glass floor gives passengers views of the valley canopies 200m below.

BLACKHEATH TOWN

The crowds and commercial frenzy fizzle considerably 10km north of Katoomba in neat, petite Blackheath. The town measures up in the accommodation, food and scenery stakes, and it's an excellent base for visiting the Grose and Megalong Valleys.

East of town are **Evans Lookout** (turn off the highway just south of Blackheath) and **Govetts Leap**, offering views of the highest falls in the Blue Mountains. To the northeast, via Hat Hill Rd, are **Pulpit Rock**, **Perrys Lookdown** and **Anvil Rock**. To the west and southwest lie the Kanimbla and Megalong Valleys, with spectacular views from **Hargraves Lookout**.

LEURA

TOWN

Leura, 3km east of Katoomba, is a gracious, affluent town, fashioned around undulating streets, unparalleled gardens and sweeping Victorian verandahs. The Mall, the tree-lined main street, offers rows of country craft stores and cafes for the daily tourist influx.

WENTWORTH FALLS

TOWN, WATERFALL

As you head into the town of Wentworth Falls, you'll get your first real taste of Blue Mountains' scenery: views to the south open out across the majestic Jamison Valley. Wentworth Falls, which lend the town its name, launch a plume of droplets over a 300m drop. Check them out at **Falls Reserve**. This is also the starting point of a network of walking tracks, which delve into the sublime **Valley of the Waters**, with waterfalls, gorges, woodlands and rainforests.

KATOOMBA

TOWN

Swirling otherworldly mists, steep streets lined with art deco buildings, astonishing valley views and a quirky miscellany of restaurants, buskers, artists, galleries, homeless people, bawdy pubs and classy hotels – Katoomba, the biggest town in the mountains, manages to be bohemian and bourgeois, embracing and menacing all at once.

Locals are beautifully dissolute – everybody seems to be smoking, growing a beard and wearing a beanie. A vague sniff of 'herb' wafts between cafes and camping-supply shops.

PARAGON

HISTORIC BUILDING

(65 Katoomba St; mains $10-17; ⊘breakfast & lunch) This heritage-listed 1916 cafe is Katoomba's undisputed art deco masterpiece, filled with dark wood and classical reliefs. It's not one of Katoomba's better cafes, but sampling handmade chocolates in

Katoomba

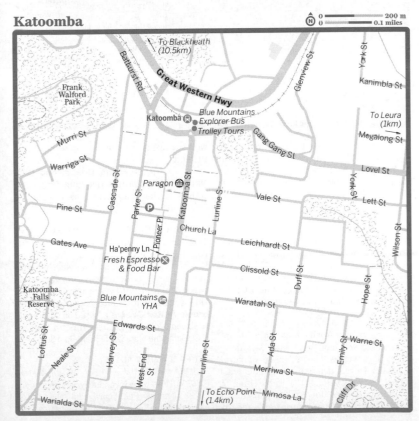

Blue Mountains

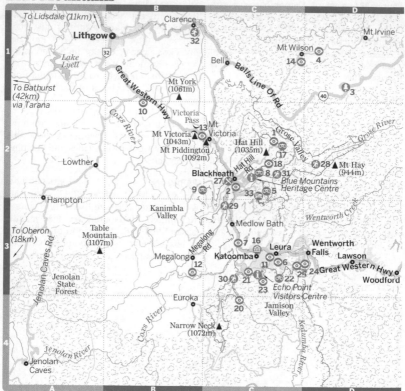

its salubrious surrounds is a compulsory Blue Mountains experience (Bob Dylan and Ginger Rogers both seemed to enjoy themselves). Wander through to the *Great Gatsby*-esque mirrored cocktail bar at the rear.

MT VICTORIA   VILLAGE

With its isolated village vibe, National Trust–classified Mt Victoria was once more influential than Katoomba. At 1043m, it's the highest town in the mountains. Crisp air, solitude, towering foliage and historic buildings are what bring you here.

MEGALONG VALLEY   OUTDOORS

(Megalong Valley Rd) The only Blue Mountains gorge you can drive into, Megalong Valley is a straw-coloured slice of rural Australia – a real departure from the quasi suburbs strung along the ridge line. A 15km road snakes down from Blackheath through pockets of rainforest; it's mostly well-surfaced, but gets rougher towards the end.

En route, the 600m **Coachwood Glen Nature Trail** features dripping fern dells, stands of mountain ash and sun-stained sandstone cliffs.

RED HANDS CAVE   ARCHAEOLOGICAL SITE

The section of Blue Mountains National Park southwest of Glenbrook contains Red Hands Cave, an Aboriginal shelter with hand stencils on the walls dating to between 500 and 1600 years ago. It's an easy, 7km return walk southwest of the **Glenbrook Visitor Centre** (1300 653 408; www.visitbluemountains.org; Great Western Highway; ⊙8.30am-4pm Mon-Sat, 8.30am-3pm Sun).

LEURALLA NSW TOY &
RAILWAY MUSEUM   MUSEUM, GARDENS

(4784 1169; www.toyandrailwaymuseum.au; 36 Olympian Pde, Leura; adult/child $14/6, gardens only $10/5; ⊙10am-5pm) Leuralla is

an art deco mansion set amid 4.9 misty hectares of handsome English gardens. The house is a memorial to HV 'Doc' Evatt, a former Australian Labor Party leader and the first UN president. Kids love the toy and model-railway museum (everything from Barbie to Bob the Builder). Cross the road to check out the awesome valley view.

EVERGLADES   GARDENS

(☑4784 1938; www.everglades.org.au; 37 Everglades Ave, Leura; adult/child $8/4; ☉10am-4pm) National Trust–owned Everglades was built in the 1930s and while the house is interesting, it's the magnificent garden created by Danish 'master gardener' Paul Sorenson that's the main drawcard. Fountains, waterfalls, terraced lawns, freestone walls, a museum, an art gallery and tearooms – Everglades is a must for green thumbs.

NORMAN LINDSAY GALLERY
& MUSEUM   MUSEUM

(☑4751 1067; www.normanlindsay.com.au; 14 Norman Lindsay Cres, Faulconbridge; adult/child $12/6; ☉10am-4pm) Celebrated artist, author and bon vivant Norman Lindsay, famed for his saucy artworks, lived in Faulconbridge from 1912 until his death in 1969. His home and studio holds a significant collection of his paintings, watercolours, drawings and sculptures. There's a cafe here, too.

BLUE MOUNTAINS NATIONAL PARK

What is known as the Blue Mountains is actually a sandstone plateau riddled with steep gullies eroded by rivers over thousands of years. The purple haze that gives the mountains their name comes from a fine mist of oil exuded by eucalyptus trees.

Initially thought to be impenetrable, the mountains were first crossed by European explorers in 1813. On this epic quest, Gregory Blaxland, William Wentworth and William Lawson followed the mountain ridges up over the top; today, their route is pretty much traced by the Great Western Hwy.

More than three million people a year visit the scenic lookouts and waterfalls of **Blue Mountains National Park** (☑4787 8877; www.environment.nsw.gov.au/nationalparks; per car $7 in the Glenbrook area only), the most popular and accessible part of the Greater Blue Mountains World Heritage Area. There are bushwalks for everyone, from pensioners to the downright intrepid, lasting from a few minutes to several days.

As you'd expect in such rugged terrain, there are hazards: walkers get lost, bushfires flare up and there are definitely snakes in the grass. These are relatively rare occurrences, but it pays to get some up-to-date advice from the visitors centres before you propel yourself into the wilderness.

Blue Mountains

⊙ Sights (p167)

1	Anvil Rock	C2
2	Blackheath	C2
3	Blue Mountains Botanic Gardens, Mount Tomah	D1
4	Cathedral of Ferns	D1
	Echo Point	(see 23)
5	Evans Lookout	C2
6	Everglades	C3
7	Explorers' Tree	C3
	Falls Gallery	(see 25)
	Falls Reserve	(see 25)
8	Govetts Leap	C2
9	Hargraves Lookout	B2
10	Hartley	B2
11	Leura	C3
	Leuralla NSW Toy & Railway Museum	(see 6)
12	Megalong Valley	B3
13	Mt Victoria	B2
14	Mt Wilson	C1
15	Norman Lindsay Gallery & Museum	E3
16	Paragon	C3
17	Perrys Lookdown	C2
18	Pulpit Rock	C2
19	Red Hands Cave	E4
20	Ruined Castle	C4
21	Scenic World	C3
22	Sublime Point	C3
23	Three Sisters	C3
24	Valley of the Waters	C3
25	Wentworth Falls	D3
26	Wollemi National Park	E1

⊗ Eating (p172)

27	Ashcrofts	C2
	Escarpment	(see 27)
	Fresh Espresso & Food Bar	(see 16)
	Leura Garage	(see 11)
	Silk's Brasserie	(see 11)

⊙ Sports & Activities (p173)

28	Blue Gum Forest	D2
	Blue Mountains Explorer Bus	(see 16)
29	Coachwood Glen Nature Trail	C3
30	Golden Stairs Walk	C3
31	Junction Rock	C2
	Trolley Tours	(see 16)
32	Zig Zag Railway	B1

⊜ Sleeping (p173)

	Blue Mountains YHA	(see 16)
	Broomelea Bed & Breakfast	(see 6)
33	Jemby-Rinjah Eco Lodge	C2

FALLS GALLERY   GALLERY
(☑4757 1139; www.fallsgallery.com.au; 161 Falls Rd, Wentworth Falls; admission $2; ⊙10am-5pm Wed-Sun) Housed in a restored weatherboard house surrounded by precisely maintained gardens, this is one of the Blue Mountains' best privately run galleries. It's devoted to ceramics and works on paper.

EXPLORERS' TREE   LANDMARK
(Great Western Hwy) Just west of Katoomba, on the edge of the highway, intrepid trio Wentworth, Blaxland and Lawson notched the Explorers' Tree to mark their trail. This sad, bushfire-ravaged stump has been amputated, gored by termites and filled with concrete, earning it the title Eucalyptus concretus.

✕ EATING & DRINKING

SILK'S BRASSERIE   MODERN AUSTRALIAN **$$**
(☑4784 2534; www.silksleura.com; 128 Leura Mall, Leura; lunch $24-39, dinner $35-39; ⊙lunch & dinner) A warm welcome awaits at this fine Leura diner. The dishes can sometimes be overworked, but the serves are generous and flavourful. Save room for the decadent chocolate fondant.

LEURA GARAGE   MEDITERRANEAN **$$**
(☑4784 3391; www.leuragarage.com.au; 84 Railway Pde, Leura; breakfast $12-17, shared plates $10-28; ⊙breakfast Sat & Sun, lunch & dinner Thu-Mon) If you were in any doubt that this cool joint was an actual old garage, the suspended mufflers and stacks of old tires press the point. Served on wooden slabs, the rustic shared plates, including deli-laden pizza, will rev up your taste buds.

ESCARPMENT   MODERN AUSTRALIAN **$$$**
(☑4787 7269; www.escarpmentblackheath.com; 246 Great Western Hwy, Blackheath; mains $33-38; ⊙lunch Sun, dinner Fri-Mon) The decor at this unassuming bistro features attractive artwork and an old-fashioned espresso machine. There's nothing old-fashioned about the menu, though – it changes with the season and makes the most of local produce.

FRESH ESPRESSO & FOOD BAR   CAFE **$**
(www.freshcafe.com.au; 181 Katoomba St, Katoomba; mains $11-20; ⊘breakfast & lunch) The organic, rainforest-alliance, fair-trade coffee served at Fresh attracts a devoted local following. Excellent all-day breakfasts are popular, too. The Katoomba branch is small and tightly packed with tables but the Leura branch on the corner of Megalong St and the Mall has plenty of space.

ASHCROFTS   MODERN AUSTRALIAN **$$$**
(☑4787 8297; www.ashcrofts.com; 18 Govetts Leap Rd, Blackheath; 2-/3-courses $75/88; ⊘dinner Wed-Sun, lunch Sun) Chef Corinne Evatt has been wooing locals and visitors alike with her flavoursome, globally inspired dishes for the past decade. The wine list is among the best in the mountains and service is exemplary.

🏃 SPORTS & ACTIVITIES

**BLUE MOUNTAINS
WALKABOUT**   CULTURAL TOUR
(☑0408 443 822; www.bluemountainswalkabout.com; half day/day $75/95) Aboriginal-owned and guided adventurous treks with spiritual themes; start at Faulconbridge train station and end at Springwood station.

TROLLEY TOURS   BUS TOUR
(☑4782 7999; www.trolleytours.com.au; 76 Bathurst Rd, Katoomba; ticket $25; ⊘9.45am-5.42pm) Runs a hop-on, hop-off bus barely disguised as a trolley, looping around 29 stops in Katoomba and Leura.

**BLUE MOUNTAINS
EXPLORER BUS**   BUS TOUR
(☑1300 300 915; www.explorerbus.com.au; 283 Bathurst Rd, Katoomba; adult/child $36/18; ⊘9.45am-4.54pm) Offers hop-on/hop-off service on a 26-stop Katoomba/Leura loop. Leaves from Katoomba station every 30 minutes to one hour.

GOLDEN STAIRS WALK   HIKING
(Glenraphael Dr, Katoomba) If you have your own transport, you can tackle the Golden Stairs Walk, a less-congested route down to the Ruined Castle. To get there, continue along Cliff Dr from Scenic World for 1km and look for Glenraphael Dr on your left. It quickly becomes rough and unsealed. Watch out for the signs to the Golden Stairs on the left after a couple of kilometres. It is a steep, exhilarating trail down into the valley (about 8km, five hours return).

WALKS AROUND BLACKHEATH   HIKING
There are steep walks into the Grose Valley from Govetts Leap. Perrys Lookdown is the

---

SLEEPING IN THE BLUE MOUNTAINS

The Blue Mountains is the home of the comfy B&B, welcoming city escapees for weekend retreats. Many places require a minimum two-night stay at the weekend; during the week, they tend to be more flexible and much cheaper.

➡ **Broomelea Bed & Breakfast** (☑4784 2940; www.broomelea.com.au; 273 Leura Mall, Leura; r $175-195; @🛜) This fine Edwardian cottage offers four-poster beds, manicured gardens, cane furniture on the verandah, an open fire and a snug lounge. There's also a self-contained cottage for families.

➡ **Jemby-Rinjah Eco Lodge** (☑4787 7622; www.jemby.com.au; 336 Evans Lookout Rd, Blackheath; from $165) These secluded, ecofriendly cabins (all with composting toilets and wood burners, and one with a rainwater hot tub) are lodged so deeply in the bottlebrush you'll have to bump into one to find it. A purist might argue against the TVs, but that's a minor quibble. There's bird feeding daily at 8.30am. The cabins easily sleep two adults and two children.

➡ **Blue Mountains YHA** (☑4782 1416; www.yha.com.au; 207 Katoomba St, Katoomba; dm $30-32, r without/with bathroom $90/100; @🛜) The austere art deco exterior of this much-lauded hostel belies its cavernous, sparkling innards. Dorms and family rooms are spotlessly bright; common areas have more beanbags than bums. Extras include a pinball machine, pool tables, open fires, a giant chess set, central heating, barbecues and curry nights. Clued-up staff are on hand to help you get the most out of your Blue Mountains experience. Hard to fault.

start of the shortest route to the magical **Blue Gum Forest** (five hours return). From Evans Lookout there are tracks to Govetts Leap (1½ hours one-way) and to **Junction Rock**, continuing to the Blue Gum Forest (six hours one-way). Register your walk and get trail condition updates from the **Blue Mountains Heritage Centre** (☑4787 8877; www.environment.nsw.gov.au; end of Govetts Leap Rd, Blackheath; ◷9am-4.30pm).

ZIG ZAG RAILWAY   RAILWAY
(☑6355 2955; www.zigzagrailway.com.au; Clarence Station, Bells Line of Road; adult/child/family $30/15/74; ◷11am, 1pm & 3pm daily) One for the trainspotters, the Zig Zag Railway was designed to bring the Great Western Railway tracks down from the mountains to Lithgow, gently zigzagging down the precipice. It's a 1½-hour return train ride.

Royal National Park

Explore

The traditional lands of the Dharawal people, the 165-sq-km **Royal National Park** (☑02 9542 0648; www.environment.nsw.gov.au; cars $11, pedestrians & cyclists free; ◷gates to park areas locked at 8.30pm daily) was established in 1879, making it the second-oldest national park in the world (behind the USA's Yellowstone). It stretches for 20km south from Port Hacking, forming Sydney's southern border.

The sandstone plateau at the northern end of the park is an ocean of low scrub, the fuel for regular bushfires. One in 1994 destroyed 95% of the park; stricter fire prevention measures have been implemented since. You'll find taller forest in the Hacking River valley and at the park's southern boundary on the edge of the Illawarra Escarpment. In late winter and early spring the park is carpeted with wildflowers.

The park visitors centre can assist with camping permits, maps and bushwalking.

The Best...
➜ **Swimming Beach Jibbon Beach**
➜ **Surf Beach** Garie Beach (p175)
➜ **Cycling Route** Lady Carrington Drive (p176)

Top Tip
If you're driving, consider continuing south to the amazing Sea Cliff Bridge, a magnificent 665m stretch of elevated road hugging the coast between Coalcliff and Clifton.

Getting There & Away
➜ **Car** You'll need a car to explore the park easily. From Sydney, take the Princes Hwy south.
➜ **Ferry** Catch the train to Cronulla, then a **Cronulla National Park Ferry** (☑02-9523 2990; www.cronullaferries.com.au; Cronulla Wharf) from Cronulla to Bundeena (30 minutes).
➜ **Train** If you're prepared for a lengthy hike from the station, take the Eastern Suburbs & Illawarra line to Loftus, Engadine, Heathcote and Waterfall, or continue on the South Coast line to Helensburgh or Otford (all adult/child $6.40/3.20, allow an hour).

SLEEPING IN ROYAL NATIONAL PARK

Since bushfires destroyed the Garie Beach YHA in 2010, camping is the only option within the park. Bookings are essential; call 9542 0683.
➜ **Bonnie Vale Camping Ground** (Sea Breeze Lane; adult/child $14/7) This 74-space drive-in site on Port Hacking near Bundeena is equipped with toilets, drinking water, hot showers, gas barbecues and picnic tables.
➜ **North Era Camping Ground** (adult/child $5/3) A walk-in, 12-site campground on the coastal track south of Garie Beach with only drop toilets provided. You'll need to bring drinking water and everything else. Wood fires are forbidden.
➜ **Uloola Falls Camping Ground** (adult/child $5/3) On the Uloola Track, this walk-in campground has only six sites and drop toilets.

Royal National Park

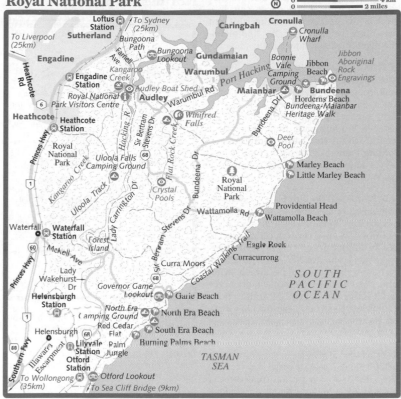

Need to Know

➔ **Area Code** 02

➔ **Location** Twenty-nine kilometres from central Sydney

➔ **Tourist Office** (📞02 9542 0648; www.environment.nsw.gov.au/nationalparks; Farnell Ave; ⊙9am-4pm)

👁 SIGHTS

BUNDEENA   TOWN

(Bundeena Dr) Isolated Bundeena (population 3500) sits near the mouth of Port Hacking, surrounded by national park. The main drawcards are its beaches: beautiful Horderns Beach and, further east, even lovelier Jibbon Beach. On Jibbon Beach's eastern headland there is a large Aboriginal rock-engraving site, where you can see outlines of the animals the Dharawal people used to hunt. Heading in the other

direction, west from Bundeena, is the Bundeena-Maianbar Heritage Walk.

WATTAMOLLA BEACH   BEACH

(Wattamolla Rd) About halfway along the coast, Wattamolla Beach is one of the park's favourite picnic spots. It has the great advantage of having both a surf beach and a lagoon, allowing for safe swimming.

GARIE BEACH   BEACH

(Garie Beach Rd) An excellent surf beach with road access. Like all of these surf beaches, swimming can be treacherous.

🏃 SPORTS & ACTIVITIES

AUDLEY BOAT SHED   KAYAKING, CYCLING

(📞9545 4967; www.audleyboatshed.com; 6 Farnell Ave) At this historic boat shed you can hire rowboats, canoes and kayaks (per hour/day $20/45) for a paddle up Kangaroo Creek or the Hacking River. They also rent aqua bikes (per half-hour $15) and mountain bikes (per hour/day $16/34).

COASTAL WALKING TRAIL HIKING

This spectacular two-day, 28km coastal walking trail connects various beaches which don't have road access. It can be easily broken into bite-sized sections: for instance, heading south from Garie Beach you'll reach the **North Era**, **South Era** and **Burning Palms** surf beaches. Take special care at **Marley Beach**, between Bundeena and Wattamolla.

LADY CARRINGTON DRIVE HIKING, CYCLING

Now closed to motor vehicles, this historic carriageway follows the Hacking River south from Audley, through rainforest and past two picnic areas. This is one of many walks and cycling tracks in the park, leading to waterfalls, tranquil freshwater swimming holes and picnic spots; enquire at the park visitors centre for other tracks. Note: it's not safe to swim in the Hacking River but you can swim in the upper reaches of Kangaroo Creek.

WAVES SURF SCHOOL SURFING

(☏1800 616 667; www.wavessurfschool.com.au) This crew will pick you up from the city and whisk you to Royal National Park for a day of surfing lessons and a barbecue lunch ($89). They also lead longer 'surfaris', heading as far north as Byron Bay.

Northern Beaches

Explore

For surf fiends and *Home & Away* devotees, the Northern Beaches are a must-see. Although we've listed them as a day trip (that's most likely how you'll approach them), they're very much a part of the city, with the suburbs pushing right up to the water's edge. Some neighbourhoods are more ritzy than others, but what they all have in common is a devotion to the beach.

Northern Beaches

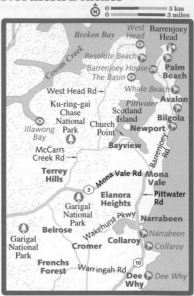

Consider hiring a car to beach-bum at your leisure. We've arranged our listings as you'll reach them, driving north. Palm Beach, the farthest flung, is the least built up and the best. From here it's a quick hop by ferry across Pittwater to untamed Ku-ring-gai Chase National Park.

The Best...

➤ **Beach** Palm Beach (p178)

➤ **Surfing** Narrabeen (p177)

➤ **Place to Eat** Barrenjoey House (p178)

Top Tip

The patrolled ocean beaches are good for swimming, but sharks make Pittwater and Broken Bay risky unless you head to the netted areas at Illawong Bay and The Basin.

Getting There & Away

➤ **Car** Driving is by far the best way to explore this stretch. From the city, take the bridge or tunnel north and exit at Military Rd. Continue on to Spit Rd and keep heading straight ahead after crossing the Spit Bridge. This eventually becomes Pittwater Rd, which reaches the coast at Dee Why.

➡ **Bus** Various routes terminate along the way but L90 (from Railway Sq and Wynyard) goes all the way to Palm Beach ($4.50, 1¾ hours).

Need to Know

➡ **Area Code** 02

➡ **Location** Between 18km and 41km from central Sydney.

◉ SIGHTS

DEE WHY   BEACH

(The Strand; 🚌176) A no-fuss family beach fronted by chunky apartments, some good cafes and ubiquitous surf shops. Grommets hit the waves and mums hit the rock pool.

COLLAROY   BEACH

(Pittwater Rd; 🚌L88, L90) A long beach chasing the *Endless Summer* north to Narrabeen. Good for learning to surf, or catching a flick in the little art deco cinema.

NARRABEEN   BEACH

(Ocean St; 🚌L88, L90) Immortalised by the Beach Boys in *Surfin' USA,* Narrabeen is hard-core surf turf – get some experience before hitting the breaks. Not the best swimming, but there's a pool and a lagoon.

BILGOLA   BEACH

(Bilgola Ave; 🚌L88, L90) With its saltwater pool, Bilgola feels like a bit of a secret gem. Good swimming.

AVALON   BEACH

(Barrenjoey Rd; 🚌L88, L90) Caught in a sandy '70s time warp, Avalon is the mythical Australian beach you always dreamt was there but could never find. Challenging surf and tangerine sand.

WHALE BEACH   BEACH

(Whale Beach Rd; 🚌L90) Sleepy Whale Beach is underrated – a paradisaical slice of deep, orange sand flanked by steep cliffs; good for surfers and families.

KU-RING-GAI CHASE NATIONAL PARK

Ku-ring-gai Chase National Park (www.nationalparks.nsw.gov.au; admission per car $11) sits across Pittwater from the narrow peninsula containing Palm Beach and stretches for a vast 150-sq-km from Broken Bay. On display is that classic Sydney cocktail of bushland, sandstone outcrops and water vistas, plus walking tracks, horse-riding trails, picnic areas and Aboriginal rock engravings.

The park has over 100km of shoreline and several through roads (enter from Bobbin Head Rd, North Turramurra; Ku-ring-gai Chase Rd off Pacific Hwy, Mt Colah; or McCarrs Creek Rd, Terrey Hills). The **Palm Beach Ferry** (☑9974 2411; www.palm beachferry.com.au; adult/child $7.20/3.60; ⊙9am-7pm Mon-Fri, to 6pm Sat & Sun) leaves Palm Beach Wharf on the hour from at least 9am to 5pm, heading to The Basin (landing fee $3) and other Pittwater wharves.

Staffed by friendly volunteers, the **Kalkari Discovery Centre** (☑9472 9300; Ku-ring-gai Chase Rd; ⊙9am-5pm) books walking tours and Aboriginal-led kayaking tours. It's 2.5km from the Mt Colah entrance. The road descends from Kalkari to the Bobbin Head picnic area and **Bobbin Head Information Centre** (☑9472 8949; Bobbin Head, Bobbin Inn; ⊙10am-4pm) at the Bobbin Inn on Cowan Creek, then climbs to the Turramurra entrance. Also at Bobbin Head are a cafe and a mangrove boardwalk.

Elevated terrain offers glorious views over Cowan Creek, Broken Bay and Pittwater. The view from **West Head** across Pittwater to Barrenjoey Lighthouse is a winner.

Normally elusive, lyrebirds are conspicuous at West Head during their mating season, from May to July. West Head Rd also offers access to **Aboriginal engravings and handprints**: from the Resolute picnic area it's 100m to some faint ochre handprints at Red Hands Cave. Another 500m along Resolute Track is an engraving site. A 3km loop from here takes in **Resolute Beach** and another engraving site. The Basin Track makes an easy stroll to some well-preserved engravings; the Echidna Track (off West Head Rd) has boardwalk access to engravings.

PALM BEACH BEACH
(Ocean Rd; ☐L90) Long, lovely Palm Beach is a meniscus of bliss, famous as the setting for the cheesy TV soap *Home & Away*. The 1881 **Barrenjoey Lighthouse** punctuates the northern tip of the headland in an annexe of Ku-ring-gai Chase National Park. You'll need some decent shoes for the steep 20-minute hike (no toilets!), but the views across Pittwater are worth the effort. On Sundays short tours run every half-hour from 11am to 3pm; no need to book ahead.

 **EATING**

BARRENJOEY HOUSE EUROPEAN **$$**
(☑9974 4001; www.barrenjoeyhouse.com; 1108 Barrenjoey Rd, Palm Beach; mains $27-39; ◎lunch & dinner; ☐L90) Overlooking picturesque Pittwater from opposite the ferry wharf, Barrenjoey House is the perfect location for a leisurely lunch. The menu is casual but assured, with a selection that will please most palates, even junior ones. It also has B&B rooms upstairs (from $180).

BOATHOUSE CAFE **$$**
(www.theboathousepb.com.au; Governor Phillip Park, Palm Beach; breakfast $8-20, lunch $15-36; ◎7.30am-4pm; ☐L90) Sit on the large timber deck facing Pittwater or grab a table on the lawn out front – either option is alluring at Palm Beach's most popular cafe. The food is nearly as impressive as the views, and that's really saying something.

🛏 Sleeping

Sydney offers both a huge quantity and variety of accommodation, with solid options in every price range. Even so, the supply shrivels up under the summer sun, particularly around weekends and big events. Predictably, views play a big part in determining room prices here: your wallet will shed kilos as you ride the hotel elevator up to your lofty harbour-view suite.

Rates & Seasons

These days, all but the smallest hotels vary their prices from day to day, depending on the season, special events, day of the week (Fridays and Saturdays tend to be more expensive in all but the most business-focused hotels, while Sundays are cheapest) and, most importantly, occupancy. Where prices vary widely, we've listed a 'from' amount, basing this on the cheapest room available given a reasonable amount of notice in the high (but not necessarily peak) season. If you leave booking until the last minute, you may find yourself paying considerably more.

The summer high season lasts from around December to March, with the absolute peak being between Christmas and New Year (especially New Year's Eve). Prices also shoot up again in late February/early March in the lead up to Mardi Gras.

Hotels

There are hotels scattered throughout Sydney, but you'll find the biggest of the international chains following in the footsteps of the first convicts by pitching their tents in Circular Quay, The Rocks and the city centre. Given their location they cater in equal parts to business people and cashed-up holiday-makers, and they tend to offer all the bells and whistles: 24-hour room service, restaurant, bar, swimming pool, gym, spa, valet parking etc. Internet access is ubiquitous but rarely free.

Boutique hotels are differentiated by their much smaller size and, usually, less generic design aesthetic. Some occupy historic buildings, and the better ones have idiosyncratic features such as iPod docks and eclectic art.

Hostels

Sydney's hostels range from the sublime to the sublimely grotty. A clump of large flashpacker-style blocks encircling Central station have raised the bar, offering en suites, air-conditioning, rooftop decks and, in one case, a swimming pool. Private rooms in such places are often more comfortable than a midrange hotel – and in many cases the prices aren't all that different either.

You'll find smaller, cheaper hostels in Kings Cross, Glebe and at the beaches. In Kings Cross, in particular, the competition is high – and enticements such as free wi-fi and breakfast are offered to sweeten the deal.

B&Bs & Guesthouses

Bed and breakfasts don't play as large a role in the accommodation scene here as they do in, say, the Blue Mountains. Manly has a good crop of boutique operators that only cater to one party at a time; get in quick, as they book up fast. We've used the term guesthouses to refer to places that are bigger and less personal than the average B&B, but are smaller and offer less services than your average hotel. Guesthouses may or may not offer free breakfast.

SLEEPING

NEED TO KNOW

Price Ranges
In reviews the following codes represent the price of accommodation for two people in high season:

$ doubles under $100

$$ doubles $100 to $220

$$$ doubles over $220

Checking In & Out
Check in is normally 2pm, although most places will let you check in earlier if the room is ready, or at least let you stow your luggage. Check out is often as early as 10am but sometimes stretches until noon; it doesn't hurt to request a later time.

Breakfast
Many hotels offer a continental buffet breakfast, but it's worth asking about room-only rates, as they can be much cheaper – and exploring Sydney's cafes is part of the fun. Some hostels offer free toast and cereal. Not all B&Bs offer full cooked breakfasts; check in advance.

Websites
➡ Wotif (www.wotif. com) Bookings, including 'mystery deals'.

➡ Trip Advisor (www. tripadvisor.com) Unvetted, user-generated ratings.

➡ Lonely Planet (hotels. lonelyplanet.com) Listings.

Lonely Planet's Top Choices

Sydney Harbour YHA (p182) Million-dollar harbour views on a youth-hostel budget.

Tara (p185) Suburban B&B riding high on charm.

Cockatoo Island (p183) Island camping in the heart of the city.

Simpsons of Potts Point (p187) An oasis of boutique luxury within cooee of gritty Kings Cross.

Park Hyatt (p182) There's no better location for Sydney razzle-dazzle.

Best by Budget

$
Wake Up! (p184)
Railway Square YHA (p184)

$$
Adina Apartment Hotel Sydney (p186)
Medusa (p186)

$$$
Observatory (p182)
Westin Sydney (p183)

Best for Views
Shangri-La (p183)
Quay West (p182)
Quay Grand (p182)
Meriton Serviced Apartments Kent St (p183)
Vibe Hotel North Sydney (p183)

Best for Heritage
Lord Nelson Brewery Hotel (p182)
The Russell (p182)
Bed & Breakfast Sydney Harbour (p182)
Victoria Court Hotel (p187)
Manor House (p186)

Best Serviced Apartments
Quay Grand (p182)
Adina Apartment Hotel Sydney (p186)
Meriton Serviced Apartments Kent St (p183)
Quay West (p182)
Medina Grand Harbourside (p185)

Best Boutique Hotels
Medusa (p186)
Establishment Hotel (p184)
Park8 (p184)
Hotel Altamont (p186)
Dive Hotel (p189)

Best B&Bs
Beaufort at the Beach (p189)
Kathryn's on Queen (p188)
101 Addison Road (p189)
Victoria Court Hotel (p187)
Bed & Breakfast Sydney Harbour (p182)

Best for Swimming Pools
Observatory (p182)
Quay West (p182)
Vibe Hotel North Sydney (p183)
Adina Apartment Hotel Sydney (p186)
Medina Grand Harbourside (p185)

Best Hostels
Wake Up! (p184)
Railway Square YHA (p184)
Blue Parrot (p187)
Bounce (p185)
Sydney Central YHA (p184)

Where to Stay

Neighbourhood	For	Against
Circular Quay & The Rocks	Big-ticket sights; vibrant nightlife; top hotels and restaurants	Tourist central, expensive, few affordable eateries
Sydney Harbour	Everywhere is a pleasant ferry journey from town	Can be isolated; difficult to access nightlife
City Centre & Haymarket	Good transport links; lots of sights, bars, eateries, hostels and hotels	Can be noisy and, in parts, ugly
Darling Harbour & Pyrmont	Plenty to see and do; lively nightlife	Soulless; few affordable restaurants
Glebe & Newtown	Bohemian; great coffee; interesting shops; priced for locals	Few sights or hotels; getting to beaches requires effort
Surry Hills & Darlinghurst	Sydney's hippest eating and drinking precinct; heart of gay scene	Few actual sights; gritty in parts
Kings Cross & Potts Point	Interesting and idiosyncratic; numerous hostels, bars and clubs; good transport links	Vomiting teenagers; sleazy stripclub touts; regular alcohol-fuelled stoushes
Paddington & Centennial Park	Leafy and genteel; top shopping; bus access to city and beaches	No train service; few sights; limited accommodation options
Bondi to Coogee	Sand, surf and sexy bods	No trains and a slow bus ride to the city; not for the body conscious
Manly	Beautiful beaches; excellent B&Bs	Not much to do if the weather's bad

SLEEPING

🏨 Circular Quay & The Rocks

TOP CHOICE SYDNEY HARBOUR YHA   HOSTEL $

Map p248 (☑8272 0900; www.yha.com.au; 110 Cumberland St; dm $47-48, r $162-180; ❋ @ 🛜; 🚇Circular Quay) Any qualms about the un-hostel-like prices will be shelved the moment you head up to the roof terrace of this singular, custom-built YHA and see Circular Quay laid bare before you. All of the rooms, including the dorms, have private bathrooms. The building, hovering over exposed foundations, incorporates a major archaeological dig into its footprint.

TOP CHOICE PARK HYATT   HOTEL $$$

Map p248 (☑9256 1234; www.sydney.park. hyatt.com; 7 Hickson Rd; r from $795; ❋ @ 🛜 ⛱; 🚇Circular Quay) Luxury meets location at Sydney's most expensive hotel, where the service levels and facilities are second to none. The Park Hyatt was never going to win the architectural face-off across Circular Quay with the Opera House and so opts instead for discreet low-slung curves in Sydney sandstone.

OBSERVATORY   HOTEL $$$

Map p248 (☑9256 2222; www.observatoryhotel. com.au; 89-113 Kent St; r from $520; ❋ @ 🛜 ⛱; 🚇Wynyard) When the owner's other properties include the Orient Express, you expect opulence. That said, the Observatory is remarkably restrained, eschewing excessive glitz in favour of an elegant antique ambience. The rooms are big 'uns, with equally spacious marble bathrooms. Some have views and four-poster beds.

QUAY GRAND   APARTMENTS $$$

Map p248 (☑9256 4000; www.mirvachotels.com; 61 Macquarie St; apt from $399; ❋ 🛜; 🚇Circular Quay) With the Opera House as its neighbour, the building known locally as 'the toaster' has a scorching-hot location – so much so that it might burn a hole right through your wallet. These well-designed contemporary apartments set you in the glitzy heart of Sydney, encircled by top restaurants, cocktail bars and that attention-seeking harbour.

LORD NELSON BREWERY HOTEL   PUB $$

Map p248 (☑9251 4044; www.lordnelson.com. au; 19 Kent St; r with/without bathroom $190/130;

🚇Circular Quay) Built in 1836, this boutique sandstone pub has a tidy set of upstairs rooms with exposed stone walls and dormer windows. Thankfully the owners have resisted the urge to spew flowers and lace all over the place. Most of the nine rooms are spacious and have en suites; there are also cheaper, smaller rooms with shared facilities.

BED & BREAKFAST SYDNEY HARBOUR   B&B $$

Map p248 (☑9247 1130; www.bbsydneyharbour. com.au; 142 Cumberland St; s $140-235, d $155-249; ❋ 🛜; 🚇Circular Quay) This 100-year-old guesthouse boldly claims to be the 'world's best-located B&B'. With The Rocks and the city on its doorstep, it's certainly in contention. It even manages to squeeze out some Opera House views, despite being hemmed in by high-rise hotels. En suite rooms have an Australian flavour without straying into twee territory. Smaller shared-bathroom rooms are also available.

RUSSELL   HOTEL $$

Map p248 (☑9241 3543; www.therussell.com. au; 143A George St; r $159-299; ❋ @ 🛜; 🚇Circular Quay) A recent renovation has seen this long-standing favourite divest itself of frills and furbelows and achieve some contemporary style as well as a downstairs wine bar. The rooftop garden and the location just minutes from Circular Quay are major drawcards, but only a few rooms have air-con and the cheaper ones share bathrooms.

QUAY WEST   APARTMENTS $$$

Map p248 (☑9240 6000; www.mirvachotels.com; 98 Gloucester St; apt from $387; ❋ @ ⛱; 🚇Circular Quay) One of the older apartment-style high-rise hotels, Quay West's early-1990s decor could just about qualify as retro; we love the brass ornamentation in the reception and the cheesy columns of the 'Roman-style' pool on level 24. The roomy apartments are a home away from home, each with a full kitchen, lounge and laundry room. The views are extraordinary.

SIR STAMFORD   HOTEL $$$

Map p248 (☑9252 4600; www.stamford.com.au; 93 Macquarie St; r from $280; ❋ ⛱; 🚇Circular Quay) Going for a stiff upper lip, old-world ambience, Sir Stamford leaves a grand first impression with its red-carpet entry, waist-coated staff, glittering chandeliers and gilt-framed portraits. The rooms themselves are a little dated but comfortable nonetheless. Formality is eschewed on the sundeck facing the tiny outdoor pool.

SHANGRI-LA HOTEL **$$$**
Map p248 (☑9250 6000; www.shangri-la.com; 176 Cumberland St; r from $395; ✿🏧🖥; 🚇Circular Quay) The Hong Kong–based chain's Sydney offering is a suitably upmarket tower with large, extremely comfortable rooms. While there's nothing all that special about the decor or ambience, the wow factor comes from Sydney itself – in the form of extraordinary views from the higher floors. Charming customer service staff, impeccably clad in Chinese-style silk jackets, add a touch of class.

🛏 Sydney Harbour

TOP CHOICE COCKATOO ISLAND CAMPGROUND **$**
(☑8898 9774; www.cockatooisland.gov.au; site from $45, 2-bed tent from $135, 10-bed house $545; 🚢Cockatoo Island) For a truly surreal experience, stay under canvas amid the convict and industrial detritus of Cockatoo Island. You can pitch your own tent; 'glamp' in a pre-pitched two-person tent complete with made-up beds; or rent one of two beautifully restored, self-contained Federation houses. It's only a 15-minute ferry ride upstream from Circular Quay, but ferries don't run much past 10pm.

VIBE HOTEL NORTH SYDNEY HOTEL **$$**
Map p270 (☑9955 1111; www.vibehotels.com.au; 88 Alfred St South; r from $143; ✿@🖥; 🚇Milsons Point) Dappled with Vibe's trademark lime and aubergine colour scheme, this slick hotel sports 165 rooms and 36 suites, the best of which offer a choice of Lavender Bay or Kirribilli views. During the week it pulls the business crowd and commands top dollar, but you can often nab a good deal on weekends.

SAVOY HOTEL HOTEL **$$**
(☑9326 1411; www.savoyhotel.com.au; 41 Knox St; d $135-165, ste $195-260; ✿🏧; 🚢Double Bay) Offers surprisingly good value on the 'Double Pay' coffee strip. The only thing with a whiff of pretension at this friendly place is the name. Atrium-view rooms are the cheapest, facing an internal courtyard; strive for a loft room or a suite looking towards the bay.

WATSONS BAY HOTEL PUB **$$**
(☑9337 5444; www.watsonsbayhotel.com.au; 10 Marine Parade; r $190-390, ste $400-620; 🏧; 🚢Watsons Bay) With the ferry right on the doorstep and amazing harbour views, this is a winning spot for keeping the city accessible but at arm's length. Yes, it is a pub, but expect boutique hotel features such as comfy beds, crisp linen and slick glassed-in en suites (privacy can be an issue). It's a busy daytime pub, but quietens down reasonably early.

GLENFERRIE LODGE GUESTHOUSE **$**
Map p270 (☑9955 1685; www.glenferrielodge.com; 12a Carabella St, Kirribilli; dm $45, s $69-99, d $149-249; 🏧; 🚢Kirribilli) Ignore the ridiculous sculpture (and the prime minister, who lives around the corner) and head inside the large 1880s house, where you'll find dozens of rooms of various configurations, spotless shared bathrooms and helpful management. Long-term rates and luggage lockers available, and buffet breakfast included.

🛏 City Centre & Haymarket

WESTIN SYDNEY HOTEL **$$$**
Map p250 (☑8223 1111; www.westin.com/sydney; 1 Martin Pl; r from $310; ✿@🏧🖥; 🚇Martin Place) Spreading half of its tentacles into the grand General Post Office building and the others into a contemporary tower, this is one luxurious address. Choose between heritage rooms with high ceilings and modern tower rooms; all have quality linen and supercomfy beds.

HILTON HOTEL **$$$**
Map p250 (☑9266 2000; www.sydney.hilton.com; 488 George St; r from $279; ✿@🏧🖥; 🚇Town Hall) Try to contain your glee as you waltz into the deluxe Hilton. Cooler-than-cool rooms feature black timber bedheads, flatscreen TVs, DVD players and internet telephony. Superchef Luke Mangan handles the restaurant; Zeta and Marble Bar lure the beautiful people; business facilities are state-of-the-art.

MERITON SERVICED APARTMENTS KENT ST APARTMENTS **$$**
Map p250 (☑8263 5500; www.staymsa.com/kent; 528 Kent St; apt from $205; ✿🏧🖥; 🚇Town Hall) There's a lot to be said for staying in a serviced apartment, not least the ability to be able to wash your smalls whenever

the need arises. Each of the one- to three-bedroom apartments in this modern tower has laundry facilities and a full kitchen complete with a dishwasher. Not that you'll want to cook, with Chinatown at your feet.

WAKE UP!
HOSTEL $

Map p255 (⌨9288 7888; www.wakeup.com.au; 509 Pitt St; dm $34-42, s $98, d $108-118; ✸@🛜; 🚇Central) Flashpackers sleep soundly in this converted 1900 department store on top of Sydney's busiest intersection. It's a convivial, colourful, professionally run hostel with 520 beds, lots of activities, a tour desk, 24-hour check-in, a sunny cafe, a bar and no excuse for neglecting your inner party animal.

RAILWAY SQUARE YHA
HOSTEL $

Map p255 (⌨9281 9666; www.yha.com.au; 8-10 Lee St; dm $37-44, r $107; @🛜🏊; 🚇Central) This hostel's not just central, it's actually in Central station. A nouveau-industrial renovation has turned a former parcel shed (complete with platform) into a hip hostel. You can even sleep in dorms in converted train carriages. The kids will love it (but bring earplugs). Private en suite rooms also available.

SYDNEY CENTRAL YHA
HOSTEL $

Map p255 (⌨9218 9000; www.yha.com.au; 11 Rawson Pl; dm $40-46, r $115-134; @🛜🏊; 🚇Central) Near Central station, this 1913 heritage-listed monolith has been renovated to within an inch of its life. Rooms are brightly painted and the kitchens are great, but the highlight is sitting in the rooftop pool making faces at the government workers in the office tower across the street.

ESTABLISHMENT HOTEL
BOUTIQUE HOTEL $$$

Map p250 (⌨9240 3100; www.merivale.com.au; 5 Bridge Lane; r from $299; ✸@🛜; 🚇Wynyard) Hidden down a nondescript lane, this so-hip-it-hurts boutique hotel attracts discreet celebrities, style-conscious couples and cashed-up execs dreaming of a nooner with their assistants. What the hotel lacks in facilities it more than makes up for in glamour. And by staying here you'll have VIP access into all the 'it' bars of the Merivale empire.

PARK8
BOUTIQUE HOTEL $$$

Map p250 (⌨9283 2488; www.8hotels.com; 185 Castlereagh St; r $225-275; ✸🛜; 🚇Town Hall) Hidden in plain sight behind a

hole-in-the-wall cafe in the centre of town, this boutique hotel has irrepressibly perky staff (maybe its something to do with all that caffeine), who alternate between frothing milk and welcoming guests. The rooms are comfortable and chic; choose between quieter standard rooms with frosted-glass windows or deluxe rooms with proper windows opening on to the noisy-by-day street.

RADISSON BLU
HOTEL $$$

Map p250 (⌨8214 0000; www.radissonblu.com/plazahotel-sydney; 27 O'Connell St; r from $350; ✸@🛜🏊) Would-be Clark Kents will feel right at home in this wedge-shaped sandstone building, built for the hardened hacks of the *Sydney Morning Herald* in the 1920s. The rooms are spacious, if a little generic, with marble bathrooms and all the typical big-hotel comforts. Plus there's a health club and spa, with an indoor lap pool and small gym.

HYDE PARK INN
APARTMENTS $$

Map p250 (⌨9264 6001; www.hydeparkinn.com.au; 271 Elizabeth St; s $176-193, d $193-209; ✸@; 🚇Museum) Right on the park, this relaxed place offers studio rooms with kitchenettes, deluxe rooms with balconies and full kitchens, and some two-bedroom apartments. All have flat-screen TVs with cable access.

MEDINA GRAND SYDNEY
APARTMENTS $$

Map p250 (⌨9274 0000; www.medina.com.au; 511 Kent St; apt from $160; ✸🛜🏊; 🚇Town Hall) Near both Chinatown and Darling Harbour but with double-glazed windows to ensure a good night's sleep, this apartment hotel offers spacious, fully equipped apartments and smaller studio rooms with kitchenettes. The larger apartments offer the best value.

MERITON SERVICED
APARTMENTS PITT ST
APARTMENTS $$

Map p250 (⌨8263 7400; www.staymsa.com/pitt; 329 Pitt St; apt from $205; ✸🛜🏊; 🚇Town Hall) Forget their most famous project, Wembley Stadium, Meriton is known in Sydney as the builder of swanky but soulless apartment complexes. This huge tower (42 floors above ground) offers Smeg appliances and spectacular views. BYO soul.

VIBE HOTEL SYDNEY
HOTEL $$

Map p255 (⌨8272 3300; www.vibehotels.com.au; 111 Goulburn St; r from $165; ✸@🛜🏊; 🚇Museum) The rooms are spacious and well priced at this handy midrange hotel near Museum and Central train stations and on the fringe of Surry Hills. All have a seating area, flat-screen TV, work desk and large closet. It has a ground-floor cafe and a gym, sauna and good-sized pool on the outdoor deck.

PENSIONE HOTEL HOTEL $$

Map p255 (✆9265 8888; www.pensione.com.au; 631-635 George St; r from $103; ❋@☎; ❑Central) This tastefully reworked post office (derelict for 40 years) features smart, neutrally shaded rooms with TVs and fridges. Mark Rothko prints and a wooden staircase warm the simple, restrained surrounds. The windows facing George St are double-glazed but don't open. The quietest rooms are those facing the central lightwell.

🛏 Darling Harbour & Pyrmont

MEDINA GRAND HARBOURSIDE APARTMENTS $$

Map p254 (✆9249 7000; www.medina.com.au; 55 Shelley St; apt from $155; ❋❄; ☻Darling Harbour) Heaven is a swish, spacious apartment where people clean up after you. That's exactly what happens at this newish low-rise development, just off King St Wharf. All apartments have kitchens, and all but the studios have laundry facilities and balconies.

🛏 Inner West

TOP CHOICE **TARA** B&B $$

Map p256 (✆9519 4809; www.taraguesthouse.com.au; 13 Edgeware Rd; r without/with bathroom $176/204; ☎; ❑Newtown) You could imagine Scarlett O'Hara and Rhett Butler trading insults beneath the high ceilings of this 1886 mansion, if it weren't for the eclectic art scattered about and the steady stream of traffic outside. Frankly, my dear, you might give a damn that only one of the four bedrooms has an en suite, but that's all part of the period charm.

GLEBE POINT YHA HOSTEL $

(✆9692 8418; www.yha.com.au; 262 Glebe Point Rd; dm $30-35, s $70, d $84; @☎; ❑431) Well run and less uptight than some YHAs, this chilled-out, brightly painted hostel has decent facilities, plenty of organised activities and simple, clean rooms with sinks. The

main lure for party people is the rooftop terrace with its barbecue nights, speed-dating extravaganzas and salsa showdowns.

VULCAN HOTEL BOUTIQUE HOTEL $$

Map p256 (✆9211 3283; www.vulcanhotel.com.au; 500 Wattle St; r from $149; ❋@☎; ❑Central) Vulcan was a watering hole well into the 1990s before the lousy pub rooms were converted into boutique budget accommodation. Discreet international staff direct you to minimalist grey and white en suite rooms, complete with TV and minibar. No sign of Dr Spock...

BILLABONG GARDENS HOSTEL $

Map p256 (✆9550 3236; www.billabonggardens.com.au; 5-11 Egan St; dm $26-28, s $55-75, d $75-95; @☎❄; ❑Newtown) This enduring motel-like hostel offers a broader experience than most backpacker joints, with travellers, touring rock bands and urbanites of all persuasions lobbing up on the doorstep. Rooms come with or without bathrooms, and encircle a central solar-heated pool.

ALISHAN INTERNATIONAL GUEST HOUSE GUESTHOUSE $$

Map p256 (✆9566 4048; www.alishan.com.au; 100 Glebe Point Rd; dm/s/d from $35/70/120; ☎; ❑431-434) In a substantial Victorian house in the centre of Glebe, the Alishan (an area of Taiwan, don't you know) is clean, quiet and well run, with spacious communal areas including a modern kitchen and a garden with a barbecue. All rooms have TVs and fridges, although some of the cheapies share bathrooms.

GLEBE VILLAGE HOSTEL $

(✆9660 8878; www.glebevillage.com; 256 Glebe Point Rd; dm $23-27, s/d $65/90; @☎; ❑431) Straddling four Victorian houses, Glebe Village is a bit like a grungy collection of student flats – perfect for those less hung-up on comfort than good times. It offers a mix of shared bathrooms and en suites, plus lively communal areas and sunny tables. Breakfast (included) might be pancakes if you're lucky.

🛏 Surry Hills & Darlinghurst

🖉 **BOUNCE** HOSTEL $

Map p260 (✆9281 2222; www.bouncehotel.com.au; 28 Chalmers St; dm $32-43, r $139-149;

✹@🤶; 🅁Central) Bounce positions itself 'where budget and boutique meet', which is a spot-on description. All dorms and rooms are air-conditioned, female-only dorms have private bathrooms, beds have inner-spring mattresses and bathrooms are sleek. Chuck another prawn on the roof terrace's barbie and soak up those skyline views.

ADINA APARTMENT
HOTEL SYDNEY
APARTMENTS $$

Map p260 (☑8302 1000; www.adinahotels.com.au; 359 Crown St; apt from $190; ✹@🤶🛏; 🅁Central) As one of the main pastimes in Surry Hills is eating out, you may find the well-equipped kitchenette of your slick, spacious apartment doesn't get a lot of use – the Adina building alone is home to three exalted eateries. The gym, sauna and leafy pool area are plenty popular over Mardi Gras.

MEDUSA
BOUTIQUE HOTEL $$

Map p260 (☑9331 1000; www.medusa.com.au; 267 Darlinghurst Rd; r from $195; ✹🤶; 🅁Kings Cross) Medusa the seducer's shocking pink exterior hints at the witty, luscious decor inside. Small colour-saturated suites with large beds, mod-con bathrooms and regal furnishings open onto a courtyard with a surprisingly noisy water feature. If your hair turns into snakes, Medusa is pet-friendly.

BIG HOSTEL
HOSTEL $

Map p260 (☑9281 6030; www.bighostel.com; 212 Elizabeth St; dm $30-34, s/d $85/99; ✹🤶; 🅁Central) If it weren't for the bunks, the backpacks and the snoring strangers, you might forget you're in a hostel. Mr Big has snazzy communal areas, clean bathrooms and a cool rooftop terrace. Elizabeth St's dark hollows aren't Sydney's most salubrious spaces, but there's good security and Central station is just across the road.

HOTEL ALTAMONT
BOUTIQUE HOTEL $$

Map p260 (☑9360 6000; www.altamont.com.au; 207 Darlinghurst Rd; d from $155; ✹@🤶; 🅁Kings Cross) Altamont flagged the end of '60s peace and love, but here in Darlinghurst, the good times continue unabated. Spiffy-looking en suite doubles feel like they should cost more than they do, staff and communal areas are welcoming (especially the terrace), and it's tantalisingly close to the Cross. Breakfast included.

MANOR HOUSE
BOUTIQUE HOTEL $$

Map p260 (☑9380 6633; www.manorhouse.com.au; 86 Flinders St; r from $160; 🛏; 🅁Central) Sashay from Taylor Sq into this time-tripping 1850s mansion, complete with extravagant chandeliers, moulded ceilings, Victorian tiling and fountains tinkling in the garden. Even an ugly green carpet and dated bathrooms don't detract from the character. It's filled to the gills around Mardi Gras time, being right on the parade route and within staggering distance of the party.

KIRKETON HOTEL
BOUTIQUE HOTEL $$

Map p260 (☑9332 2011; www.kirketon.com.au; 229 Darlinghurst Rd; r from $144; 🛏; 🅁Kings Cross) You might feel like you're in a David Lynch movie as you wander the darkened, mirror-lined corridors to your room, one of 40 spread over two levels. Even the cramped standard rooms have classy trimmings such as gilt-edged mirrors, superior linen and plasma screens.

CITY CROWN MOTEL
MOTEL $$

Map p260 (☑9331 2433; www.citycrownmotel.com.au; 289 Crown St; r from $125; ✹@🤶; 🅁Central) The location is the clincher for this otherwise run-of-the-mill, brown-brick motel offering simple rooms, some with a balcony or a patio. Helpful management, DVD players and an on-site cafe are bonuses. Rates rise 50% for Mardi Gras, but drop substantially in the low season.

HOTEL STELLAR
HOTEL $$

Map p260 (☑9264 9754; www.hotelstellar.com; 4 Wentworth Ave; r from $169; ✹@🤶; 🅁Museum) After doing a spell as a hip boutique hotel this Victorian office building is now a Best Western, and while it retains plenty of character, it's not as cool (or as expensive) as it once was. Rooms have kitchenettes, flat-screen TVs, DVD players and, when we last visited, conspicuous mouse traps.

ROYAL SOVEREIGN HOTEL
PUB $

Map p260 (☑9331 3672; www.darlobar.com.au; cnr Liverpool St & Darlinghurst Rd; r with shared bathroom $77; 🅁Kings Cross) With one of Darlinghurst's favourite drinking dens downstairs (the Darlo Bar), these eight nifty cheapies are an appealing proposition. The bathrooms are shared, the rooms are small and the beds are a bit saggy, but they're smartly painted and come with TVs. Not for light sleepers.

ALFRED PARK HOSTEL $
(☏9319 4031; www.alfredpark.com.au; 207 Cleveland St; dm $27-31, s with/without bathroom $72/62, tw $82/102; ✳@令; 闫Redfern) Housed in an ageing two-storey house on the Redfern side of busy Cleveland St, this hostel is well located for unfussy travellers keen to explore the increasingly hip Surry Hills/Redfern/Chippendale fringe. It's a little down-at-heel, but extras include free wi-fi, air-conditioning and friendly staff.

Kings Cross & Potts Point

TOP CHOICE **SIMPSONS OF POTTS POINT** BOUTIQUE HOTEL $$$
Map p259 (☏9356 2199; www.simpsonshotel.com; 8 Challis Ave; r from $235; ✳@令; 闫Kings Cross) An 1892 red-brick villa at the quiet end of a busy cafe strip, the perennially popular Simpsons looks to yesteryear for decorative flourishes. The downstairs lounge and breakfast room are lovely, and rooms are both comfortable and impeccably clean.

BLUE SYDNEY HOTEL $$$
Map p260 (☏9331 9000; www.taihotels.com/sydney; 6 Cowper Wharf Rd; r from $275; ✳@令≋; 闫Kings Cross) Once you could stay here for the night and boast that you slept next to Russell Crowe (he used to live in one of the apartments at the end of the wharf). Even so, you're sure to enjoy the boutique sensibilities and excellent location of this hotel carved out of the historic Woolloomooloo finger wharf.

DIAMANT HOTEL $$
Map p259 (☏9295 8888; www.diamant.com.au; 14 Kings Cross Rd; r from $175; ✳令; 闫Kings Cross) The new kid on the Kings Cross block is the swish, noir Diamant, a 76-room hilltop high-rise. Space-age corridors open onto slick, spacious rooms, all with king-size beds, quality linen, huge plasma screens and iPod docks. Choose from bridge, harbour or city views. Affable staff complete a very impressive package.

VICTORIA COURT HOTEL B&B $$
Map p259 (☏9357 3200; www.victoriacourt.com.au; 122 Victoria St; d $138-380; ✳令; 闫Kings Cross) Chintzy charm reigns supreme at this faded but well-run B&B, which has 25 rooms in a pair of three-storey 1881 terrace houses.

The more expensive rooms are larger and have balconies.

HOTEL 59 GUESTHOUSE $$
Map p259 (☏9360 5900; www.hotel59.com.au; 59 Bayswater Rd; s $99, d $125-132; ✳令; 闫Kings Cross) Hotel 59 is good bang for your buck on the quiet part of Bayswater Rd, with nouveau-Med rooms and smiley staff who go out of their way not to get in your way. The cafe downstairs does whopping cooked breakfasts (included in the price) for those barbarous Kings Cross hangovers. Two-night minimum.

WALDORF WOOLLOOMOOLOO WATERS APARTMENTS $$
Map p259 (☏8356 1500; www.woolloomooloo-waldorf-apartments.com.au; 88 Dowling St; apt from $220; ✳令; 闫Kings Cross) Despite its proximity to Kings Cross and the city, Woolloomooloo is a relatively quiet place to stay. This tidy backstreet block offers spacious apartments ranging from roomy studios to two-bedrooms. The decor is beyond dated (we doubt the stained-glass partitions were ever 'on trend'), but the apartments all have kitchens and some also have balconies and laundries.

BLUE PARROT HOSTEL $
Map p259 (☏9356 4888; www.blueparrot.com.au; 87 Macleay St; dm $35-40; @令; 闫Kings Cross) Polly want a cracker little hostel? Behind the shocking blue-and-mustard-painted bricks is a well-maintained, secure little place with a lazy courtyard strung with hammocks. There are no private rooms, just dorms. Renovations in progress at the time of research (we told you it was well-maintained) hampered some of our usual snooping.

JACKAROO HOSTEL $
Map p259 (☏9332 2244; www.jackaroohostel.com; 107-109 Darlinghurst Rd; dm $33, r with/without bathroom $90/80; @令; 闫Kings Cross) There's no accommodation positioned closer to the heart of the action than this hostel directly above Kings Cross station. Ordinarily that wouldn't be a good thing, but Jackaroo passes muster as the least trashy place on Sydney's most trashy strip. Try to nab a rear-facing room but pack earplugs regardless. The vibe is bright, bustling and (extremely) youthful.

BACKPACKERS HQ
HOSTEL $

Map p259 (📞9356 4551; www.backpackershq. com.au; 174 Victoria St; dm $32-37, r with/without bathroom $95/80; 🛜; 🚇Kings Cross) Revolving around an attractive central courtyard with a slick indoor/outdoor kitchen, this newly renovated hostel has shed some of its laidback Bohemian vibe in favour of designer touches and splashes of bright orange paint. All rooms have TVs and fridges; the pricier ones have en suites. Free internet and breakfast.

EVA'S BACKPACKERS
HOSTEL $

Map p259 (📞9358 2185; www.evasbackpackers. com.au; 6-8 Orwell St; dm/r $32/85; 🛜; 🚇Kings Cross) Eva's is a perennial backpacker favourite, probably because it's far enough from the Kings Cross fray to maintain some composure and dignity. Free breakfast and wi-fi, plus an ace rooftop barbecue area and a sociable kitchen-dining room. Clean and secure.

MAISONETTE HOTEL
GUESTHOUSE $$

Map p259 (📞9357 3878; www.maisonettehotel. com; 31 Challis Ave; s/d from $64/106; 🛜; 🚇Kings Cross) Wake up and smell the coffee above Potts Point's hip cafe strip. The rooms range from small, bright doubles with en suites to little singles with shared bathrooms; all have TVs and kitchenettes.

ORIGINAL BACKPACKERS LODGE
HOSTEL $

Map p259 (📞9356 3232; www.originalback packers.com.au; 160-162 Victoria St; dm $28-32, s with/without bathroom $80/70, d $90/80; 🚇Kings Cross) This long-standing hostel meanders through two historic mansions, offering dozens of beds and great (if a little noisy) outdoor spaces. Rooms have high ceilings, fridges, fans and shared bathrooms (some singles and doubles have en suites). There's a busy schedule of activities to get you out and socialising.

MARINERS COURT
HOTEL $$

Map p259 (📞9320 3888; www.marinerscourt. com.au; 44-50 McElhone St; r $135-155; 🚇Kings Cross) A tucked-away treasure, this ship-shape port-in-a-storm won't be the flashest place you'll stay in Sydney (the vibe is kinda 1994), but it offers that rare combination of location, price and a bit of elbow room. All rooms have courtyards or balconies, some with leafy outlooks. Good wheelchair access.

O'MALLEY'S HOTEL
PUB $

Map p259 (📞9357 2211; www.omalleyshotel.com. au; 228 William St; r $89-139; 🌀; 🚇Kings Cross) This raucous Irish pub has 15 simple rooms upstairs (all with private bathrooms and TVs), which are surprisingly quiet, given the William St traffic and nightly twiddle-dee-dee live music downstairs. The two harbour-view rooms are winners; one has a full kitchen.

ELEPHANT BACKPACKER
HOSTEL $

Map p259 (📞9380 2922; www.elephantback packer.com.au; 50 Sir John Young Cres; dm $24-28, r $90; @🛜; 🚇St James) Supremely grungy but not without charm, this 1892-built building has an awesome roof terrace that floats you up into the city lights. It's a huge place (250 beds), but the ceilings are high and the rooms airy – you'll never feel like you're stuffed into someone else's backpack. The downside? Peeling paint, disinterested staff and traffic noise.

🛏 Paddington & Centennial Park

KATHRYN'S ON QUEEN
B&B $$

Map p264 (📞9327 4535; www.kathryns.com.au; 20 Queen St; r $180-260; 🚌380) Deftly run by the ever-smiley Kathryn, this grandiose 1888 Victorian terrace at the top end of ooh-la-la Queen St has just two rooms. Dotted with antiques, the rooms are tastefully decorated in cream and white; choose between the en suite attic room or the 1st-floor room with a balcony overlooking the street.

ARTS
HOTEL $$

Map p264 (📞9361 0211; www.artshotel.com.au; 21 Oxford St; r $178-198; 🌀@🛜🌊; 🚌380) Popular with gay travellers, this well-managed 64-room hotel has simple but comfortable rooms in a handy location on the Paddington-Darlinghurst border. There's heavy-duty triple-glazing on the Oxford St frontage, while the rear rooms face a quiet lane. The brick-paved central courtyard has a small solar-heated pool.

HUGHENDEN
HOTEL $$

Map p264 (📞9363 4863; www.thehughenden. com.au; 14 Queen St; r/apt from $138/225; 🌀🛜; 🚌380) Just a lofted hook shot from the Sydney Cricket Ground, Oxford St and Centennial Park, this quirky Victorian Italianate guesthouse has plenty of charm without much style. Room categories range from 'cosy' (a euphemism for small and dark with a window facing the corridor) to comfortable terrace apartments on the roof. For your distraction there's Sunday high tea and story-telling evenings.

Bondi to Coogee

BONDI BEACH HOUSE
GUESTHOUSE **$$**

Map p266 (☑9300 0369; www.bondibeachhouse. com.au; 28 Sir Thomas Mitchell Rd; s $110-135, d $160-275, ste $280-305; ✳☎; ☐380) Tucked away in a tranquil pocket behind Campbell Pde, this charming place offers a real home-away-from-home atmosphere. Though only a five-minute walk from the beach, you may well be tempted to stay in all day – the rear courtyard and front terrace are great spots for relaxing, and the rooms (particularly the suites) are conducive to long sleep ins.

HOTEL BONDI
HOTEL **$$**

Map p266 (☑9130 3271; www.hotelbondi.com.au; 178 Campbell Pde; s $90, d $125-165; ✳☎; ☐380) At the time of research Bondi's grand dame had shed her Barbara Cartland-esque pink wrap and was in the process of an extreme makeover, creating two larger rooms out of every three 1920s shoeboxes. By the time you're reading this there should be air-conditioning and double-glazing throughout (we suspect the prices might creep up as well).

DIVE HOTEL
BOUTIQUE HOTEL **$$**

Map p267 (☑9665 5538; www.divehotel.com. au; 234 Arden St; r $180-315; ☎☎; ☐372-374) Plenty of hotels don't live up to their name ('grand', 'palace' and 'central' are often less than literal) and thankfully neither does this one. The 14 boutique rooms here are well designed and come with kitchenettes and small groovy bathrooms. Breakfast included.

COOGEE SANDS
APARTMENTS **$$**

Map p267 (☑9665 8588; www.coogeesands.com. au; 161 Dolphin St; apt from $190; ✳☎; ☐372-374) The decor is dated but the golden sands of Coogee Beach are just across the street from this apartment hotel. Standard studios are a decent size; add about $10 for a shady courtyard and $90 for an ocean view.

COOGEE BEACH HOUSE
HOSTEL **$**

Map p267 (☑9665 1162; www.coogeebeach house.com; 171 Arden St; dm/s/tw $33/81/86; ☎☎; ☐372-374) This affable, alcohol-free hostel has four-bed dorms and basic private rooms (all with shared bathrooms), a barbecue terrace and a homely living room for rainy days. Freebies include a simple breakfast and a DVD and book library, and surfboards can be hired.

BONDI BEACHHOUSE YHA
HOSTEL **$**

Map p266 (☑9365 2088; www.yha.com.au; 63 Fletcher St; dm $35, r with/without bathroom $100/80; ☎☎; ☐381) A steep stroll from the beach, this 95-bed art-deco hostel is the best in Bondi. Dorms sleep between four and eight, and some of the private rooms have ocean views – all are clean and well maintained. Facilities include a table-tennis table, games room, barbecue, free bodyboard and snorkel use, and a rooftop deck with views over Tamarama Beach.

RAVESI'S
BOUTIQUE HOTEL **$$$**

Map p266 (☑9365 4422; www.ravesis.com. au; 118 Campbell Pde; r/ste from $249/299; ☎; ☐380) Ravesi's fits into the Bondi's shaggy surfer scene like a briefcase on a beach – its sleek chocolate and grey rooms are positioned above one of the strip's busiest bars. At the very top, the best rooms have deep balconies with five-star ocean views. Pack earplugs for the standard rooms above the bar.

Manly

BEAUFORT AT THE BEACH
B&B **$$$**

Map p268 (☑9977 2968; www.beaufort.com. au; 8 Quinton Rd; r $225-275; ✳☎☎; ☎Manly) Behind the boxed hedges and manicured lawn, this two-storey Federation-era wooden house on a quiet residential street is Manly's most elegant and luxurious accommodation option. The two tastefully decorated guest rooms form a suite, which is only let to one party at a time – so book well ahead. Treats include a deep bathtub, waffle bathrobes and large beach towels.

101 ADDISON ROAD
B&B **$$**

Map p268 (☑9977 6216; www.bb-manly.com; 101 Addison Rd; s/d $150/170; ☎Manly) At the risk of sounding like a Victorian matron, the only word to describe this 1880 cottage on a quiet street is 'delightful'. Two rooms are available, but single-group bookings are the name of the game (from one to four people) – meaning you'll have free reign of the antique-strewn accommodation, including a private lounge with an open fire.

WINDERMERE
B&B $$

Map p268 (☑9977 7363; www.windermeremanly. com; 31 Cliff St; r $140; ☞; ☑Manly) If you miss out on a room at 101 Addison Road, this pleasant place nearby offers a very similar setup (two bedrooms, but only one booking accepted at a time). While it doesn't have quite the same sumptuous historic charm, it's still an extremely good proposition.

OUTBACK LODGE
GUESTHOUSE $$

Map p268 (☑0412 613 401; www.theoutback lodge.com.au; 5 Smith St; r $100-120; ☞; ☑Manly) Manly is hardly the outback, and if it was, this salmon-pink stucco house with a little windmill on its lawn would scarcely blend in. Even on a quiet Manly backstreet it's conspicuous, not least for the excellent value for money of its tidy, unassuming rooms. Each has an ensuite bathroom and either a kitchenette or full kitchen.

PERIWINKLE
B&B $$

Map p268 (☑9977 4668; www.periwinkleguest house.com.au; 18-19 East Esplanade; s with/without bathroom from $157/127, d from $182/150; ☞; ☑Manly) This lavishly restored Victorian manor faces the sunset across Manly Cove. Twelve en suite rooms are elegant and well appointed, and there's a cosy kitchen. If your wallet can stand the heat, avoid the ground-floor rooms facing the courtyard, which can get a bit stuffy. Rates include breakfast.

NOVOTEL SYDNEY MANLY PACIFIC
HOTEL $$$

Map p268 (☑9977 7666; www.novotelmanly pacific.com.au; 55 North Steyne; r from $279; @☞☒; ☑Manly) Right on Manly's ocean beach, this midriser has a dated corporate vibe but is a million miles from the city's business

hustle. Check the surf from ocean-front balconies, or hit the rooftop pool if you don't want sand in your laptop. Courtyard-view rooms aren't nearly as good as the ocean-view versions.

Other Suburbs

LANE COVE RIVER TOURIST PARK
CAMPGROUND $

(☑9888 9133; www.lcrtp.com.au; Plassey Rd, Macquarie Park; unpowered/powered sites per 2 people $35/37, cabins from $130; @☞☒; ☑North Ryde) Have a back-to-nature experience in the heart of suburbia, staying in this national park campsite 14km northwest of the city centre. There are caravan and camping sites, cabins and a pool to cool off in when the city swelters. Park admission is included in the rates.

CRONULLA BEACH YHA
HOSTEL $

(☑9527 7772; www.cronullabeachyha.com; 40-42 Kingsway; dm $34-35, s/d $75/100; @; ☑Cronulla) Given that 90% of the clientele are shaggy surfer dudes, no-one's going to get too hung up if the showers aren't totally immaculate. Comfortable in its own skin, this is a great party hostel with a free pool table and bodyboards for the beach. En suite doubles approach motel quality. Cronulla is 30km south of the city centre.

Understand Sydney

SYDNEY TODAY 192

Amid global financial meltdowns, soaring housing costs, gang turf wars and transport snags, Sydney remains reasonably upbeat.

HISTORY 194

From millennia of Eora rule to a colony founded on convicts and rum, to today's thriving metropolis.

FOOD CULTURE 200

How waves of migration and an abundance of fresh Australian produce created a New World cuisine.

THE ARTS 204

Sydneysiders taking their place among the world's best across the artistic spectrum.

ARCHITECTURE 209

From the colonial to the contemporary, with a global architectural icon in between.

SPORTY SYDNEY.......................... 213

Getting under the skin of the national obsession as it plays out in the Harbour City.

Sydney Today

With around 4.3 million residents, Sydney is Oceania's biggest and brightest city, and it dominates its home state of New South Wales politically and economically. Australia may have escaped recession during the recent global economic turmoil but much of that was due to a resources boom on the other side of the country. While plenty of Sydney-siders are feeling the pinch, the city remains reasonably upbeat, taking solace in the knowledge that it could have been much worse.

Best on Film

Finding Nemo (2003) Animated feature following an adventurous clownfish who finds himself captive in a Sydney aquarium.
The Adventures of Priscilla, Queen of the Desert (1994) Sydney drag queens road-tripping to Alice Springs.
Muriel's Wedding (1994) Both a good laugh and genuinely affecting; Toni Collette's Muriel reinvents her frumpy Abba-tragic self.
Strictly Ballroom (1992) Breakthrough Aussie comedy set in the surreal world of competitive ballroom dancing.

Best in Print

The Lieutenant (Kate Grenville, 2008) The names are changed but Grenville's fascinating chronicle of first contacts with the Eora people rings true.
Leviathan (John Birmingham, 1999) A gritty history exploring Sydney's seamier side, written in the tone of an unauthorised biography.
The Playmaker (Thomas Keneally, 1987) A fictionalised account of First Fleet life.
Voss (Patrick White, 1957) Nobel Prize–winner White contrasts the unforgiving outback with Sydney colonial life.

Sydney Style

Despite recent economic events, Sydneysiders remain optimistic. Most Sydney living happens under the sun and the stars: street cafes, alfresco restaurants, moonlight cinemas, beer gardens, parades... It follows that locals have an almost pathological disdain for over-dressing. As the innumerable supermodel-spangled billboards around town attest, less is more in the Sydney fashion stakes, and showing some skin is de rigueur. And if you've got a hot bod, why not decorate it? Full-sleeve tattoos have become mainstream, while hospitality workers sans piercings are rare. Smoking is as popular as ever – will future Sydney echo with an emphysematic death rattle?

Ultimately, Sydney's relentlessly chipper attitude tends to bowl over (or at least distract from) any obstacle. A swim in the surf, a bucket of prawns by the harbour, a kickin' DJ set or a multicultural meal goes a long way toward convincing the majority of residents that life here is pretty darn good.

Housing Woes

If Sydneysiders seem utterly obsessed by real estate, it's for good reason. A 2012 Demographia survey rated Sydney as the third least affordable city (behind Vancouver and Hong Kong) in which to buy a house within the English-speaking world. Median house prices ($637,600) are 9.2 times higher than median household incomes ($69,400) – a ratio of 3:1 is considered affordable, above 5:1 severely unaffordable.

For those Sydneysiders for whom home ownership seems like an unattainable dream, there's a double whammy to face: renting is increasingly unaffordable too. The median asking price is now $485 per week (in Melbourne it's $360) and stories abound of hordes of people turning up to showings of even the crummiest flats. For those on the fringes, it's hardest: Anglicare estimated that out of 9400 properties advertised for rent in April 2011, only 72 were affordable for those on the government pension or single-parent payment.

Part of the challenge is geographical. The city is hemmed in between ocean, mountains and national parks, restraining the ability for new housing to expand on its fringes. Then there's Australia's perennial problem – how to provide enough water for an expanding city?

The silver lining? In most surveys of the world's most liveable cities, Sydney rates in the top 10.

Transport

Transport is one of the city's biggest political hot potatoes. Most travellers will find it suprisingly easy and reasonably pleasant to get around using public transport, but for those residents not living in suburbs served by train lines, the daily commute involves traffic snarls or expensive tolls... or both.

In 2012 the state government trumpeted its purchase of the company running the monorail and light rail as a 'once-in-a-generation opportunity' to fix the transport issues in the city centre. By 2014 they're promising that the Opal Card, a new smart ticketing system (similar to London's Oyster Card) will be fully operational on all trains, ferries, buses and trams.

And the monorail? While it must have seemed like the way of the future when it opened in 1988, its pointless loop through Darling Harbour and Haymarket is soon to be a thing of the past (probably by the time you're reading this, in fact). It was always more of a tourist attraction than a serious transport option anyway, and the city's transport boffins hope that the space saved by its removal can be used to extend the tram lines.

Gang Turf Wars

Sydneysiders have long taken a prurient interest in the power struggles between criminal families that have plagued Melbourne for decades. Of course, Sydney's not without form in this regard: bitter clashes between 'razor gangs' terrorised Surry Hills and Kings Cross in the 1930s. Yet the current wave of violence between rival bikie gangs has rattled the city.

Between August 2011 and April 2012 there were 60 gun attacks linked to turf disputes, and while the violence appears to have been mainly criminal-on-criminal, there's a very real fear that innocent bystanders may get caught in the fray. Travellers shouldn't be too concerned – unless you're frequenting gang hangouts in the outer suburbs, you're unlikely to be at risk.

if Sydney were 100 people

70 would be born in Australia
12 would be born in Asia
10 would be born in Europe
2 would be born in New Zealand
6 would be born elsewhere

belief systems
(% of population)

64 Christian
14 No religion
4 Muslim
4 Buddhist
2 Hindu
12 Other

population per sq km

SYDNEY MELBOURNE

≈ 313 people

History

Although go-getting modern Sydney may not seem particularly interested in the past, it's surprisingly easy to catch glimpses of what's gone before. Ancient rock carvings still adorn the headlands, people continue to travel along convict-hewn roads and large chunks of the harbour look much as they did when the First Fleet breezed in and changed absolutely everything.

ABORIGINAL AUSTRALIA

Australian Aboriginal society has the longest continuous cultural history in the world, its origins dating back to at least the last ice age. Mystery shrouds many aspects of Australian prehistory, but it's thought that the first humans probably came here from Southeast Asia more than 50,000 years ago. Archaeological evidence suggests that descendants of these first arrivals colonised the continent within a few thousand years.

Aborigines were traditionally tribal people, living in extended family groups. Knowledge and skills obtained over millennia enabled them to use their environment extensively and sustainably. Their intimate knowledge of animal behaviour and plant harvesting ensured that food shortages were rare.

The simplicity of Aboriginal technology contrasted with a sophisticated cultural life. Religion, history, law and art were integrated in complex ceremonies, which depicted ancestral beings who created the land and its people, as well as prescribing codes of behaviour. Aborigines continue to perform traditional ceremonies in many parts of Australia.

When the British arrived at Sydney Cove in 1788, it's estimated that there were between 500,000 and one million Aborigines across Australia, with between 200 and 250 distinct regional languages. Governor Arthur Phillip estimated that around 1500 Aborigines lived around Sydney at first contact, but his figures can't be relied upon.

The coastal people around Sydney were known as the Eora (which literally means 'from this place'), broken into clans such as the Cadigal and the Wangal. Three main languages were used by Aborigines in the area, encompassing several dialects and subgroups. Although there was

TIMELINE	40,000 BC	AD 1770	1788
	The Eora people live in Sydney, split into several separate tribes including the Dharug-speaking Cadigal around Sydney Cove. Ku-ring-gai people occupied the North Shore.	Lieutenant James Cook lands at Botany Bay and claims Australia for the British; he writes of the indigenous population: 'all they seem'd to want was us to be gone'.	The First Fleet drops anchor in Botany Bay, followed by Frenchman La Pérouse five days later; the British decide Botany Bay is unsuitable and head north to Port Jackson.

considerable overlap, Ku-ring-gai was generally spoken on the northern shore, Dharawal along the coast south of Botany Bay, and Dharug and its dialects around Parramatta on the plains to the Blue Mountains.

As Aboriginal society was based on tribal family groups, a coordinated response to the European colonisers wasn't possible. Without any 'legal right' to the lands they lived on – the British declared Australia to be terra nullius, meaning 'land belonging to no one' – Australia's Aborigines were dispossessed. Some were driven away by force, some were killed, many were shifted onto government reserves and missions, and thousands, including most of the Cadigal, succumbed to foreign diseases introduced by the Europeans.

Communities that had survived for millennia before the arrival of the settlers were changed – often shattered – forever.

Australia's Aborigines were the first people in the world to make polished, edge-ground stone tools; to cremate their dead; and to engrave and paint representations of themselves and the animals they hunted.

THE BLOOM OF BRITISH SAILS

When the American War of Independence disrupted the transportation of convicts to North America, Britain lost its main dumping ground for undesirables and needed somewhere else to put them. Joseph Banks, who had been Lieutenant James Cook's scientific leader during the expedition in 1770, piped up with the suggestion that Botany Bay would be a fine new site for criminals.

The 11 ships of the First Fleet landed at Botany Bay in January 1788 – a motley crew of 730 male and female convicts, 400 sailors, four companies of marines, and enough livestock and booze to last two years. Captain Arthur Phillip, eager to be the colony's first governor, didn't take to Botany Bay's meagre natural supplies. He weighed anchor after only a few days and sailed 25km north to the harbour Cook had named Port Jackson, where he discovered a crucial source of fresh water in what he called Sydney Cove (Circular Quay). The day was 26 January 1788, now celebrated as Australia Day (many Aborigines refer to it as 'Invasion Day' or 'Survival Day').

Convicts were put to work on farms, roads and government building projects, but Governor Phillip was convinced that the colony wouldn't progress if it relied solely on convict blood and sweat. He believed prosperity depended on attracting free settlers (to whom convicts would be assigned as labourers) and on the granting of land to officers, soldiers and worthy emancipists (convicts who had served their time). In 1791 James Ruse was the first former convict to be granted land by Governor Phillip; he was given 12 hectares as reward for his successful work in agriculture.

1791	1825	1836	1842
It's estimated that only three Cadigal people survive, their numbers decimated by the smallpox that arrived with the First Fleet. The Cadigal had no natural immunity to the disease.	Van Diemen's Land (Tasmania) is split off from NSW and declared a colony in its own right, followed by South Australia (1836), Victoria (1851) and Queensland (1859).	The state of NSW shrinks, with South Australia declared a separate colony. Victoria would be carved off in 1851 and Queensland in 1859.	The transportation of convicts to New South Wales effectively ceases; over the course of the previous half-century 150,000 people had been dumped in the colony.

WILD COLONIAL BOYS

EARLY DAYS

The early days of the colony weren't for softies – the threat of starvation hung over the settlement for at least 16 years. The Second Fleet arrived in 1790 with more convicts and supplies. A year later, following the landing of the Third Fleet, Sydney's population had swelled to around 4000.

When Governor Phillip went back to England in 1792 due to failing health, Francis Grose took over. Grose granted land to officers of the New South Wales Corps, nicknamed the Rum Corps. With so much money, land and cheap labour in their hands, this military leadership made huge profits at the expense of small farmers. They began paying for labour and local products in rum. Meeting little resistance (everyone was drunk), they managed to upset, defy, outmanoeuvre and outlast three governors, the last of which was William Bligh, the famed captain of the mutinous ship HMAV *Bounty*. In 1808 the Rum Corps, in cahoots with powerful agriculturalist John Macarthur, ousted Bligh from power in what became known as the Rum Rebellion.

The Rum Rebellion was the final straw for the British government – in 1809 it decided to punish its unruly child. Lieutenant Colonel Lachlan Macquarie was dispatched with his own regiment and ordered the New South Wales Corps to return to London to get their knuckles rapped. Having broken the stranglehold of the Rum Corps, Governor Macquarie began laying the groundwork for social reforms.

Until 1803, when a second penal outpost was established in Van Diemen's Land (today's Tasmania), Sydney was still the only European settlement in Australia. Inroads into the vast interior of the continent were only made in the ensuing 40 years.

In 1851 the discovery of large gold deposits near Bathurst, 200km west of Sydney, sparked Australia's first gold rush. Another massive find in the southern colony of Victoria shortly afterwards reduced Sydney to secondary size and importance to Melbourne. Melbourne's ascendency lasted from the 1850s until the economic depression of the 1890s, when Sydney swung back into national favour...and so the Sydney-Melbourne rivalry began.

THE AUSTRALIAN CENTURY

The Commonwealth of Australia came into being on 1 January 1901 and New South Wales (NSW) became a state of the new Australian nation. Yet Australia's legal ties with, loyalty to, and dependency on Britain remained strong. When WWI broke out in Europe, Australian troops were sent to fight in the trenches of France, at Gallipoli in Turkey and in the Middle East. This was a first test of physical stamina and strength for the nation, and it held its own, although almost 60,000 of the 330,000 troops perished in the war. A renewed patriotism cemented the country's confidence in itself. But, in the wake of so much slaughter, many

1842	1900	1902	1932
Sydney is officially declared a city, and London-born merchant John Hosking is elected as its first mayor.	Bubonic plague kills 103 people in Sydney's overcrowded and unhygienic slums; as a result, large areas of substandard housing, particularly around The Rocks, are cleared and rebuilt.	Women are granted the right to vote; the same right isn't extended to indigenous Australians until almost 70 years later, the result of a referendum.	Sydney's second-most-famous icon, the Sydney Harbour Bridge, opens to traffic; the vast structure is immediately loved by Sydney residents for both aesthetic and practical reasons.

Australians also questioned their relationship with their old colonial overlords. The bond between Britain and Australia was never quite the same.

If Australia was now notionally independent, the same could not be said for its indigenous peoples. From 1910 to the end of the 1960s, a policy of 'cultural assimilation' allowed Aboriginal children (usually of mixed race) to be forcibly removed from their families and schooled in the ways of white society and Christianity. Around 100,000 children (dubbed the 'stolen generation') were separated from their parents in this way, causing untold stress and damage to the nation's indigenous community.

Meanwhile, Australia's economy grew through the 1920s until the Great Depression hit the country hard. By 1932, however, Australia was starting to recover due to rises in wool prices and a revival of manufacturing. With the opening of the Harbour Bridge in the same year, Sydney's building industry gained momentum and its northern suburbs began to develop.

In the years before WWII, Australia became increasingly fearful of the threat to national security posed by expansionist Japan. When war broke out, Australian troops again fought beside the British in Europe. Only after the Japanese bombed Pearl Harbor did Australia's own national security begin to take priority. A boom with a net barrage to prevent submarine access was stretched across the entrance channels of Sydney Harbour, and gun fortifications were set up on rocky harbour headlands.

Unlike the Northern Territory's capital city, Darwin, which was pretty much razed by Japanese bombings, Sydney escaped WWII virtually unscathed – although on 31 May 1942, three Japanese M24 midget submarines entered Sydney Harbour, sank a small supply vessel and lobbed a few shells into the suburbs of Bondi and Rose Bay.

Ultimately, US victory in the Battle of the Coral Sea protected Australia from Japanese invasion and pushed along Australia's shift of allegiance from mother Britain to the USA.

The aftermath of WWII, along with postwar immigration programs, made Australia more appealing to migrants from Europe. Australia experienced new growth and prosperity, Sydney's population exploded and the city's borders spread west.

Despite a strong trade-union movement, Australia came to accept the US view that communism threatened the increasingly Americanised Australian way of life. In 1965 the Liberal Party government sent troops to serve in the Vietnam War, even though Britain did not.

Early History Online

Barani (www.cityofsydney.nsw.gov.au/barani)

Dictionary of Sydney Project (www.dictionaryofsydney.org)

First Fleet Online (http://firstfleet.uow.edu.au/index.html)

Australian History Selected Websites (http://www.nla.gov.au/australiana/australian-history-selected-websites)

The Sydney Harbour Bridge during construction

FOX PHOTOS / STRINGER / GETTY IMAGES ©

1942

Japanese submarines enter Sydney Harbour and fire torpedos. Two subs are destroyed in the harbour boom net; the wreckage of a third is discovered off Sydney's Northern Beaches in 2006.

1959

Construction of the much-admired Sydney Opera House gets underway, but it doesn't open for performances until 1973, after a long and turbulent period of construction.

In 1967 a national referendum was held on whether to allow Aboriginal people the right to vote, which was passed by 90% of eligible voters. Meanwhile, civil unrest over conscription to Vietnam eventually helped to bring about the election of the left-wing Australian Labor Party (ALP) in 1972, the first time in 23 years that it had held power.

During Labor leader Gough Whitlam's short stint as Prime Minister, the government withdrew Australian troops from Vietnam, abolished national military service and put the final nail in the coffin of the White Australia Policy (p101). His ousting by the Governor General in 1975 fuelled unease with the constitutional system and generated calls for a republic (a referendum on the issue was voted down in 1999).

INTO THE NEW MILLENNIUM

A booming 1980s economy saw Sydney skyscrapers spring up, while the bicentennial celebrations in 1988 also boosted the city's ego. The subsequent economic bust in 1989 left a number of abandoned construction holes in the city centre, but with the announcement of the 2000 Olympic Games, Sydney reinvigorated itself and put on a great show for the world.

Australian indigenous issues have been to the fore over the last couple of decades. In 1992 a landmark High Court case overturned the principle of terra nullius and in a later court case, the Wik decision declared that pastoral leases do not necessarily extinguish native title, and that Aborigines could still claim ancestral land under white ownership. The implications of this ruling are still being resolved.

In 1997 the damning *Bringing Them Home* report was tabled in federal parliament, which graphically detailed the harm done to the stolen generation of Indigenous Australians. A quarter of a million Sydneysiders marched across Sydney Harbour Bridge in 2000, calling on the government to apologise for the historical systematic ill treatment of Australia's first people. It took until 2008 and a change of federal government for the apology to take place.

Sydney welcomed the millennia with a boom of fireworks and a combination of excitement and scepticism about the upcoming Olympics. Once they rolled around, all doubts were dispelled and Sydneysiders embraced the Games with much passion and good cheer. The rosy glow lingered long after the flame was extinguished, and the effect on tourism to the city has been pronounced.

During the Vietnam War years, the face of Sydney changed again, as American GIs flooded the city. Kings Cross provided the kind of belt-level R&R the troops desired.

Riveting Historical Reads

The Lieutenant (Kate Grenville)

The Playmaker (Thomas Keneally)

Oscar & Lucinda (Peter Carey)

The Harp in the South (Ruth Park)

1984	1990s	1999	2000
Homosexuality is decriminalised in NSW. Today, Sydney is considered one of the world's most gay-friendly cities.	Sydney booms as a film-making centre, churning out classics such as *The Matrix*, *Strictly Ballroom*, *Shine*, *Muriel's Wedding* and *The Adventures* of *Priscilla, Queen of the Desert*.	A referendum seeking to abandon the monarchy and turn Australia into a republic is defeated, with 55% of voters against. However, in Sydney, 68% voted in favour of a republic.	Sydney stages a dazzling Olympic Games, at which Australia wins 16 gold medals – in fourth place overall after traditional powerhouse nations USA, Russia and China.

The 2004 election of colourful Clover Moore as lord mayor was perhaps a reaction to a growing frustration with state politics. An independent politician, she came with none of the baggage of her rivals on either side of Australia's left-right divide. She also embraces many of the issues for which Sydney is famed, such as environmental sustainability and gay rights.

In the 2011 state elections, the Liberal-National Coalition celebrated a landslide win over Labor who had been in power for the previous 16 years (but had been through four leaders since 2008). When it comes to politics, Sydneysiders are a cynical bunch, and many view both major political parties with similar mistrust.

2003	2004	2005	2008
In February, an estimated 250,000 people take to the streets of Sydney to protest against the looming war in Iraq. Australian troops are part of the invasion the following month.	Redfern erupts in a night of rioting following the death of an Aboriginal teenager who was impaled on a fence after falling off his bike while being pursued by police.	Race riots break out in Cronulla following an assault on local surf lifesavers, with drunken mob attacks on people of Middle Eastern appearance.	Architect Jørn Utzon dies, having never seen his famous Sydney Opera House. The lights on the Opera House sails are dimmed to mourn his passing.

Food Culture

Food is so hot right now – even the cold stuff. It's almost as if Sydneysiders couldn't live without it. Switch on Australian TV and every other show is a cooking competition or a celebrity-chef-led expedition to discover the taste sensations of outer Mongolia. This chapter aims to help you make sense of the city's dynamic dining scene.

ADVANCE AUSTRALIAN FARE

Australia is blessed with brilliant produce from farms and fisheries across the nation. The tropical north provides pineapples, mangoes and even winter strawberries, while cooler southern climes lend themselves to fine wines and cheeses. These come together in a fresh, flavoursome, multicultural collision on dining tables across Sydney.

It's through food that the last lingering limitations of colonial Australia are being dissolved. These days Sharon and Darren from Rooty Hill are just as likely to head out for Thai, Vietnamese or Lebanese as they are for fish and chips or a roast.

HISTORY & CULTURAL INFLUENCES

While the First Fleeters came close to starvation in the early years of Sydney Town, the local Aboriginal tribes had millennia of experience in living from the land. You can check out examples of edible plants harvested by the Cadigal, Dharug and Dharawal peoples in the *Cadi Jam Ora* (First Encounters) beds of the Royal Botanic Gardens. The existence of huge middens under the city centre shows that shellfish were a staple, with fish, birds, snakes and kangaroo providing further protein.

The nearest wine-growing region to Sydney is the Hunter Valley, 150km north of the city. It's the oldest wine region in Australia, with the first vines planted here in 1831. Semillon, shiraz and, more recently, chardonnay are the specialities, with more than 100 vineyards blanketing the valley slopes.

The colonists, though, hankered for their bland English food – roast meat, pies and boiled vegetables. In lean times, the city's poor would fall back on rabbit. Eventually, 'meat and three veg' followed by tinned fruit with cream became the standard Australian home-cooked meal, with 'throwing some prawns on the barbie' the domain of the adventurous.

Waves of immigrants brought their cuisine with them, starting with the Chinese in the 1850s. Mediterranean migrants (particularly Italians, Greeks and southern Slavs) influenced local fare from the early 20th century, especially around Kings Cross. They also started Sydney's love affair with coffee, which has spread to every corner of the city.

In the latter half of last century, wars in Vietnam and Lebanon brought new refugees and new ways of cooking – although it's only recently that these cuisines have crossed into the mainstream. In the 1980s and '90s the number of young Thai students burgeoned, firmly establishing Thai as one of Sydney's most popular ethnic cuisines.

In Sydney today you can experience a different culture's cuisine every night for a month without doubling up – everything from Cambodian to Colombian can be found within a few kilometres of the city centre.

ETHNIC EAT STREETS

⇒ **Thai** Campbell St, Haymarket; King St, Newtown
⇒ **Chinese** Chinatown; Chatswood
⇒ **Korean** Pitt St near Liverpool St in the city
⇒ **Indian** Cleveland St, Surry Hills
⇒ **Italian** Norton St, Leichhardt; Stanley St, East Sydney
⇒ **Vietnamese** Chinatown; King St, Newtown; Cabramatta

MOD OZ

Those making the case for a distinctly Australian cuisine might point to 'bush tucker' or a degustation menu of pavlova, lamingtons, Vegemite sandwiches and Anzac biscuits. Patriots might suggest eating the coat of arms: kangaroo and emu, with a crocodile starter. A more reasoned approach has been taken by Australia's more innovative chefs, reverting to convict stereotypes: eyeing the surroundings, determining what to steal and weaving it all into something better than the sum of its parts – something perfect for the location and the climate.

This mix of European traditions with exotic flavours is casually termed Modern Australian cuisine – an amalgamation of Mediterranean, Asian, Middle Eastern and Californian cooking practices that emphasise lightness, experimentation and healthy eating. It's a hybrid style, shaped by migrant influences, climatic conditions and local ingredients – a culinary adventure built around local, seasonal produce that plays freely with imported ingredients and their accompanying cooking techniques and traditions. In Sydney this light-fingered culinary style has filtered down from sophisticated restaurants to modest main-street bistros and pubs.

The once ubiquitous phrase 'Mod Oz' may have fallen out of vogue, but the style of cooking is very much alive and well.

CURRENT TRENDS

A craze for Latin American street food has seen tangy soft-shell tacos replace salt and pepper squid as the bar snack of choice in hipper establishments. A similar fad for 'dude food' has seen posh places adding fancy burgers (called 'sliders' by those chefs who watch far too much American TV), pulled-pork sandwiches and big slabs of meat to their menus, often with a liberal side-serve of irony.

In an extension of the tapas trend that's been rolling for several years, 'shared plates' are all the rage. Bigger than tapas and not necessarily Spanish, this style of eating favours groups with adventurous palates. Fussy eaters and those from cultures that prefer their own portions on their own plates might find it more challenging.

The move towards favouring quality local, seasonal, organic, sustainable, free-range and fair-trade produce is now so ingrained in the culture of the very best restaurants that it can barely be called a trend any more. While ethical eating seems to be here to stay, you'll still see unsustainable fish species and controversial products like foie gras popping up on Sydney menus. Cheaper restaurants with lower margins are usually less inclined to pay the premium for ethical products, but there are worthy exceptions. Fair-trade coffee and free-range eggs are quickly becoming the norm at the better cafes.

CELEBRITY CHEFS

Not content with proving themselves world beaters in the swimming pool, on the cricket pitch and on the big screen, Australians have taken the competition into the kitchen, where old-fashioned Aussie hero worship has turned a crop of local chefs into minor celebrities. You might find this glossy cult of the celebrity chef a bit nauseating – the food isn't always unbeatable, and unless you book weeks in advance you mightn't even be able to get a table. Still, such competitive kitchen vigour makes for interesting conversation.

Major players include the following:

➡ **Adriano Zumbo** Australia's highest-profile pastry chef introduced the nation to macarons during a stint on TV's *MasterChef*, and has gone on to sell his 'zumbarons' through four eponymous patisseries.

➡ **Manu Feildel** Bringing sexy Gallic swagger to the TV in *My Kitchen Rules* and to Paddington where he is the chef, owner and star of L'etoile.

➡ **Luke Nguyen** Mainstream fame came with SBS TV series *Luke Nguyen's Vietnam*; try his food at Red Lantern in Surry Hills.

➡ **Peter Gilmore** Rated Sydney's best chef in 2012, Gilmore's Quay restaurant is currently the only one in Australia to make *Restaurant* magazine's prestigious list of the top 50 restaurants in the world.

➡ **Matt Moran** Handsome bald-headed *MasterChef* judge and chef at Circular Quay's excellent Aria restaurant.

➡ **Kylie Kwong** Flying the flag for both sustainable food and modern Chinese cuisine, Kylie runs Billy Kwong restaurant (named after her father) and can often be spotted cooking up a storm at Eveleigh Farmers' Market in the Inner West.

➡ **Bill Granger** Credited with kicking Sydney's brunch scene into high gear; taste Mr Scrambled Eggs' handiwork at his three 'bills' cafes, the original of which is in Darlinghurst.

➡ **Tetsuya Wakuda** His landmark Tetsuya's, in the city centre, was once ranked among the top five restaurants in the world. His innovative blend of Japanese and French cuisine raised standards in Sydney, so much so that he's now forced to share the limelight with several protégés.

➡ **Neil Perry** Pony-tailed veteran with a passion for seafood and Chinese flavours, and with numerous books and TV shows under his apron. Sample his stuff at Rockpool, in The Rocks; Rockpool Bar & Grill and Spice Temple, in the city centre; and on Qantas planes.

➡ **Christine Manfield** Platinum-haired fusion queen, currently marrying East with West at her Darlinghurst signature restaurant, Universal.

VEGETARIANS & VEGANS

Sydney is great for herbivores. Unless you wander into a steak house by mistake, vegetarians should have no trouble finding satisfying choices on most menus. Some leading restaurants offer separate vegetarian menus; at Tetsuya's and the Bathers' Pavilion these stretch to multiple-course degustation.

At Asian eateries it pays to ask whether the vegetable dishes are cooked with oyster or fish sauce – they'll usually be happy to make soy-based substitutions. Many of the more established restaurants such as Thai Pothong in Newtown specifically mark strictly vegetarian options on the menu. Southeast Asian vegetarian dishes are usually a good option for vegans also, but again, it pays to check.

The more socially progressive suburbs such as Newtown and Glebe have the widest range of veggie options. Also worth checking out is the cluster of mainly vegetarian South Indian restaurants on Cleveland St, Surry Hills, between Crown and Bourke Sts.

Catering specifically to vegans are the chain Iku Wholefood, which has 13 cafes throughout Sydney, and Pure Wholefoods (p164).

HOW SYDNEYSIDERS EAT

It might be something to do with long nights of partying, but breakfast is something Sydney cafes do particularly well. Many locals prefer to conduct business over a morning latte instead of a power lunch or an upmarket dinner, and friends often launch the day with scrambled eggs, carrot juice and a few laughs. The prime breakfasting 'hoods are Potts Point, Surry Hills and the beaches, but it'd be weird not to find a decent brekky cafe in any inner-city 'burb.

Breakfast can happen anytime from 6am to late morning, although many cafes serve all-day breakfasts, especially on weekends. The all-day option is perfect for hardened party animals, and is therefore more common in the inner east and west. If you're an early riser, pull up a window seat in Darlinghurst or Kings Cross and watch the nocturnal detritus spilling out of the clubs – think of yourself as a seat warmer for when they wake up in the afternoon. Yum cha in Chinatown is also a hugely popular weekend brunch option (expect to queue).

It's in the caffeine stakes that Sydney wipes the floor with London and Los Angeles (as do most Australasian cities). You won't have to settle for wussy drip-filtered pap here – it's espresso all the way. The big international chains have sprouted up, but they're generally considered the last refuge of the unimaginative. Choose a local cafe instead and order a flat white (espresso with milk that's been perfectly warmed but not bubbled – it's an art all of its own), caffe latte (similar but milkier, often served in a glass), a cappuccino (espresso topped with frothed milk and chocolate or cinnamon), a long or short black (espresso without milk and with varying amounts of water), a *macchiato* (a short black with a tiny splash of milk) or a *ristretto* (very concentrated espresso). Most cafes also offer soy or 'skinny' (skim) milk.

For Sydney's workaday warriors, lunch means a quick sandwich or salad inhaled at their desk or in a nearby park. Others hit the shopping centre food courts, which offer ethnically diverse bain-marie fodder – though many restaurants provide more atmospheric versions of the same. Chinatown, in particular, sees corporate-casual lunchtime crowds jamming its good-value eateries.

Dinner weighs more heavily on the social scales, but unless it's a special event, casual is usually the go: jeans, T-shirts and trainers are usually OK in all but the most ritzy joints.

At many restaurants, but particularly Asian, Middle Eastern and Indian restaurants, sharing dishes is the norm (unless you're the only vegetarian). At European-style restaurants many Sydneysiders stop at two courses, only ordering an entrée (Americans take note: this is the starter served before the main course, not the main course, which is called a 'main') or dessert on special occasions (or when the boss is paying).

When it comes to the pointy end of the night, there's usually a discussion as to whether to split the bill or pay for your own. Splitting is common, but if you've knocked back the crayfish and a bottle of Dom Perignon you'd better shell out some extra. Unlike in some cultures, there's no expectation that the person doing the inviting will pay the whole bill. Even if you're out on a date, women shouldn't expect that their meal will be bought for them. Gender inequality is *soooo* last millennium.

Food Festivals

Taste of Sydney (www.tasteof sydney.com. au) Early March; Centennial Park

Crave (www. cravesydney.com) October; city-wide.

Food & Wine Fair (www.aidstrust. com.au) Late October; Hyde Park.

The Arts

While it can't match New York or London in terms of the volume of theatres, galleries or performance venues, Sydney nevertheless lays claim to a robust arts scene. And as opposed to taking the sniffy, superior attitude so prevalent in many artsy societies, Sydney has a laidback, open-minded approach to its artistic pursuits. Influencing the local arts scene is the constant redefinition of the city's identity, with the beach and Sydney's many multicultural facets also chiming in.

CINEMA

Since Fox Studios opened in Moore Park in 1998, Sydney has starred in various big-budget blockbusters such as *The Matrix* trilogy (featuring numerous Sydney skyscrapers), *Mission Impossible 2* (Elizabeth Bay and Sydney Harbour) and *X-Men Origins: Wolverine* (Cockatoo Island). Sydneysider Baz Luhrmann's *Moulin Rouge*, *Australia* and *The Great Gatsby* were made here, as were numerous other films set everywhere from Antarctica (*Happy Feet II*) to a galaxy far, far away (the *Star Wars* prequels).

Yet more emblematic of the soul of Sydney cinema is the decidedly low budget Tropfest (p21), where thousands of locals shake out their blankets in the Domain to watch entries in the largest short-film festival in the world.

One of the most successful early Australian films was *The Sentimental Bloke* (1919), which included scenes filmed in Manly, the Royal Botanic Gardens and Woolloomooloo. The cavalry epic *Forty Thousand Horsemen* (1940), in which Cronulla's sand dunes stood in for the Sinai, was a highlight of the locally produced films of the 1930s to the 1950s, many of which were based on Australian history or literature.

Government intervention reshaped the future of the country's film industry through the 1970s. This took the form of both state and federal subsidies, tax breaks and the creation of the Australian Film Commission (AFC) in 1975. Sydneysiders who benefited from the subsequent renaissance in the Australian industry included Oscar-nominated director Peter Weir (who made such films as *Gallipoli*, *Dead Poets Society*, *The Truman Show* and *Master and Commander*) and Oscar-winners Mel Gibson and Nicole Kidman.

The 1990s saw films that cemented Australia's reputation as a producer of quirky comedies about local misfits: *Strictly Ballroom* (with locations in Pyrmont and Marrickville), *Muriel's Wedding* (Parramatta, Darlinghurst, Darling Point and Ryde) and *The Adventures of Priscilla, Queen of the Desert* (Erskineville). Sydney actors who got their cinematic start around this time include Hugo Weaving, David Wenham, NZ-born Russell Crowe, Cate Blanchett, Heath Ledger and Toni Collette (p192).

The new millennium got off to a good start with the likes of *Lantana* and *Finding Nemo*, but since then it's fair to say that Sydney has failed to set big screens alight.

Australia saw some of the world's earliest attempts at cinematography. In 1896, just one year after the Lumière brothers opened the world's first cinema in Paris, one of their photographers, Maurice Sestier, came to Sydney where he made the country's first films and opened its first cinema.

FILM

SYDNEY CINEMA

Sydney sure is good-lookin' – a fact not overlooked in its filmography.

➡ *Puberty Blues* (1981) Southern Sydney's 1970s surf culture at its most 'perf'. Directed by Bruce Beresford.

➡ *The Sum of Us* (1994) A touching father-son tale where a young Russell Crowe jogs round Sydney in his footie shorts as the gay lead. Directed by Geoff Burton and Kevin Dowling Lucas.

➡ *Two Hands* (1999) A black-humoured look at the Kings Cross criminal underworld, starring a young Heath Ledger. Directed by Gregor Jordan.

➡ The Matrix trilogy (1999–2003) A trio of futuristic, mind-bending flicks with plenty of martial-arts action, slick costumes and noir themes. Filmed in Sydney's streets and soundstages. Directed by Andy and Larry Wachowski.

➡ *Looking for Alibrandi* (2000) An endearing story about growing up Italian in modern Sydney. Directed by Kate Woods.

➡ *Lantana* (2001) 'Mystery for grown-ups', this extraordinary ensemble piece is a deeply moving meditation on life, love, truth and grief. Directed by Ray Lawrence.

➡ *Candy* (2006) Abbie Cornish and Heath Ledger play drug-addicted lovers in the film adaptation of Luke Davies' 1998 grunge novel. Directed by Neil Armfield.

➡ *Bra Boys* (2007) Maroubra's bad-boy surf gang in stark profile. Narrated by the dulcet Russell Crowe; directed by real-life Bra Boy Sunny Abberton.

THEATRE

Sydney provides something for all thespian tastes, from mainstream blockbuster musicals at major venues to small theatre companies staging experimental, exciting works in the inner-city suburbs. That said, Sydney's theatrical tastes do tend towards the unadventurous end of the spectrum.

While the bulk of Australian actors live and work in Sydney, Australia's geographic isolation and a lingering sense of 'cultural cringe' mean that truly local theatre gigs are thin on the ground and not particularly well paid. Thus, many actors prefer to get as much film and TV work as they can or, better yet, go overseas. The National Institute of Dramatic Art (NIDA) in Kensington is a breeding ground for new talent, and stages performances of students' work.

The city's biggest name in theatre is the Sydney Theatre Company (STC). Established in 1978, it provides a balanced program of modern, classical, local and foreign drama, and attracts solid talent across the board. Since 2008 Cate Blanchett and playwright hubbie Andrew Upton have been the company's artistic directors, their star-power bringing plenty of media attention to the company. Their stint will come to an end in 2013.

Smaller theatre companies presenting genuinely innovative work include the much-loved Company B at the Belvoir St Theatre; the Griffin Theatre Co at the Stables; and the Tamarama Rock Surfers at the Old Fitzroy and Bondi Pavilion.

Stage performers to watch for in local productions include Deborah Mailman, Oscar-nominee Jackie Weaver, Marcus Graham, John Howard (not that one), Robyn Nevin and Barry Otto. And, of course, Sydney's resident colony of movie stars pop up from time to time in stage roles.

VISUAL ART

Sydney's first artists were the people of the indigenous Eora nation. Figures of animals, fish and humans can still be seen engraved into sandstone outcrops in Bondi and around the harbour. In the Blue Mountains, ancient hand stencils decorate cave walls.

In the colony's early days, the first foreign-born painters applied traditional European aesthetic standards to Australia's bleached light, raggedy forests and earthy colours: as such, they failed to capture the landscape with any certainty. In the early 19th century, John Glover (a convict) adopted a different Australian landscape-painting style, using warm earth tones and more precise depictions of gum trees and mountains in his work. Conrad Martens, a friend of Charles Darwin, painted accurate landscapes of a surprisingly busy Sydney Harbour in the 1850s (where did all the trees go?).

Australian Aboriginal art is one of the oldest forms of creativity in the world, dating back more than 50,000 years. Art has always been integral to Aboriginal life – a connection between the past and the present, the supernatural and the earthly, the people and the land.

The first significant art movement in Australia, the Heidelberg School, emerged around the 1890s. Using impressionistic techniques and favouring outdoor painting, the school represented a major break with prevailing European tastes. Painters such as Tom Roberts and Arthur Streeton were the first to render Australian light and colour in this naturalistic fashion. Originally from Melbourne, they came to Sydney and established an artists' camp at Little Sirius Cove in Mosman in 1891, which became a focal point for Sydney artists. Roberts and Streeton depicted what are now considered typically Australian scenes: sheep shearers, pioneers, bushrangers...all powerful stimulants in the development of an enduring national mythology.

At the beginning of the 20th century, Sydney painters such as Grace Cossington Smith and Margaret Preston began to flirt with modernism. French-influenced Nora Simpson kick-started the innovative movement, experimenting with cubism and expressionism.

In the 1960s Australian art drew on multiculturalism and abstract trends, an eclecticism best represented by the work of Sydney artist Brett Whiteley, an internationally celebrated *enfant terrible* who died in 1992. He painted sexy, colourful canvases, often depicting distorted figures, as well as landscapes of Sydney Harbour. His Surry Hills studio, containing many of his works, has been preserved as a gallery.

On the design front, Australia's most successful export has been the work of Marc Newson, a graduate of the Sydney College of the Arts. His aerodynamic Lockheed Lounge (1985–86) has been snapped up by savvy furniture collectors and design buffs worldwide.

Drawing on pop culture images for much of his work, Martin Sharp rose to prominence in the 1960s as cofounder of the satirical magazine *Oz*. In the 1970s he helped restore the 'face' at Luna Park, but he is most famous for his theatrical posters and record covers (including Cream's *Disraeli Gears* and *Wheels of Fire*).

Performance art happens at galleries around Sydney, including Artspace in Woolloomooloo – some of it is most certainly not for the fainthearted. In 2003 Mike Parr performed a piece at Artspace titled *Democratic Torture,* in which people could deliver electric shocks to him via the internet; he also nailed himself to a wall here in *Malevich: A Political Arm.*

Other contemporary artists of note include photographers Tracey Moffatt and William Yang, and painters Tim Storrier, Ben Quilty, Keith Looby, Judy Cassab and John Olsen. For some quirky wearable art, check out artist Reg Mombassa's work for surfwear label Mambo, available at most surf shops.

LITERATURE

Australia's literary history harks back to Sydney's convict days. New experiences and landscapes inspired the colonists to commit their stories to the page. Though many early works have been lost, some – like Marcus Clarke's convict drama *For the Term of His Natural Life* (1870) – have become legendary.

By the late 19th century, a more formal Australian literary movement was developing with the *Bulletin,* an influential magazine promoting

SYDNEY ON THE SHELF

Sydney has been a rich setting and source material for the written word.

➡ *Sydney*, Delia Falconer (2010) An insightful dissection of the Harbour City by one of its own.

➡ *The Secret River*, Kate Grenville (2005) Grenville's Commonwealth Prize–winning and Booker-nominated story of 19th-century convict life in Sydney and around the Hawkesbury River.

➡ *Sydney Architecture*, Paul McGillick and Patrick Bingham-Hall (2005) One for the coffee table, with beautiful photographs and text showcasing 100-plus stunning Sydney buildings.

➡ *30 Days in Sydney*, Peter Carey (2001) A richly nostalgic account of Carey's return to Sydney after 10 years in New York. His emotions and experiences read like a diary, thematically spanning the four elements of earth, air, fire and water.

➡ *Quill*, Neal Drinnan (2001) A sassy and moving tale of gay love, life and death in Sydney, with party scenes that many Sydneysiders will relate to.

➡ *In the Gutter...Looking at the Stars*, ed Mandy Sayer and Louis Nowra (2000) A spellbinding compilation of Kings Cross musings, painting a vivid, decade-by-decade portrait of the area.

➡ *The Cross*, Mandy Sayer (1995) Set in Kings Cross, and based on the life and unsolved 1975 disappearance of Sydney publisher Juanita Nielson.

➡ *Oscar & Lucinda*, Peter Carey (1988) This unusual tale of 19th-century misfits won Carey his first Booker prize.

➡ *The Bodysurfers*, Robert Drewe (1983) Seductive stories from Sydney's Northern Beaches, calmly tearing shreds off the Australian suburban idyll.

➡ *The Harp in the South* and *Poor Man's Orange*, Ruth Park (1948 & 1949) Gripping and touching accounts of impoverished family life in Surry Hills when the suburb was a crowded slum.

egalitarian and unionist thinking. Well-known contributing authors of the time included Henry Lawson (1867–1922), who wrote short stories about the Australian bush, and poet AB 'Banjo' Paterson (1864–1941), who penned *Waltzing Matilda* and *The Man from Snowy River*.

My Brilliant Career (1901), by Miles Franklin (1879–1954), is considered the first authentic Australian novel. The book caused a sensation when it was revealed that Miles was actually a woman.

Australian authors of international stature include Patrick White (Nobel Prize in Literature, 1973), Thomas Keneally (Booker Prize winner, 1982), Peter Carey (Booker Prize winner 1988 and 2001) and Kate Grenville (Commonwealth Writers' Prize winner 2006). Other Sydney authors of note include David Malouf, Mandy Sayer, Shirley Hazzard, Eleanor Dark and Ruth Park. For a list of some classic Sydney titles see p192.

MUSIC

Sydney offers the traveller everything from world-class opera and intimate jazz to indigenous hip hop, live electronic beats and raucous pub rock. Gigs happen every night in the city's pubs and performance halls, with plenty of big-name touring artists enriching the mix.

In the 1970s and '80s Australia churned out a swag of iconic pub rockers, with Sydney bands INXS and Midnight Oil at the forefront. During the '90s and noughties, when guitar bands came back into vogue, contrary Sydney popped a pill and headed to the disco. Most of the significant Australian acts of the era formed elsewhere, with the

SYDNEY PLAYLIST

➡ 'Khe Sanh' (Cold Chisel, 1978) Classic Oz rock song about a Vietnam vet's return. Other Sydney songs by Cold Chisel include 'Tomorrow', 'Numbers Fall' and 'Letter to Alan'.

➡ 'Bliss' (Th' Dudes, 1979) Kiwi rockers score speed in Coogee and falafels in Kings Cross.

➡ 'Power and the Passion' (Midnight Oil, 1982) Peter Garrett, now a federal MP, vents about Sydney 'wasting away in paradise'. Listen also to Midnight Oil songs 'Wedding Cake Island' and 'Section 5 (Bus to Bondi)'.

➡ 'Reckless' (Australian Crawl, 1983) Glacial '80s pop: 'as the Manly ferry cuts its way to Circular Quay'.

➡ 'Incident on South Dowling' (Paul Kelly, 1986) The Melbourne bard turns his pen to Sydney. Listen also to Kelly's 'From St Kilda to Kings Cross', 'Randwick Bells' and 'Darlin' It Hurts'.

➡ 'My Drug Buddy' (the Lemonheads, 1992) Evan Dando gets wasted in Newtown.

➡ 'Purple Sneakers' (You Am I, 1995) 'Had a scratch only you could itch, underneath the Glebe Point Bridge'.

➡ 'God Drinks at the Sando' (the Whitlams, 1999) The band named after Australia's grooviest Prime Minister digs into Sydney's best and worst on *Love this City*.

➡ 'Never Had So Much Fun' (Frenzal Rhomb, 1999) Local punks advise against drinking the water.

➡ 'Sydney Song' (Eskimo Joe, 2001) Ode to Sydney wannabes.

➡ 'Darlinghurst Nights' (the Go-Betweens, 2005) Sad Darlinghurst memories get an airing.

exception of garage rockers the Vines and the Cops, cartoon punks Frenzal Rhomb, singer-songwriter Alex Lloyd and jangly sentimentalists the Whitlams. In the meantime, Sydney's most successful musical export was children's novelty act the Wiggles.

However, things have been looking up in recent years, with the city turning out the likes of electro popsters the Presets, hard rockers Front End Loader, folky siblings Angus & Julia Stone, alternative rock lads Boy & Bear and indie disco kids the Jezabels.

Australia loves its pop stars and dance divas, and is currently churning them out at a rate of knots in reality-TV shows. While most inevitably sink without a trace, Sydneysiders Guy Sebastian and Altiyan Childs have gone on to have considerable hits. Others have taken the more traditional route to pop stardom: starring in a cheesy soap opera. Melbourne can lay claim to Kylie, but Sydney makes do with Delta Goodrem and Natalie Imbruglia.

Sydney loves to cut a rug, and you'll find a bit of everything being played around the dance clubs, from drum and bass to electro. Homegrown dance music is made by the likes of Bag Raiders and Art vs Science, and spun by popular DJs such as Tom Piper, Timmy Trumpet, Kid Kenobi and Ajax.

With an opera house as its very symbol, no discussion of Sydney's musical legacy is complete without mentioning Dame Joan Sutherland (1926–2010), the Eastern Beaches lass who became one of the greatest opera singers of the 20th century. Her legacy can be seen in the success of Opera Australia and singers such as Cheryl Barker.

Architecture

Modern Sydney began life in Sydney Cove and the area immediately around it has been the hub of the city ever since. It's no surprise, then, that central Sydney gives the best insight into how the city's architecture has matured from shaky, poorly crafted imitation to confident autonomy, peaking with its glorious opera house.

THE LAY OF THE LAND

Ever since Captain Arthur Phillip slurped from the Tank Stream, water has shaped Sydney's development. The Tank Stream now runs in brick culverts beneath the city, but in the early days of the First Fleet it defined Sydney. Phillip used the stream to separate convicts on the rocky west from the officers on the gentler eastern slopes, hemming in the convicts between the sea on one side and the soldiers on the other. Following this pattern, government institutions were concentrated to the east of the stream, while industry set up shop on the western side of town. Social differences were thus articulated, establishing a pattern that can still be seen in Sydney more than 200 years later.

According to scientist and author Dr Tim Flannery, many Aboriginal campsites used to lie near fresh water on Sydney Harbour's north-facing shore – and the colonists took their cue from the original inhabitants. Topographically, it makes sense. The area catches the winter sun, and is relatively sheltered from chilly southerly and bullying westerly winds. The northeasterly breeze, meanwhile, comes straight through the mouth of the harbour, delivering warm winter and cool summer breezes.

In one of history's great coincidences, Frenchman Jean Compte de la Pérouse arrived at Botany Bay days after the First Fleet. That event and fierce competition from other colonial powers meant there was a perceived threat of invasion from the outset. As a consequence, the navy appropriated much of the harbour foreshore. This was fortunate indeed – much of the land was not built upon, conserving these regions as wilderness while the rest of Sydney clambered up around them.

LITTLE BRITAIN

The men and women who arrived in the First Fleet were staggeringly ill-prepared for the realities of building in their new, raw environment. The British powers-that-be had failed to include an architect on board, so design and construction duties largely fell to the convict bricklayer James Bloodsworth. Inevitably the early builders looked to the 'mother' country for inspiration, but shoddy workmanship, poor tools and the colony's temporary vibe conspired against long-term success.

A significant change to this ad-hoc approach was heralded by the appointment of Governor Lachlan Macquarie in 1810, who viewed good architecture as an essential component of a thriving, healthy society. The arrival of several architects, including the transfigurative Francis Greenway, a convict transported for forgery, helped change Sydney's

If the city centre is ideal for tracing the development of institutional and financial building styles, The Rocks is the place to gain an understanding of the social structures behind Sydney architecture. Millers Point highlights some impressive social housing policies and the area's strong industrial maritime heritage

THE ROCKS

built environment. The prevailing Georgian architecture of Britain was echoed in many buildings that sprang up at this time.

As the 19th century kicked on, colonial architects still looked to Britain for inspiration, but broader European influences were also seen, from the neoclassical Town Hall (p89) to the early-Gothic-style spires of St Mary's Cathedral (p85).

When Australia became a fully fledged country in its own right in 1901, increasing architectural autonomy ensued. Architects questioned traditional approaches and sought new ways to adapt buildings to Sydney's extraordinary setting – particularly in the residential areas. In the city centre, meanwhile, the scrapping of height restrictions in the 1950s sparked Sydney's love affair with skyscrapers. Modernism was influential, with such architects as Harry Seidler focusing on Sydney Harbour and embracing diverse international attitudes. Of course, a walk around central Sydney still shows the legacy of British influence. Today's buildings, however, are much more locally sensitive.

THE UTILITARIAN HARBOUR

Sydney has always relied on its harbour. All sorts of cargo (including human) has been unloaded here, and some of the more interesting Sydney buildings are the utilitarian wharves and warehouses still lining parts of the harbour's inner shores. After the bubonic plague arrived in Sydney in 1900 (killing 103 Sydneysiders), the government took control of the old, privately owned wharves. Many ageing neoclassical warehouses were razed and replaced with new utilitarian buildings, but the 'containerisation' of shipping in the 1960s and '70s made many of these facilities redundant almost overnight.

Now, Sydneysiders' obsession with harbourside living is also putting many of these historic sites at risk. Fortunately, some have been transformed through inspired redevelopment – once-dilapidated sheds morphing into top-notch cafes, restaurants and apartments. Woolloomooloo's

SYDNEY OPERA HOUSE

Frank Lloyd Wright called it a 'circus tent' and Mies van der Rohe thought it the work of the devil, yet Danish architect Jørn Utzon (1918–2008) bequeathed Sydney one of the 20th century's defining architectural monuments.

Utzon was 38 when he entered the NSW government's competition to design the Opera House in 1956 and, remarkably, had only realised a few small houses by this age. Working from navigational maps of the site and memories of his travels to the great pre-Columbian platforms in Mexico, Utzon achieved the unimaginable. His great architectural gesture – billowing white sails hovering above a heavy stone platform – tapped into the essence of Sydney, almost as if both building and site had grown from the same founding principles.

Eight years on, having realised his designs for the platform, concrete shells and ceramic skin, Utzon had a change of client following the election of new NSW Premier Robert Askin. By April 1966, owed hundreds of thousands of dollars in unpaid fees, Utzon was unceremoniously forced to leave his building half-finished. He afterward commented that the six years he spent developing the house's interiors and glass walls, for which there is nothing to show, were the most productive of his working life.

Attempts at reconciliation with Utzon began in the 1990s, and in 1999 he agreed to be taken on as a consultant for a new acoustic interior for the building. Sadly, Utzon died in 2008 having never returned to Australia to see his masterpiece.

Finger Wharf (p132), and the Walsh Bay (p60) and Pyrmont wharves are classic examples. One of Sydney's big architectural challenges is to retain the richness of a working harbour and to ensure these sites have a successful, working role in the modern city.

MODERNISM ARRIVES

Between the two world wars Sydney boomed, and Australia looked to the USA for architectural inspiration. Martin Place (p87), with its granite-faced art-deco temples to commerce, is a well-preserved example. Similarly lavish buildings began to dot the eastern suburbs skyline, giving a stylish look to many suburbs, although there have since been some hideous modern incursions.

The opening of the Sydney Harbour Bridge (p55) in 1932 was a seminal moment for Sydney architecture, opening up the densely forested North Shore to development. Much of this shoreline retains a bushy character, reflecting local architects' determination to engage with Sydney's natural charms.

Some good news in the 1950s and '60s came via the Sydney School, which pioneered a distinctively Australian architecture, characterised by the appreciation of native landscapes and natural materials, and the avoidance of conventional and historic features. Further steps were taken as 'new Australians' such as Seidler and Hugh Buhrich brought to the local architectural scene a sensitivity to place, infused with Bauhaus and modernist concepts.

Since the 1960s, central Sydney has become a mini-Manhattan of tall buildings vying for harbour views, thanks to the lifting in the late 1950s of the 150ft (46m) height limit. The best early modernist examples are Seidler's Australia Square (p89) and MLC buildings. Plans for an almost total redevelopment of the city's historic districts were afoot in the 1960s as the irascible Askin Liberal Government (which kicked Sydney Opera House designer Jørn Utzon out of Sydney) deemed many Victorian and early-20th-century buildings undesirable in its race to construct an 'all new' metropolis. Thankfully, union green bans and plenty of vociferous local protests managed to save large chunks of The Rocks and areas such as Kings Cross, Paddington and Woolloomooloo.

Many buildings from the 1970s and '80s are forgettable, but striking exceptions include the Capita Centre on Castlereagh St and Governors Phillip & Macquarie Towers (p89) on Phillip St.

CONTEMPORARY DESIGN

The spate of skyscraper construction that hit central Sydney following the lifting of height restrictions has defined the skyline. For a while, the city's older buildings were in danger of being neglected. That changed for the bicentennial celebrations of 1988, when cultural heritage soared up the agenda. As well as the refurbishment of Macquarie St and Circular Quay, developers turned their eye towards Darling Harbour. Critics condemn today's Darling Harbour as a tacky Las Vegan aberration, but few fail to be amazed at how completely this once-disused industrial space has been transformed.

Historic buildings that have been redeveloped for new uses with effect include the Mint (p86) and the Sydney Conservatorium of Music (p58) on Macquarie St, the Customs House (p57) at Circular Quay, and the wharves at Walsh Bay – all great examples of how thoughtful and

For some glimpses of typical Sydney inner-city residential styles, make your way to Paddington, Potts Point or Elizabeth Bay. The backstreets of these dense suburbs include superbly restored Victorian terrace houses, art deco apartments and modern housing.

Some of the more innovative contemporary work in Sydney often happens far from the public gaze in the realm of the family house, where progressive clients bankroll the creative ambitions of architects.

GREEN BUILDINGS

Environmental concerns have rocketed up the agenda in Sydney over the past decade, and local architecture hasn't been immune. The Olympic Games quickened architects' thinking on sustainability issues, and there are several developments around Olympic Park that highlight the 'sustainable' agenda of the Games. The first thing you'll probably see when you arrive is the Olympic Park Rail Station, admired for its natural light, ventilation and striking shell-like design. The modernist blocks of Newington Apartments, originally the Olympic Village, also emphasise natural light, energy conservation and water recycling. While you're in the 'hood, sneak a peek at the sleek grace of Peter Stutchbury's Archery Pavilion.

Since the Olympics, 30 The Bond on Hickson Rd in Millers Point has become the benchmark for Sydney's green buildings. Its adjustable facade, chilled beam air-conditioning and abundant natural light make it the most energy-efficient building in Sydney. Its developers were the first to pledge to achieving a five-star Australian Building Greenhouse rating.

Of course, sustainable building isn't limited to big financial and infrastructure developments – new and recycled 'green' residential projects are also coming on apace. One stellar example is the converted 19th-century Chippendale terrace house at 58 Myrtle St, which the owner/designer bills as 'Sydney's first sustainable house' (see www.sustainablehouse.com.au).

It seems like a regulation Sydney terrace from the front, one of thousands in the inner city, but some ingenious and surprisingly simple design means that all the house's requisite energy and water needs are supplied on site. The house consumes just 220L of water per day (the Sydney average is 274L), and only six kilowatts of electricity, down from an average of 24. In fact, the house exports more energy to the national grid than it uses. Simple but effective fittings include rooftop solar panels, a rainwater filter on the drainpipe, a doorbell on a string, a super-energy-efficient fridge, and stainless-steel benches that magnify sunlight and prevent the need for daytime electric light during the day. Check it out in the book *Sustainable House* by owner Michael Mobbs.

sympathetic contemporary design can inject new life and energy into an area.

The other defining event that cemented Sydney architecture's place on the world map was the 2000 Olympic Games. Many of the buildings and infrastructure developed around Homebush Bay, where the Games were based, were world class.

At the time of writing, major new buildings by internationally acclaimed architects Jean Nouvel, Sir Norman Foster and Frank Gehry were being raised in Ultimo and Chippendale, at the southern end of the city.

Sporty Sydney

Sydneysiders – like most Aussies – are nuts about sport: watching it, playing it and betting on it. Australia's national self-esteem is so intertwined with sporting success that locals worship their teams as they would a religion. This national obsession makes for heady times in front of the big screen at the local pub, and certainly contributed to Sydney's overwhelmingly successful 2000 Olympic Games. Sport dominates weekend TV schedules, but nothing beats catching a game live. Sydney's all-consuming passion is rugby league – a superfast, supermacho game with a frenzied atmosphere for spectators.

RUGBY LEAGUE

There's plenty to yell about if you arrive during the winter footy season. 'Footy' can mean a number of things: in Sydney's it's usually rugby league, but the term is also used for Australian Rules football (Aussie Rules), rugby union and soccer.

In this big, dirty city, rugby league is the big, dirty game: mud, swearing, broken bones, cheerleaders...and that's just in the stands! Rugby league is king in NSW, and Sydney is considered one of the world capitals for the code. The pinnacle of the game is widely held to be the annual State of Origin where NSW battles Queensland (and Queensland usually wins). This best-of-three series even overshadows test matches, such as the annual ANZAC Test between Australia's Kangaroos and New Zealand's Kiwis.

The National Rugby League (www.nrl.com) comp runs from March to October, climaxing in the sell-out Grand Final at ANZ Stadium. You can catch games every weekend during the season, played at the home

GO RABBITOHS! GO RUSS!

For a rugby league team in need of friends in high places, South Sydney (aka Souths, aka the Rabbitohs) has certainly managed to pull some bunnies out of the hat. Big-name fans waving their green and red scarves around include TV host Ray Martin, comedian Andrew Denton, Australia's favourite ex-son-in-law Tom Cruise and actor Russell Crowe, who loved the team so much he bought the franchise in 2006.

Despite being the only surviving team from the seminal 1908 season and having won more premierships than any other team (20, although the last one was in 1971), South Sydney was on the scrap heap in the late 1990s. The ill-fated '1997 Super League' saw the competition slashed from 17 teams to 14, omitting the Rabbitohs. Souths' passionate supporters didn't appreciate this 'redundancy' and weren't going to go quietly. In June 2001, 80,000 green-and-red-clad supporters paraded from Redfern Oval to the Town Hall in a 'Save the Game' rally. On 6 July 2001 the Federal Court of Australia gave the Bunnies back their footy-playing rights and the number of teams in the comp was raised to 15.

While the Rabbitohs rarely threatens the top of the now 16-team NRL ladder, it's good to know they're here to stay. And since Russ bought the club, its run of bad luck and heavy on-field losses seems to have ended. For current Bunny stats, see www.rabbitohs.com.au.

grounds of Sydney's various tribes. The easiest ground to access is the 45,500-seat Sydney Football Stadium, home of the Sydney Roosters, but nothing beats a Wests Tigers home match at Leichhardt Oval.

The main Sydney teams are the Sydney Roosters, the South Sydney Rabbitohs, the Wests Tigers, the Canterbury Bulldogs, the Cronulla Sharks, the Parramatta Eels, the Manly-Warringah Sea Eagles and the Penrith Panthers. The St George Illawarra Dragons are based in Wollongong, but also in Kogarah in Sydney's southern 'burbs.

Not many people have a ferry and a swimming pool named after them, but Dawn Fraser is quite extraordinary. One of Sydney's most loved sportspeople, she is one of only two swimmers to have won the same event at three successive Olympics (the 100m freestyle in 1956, 1960 and 1964).

NETBALL

Despite Australia being world champs since 2007, and it being one of the most-played sports in the country, netball gets neither the coverage nor the money that the football boys rake in. During the winter season, catch test internationals or Sydney's team the NSW Swifts (www.nswswifts.com.au) in the trans-Tasman ANZ Championship (www.anz-championship.com). The team won the inaugural championship when it was held in 2008; catch them at Sydney Olympic Park Sports Centre.

CRICKET

Cricket is the major summer sport, and one in which Australia does very well (at the time of writing, the national team ranked fourth in the world for test matches and first for One Day Internationals (ODI). From October to March, Sydney hosts interstate Sheffield Shield and one-day matches, and international Test, ODI and 20/20 cricket matches; see Cricinfo (www.espncricinfo.com) for details. Cricket matches are held at the elegant old Sydney Cricket Ground.

RUGBY UNION

Rugby Union (www.rugby.com.au), which despite its punishing physical component, has a more upper-class rep than rugby league and a less fanatical following in Sydney. Since winning the Rugby World Cup in 1991 and 1999, Australia's national team, the Wallabies, has been a bit off the boil. The annual southern hemisphere Rugby Championship (formerly the Tri-Nations) between Australia's Wallabies, New Zealand's All Blacks, South Africa's Springboks and Argentina's Pumas provokes plenty of passion – particularly the matches against New Zealand, which determine the holders of the ultimate symbol of Trans-Tasman rivalry, the Bledisloe Cup (mostly because the Aussies haven't won it since 2002).

In the SuperRugby competition, the NSW Waratahs bang heads with 14 other teams from Australia, New Zealand and South Africa.

AUSTRALIAN RULES

In Aussie Rules football, the Australian Football League (www.afl.com.au) is growing in popularity since Sydney's beloved Swans won the 2005 premiership – the first time the Swans had won it since 1933, when they were still the South Melbourne Swans (they relocated to Sydney in 1982). Traditionally much more popular in the southern states and Western Australia, the future of Aussie Rules is looking rosy in NSW, with the addition of the new Greater Western Sydney Giants team to the AFL in 2012.

SOCCER (FOOTBALL)

Soccer comes a lowly fourth in the popularity race between Sydney's football codes, but received a boost when Australia qualified for the FIFA World Cup in 2006 and again in 2010 – the last time they qualified before that was 1974.

European immigrants kickstarted many of the city's local teams, which became strongly associated with particular ethnicities. Fan tensions were particularly pronounced in matches between the Croatian-dominated Sydney United and Serbian-dominated Bonnyrigg White Eagles, culminating in a riot in 2005.

Things have settled down since the creation of the A-League (www. footballaustralia.com.au/aleague) (consisting of nine Australian and one New Zealand team) and the multi-ethnic Sydney FC (www.footballaustralia.com.au/sydneyfc), which won the championship in 2006 and 2010. The league bucks convention, playing games from late August to February rather than through the depths of winter.

BASKETBALL

Sydney is represented in the National Basketball League (www.nbl.com. au) by the Sydney Kings, who had a run of three wins in the first decade of this century. Home games are held at the Entertainment Centre – christened the Kingdome for the events. In the Women's National Basketball League (www.wnbl.com.au), the Sydney Flames haven't won a championship since 1997.

SURF LIFESAVING

Surf lifesaving originated in Sydney, although red-and-yellow-capped volunteer lifesavers have since assumed iconic status across Australia. Despite the macho image, many lifesavers are women, and a contingent of gay and lesbian lifesavers march in the Sydney Mardi Gras Parade.

At summer surf carnivals all along the coast you can see these dedicated athletes wedge their speedos up their butt cracks and launch their surf boats (butt cheeks grip the seats better than speedos, apparently). Ask a local surf lifesaving club for dates, or contact Surf Life Saving Australia (www.sls.com.au) for info.

SAILING

The racing season for 18ft skiff yachts runs from September to April, with a whole messy wake of races across the harbour. South Head offers a good vantage point or head out on a Sydney Flying Squadron (www. sydneyflyingsquadron.com.au) viewing boat. On Boxing Day (26 December), Sydney Harbour hosts the start of the harrowing Sydney to Hobart Yacht Race (www.rolexsydneyhobart.com).

TENNIS

Tennis is much played in Sydney, with plenty of good courts scattered about, but Melbourne is home to the Australian Open. A prelude to that event, January's Apia International Sydney tennis tournament (www. apiainternational.com.au) takes place at Sydney Olympic Park.

Formerly the domain of dapper septuagenarians, lawn bowls has become inexplicably hip for a certain demographic in recent years. Young folks have learned to appreciate the sport's affordability, retro-kitsch vibe and the time-honoured traditions of drinking and smoking while the balls are rolling. Jack high!

Survival Guide

TRANSPORT **218**

GETTING TO SYDNEY 218
Air 218
Train 218
Bus 218
GETTING AROUND SYDNEY 218
Train 219
Bus 219
Light Rail 219
Boat 219
Bicycle 220
Car & Motorcycle 221
Taxi 221
TOURS 222

DIRECTORY A–Z **223**

Business Hours 223
Customs Regulations 223
Discount Cards 223
Electricity 224
Embassies & Consulates 224
Emergency 224
Internet Access 224
Legal Matters 224
Medical Services 224
Money 225
Post 225
Public Holidays 226
Taxes & Refunds 226
Telephone 226
Time 226
Tourist Information 226
Travellers with Disabilities 227
Visas 227
Women Travellers 228

Transport

GETTING TO SYDNEY

The vast majority of visitors to Sydney (and to Australia, for that matter) arrive at Sydney Airport, 10km south of the city centre. Trains chug into Sydney's Central station from as far north as Brisbane (13½ hours), as far south as Melbourne (11½ hours) and as far west as Perth (four days!). Long-distance buses pull up to the Sydney Coach Terminal beneath Central station.

Flights, tours and rail tickets can be booked online at lonelyplanet.com/bookings.

Air

Also known as Kingsford Smith Airport, **Sydney Airport** (☑9667 9111; www. sydneyairport.com.au) has separate international (T1) and domestic (T2 and T3) sections, 4km apart on either side of the runway. Each has left-luggage services, ATMs, currency exchange bureaux and rental-car counters.

Getting to/from Sydney Airport

➡ **Taxi** Allow $50 for a taxi to Circular Quay.

➡ **Shuttle** Airport shuttles head to hotels and hostels in the city centre, and some reach surrounding suburbs and beach destinations. Operators include

Sydney Airporter (☑9666 9988; www.kst.com.au; adult/ child $14/11), **Super Shuttle** (☑9697 2322; www.signature limousinessydney.com.au; airport hotels $6) and **Manly Express** (☑8065 9524; www.manly express.com.au; to Manly $35).

➡ **Train** Trains from both the domestic and international terminals, connecting into the main train network, are run by **Airport Link** (☑8337 8417; www.airportlink.com.au; to city $17; ☺5am-midnight). They're frequent (every 10 minutes), easy to use and quick (13 minutes to Central), but airport tickets are charged at a hefty premium.

➡ **Bus** The cheapest (albeit slowest) option to Bondi Junction is the 400 bus ($4.50, 1¼ hours).

Train

CountryLink (☑13 22 32; www.countrylink.info) The government-owned network, connecting Sydney to Canberra, Melbourne, Griffith, Broken Hill, Dubbo, Moree, Armidale and Brisbane. Book tickets online or through the **CountryLink Travel Centre** (Railway Square, Central station; ☺6.15am-8.45pm; ℝCentral) near platform one. Discounts of up to 50% apply with two weeks' notice.

Indian Pacific (☑08-8213 4592; www.trainways.com.au)

The famous train that heads clear across the continent from Perth to Sydney.

Bus

Long-distance bus services arrive at **Sydney Coach Terminal** (☑9281 9366; Eddy Ave; ☺6am-6pm Mon-Fri, 8am-6pm Sat & Sun; ℝCentral), underneath Central station. As well as **CountryLink** (☑13 22 32; www.countrylink.info), major operators include the following:

Firefly (☑1300 730 740; www. fireflyexpress.com.au) Adelaide to Sydney via Melbourne and Canberra.

Greyhound (☑1300 473 946; www.greyhound.com.au) Has the most extensive nationwide network.

Murrays (☑13 22 51; www. murrays.com.au) Canberra, South Coast and Snowy Mountains to Sydney.

Premier Motor Service (☑133 410; www.premierms. com.au) Cairns to Melbourne, via Brisbane, Gold Coast and Sydney.

GETTING AROUND SYDNEY

Sydneysiders love to complain about their public transport system, but visitors should find it surprisingly easy to navigate. The train system is the linchpin, with

CLIMATE CHANGE & TRAVEL

Every form of transport that relies on carbon-based fuel generates CO_2, the main cause of human-induced climate change. Modern travel is dependent on aeroplanes, which might use less fuel per kilometre per person than most cars but travel much greater distances. The altitude at which aircraft emit gases (including CO_2) and particles also contributes to their climate change impact. Many websites offer 'carbon calculators' that allow people to estimate the carbon emissions generated by their journey and, for those who wish to do so, to offset the impact of the greenhouse gases emitted with contributions to portfolios of climate-friendly initiatives throughout the world. Lonely Planet offsets the carbon footprint of all staff and author travel.

lines radiating out from Central station. Ferries head all around the harbour and up the river to Parramatta; light rail is useful for Pyrmont and Glebe; and buses are particularly useful for getting to the beaches.

Train

Sydney has a large suburban railway web with relatively frequent services. You can reach most places by train, but lines don't extend to Balmain, Glebe or the northern or eastern beaches. Trains run from around 5am to 1am – check timetables for your line. A short innercity one-way trip on **CityRail** (☑131 500; www.cityrail.info) costs $3.40. On weekends and after 9am Monday to Friday you can buy an off-peak return ticket for not much more than a standard one-way fare.

Bus

Sydney Buses (☑131 500; www.sydneybuses.info) runs the local bus network. Fares depend upon the number of 'sections' you traverse; tickets range from $2.10 to $4.50. Discount passes will save you some bucks and are handy for 'prepay only' services.

Regular buses run between 5am and midnight, when NightRide buses take over. During peak hour, buses get crowded and sometimes fail to pick up passengers at major stops if they're full.

The major bus route hubs are Circular Quay, Argyle St in Millers Point, Wynyard Park, Queen Victoria Building and Railway Sq (near Central station). Most buses exit the city on George or Castlereagh Sts, and take George or Elizabeth Sts coming back in. Pay the driver as you enter (correct change minimises annoyance), or dunk prepaid tickets in the green ticket machines. Increasing numbers of services are 'prepay only'. Bus routes starting with an X indicate limited-stop express routes; those with an L have limited stops.

At Circular Quay there's a **TransitShop** (cnr Alfred & Loftus Sts; ⊙7am-7pm Mon-Fri, 8.30am-5pm Sat & Sun), which sells bus tickets and offers bus info. There are other TransitShops at **Wynyard Park** (Map p250; York St; ℝWynyard), the **Queen Victoria Building** (York St) and Railway Sq. Tickets can also be purchased at numerous newsagents, corner stores and supermarkets throughout the city.

If you'll be catching buses a lot (but not trains or ferries), consider a prepaid 10-ride TravelTen ticket (sections 1-2/3-5/6+ $17/28/36).

Free City Shuttle

Bus 555 is a free CBD shuttle bus, looping between Central station, George St, Circular Quay and Elizabeth St every 10 minutes from 9.30am to 3.30pm on weekdays (until 9pm Thursdays), and between 9.30am and 6pm on weekends.

Light Rail

Metro Light Rail (MLR; www.metrolightrail.com. au; zone 1 adult/concession $3.40/2.20, zone 1 & 2 adult/concession $4.40/3.40, day pass adult $9; ⊙24hr, every 10-15min 6am-midnight, every 30min midnight-6am) heads from Central to Lilyfield (via Chinatown, Darling Harbour, Pyrmont and Glebe) every 10 to 15 minutes from 6am to 11pm. There's a 24-hour service from Central to the Star, with late-night trains every 30 minutes.

Boat

Ferries

Most **Sydney Ferries** (☑131 500; www.sydneyferries.info) operate between 6am and midnight. Popular places accessible by ferry include Darling Harbour, Balmain, Cockatoo Island, Sydney Olympic Park and Parramatta to the west; Milsons Point/ Luna Park, North Sydney, Kirribilli, Neutral Bay, Cremorne, Mosman, Taronga Zoo and Manly on the North Shore; and Double Bay, Rose Bay and Watsons Bay in the Eastern Suburbs. All ferries depart from Circular Quay.

INTEGRATED PUBLIC TRANSPORT SERVICES

All of the state's public and many of its private services are gathered together under the umbrella of the **NSW Transport Infoline** (☑13 15 00; www.131500. com.au). The website has an excellent journey planner, where you can plug in your requirements and then let the system spit out a range of options. MyMulti passes allow unlimited travel on trains (except the airport stations), light rail, buses and government ferry services. Options include the following:

➡ **MyMulti DayPass** ($21) Covers the entire system.

➡ **MyMulti1** (per week/month $43/164) Includes all buses, light rail and ferries but only Zone 1 trains. Note, you can get to Parramatta and Olympic Park on this pass by ferry but not by train. This pass is the best option for most travellers.

➡ **MyMulti2** (per week/month $51/194) As above, but includes trains to places like Olympic Park and Parramatta.

➡ **MyMulti3** (per week/month $60/232) As above, but includes trains to Cronulla, the Blue Mountains and the stations on the fringes of Royal National Park.

➡ **Family Funday Sunday** If you're related and have at least one adult and one child in your party, all of you can travel anywhere within the network on Sundays for a day rate of $2.50 per person.

The standard single fare for most harbour destinations is $5.60; boats to Manly, Sydney Olympic Park and Parramatta cost $7. If you're staying near a ferry wharf and don't think you'll be using buses or trains much, consider a prepaid 10-ride MyFerryTen ticket ($44.80). If you're heading to Taronga Zoo by ferry, consider the all-inclusive ZooPass (adult/child $52/26).

Manly Fast Ferry (☑9583 1199; www.manly fastferry.com.au; adult/child $8.20/6) and **Sydney Fast Ferries** (☑9818 6000; www. sydneyfastferries.com.au; peak/offpeak $9/6) both offer boats that blast from Circular Quay to Manly in 18 minutes.

Water Taxis

Water taxis are a fast way to shunt around the harbour (Circular Quay to Watsons Bay in as little as 15 minutes). Companies will quote on any pick-up point within the harbour and the river, including private jetties, islands and other boats. Operators include the following:

Aussie Water Taxis (☑9211 7730; www.aussie watertaxis.com) The smallest seats 16 passengers. Can be rented per hour or point-to-point. Has discounted per-person prices from Darling Harbour, including Circular Quay ($15), Luna Park ($15), Fish Markets ($20) and Taronga Zoo ($25).

H2O Taxis (☑1300 420 829; www.h2owatertaxis.com. au) Smallest seats 21 people. Harbour Islands a speciality: Fort Denison/Cockatoo Island/ Shark Island cost $65/80/90 for up to six people from Circular Quay. Has a handy quote calculator on its website.

Water Taxis Combined (☑9555 8888; www.watertaxis. com.au) Fares based on up to four passengers; add $10 per person for additional passengers. Sample fares: Circular Quay to Watsons Bay $110; to Rose Bay $105; Mosman to Woolloomooloo $80. Time-based cruises are $200 per half hour for up to 16 people.

Yellow Water Taxis (☑1300 138 840; www.yellow watertaxis.com.au) Set price for up to four passengers, then $10 per person for additional people. Sample fares from King St Wharf: Circular Quay and Fort Denison $75; Taronga Zoo $95; Cockatoo Island and Shark Island $110; Watsons Bay $115.

Bicycle

Sydney traffic can be intimidating, but there are an increasing number of separated bike lanes; see www. cityofsydney.nsw.gov.au. Helmets are compulsory.

There's no charge for taking a bike on CityRail trains, except during peak hours (6am to 9am and 3.30pm to 7.30pm Monday to Friday) when you will need to purchase a child's ticket for the bike. Bikes travel for free on Sydney's ferries, which usually have bicycle racks (first come, first served). Buses are no-go zones for bikes.

Many cycle-hire shops require a hefty credit-card deposit. For hire, see the following:

Inner City Cycles (Map p256; ☑9660 6605; www. innercitycycles.com.au; 151 Glebe Point Rd; hire per day/ week $33/88; ⏱9.30am-6pm Mon-Wed & Fri, 9.30am-8pm Thu, 9.00am-4pm Sat, 11am-3pm Sun; 🚆Glebe)

Bonza Bike Tours (Map p248; ☑9247 8800; www. bonzabiketours.com; 30 Harrington St; adult/child $99/79; 🚆Circular Quay)

Bike Buffs (⌨0414 960 332; www.bikebuffs.com.au; adult/child $95/70; ☺10am-6pm)

Centennial Park Cycles (Map p264; ⌨0401 357 419; www.cyclehire.com.au; Grand Dr; ☺9am-5pm)

Skater HQ EQ (Map p264; ⌨9368 0945; www.skaterhq. com.au; Bent St; ☺10am-7pm Sun-Fri, to 9pm Sat; ▣372-374 & 391-397)

Skater HQ Manly (Map p268; ⌨8667 7892; www.skat erhq.com.au; 49 North Steyne; ☺9am-6pm; ▣Manly)

Manly Bike Tours (Map p268; ⌨8005 7368; www. manlybiketours.com.au; 54 West Promenade; hire per hr/day from $14/28; ☺9am-6pm; ▣Manly)

Bike Hire @ Sydney Olympic Park (⌨9746 1572; www.bikehiresydneyolympic park.com.au; Bicentennial Dr, Bicentennial Park; mountain bike per 1/2/4/8/24hr $15/20/30/40/50; ☺8.30am-5.30pm)

Car & Motorcycle

Avoid driving in central Sydney if you can: there's a confusing one-way street system, parking sucks (even at hotels!), and parking inspectors and tow-away zones proliferate. Conversely, a car is handy for accessing Sydney's outer reaches (particularly the beaches) and for day trips. Or you could try a moped or a motorcycle; just wear something bright so you don't get crunched by a four-wheeler.

Driving & Parking

Australians drive on the left-hand side of the road; the minimum driving age (unassisted) is 18. Overseas visitors can drive with their domestic driving licences for up to three months but must obtain a NSW driving licence after that. Speed limits in Sydney are generally 60km/h (50km/h in some areas), rising to 100km/h or

110km/h on motorways. Seat belts are compulsory; using hand-held mobile phones is prohibited. A blood-alcohol limit of 0.05% is enforced with random breath tests and hefty punishments. If you're in an accident (even if you didn't cause it) and you're over the alcohol limit, your insurance will be invalidated. For further information, see www.rta.nsw.gov.au.

Sydney's private car parks are expensive (around $15 per hour); public car parks are more affordable (sometimes under $10 per hour). The city centre and Darling Harbour have the greatest number of private car parks, but these are also the priciest. Street parking devours coins (from $2.50 to $5 per hour), although some take credit cards.

Toll Roads

Sydney's motorways are all tolled; charges vary with the distance travelled – anywhere from $2 to $15. Most are cashless, hire-car companies can provide information for setting up a temporary electronic pass.

Hire

Car-rental prices vary depending on season and demand. Read the small print to check age restrictions, exactly what your insurance covers and where you can take the car (dirt roads are sometimes off limits).

The big players have airport desks and city offices (mostly around William St). The Yellow Pages lists other local car-hire companies, some specialising in renting near-wrecks at rock-bottom prices – study the fine print to ensure you're not being lumped with a lemon.

For motorbike hire, try Bikescape (p222).

Avis (⌨9353 9000; www.avis. com.au)

Bayswater Car Rental (⌨9360 3622; www.bays watercarrental.com.au)

Budget (⌨9207 9165; www. budget.com.au)

Europcar (⌨1300 131 390; www.europcar.com.au)

Hertz (⌨133 039; www.hertz. com.au)

Thrifty (⌨8337 2700; www. thrifty.com.au)

Automobile Association

The **National Roads & Motorists Association** (NRMA; ⌨132 132; www.nrma. com.au; 74 King St; ☺9am-5pm Mon-Fri, 9.30am-12.30pm Sat; ▣Wynyard) provides 24-hour emergency roadside assistance, maps, travel advice, insurance and accommodation discounts. It has reciprocal arrangements with similar organisations interstate and overseas (bring proof of membership).

Taxi

Taxis are easy to flag down in the city and the inner suburbs, except for at 'changeover' times (3pm and 3am). Taxis are metered and drivers won't usually rip you off – but don't expect them to know how to get to where you're going! If they're unsure, ask them to turn off the meter while they check the map.

Flagfall is $3.40; the metered fare thereafter is $2.06 per kilometre. There's a 20% surcharge between 10pm and 6am, and additional charges for tolls and radio bookings ($2.30). For more on Sydney's taxis, see www. nswtaxi.org.au.

Big, reliable operators:

Legion Cabs (⌨13 14 51; www.legioncabs.com.au)

Premier Cabs (⌨13 10 17; www.premiercabs.com.au)

RSL Cabs (⌨9581 1111; www. rslcabs.com.au)

Taxis Combined (⌨13 33 00; www.taxiscombined. com.au)

TOURS

Organised tours can be a useful way to get around if you're short on time or prefer to have things organised for you. For localised tours, refer to the neighbourhood chapters.

City Sightseeing (✆9567 8400; www.city-sightseeing. com; 24/48hr ticket $40/60; ⊗every 15-30 minutes, 8.30am-7.30pm) Double-decker buses on two interlinking, 90-minute, hop-on/hop-off loops around Sydney.

Real Sydney Tours (✆0412 876 180; www.realsydneytours. com.au) A private minibus tour for two people costs $455, but enquire about openings on share tours (per person $150) and Blue Mountains trips.

Bikescape (✆02 9569 4111; www.bikescape.com.au; cnr Parramatta Rd & Young St, Annandale; tours from $130; ☒Stanmore) Harley Davidson city tours, road trips and motorbike hire (from $80 per day for a scooter to $345 for a Harley).

Runaway Tours (✆0410 545 117; www.nightcattours. com; per person $75) Small-group night-time tours, half-day city sights tours, and day trips to the Blue Mountains.

Oz Trails (✆1300 853 842; www.oztrails.com.au; adult/child $79/60) Small-group day tours to the Blue Mountains.

Directory A–Z

Business Hours

The following tables summarise standard opening hours. Reviews in this book won't list opening hours unless they significantly differ from these.

➡ **Restaurants** noon–3pm and 6pm–10pm

➡ **Cafes** 8am–4pm

➡ **Pubs** 11am–midnight Monday–Saturday, 11am–10pm Sunday

➡ **Shops** 9.30am–6pm Monday–Wednesday, Friday and Saturday, 9.30am–8pm Thursday, 11am–5pm Sunday

➡ **Banks** 9.30am–4pm Monday–Thursday, 9.30am–5pm Friday

➡ **Offices** 9am–5.30pm

Customs Regulations

Entering Australia you can bring in most articles free of duty, provided Customs is satisfied they're for personal use and that you'll be taking them with you when you leave. There's a duty-free quota per person of 2.25L of alcohol (if you're over 18), 250 cigarettes (ditto) and dutiable goods up to the value of $900 ($450 if you're under 18). Wads of more than A$10,000 cash must be declared. These values change from time to time; check current regulations with the **Australian Customs Service** (☑1300 363 263; www.customs.gov.au).

Two issues require particular attention. One is illegal drugs – don't bring any in with you. The second is animal and plant quarantine – be sure to declare all goods of animal or vegetable origin and show them to an official. Authorities are anxious to prevent pests and diseases getting into the country. Fresh food and flowers are also unpopular. If you've recently visited farmland or rural areas, it might pay to scrub your shoes before you get to the airport, and you'll also need to declare it to Customs.

Weapons and firearms are either prohibited or require a permit and safety testing. Other restricted goods include products made from protected wildlife species, nonapproved telecommunications devices and live animals.

When you leave, don't take any protected flora or fauna with you. Customs comes down hard on smugglers.

Discount Cards

See Sydney & Beyond Card (☑1300 366 476; www.seesydneycard.com; 2-/3-/7 day $155/189/270, with transport $190/245/339) Offers admission to a plethora of Sydney attractions, including sightseeing tours, harbour cruises, museums, historic buildings and wildlife parks. It's reasonably pricy, so assess how many of these attractions you think you'll actually visit in the timeframe given before purchasing. The 'with transport' option includes a MyMulti public transport pass.

Ticket Through Time (☑02-8239 2211; www.hht.net.au/visiting/ticket_through_time; adult/concession & child $30/15) Provides entry for a three-month period to the 11 Sydney museums of the Historic Houses Trust. Can be purchased online or at any HHT property.

PRACTICALITIES

➡ **Newspapers** The main daily newspaper are the *Sydney Morning Herald* (for serious news) and the *Daily Telegraph* (sports and rabble-rousing).

➡ **TV** Sydney has six free-to-air TV channels. ABC and SBS offer more worthy fare, while Seven, Nine and Ten are the main commercial channels. TVS is the free community-run channel.

➡ **Smoking** Smoking is not permitted indoors in public places (including offices, shops, bars, restaurants, cafes, hospitals) and new laws will ban smoking in playgrounds, public sports grounds, transport stops, entrances to public buildings and outdoor dining areas.

Electricity

240V/50Hz

Embassies & Consulates

Most foreign embassies are in Canberra, but many countries also maintain a consulate in Sydney. For consulates not listed here, see Consulates & Legations in the telephone directory.

British Consulate-General (☑9247 7521; www.ukinaustralia.fco.gov.uk; L16, 1 Macquarie Pl; ℝCircular Quay)

Canadian Consulate-General (☑9364 3000; www.canadainternational.gc.ca; L5, 111 Harrington St; ℝCircular Quay)

Dutch Consulate-General (http://australia.nlembassy.org; L23, 101 Grafton St, Bondi Junction; ℝBondi Junction)

French Consulate-General (☑9268 2400; www.ambafrance-au.org; L26, 31 Market St; ℝTown Hall)

German Consulate-General (☑9328 7733; www.australien.diplo.de; 13 Trelawney St, Woollahra; ℝEdgecliff)

Irish Consulate-General (☑9264 9635; www.irishconsulatesydney.net; L26, 1 Market St; ℝTown Hall)

New Zealand Consulate-General (☑8256 2000; www.nzembassy.com; L10, 55 Hunter St; ℝMartin Place)

US Consulate-General (☑8278 1420; http://sydney.usconsulate.gov; L10, MLC Centre, 19-29 Martin Pl; ℝMartin Place)

Emergency

In the event of an emergency, call 000 for the police, the ambulance or the fire brigade. Other useful contacts:

Lifeline (☑13 11 14; www.lifelinesydney.org; ⊙24hr) Round-the-clock phone counselling services, including suicide prevention.

National Roads & Motorists Association (NRMA; ☑132 132; www.nrma.com.au; 74 King St; ⊙9am-5pm Mon-Fri, 9.30am-12.30pm Sat; ℝWynyard) Provides 24-hour emergency roadside assistance, maps, travel advice, insurance and accommodation discounts. It has reciprocal arrangements with similar organisations interstate and overseas (bring proof of membership).

Rape Crisis Centre (☑1800 424 017; www.nswrapecrisis.com.au; ⊙24hr) Offers 24hr counselling.

Internet Access

➡ Most hotels and hostels now provide wi-fi connections, although many, especially top-end places, charge for the service. Many larger hotels have an in-room cable connection.

➡ The majority of hostels and some hotels provide computers for guest use. Access may or may not be charged.

➡ Many cafes and bars offer free wi-fi, particularly the big international chains (including Starbucks and most McDonald's). Most public libraries offer it, and the Broadway Shopping Centre has it in its foodcourt.

➡ Pay-as-you-go internet hotspots are common in busy areas.

➡ Because of the greater access to free connections, internet cafes are not as ubiquitous as they once were, although you'll still find them around touristy areas such as Central station, Kings Cross and Bondi. One reliable chain is **Global Gossip** (☑1300 738 353; www.globalgossip.com; 790 George St), which has terminals in many hostels.

Legal Matters

➡ Australia is very strict when it comes to driving under the influence of alcohol or other drugs. There is a significant police presence on the roads, and they have the power to stop your car and see your licence (you're required to carry it), check your vehicle for roadworthiness and insist that you take a breath test for alcohol. The legal limit is 0.05 blood alcohol content. If you're over, you may face a hefty fine.

➡ First offenders caught with small amounts of illegal drugs are likely to receive a fine rather than go to jail, but a conviction may affect your visa status.

➡ If you remain in Australia after your visa expires, you will officially be an 'overstayer' and could face detention and expulsion, and then be prevented from returning to Australia for up to three years.

Medical Services

Visitors from Belgium, Finland, Ireland, Italy, Malta, the

Netherlands, New Zealand, Norway, Slovenia, Sweden and the UK have reciprocal health rights, entitling them to 'limited subsidised health services for medically necessary treatment', including free public-hospital access and subsidised medicines. In some cases you'll have to pay upfront, then be reimbursed once you've registered with **Medicare** (☑13 20 11; www.medicareaustralia. gov.au). Travel insurance is advisable to cover other expenses (such as ambulance and repatriation).

Clinics

If you need a dentist pronto, visit www.dentist.com.au.

Kings Cross Clinic (☑9358 3066; www.kingscrossclinic.com.au; 13 Springfield Ave; ◷9am-6pm Mon-Fri, 10am-1pm Sat; ☒Kings Cross) General practitioners with a travel medicine focus, offering vaccinations, morning-after pills and dive medicals.

Travellers Medical Vaccination Centre (☑9221 7133; www.traveldoctor.com.au; L7, 428 George St; ◷9am-5.30pm Mon, Wed & Fri, 9am-8pm Tue & Thu, 9am-1pm Sat; ☒St James) Travel-related shots and medical advice.

Emergency Rooms

Hospitals with 24-hour accident and emergency departments include the following:

Royal Prince Alfred Hospital (RPA; ☑9515 6111; www.sswahs.nsw.gov.au/rpa; Missenden Rd, Camperdown; ☒Macdonaldtown)

St Vincent's Hospital (☑8382 1111; wwwsvh.stvincents.com.au; 390 Victoria St, Darlinghurst; ☒Kings Cross)

Sydney Children's Hospital (☑9382 1111; www.sch.edu. au; High St, Randwick; ▣400)

Sydney Hospital & Sydney Eye Hospital (☑9382 7111; www.sesahs.nsw.gov.

au/sydhosp; 8 Macquarie St; ☒Martin Place)

Pharmacies

Every shopping strip and mall has a pharmacy. The following have conveniently long hours:

Blakes Pharmacy (☑9358 6712; www.blakespharmacy. com.au; 20 Darlinghurst Rd, Darlinghurst; ◷9am-11pm; ☒Kings Cross)

Wu's Pharmacy (☑9281 9431; 629 George St, Haymarket; ◷9am-9pm Mon-Sat, to 7pm Sun; ☒Town Hall)

Money

➡ The unit of currency is the Australian dollar, which is divided into 100 cents.

➡ Notes are colourful, plastic and washing-machine-proof, in denominations of $100, $50, $20, $10 and $5.

➡ Coins come in $2, $1, 50c, 20c, 10c and 5c. The old 2c and 1c coins have been out of circulation for years, so shops round prices up (or down) to the nearest 5c. Curiously, $2 coins are smaller than $1.

➡ Travellers cheques are something of a dinosaur these days, and they won't be accepted everywhere. It's easier not to bother with them.

ATMs

Central Sydney is chock-full of banks with 24-hour ATMs that will accept debit and credit cards linked to international network systems (Cirrus, Maestro, Visa, MasterCard etc). Most banks place a $1000 limit on the amount you can withdraw daily. You'll also find ATMs in pubs and clubs, although these usually charge slightly higher fees. Shops and retail outlets usually have EFTPOS facilities, which allow you to pay for purchases with your debit or credit card.

Changing Money

➡ Exchange bureaux are dotted around the city centre, Kings Cross and Bondi.

➡ Shop around, as rates vary and most charge some sort of commission.

➡ The counters at the airport are open until the last flight comes in; rates here aren't quite as good as they are in the city.

Credit Cards

Visa and MasterCard are widely accepted at larger shops, restaurants and hotels, but not necessarily at smaller shops or cafes. Diners Club and American Express are less widely accepted. Lost-card contact numbers:

American Express (☑1300 736 659; www.americanexpress.com)

Diners Club (☑1300 360 060; www.dinersclub.com.au)

MasterCard (☑1800 120 113; www.mastercard.com.au)

Visa (☑1800 125 440; www.visa.com.au)

Tipping

In Sydney most service providers don't expect a tip, so you shouldn't feel pressured into giving one, even at fancy restaurants. If the service is good, however, it is customary to tip porters (gold coin), wait staff in restaurants (up to 10%, but only for good service) and taxi drivers (round up to the nearest dollar).

Post

Australia Post (☑13 76 78; www.auspost.com.au) has efficient branches throughout Sydney. It costs 60c to send a postcard or standard letter within Australia. Airmail letters (weighing up to 50g) cost $1.65 to the Asia Pacific region and $2.35 to the rest of the world. Mailing postcards anywhere outside Australia costs a flat $1.60.

Public Holidays

On public holidays, government departments, banks, offices and post offices shut up shop. On Good Friday, Easter Sunday, ANZAC Day and Christmas Day, most shops are closed. Public holidays include the following:

→ **New Year's Day** 1 January

→ **Australia Day** 26 January

→ **Easter** (Good Friday to Easter Monday) March/April

→ **ANZAC Day** 25 April

→ **Queen's Birthday** Second Monday in June

→ **Bank Holiday** First Monday in August (only banks are closed)

→ **Labour Day** First Monday in October

→ **Christmas Day** 25 December

→ **Boxing Day** 26 December

Most public holidays cleverly morph into long weekends (three days), so if a holiday such as New Year's Day falls on a weekend, the following Monday is usually a holiday.

Something else to consider when planning a Sydney visit is school holidays, when accommodation rates soar and everything gets decidedly hectic. Sydney students have a long summer break that includes Christmas and most of January. Other school holidays fall around March to April (Easter), late June to mid-July, and late September to early October.

Taxes & Refunds

There's a 10% goods and services tax (GST) automatically added to almost everything you buy, Australiawide. If you purchase goods with a total minimum value of $300 from any one store within 30 days of departure from Australia, the Tourist Refund Scheme entitles you to a refund of any GST paid. Keep your receipts and carry the items on board your flight as hand luggage; you can get a cheque refund or a credit card refund at the designated booth located past Customs at Sydney airport (see www.customs.gov.au for more information).

Telephone

→ Public telephones, which can be found all over the city, take phonecards, credit cards and occasionally (if the coin slots aren't jammed up) coins.

→ Australia's country code: 61

→ Sydney's area code: 02 (drop the zero when dialling into Australia)

→ International access code: 0011 (used when dialling other countries from Australia)

→ Toll-free numbers start with the prefix 1800, while numbers that start with 1300 are only the cost of a local call.

Mobile Phones

→ Australian mobile-phone numbers have four-digit prefixes starting with 04.

→ Australia's digital network is compatible with GSM 900 and 1800 handsets (used in Europe). Quad-band US phones will work, but to avoid global-roaming charges, you need an unlocked handset that takes prepaid SIM cards from Australian providers.

→ It's illegal to talk on a hand-held mobile phone while driving.

Phonecards

Local and international phonecards range in value from $5 to $50 – look for the phonecard logo at retail outlets, such as newsagents. There is a bewildering variety of cards available, with all sorts of deals aimed at visitors wanting to get in touch with loved ones in Europe, Asia and the Americas. Shop around.

Time

Sydney is on Eastern Standard Time (EST), which is 10 hours ahead of GMT/UTC. That means that when it's noon in Sydney it's 6pm the day before in Los Angeles, 9pm the day before in New York, 2am in London, 4am in Johannesburg, 11am in Tokyo and 2pm in Auckland. Running from the first Sunday in October to the first Sunday in April, Daylight Savings Time is one hour ahead of standard time.

Tourist Information

The following opening hours vary with the seasons (summer hours tend to be longer).

City Host Information Kiosks (www.cityofsydney. nsw.gov.au) **Circular Quay** (cnr Pitt & Alfred Sts; ⊘9am-5pm; ℞Circular Quay); **Town Hall** (George St; ⊘9am-5pm; ℞Town Hall); **Haymarket** (Dixon St; ⊘11am-7pm; ℞Town Hall)

Manly Visitor Information Centre (☑9976 1430; www.manlyaustralia.com. au; Manly Wharf; ⊘9am-5pm Mon-Fri, 10am-4pm Sat & Sun; ☒Manly) This helpful visitors centre, just outside the ferry wharf and alongside the bus interchange, has free pamphlets covering the Manly Scenic Walkway and other Manly attractions, plus loads of local bus information.

Parramatta Heritage & Visitor Information Centre (☑1300 889 714; www. discoverparramatta.com.au; 346a Church St; ⊘9am-5pm; ☒Parramatta) Knowledgeable staff will point you in the right direction with loads of brochures and leaflets, info on access for visitors with impaired mobility and details on local Aboriginal cultural sites.

Sydney Coach Terminal (☑9281 9366; Eddy Ave; ⊘6am-6pm Mon-Fri, 8am-6pm Sat & Sun; ℞Central) Bus and hotel bookings, internet access and luggage storage. Not radically helpful, but then again, it could just be the location, which has extremely bad feng shui.

Sydney Harbour National Park Information Centre (Map p248; ☑9253 0888; www.environment.nsw.gov.au; Cadman's Cottage, 110 George St; ☉10am-4.30pm; ⓇCircular Quay) Has maps of walks in different parts of the park and organises tours of the harbour islands.

Sydney Visitor Centre – Darling Harbour (☑9240 8788; www.darlingharbour. com; ☉9.30am-5.30pm; ⓇTown Hall) Behind the IMAX Theatre, with bountiful info about NSW, tours, hotels and entertainment options.

Sydney Visitor Centre – The Rocks (☑9240 8788; www.sydneyvisitorcentre. com; cnr Argyle & Playfair Sts; ☉9.30am-5.30pm; ⓇCircular Quay) Sydney's main visitors centre, with walls of brochures and information on Sydney and regional NSW. Knowledgeable staff can help you find a hotel or a restaurant with harbour views, book a tour, hire a car and arrange transport for day trips out of town. Info on exploring The Rocks is the obvious speciality.

Travellers with Disabilities

Compared with many other major cities, Sydney has great access for citizens and visitors with disabilities. Most of Sydney's main attractions are accessible by wheelchair, and all new or renovated buildings must, by law, include wheelchair access. Older buildings can pose some problems, however, and some restaurants and entertainment venues aren't quite up to scratch. Most of

the National Trust's historic houses are at least partially accessible, and abashed attendants can usually show you photos of inaccessible areas. Some taxis accommodate wheelchairs – request them when you make your booking.

Most of Sydney's major attractions offer hearing loops and sign-language interpreters for hearing-impaired travellers. To expedite proceedings, make contact with venue staff in advance.

Many new buildings incorporate architectural features that are helpful to the vision impaired, such as textured floor details at the top and bottom of stairs. Sydney's pedestrian crossings feature catchy beep-and-buzz sound cues.

Sydney also has lots of parking spaces reserved for drivers with disabilities; see the City of Sydney website for information.

Organisations

City of Sydney (☑9265 9333; www.cityofsydney. nsw.gov.au) Lists parking spaces, transport information, CBD access maps and other information.

Deaf Society of NSW (☑9893 8555; www.deaf societynsw.org.au)

Roads and Traffic Authority (RTA; ☑13 22 13; www.rta.nsw.gov.au) Supplies temporary parking permits for international drivers with disabilities.

Spinal Cord Injuries Australia (www.spinalcord injuries.com.au)

Vision Australia (☑1300 847 466; www.visionaustralia. org.au)

Visas

➡ All visitors to Australia need a visa – only New Zealand nationals are exempt, and even they

receive a 'special category' visa on arrival. Visa application forms are available from Australian diplomatic missions overseas, travel agents or the website of the **Department of Immigration & Citizenship** (DIAC; ☑13 18 81; www. immi.gov.au).

➡ Citizens of European Union member countries, Andorra, Iceland, Liechtenstein, Monaco, Norway, San Marino and Switzerland are eligible for an eVisitor, which is free and allows visitors to stay in Australia for up to three months. These must be applied for online, and they are electronically stored and linked to individual passport numbers, so no stamp in your passport is required. It's advisable to apply at least 14 days prior to the proposed date of travel to Australia. Applications are made on the Department of Immigration & Citizenship website.

➡ An Electronic Travel Authority (ETA) allows visitors to enter Australia any time within a 12-month period and stay for up to three months at a time (unlike eVisitor, multiple entries are permitted). Travellers from qualifying countries can get an ETA through any International Air Transport Association (IATA)-registered travel agent or overseas airline. They make the application for you when you buy a ticket and they issue the ETA, which replaces the usual visa stamped in your passport. It's common practice for travel agents to charge a fee for issuing an ETA (in the vicinity of US$25). This system is available to passport holders of some 33 countries, including all of the countries that are eligible for eVisitor.

➡ The eight countries that are eligible for ETA but not eVisitor can make their application online at www.eta.immi.gov.au, where a $20 fee applies. Those countries are Brunei, Canada, Hong Kong, Japan, Malaysia, Singapore, South Korea and the USA.

➡ If you are from a country not covered by eVisitor or ETA, or you want to stay longer than three months, you'll need to apply for a visa. Tourist visas cost $110 and allow single or multiple entry for stays of three, six or 12 months and are valid for use within 12 months of issue.

➡ Visitors are allowed a maximum stay of 12 months, including extensions. Visa extensions are made through the Department of Immigration & Citizenship, and it's best to apply at least two or three weeks before your visa expires. The application fee is $290 – it's nonrefundable, even if your application is rejected.

➡ Young (aged 18 to 30) visitors from Belgium, Canada, Cyprus, Denmark, Estonia, Finland, France, Germany, Hong Kong, Ireland, Italy, Japan, Korea, Malta, the Netherlands, Norway, Sweden, Taiwan and the UK are eligible for a Working Holiday Maker (WHM) Visa (417), which allows you to visit for up to one year and gain casual employment. The emphasis of this visa is on casual and not full-time employment, so you're only supposed to work for any one employer for a maximum of six months. A first WHM visa must be obtained prior to entry to Australia and can be applied for at Australian diplomatic missions abroad or online. You can't change from a tourist visa to a WHM visa once you're in Australia. You can apply for this visa up to a year in advance, which is worthwhile doing, as there's a limit on the number issued each year. Conditions include having a return air ticket or sufficient funds for a return or onward fare, and an application fee of $270 is charged.

➡ Nationals from Argentina, Bangladesh, Chile, Indonesia, Malaysia, Thailand, Turkey and the USA between the ages of 18 and 30 can apply for a Work & Holiday Visa (462) prior to entry to Australia. Once granted, this visa allows the holder to stay for up to 12 months and undertake temporary employment to supplement a trip. Conditions vary depending on nationality. The application fee is also $270.

Women Travellers

Sydney is generally safe for women travellers, although you should avoid walking alone late at night. Sexual harassment and discrimination, while uncommon, can occur and shouldn't be tolerated. If you do encounter infantile sexism from drunken louts, the safest option is to leave without making any comment. In bars, use common sense and don't accept drinks from people you don't know or leave your drink unattended. Drink spiking isn't a common practice, but it has occurred in the past.

Behind the Scenes

SEND US YOUR FEEDBACK

We love to hear from travellers – your comments keep us on our toes and help make our books better. Our well-travelled team reads every word on what you loved or loathed about this book. Although we cannot reply individually to postal submissions, we always guarantee that your feedback goes straight to the appropriate authors, in time for the next edition. Each person who sends us information is thanked in the next edition – and the most useful submissions are rewarded with a selection of digital PDF chapters.

Visit **lonelyplanet.com/contact** to submit your updates and suggestions or to ask for help. Our award-winning website also features inspirational travel stories, news and discussions.

Note: We may edit, reproduce and incorporate your comments in Lonely Planet products such as guidebooks, websites and digital products, so let us know if you don't want your comments reproduced or your name acknowledged. For a copy of our privacy policy visit lonelyplanet.com/privacy.

OUR READERS

Many thanks to the travellers who used the last edition and wrote to us with helpful hints, useful advice and interesting anecdotes:

Courtney Chute, Ben Dewis, Mick Garton, Jeri Gertz, Liz Heynes, Anne Matheson, Katy Pickvance, Erick Strauss, Christopher Tudehope.

AUTHOR THANKS
Peter Dragicevich

I would like to offer heartfelt thanks to Mandy Sayer, David Mills, Barry Sawtell, Michael Woodhouse, Tim Moyes and especially Tony Dragicevich and Debbie Debono (sorry about the Batmobile). Thanks also to Shenita Prasad, Shelley Mulhern, Jo Brook, Sue Ostler, John Burfitt, Braith Bamkin, Daniel Dragicevich, Lauren Dragicevich and Matt Dragicevich for on-the-road advice and company.

ACKNOWLEDGMENTS

Illustration p70-1 by Javier Zarracina.
Cover photograph: George St in The Rocks with Sydney Harbour Bridge in the background/Andrew Watson/Getty Images ©.

THIS BOOK

This 10th edition of Lonely Planet's *Sydney* guidebook was researched and written by Peter Dragicevich. The previous edition was written by Charles Rawlings-Way. *Sydney* 8 was written by Peter Dragicevich and Jolyon Attwooll. This guidebook was commissioned in Lonely Planet's Melbourne office, and produced by the following:

Commissioning Editor Maryanne Netto

Coordinating Editors Ross Taylor, Simon Williamson
Coordinating Cartographer Jeff Cameron
Coordinating Layout Designer Lauren Egan
Managing Editor Barbara Delissen
Senior Editor Andi Jones
Managing Cartographers Shahara Ahmed, Anita Banh, Corey Hutchison
Managing Layout Designers Chris Girdler, Jane Hart
Assisting Editors Kate Morgan, Charlotte Orr, Angela Tinson

Assisting Cartographer Alex Leung
Cover Research Naomi Parker
Assisting Layout Designer Adrian Blackburn
Internal Image Research Rebecca Skinner
Illustrator Javier Zarracina
Thanks to Dan Austin, Laura Crawford, Ryan Evans, Jouve India, Asha Ioculari, Kate McDonell, Erin McManus, Trent Paton, Averil Robertson, Fiona Siseman, Lieu Thi Pham, Rob Townsend, Gerard Walker

See also separate subindexes for:

✗ **EATING P241**

🍷 **DRINKING & NIGHTLIFE P242**

☆ **ENTERTAINMENT P243**

🔒 **SHOPPING P243**

🏃 **SPORTS & ACTIVITIES P244**

📖 **SLEEPING P244**

Index

2 Danks St 124

A

Aboriginal people
  history 63, 194-5, 197, 198
  rock art 12, 152, 177, 205-6, **12**
  tours 56, 78
Aboriginal Rock Engravings 12, 152, **12**
accommodation 15, 179-90
  airport 190
  Bondi 189
  Centennial Park 188-9
  Circular Quay 182-3
  City Centre 183
  Coogee 189
  Darling Harbour 185
  Darlinghurst 185-7
  Haymarket 183
  Inner West 185
  Kings Cross 187
  Manly 189 90
  Paddington 188-9
  Potts Point 187
  Pyrmont 185
  Rocks, The 182-3
  Surry Hills 185-7
  Sydney Harbour 183
activities 21-3, 46-7, see also individual activities
air travel 218
Alexandria 110, 116
animals, 20, see also individual animals
Anna Schwartz Gallery 108
Annandale 113
Anvil Rock 168
ANZ Stadium 108
Anzac Bridge 101
Anzac Memorial 85

Sights 000
Map Pages **000**
Photo Pages **000**

Aquatic Centre 108
Archibald Prize 84
architecture 19, 20, 209-12
area codes 226
Argyle Cut 60
Argyle Place 62
art galleries 19
Art Gallery of NSW 10, 84, **3, 11**
arts 204-8
  Aboriginal art 12, 152, 177, 205-6, **12**
  dance 39, 40
  film 192, 204-5
  literature 192, 198, 206-7
  music 39, 40, 207-8
  painting 200
  theatre 39, 40, 205
  visual arts 205-6
Artspace 132
ATMs 225
Australia Day 21, 195
Australia Square 89
Australian Centre for Photography 140
Australian Museum 119
Australian National Maritime Museum 100
Australian Rules football 214
Avalon (Northern Beaches) 177

B

Balgowlah Heights 163
Balls Head Reserve 74-6
Balmain 74
Balmoral Beach 78
Banks, Joseph 195
basketball 215
beaches 31-2
  Avalon 177
  Balmoral Beach 78
  Bilgola 177
  Bondi Beach 9, 151, **9**
  Bronte Beach 152
  Burning Palms 176

Camp Cove 72
  Chinamans Beach 78
  Clontarf Beach 163
  Clovelly Beach 152
  Cobblers Beach 78
  Collaroy 177
  Coogee Beach 152, 154
  Curl Curl 163
  Dee Why 177
  Fairy Bower Beach 161
  Forty Baskets Beach 163
  Freshwater 163
  Garie Beach 175
  Lady Bay 73
  Manly Beach 161
  Manly Cove 161
  Marley Beach 176
  Maroubra 155
  McIvers Baths 154
  Narrabeen 177
  North Era 176
  Obelisk 78
  Palm Beach 178
  Parsley Bay 73
  Redleaf Pool 74
  Reef Beach 163
  Shark Beach 73
  South Era 176
  Store Beach 161
  Tamarama Beach 152
  Washaway Beach 163
  Wattamolla Beach 175
  Whale Beach 177
Bells Line of Roads 168
Ben Buckler Point 152
Bennelong 57
Bicentennial Square 75
bicycle travel, see cycling
Biennale of Sydney 22
Big Dig, The 59
Bilgola (Northern Beaches) 177
Blackheath (Blue Mountains) 168
Blanchett, Cate 204, 205
Blaxland, Gregory 171

Blaxland Riverside Park 108
Bligh, William 196
Bloodsworth, James 209
Blue Gum Forest 174
Blue Mountains 167-74, **170-1**
Blue Mountains Botanic Gardens 168
Blue Mountains Heritage Centre 174
Blue Mountains National Park 171
boat cruises 47
boat travel 219-20
Bobbin Head Information Centre 177
Bondi 51, 149-58, **149, 266, 9**
  accommodation 189
  drinking & nightlife 150, 156-7
  food 150, 155-6
  highlights 9, 149-50, 151
  shopping 157-8
  sights 151, 152
  sports & activities 158
  transport 150
  walks 153, **153**
Bondi Beach 9, 151, **9**
Bondi Pavilion 151
books 192, 198, 206-7
bookshops 45
Brett Whiteley Studio 119
Brickpit Ring Walk 108
Bronte 152, 156, **149**
Bronte Beach 152
bubonic plague 196
Bundeena (Royal National Park) 175
Burning Palms 176
bus travel 218, 219
business hours 223

C

Cadigal people 194, 195
Cadman's Cottage 58

INDEX C–G

Camp Cove 72
Campbell's Storehouses 60
Camperdown 107, 110, 115, **256-7**
Camperdown Cemetery 108
car travel 221
Carriageworks 108
Cathedral of Ferns 168
Cathermore 74
CBD, see City Centre
celebrity chefs 202
cell phones 14, 226
Centennial Park 140
Centennial Park (area) 51, 138-48, **138**, **264-5**
  accommodation 188-9
  drinking & nightlife 139
  entertainment 144-5
  food 139
  highlights 138-9
  shopping 147
  sights 140-2
  sports & activities 147-8
  transport 139
  walks 141, **141**
Central station 90, 218
chemists 225
children, travel with 24-5
Chinamans Beach 78
Chinatown 90
Chinese Garden of Friendship 100
Chinese New Year 21
Chippendale 107
Choochoo Express 56
churches 19-20
cinema 40
Circular Quay 51, 52-67, **52**, **248-9**
  accommodation 182-3
  drinking & nightlife 53, 64
  entertainment 65-6
  food 53, 62
  highlights 7, 10, 11, 52-3, 54, 56
  shopping 66
  sights 54, 56, 57-8
  sports & activities 67
  transport 53
  walks 61, **61**

Sights 000
Map Pages **000**
Photo Pages **000**

City Centre 51, 82-97, **82**, **250-1**
  accommodation 183-5
  drinking & nightlife 83, 92-4
  entertainment 94-5
  food 83, 90-1
  highlights 10, 82-3, 84
  shopping 95-7
  sights 84, 87-90
  sports & activities 97
  transport 83
  walks 88, **88**
classical music 39, 40
climate 15, 21-3
Clontarf 163
Clontarf Beach 163
Clontarf Cottage 74
Clovelly 152, 156, 157, **149**
Clovelly Beach 152
Cobblers Beach 78
Cockatoo Island 72
Cockle Bay Wharf 100
coffee 203
Collaroy (Northern Beaches) 177
Commonwealth Bank building 87
consulates 224
Coogee 51, 149-58, **149**, **267**
  accommodation 189
  drinking & nightlife 157
  highlights 149-50
  sights 152-4
  walks 153, **153**
Coogee Beach 152, 154
Cook, Captain James 194, 195
Corso, The 163
costs 14, 34, 180, 226
courses 33
credit cards 225
Cremorne Point 76
cricket 214
Cronulla 156
Crowe, Russell 204, 213
culture 192-3
Curl Curl 163
currency 14, 34, 180, 225
Customs House 57, **30**
customs regulations 223
cycling 46, 220-1

D

dance 39, 40
dangers 32
Danks St 124

Darling Harbour 51, 98-104, **98**, **254**
  accommodation 185
  drinking & nightlife 99, 104
  entertainment 104
  food 99, 103
  highlights 98-9
  sights 100-1
  sports & activities 104
  transport 99
  walks 102, **102**
Darling Point 74
Darling Walk 101
Darlinghurst 51, 117-29, **117**, **260-1**
  accommodation 185-7
  drinking & nightlife 118, 126-8
  entertainment 128
  food 118, 124-5
  highlights 117-18
  shopping 129
  sights 119-21
  transport 118
  walks 120, **120**
Darlington 108, 111, 115, **256-7**
Darren Knight Gallery 124
Dawes Point 60, 63-6
Dawn Fraser Baths 74
Dee Why (Northern Beaches) 177
disabilities, travellers with 227
discount cards 223
diving 46
Dolphin Point 154
Domain, The 86
Double Bay 74
drinking & nightlife 36-8, see also individual neighbourhoods, Drinking & Nightlife subindex
driving, see car travel
driving licences 221
dugongs 13

E

Eastern Suburbs 154
Echo Point (Blue Mountains) 167
electricity 224
Elizabeth Bay 132
Elizabeth Bay House 132
Elizabeth Farm 75
Elkington Park 74
embassies 224
emergencies 224

Enmore 112, 114
entertainment 39-40, see also individual neighbourhoods, Entertainment subindex
Entertainment Quarter 142
Eora people 152, 194, 205
Erskineville 112, 114, **256-7**
Evans Lookout 168
events 21-3, 203
Everglades (Blue Mountains) 171
Everleigh Farmers' Market 13, 111
Experiment Farm Cottage 75
Explorers' Tree (Blue Mountains) 172

F

Fairy Bower Beach 161
Falls Gallery (Blue Mountains) 172
Federation Pavilion 142
ferry travel 219-20
festivals 21-3, 203
film 192, 204-5
First Fleet 195
Fitzroy Gardens 132
Flickerfest 21
flying foxes 142
food 9, 33-5, 200-3, see also individual neighbourhoods, Eating subindex
  costs 34
  festivals 203
  opening hours 34
football 213, 214, 215
Fort Denison 72
Forty Baskets Beach 163
Foundation Park 59
Fraser, Dawn 214
free attractions 28-30
Freshwater 163

G

galleries 19
gang wars 193
gardens 18, see also individual gardens
Garie Beach (Royal National Park) 175
Garrison Church 60
gay travellers 41-3
Giles Baths 154
Gilmore, Peter 202
Glebe 107, 110, 112-13, 115
Goat Island 72
Golden Water Mouth 90

Government House 56
Governors Phillip & Macquarie Towers 89
Govetts Leap 168
GPO Sydney 87
Granger, Bill 202
Great Depression 197
Great Synagogue 86
Greek Revival Courthouse 167
Green Park 119
Greenway, Francis 209

H
Hambledon Cottage 75
Hampton Villa 74
Harbourside 101
Hargraves Lookout 168
Harry's Cafe de Wheels 132
Hartley 167
Haymarket 51, 82-97, **82, 255**
  accommodation 183-5
  drinking & nightlife 83, 92-4
  entertainment 95
  food 83, 92
  highlights 10, 82-3
  shopping 97
  sights 90
  sports & activities 97
  transport 83
  walks 88, **88**
Heidelberg School 206
hiking, see walks
historic buildings 19
history 194-9
  20th century 196-8
  Aboriginal history 63, 194-5, 197, 198
  architectural 209-12
  Chinese 101
  colonial 196
  first settlers 195
  industrial 20
  Pemulwuy 63
  Rocks, The 59
holidays 226
Hornby Lighthouse 72
Hosking, John 196
housing 192
Hyde Park 85
Hyde Park Barracks 85, **18**

I
Icebergs 151
in-line skating 46

Inner West 51, 105-16, **105, 256-7**
  accommodation 185
  drinking & nightlife 106, 112-14
  entertainment 114
  food 106, 110-12
  highlights 105-6
  shopping 114-16
  sights 107-10
  sports & activities 116
  transport 106
  walks 109, **109**
insurance 221, 225
internet access 224
Invasion Day, see Australia Day
Italian Forum 111
itineraries 16-17

J
Japanese submarines 197
jogging 47
Jubilee & Bicentennial Parks 107
Junction Rock 174
Juniper Hall 140
Justice & Police Museum 57

K
Katoomba (Blue Mountains) 169, **169**
kayaking 47
Ken Done Gallery 60
King Street Wharf 101
Kings Cross 51, 130-7, **130, 259**
  accommodation 187-8
  drinking & nightlife 131, 135-6
  entertainment 137
  food 131, 134
  highlights 130-1
  transport 131
  walks 133, **133**
Kirribilli Point 76
kiteboarding 158
Ku-ring-gai Chase National Park 177
Ku-ring-gai people 194
Kwong, Kylie 202

L
Lady Bay 73
Lane Cove National Park 163
language 14

Lawson, William 171
legal matters 224
Leichhardt 111
lesbian travellers 41-3
Leura (Blue Mountains) 169
Leuralla NSW Toy & Railway Museum (Blue Mountains) 170
light rail travel 219
Lightkeepers' Cottages 73
Lindesay 74
literature 192, 198, 206-7
live music 38, 40
local life 26-7, see also individual neighbourhoods
lookouts 20
Luna Park 76

M
Macquarie Lighthouse 73
Macquarie Place 57
Macquarie, Governor Lachlan 196, 209
Madame Tussauds 13, 100
Mahon Pool 155
Manly 51, 159-65, **159, 268, 26**
  accommodation 189-90
  beaches 160
  drinking & nightlife 160, 164-5
  food 160, 163-4
  highlights 12, 159
  sights 161-3
  sports & activities 165
  transport 160
  walks 162, **162**
Manly Art Gallery & Museum 161
Manly Beach 161
Manly Cove 161
Mardi Gras 21, 41-2
markets 45
Marley Beach 176
Maroubra 155
Martin Place 87
Mary Mackillip Place 76
Mary's Hall 74
May Gibbs' Nutcote 76
McElhone Stairs 132
McIvers Baths 154
medical services 224-5
Megalong Valley (Blue Mountains) 170
Millers Point 60-2
Mint 86
mobile phones 14, 226
money 14, 34, 180, 225, 226

Moore, Clover 199
Moore Park 142
Moore Park (area) 140-2, 144-5, 147
Mordant Family Wing 13
Mortuary Station 90
Mosman 76-8
motorcycle travel 221
Mrs Macquaries Point 57
Mt Victoria (Blue Mountains) 170
Mt Wilson 168
Museum of Contemporary Art 58
Museum of Sydney 89
museums 19
music 38, 39, 40, 207-8

N
Narrabeen (Northern Beaches) 177
National Art School 119
National Institute of Dramatic Art 144
national parks 20
Neild Avenue Maze 140
netball 214
New Year's Eve 23
Newington Nature Reserve 108
newspapers 223
Newtown 108-10, 111-12, 113, 115-16, **256-7**
Nicholson Museum 107
Nielsen Park & Shark Beach 73
nightlife, see drinking & nightlife
Norman Lindsay Gallery & Museum (Blue Mountains) 171
North Era 176
North Head 161
North Shore 77, 270-1, **77**
North Sydney 74-6
Northern Beaches 176-8, **176**

O
Obelisk 78
Object Gallery 119
Observatory Hill 60
Oceanworld 161
Old Government House 75
Olympic Games 198
opening hours 223
opera 39
Overseas Passenger Terminal 60

P

Paddington 51, 138-48, **138**, **264-5**
  accommodation 188-9
  drinking & nightlife 139, 143
  entertainment 144
  food 139, 142-3
  highlights 138-9
  shopping 145-6
  sights 140
  sports & activities 147-8
  transport 139
  walks 141, **141**
Paddington Reservoir Gardens 140
painting 84, 206
Palm Beach (Northern Beaches) 178
Palm Beach Ferry 177
Paragon (Blue Mountains) 169
parks & gardens 18, 20, see also individual parks & gardens
Parliament House 86
Parramatta River 75
Parramatta Town Hall 75
Parsley Bay 73
Pemulwuy 63
Perrys Lookdown 168
pharmacies 225
Phillip, Governor Arthur 194, 196
phonecards 226
planning, see also individual neighbourhoods
  beaches 31-2
  budgeting 14-15, 28-30, 34
  children, travel with 24-5
  climate 15
  festivals & events 21-3
  gay & lesbian travellers 41-3
  itineraries 16-17
  local life 26-7
  repeat visitors 13
  Sydney basics 14-15
  Sydney's neighbourhoods 50-1
  travel seasons 21-3
  websites 14
population 193

Sights 000
Map Pages **000**
Photo Pages **000**

postal services 225
Potts Point 51, 130-7, **130**, **259**
  accommodation 187-8
  drinking & nightlife 131, 136-7
  food 131, 134-5
  highlights 130-1
  sights 132
  transport 131
  walks 133, **133**
Powerhouse Museum 107
public holidays 226
public transport 220
Pulpit Rock 168
Pyrmont 51, 98-104, **98**, **254**
  drinking & nightlife 99, 104
  entertainment 104
  food 99, 103
  highlights 98-9
  sights 101-3
  transport 99
  walks 102, **102**

Q

Q Station 161
Queen St 140
Queen Victoria Building 87

R

Rabbitohs, South Sydney 213
Rail Heritage Centre 90
Red Hands Cave (Blue Mountains) 170
Redleaf Pool 74
Reef Beach 163
road rules 221
rock art 12, 152, 177, 205-6, **12**
Rocks, The 9, 51, 52-67, **52**, **248-9**, **8**
  accommodation 182-3
  drinking & nightlife 53, 64
  entertainment 65-6
  food 53, 62-3
  highlights 10, 11, 52-3, 55
  shopping 67
  sights 55, 58-60
  sports & activities 67
  transport 53
  walks 61, **61**
Rocks Discovery Museum, The 58
Rose Seidler House 164

Ross Jones Memorial Pool 154
Royal Botanic Gardens 11, 56, **11**
Royal Easter Show 22
Royal National Park 174-6, **175**, **7**
rugby league 213
rugby union 214
Ruined Castle 168
Rum Rebellion 196
Rushcutters Bay 140

S

safety 32
sailing 46, 47, 215
Sayer, Mandy 136
Scenic World (Blue Mountains) 168
Seidler, Harry 210
SH Ervin Gallery 62
Shark Beach 73
Shark Island 72
Sherman Contemporary Art Foundation 140
shopping 44-5, see also individual neighbourhoods, Shopping subindex
skateboarding 46
smoking 223
snorkelling 32
soccer 215
South Era 176
South Head 72
South Head Heritage Trail 72
South Sydney Rabbitohs 213
speakeasies 13
Speakers' Corner 87
sports 46-7, 213-16, see also individual sports, Sports & Activities subindex
St Andrew's Cathedral 89
St James' Church 85
St John's Cemetery 75
St John's Church 121
St Mary's Cathedral 85
St Patrick's Church 59
St Philip's 89
Star, The 13, 103
State Libary of NSW 86
State Theatre 89
Store Beach 161
Sublime Point (Blue Mountains) 167
submarines 197

Suez Canal 59
surf lifesaving 215
surfing 31, 32, 151
Surry Hills 51, 117-29, **117**, **260-1**
  accommodation 185-7
  drinking & nightlife 118, 125-6
  entertainment 128
  food 118, 121-4
  highlights 117-18
  shopping 128-9
  sights 119
  transport 118
  walks 120, **120**
Susannah Place Museum 58
swimming pools 47
Sydney Aquarium 24, 100
Sydney Carnival 22
Sydney Conservatorium of Music 58
Sydney Convention & Exhibition Centre 101
Sydney Festival 21
Sydney Film Festival 22
Sydney Fish Market 101
Sydney Harbour 51, 68-81, 183, **68**, **270-1**, **28**, **69**, **70-1**
  beaches 69
  drinking & nightlife 69, 78-9
  entertainment 79
  food 69, 78
  highlights 7, 12, 68-9
  shopping 79
  sights 72-8
  sports & activities 80-1
  transport 69
  walks 77, **77**
Sydney Harbour Bridge 10, 55, 211, **3**, **10**
Sydney Harbour National Park 7, 73, **7**
Sydney Hospital 86
Sydney Jewish Museum 119
Sydney Mardi Gras 21, 41-2
Sydney Observatory 60
Sydney Olympic Park 108
Sydney Opera House 7, 54, 210, **3**, **6-7**
Sydney Park 110
Sydney Tower Eye 87
Sydney Tropical Centre 56
Sydney Writers' Festival 22
Sydney Writers Walk 58
Sze Yup Temple 107

T

Tamarama 152, **149**
Tamarama Beach 152
Tank Stream Fountain 58
Taronga Zoo 12, 76, **12**
taxes 226
taxis 221
Taylor Square 121
telephone services 14, 226
temples 19-20
tennis 215
theatre 39, 40, 205
Three Sisters 168
time 14, 226
tipping 225
tourist information 14, 226-7
tours 222, see also boat
    cruises
    Blue Mountains 173
    walking 47
Town Hall 89
train travel 218, 219, see
    also Central station,
    light rail
transport 193
travel to Sydney 15, 218
travel within Sydney 15,
    218-21
Tropfest 21
Tumbalong Park 100
TV 223

U

Ultimo 107, 110
University of Sydney 107
Utzon, Jørn 54, 210, 211

V

vacations 226
Vaucluse 73
Vaucluse House 73
vegetarians 202
Victoria Barracks 140
Victoria Park 107
visas 14, 227-8
Vivid Sydney 22

W

walks, see also tours
    Blue Mountains 173-4
    Bondi to Coogee 153, **153**
    Circular Quay & The
        Rocks 61, **61**
    City Centre & Haymarket
        8, 97, **88**
    Darling Harbour 102,
        102

Inner West 109, **109**
Kings Cross & Potts
    Point 133, **133**
Manly 162, **162**
North Shore 77
Royal National Park 176
South Head Heritage
    Trail 72
Surry Hills & Darling-
    hurst 120, **120**
Sydney Architecture
    Walks 97
Walsh Bay Heritage
    Walk 60
Walsh Bay 60
Warringah 163-4
Washaway Beach 163
Watch House 74
water taxis 219-20
Waterloo 124
Waterman's Cottage 74
Watsons Bay 72
Watsons Bay (area) 72-3
Wattamolla Beach (Royal
    National Park) 175
Waverly Cemetery 152
weather 15, 21-3
websites 14, 180, 197
Wentworth, William 171
Wentworth Falls (Blue
    Mountains) 169
West Head 177
Westfield Sydney 13
Whale Beach (Northern
    Beaches) 177
whales 28, **28**
White Australia Policy 101
White Rabbit 13, 107
Whiteley, Brett 206
Whitlam, Prime Minister
    Gough 198
Wild Life Sydney 100
wildlife, see animals
Wollemi National Park 168
women travellers 228
Woollahra 140, 143-4, 147
Woolloomooloo 132,
    135, 137
Woolloomooloo Finger
    Wharf 132
WWII 196, 197
Wynyard Park 90

Y

Yurulbin Point 74

Z

zoos 12, 76, **12**
Zumbo, Adriano 202

EATING

13B 125

A

A Tavola 124
Adriano Zumbo 103
Aki's 135
Aria 62
Ash St Cellar 91
Ashcrofts (Blue
    Mountains) 173

B

Bangbang 122
Bar H 121
Barefoot Coffee
    Traders 163
Barrenjoey House (North-
    ern Beaches) 178
Bathers' Pavilion 78
Beach Burrito Company
    112
Belgrave Cartel 163
Benbry Burgers 164
Bentley Restaurant &
    Bar 122
bills 125
Billy Kwong 122
Bistro Moncur 143
Bistrode 122
Bistrode CBD 91
Black Star Pastry 111
Bloodwood 111
Boathouse (Northern
    Beaches) 178
Boathouse on Blackwattle
    Bay 110
Bodega 122
Bondi Trattoria 155
Book Kitchen 122
Bourke Street Bakery 122

C

Café Court 103
Cafe Dov 135
Cafe Morso 103
Cafe Sopra (Dawes Point)
    63, **8**
Cafe Sopra (Potts Point) 135
Cafe Sopra (Waterloo) 124
Cafe Sydney 62
Caffe Sicilia 124
Campos 111
Centennial Parklands
    Dining 142
Central Baking Depot 91
Chat Thai 92, 164
Chiswick Restaurant 143

Clodeli 156
Cow & the Moon 112
Crabbe Hole 155

D

Deus Cafe 110
Din Tai Fung 91
Don Don 125
Duke 124

E

Earth Food Store 155
East Ocean 92
El Capo 123
El Loco 123
Escarpment (Blue
    Mountains) 172
est. 91

F

Falconer 123
Felix 91
Firefly 63
Fish Face 124
Forbes & Burton 125
Formaggi Ocello 123
Four in Hand 142
Fouratefive 122
Fratelli Paradiso 134
Fresh Espresso & Food Bar
    (Blue Mountains) 173

G

Golden Century 92
Grappa 111
Guillaume at Bennelong 62
Guzman Y Gomez (Kings
    Cross) 134
Guzman Y Gomez (New
    Town) 112

H

Harry's Espresso Bar 155
House 121
Hugo's Bar Pizza 134
Hugos Manly 164

I

Icebergs Dining Room 155

J

Jimmy Lik's 135

K

Kazbah 103
Kingfish Bistro 112

INDEX DRINKING & NIGHTLIFE

L
La Buvette & Spring Espresso 135
Le Monde 121
Leura Garage (Blue Mountains) 172
Light Brigade Hotel 144
LL Wine & Dine 134
Longrain 121
Lord Dudley Hotel 144
Luxe 111

M
Maggie's 112
Mamak 92
Marigold Restaurant 92
Marque 121
Mecca Espresso 110
Messina 123
Ms G's 134

N
Neild Avenue 143
Norfold on Cleveland 123
North Bondi Italian Food 155

P
Pablo's Vice 125
Piccolo Bar 134
Pier 78
Pilu at Freshwater 164
Pilu Kiosk 164
Pizza Birra 123
Pompei's 155
Porteño 121
Pure Wholefoods 164

Q
Quay 62

R
Red Lantern 123
Ripples 78
Rockpool 62
Rockpool Bar & Grill 91
Room 10 134

S
Sabbaba 156
Sailors Thai Canteen 63

Sights 000
Map Pages **000**
Photo Pages **000**

Sappho Books, Cafe & Wine Bar 110
Sepia 90
Shop, the 156
Silk's Brasserie (Blue Mountains) 172
Single Origin Roasters 122
Sonoma 143
Spice I Am 122
Spice Temple 91
Sydney Kopitiam 110
Sydney Madang 91

T
Ten Buck Alley 125
Tetsuya's 90
Thai Pothong 112
Thanh Binh 111
Three Blue Ducks 156
Toby's Estate 135
Toko 123

U
Uliveto 134
Universal 124

V
Vargabar Espresso 111

W
Wilbur's Place 134
Wine Library 143
Woollahra Hotel 144

Y
Yuga 110

Z
Zaaffran 103
Zinc 134

🍷 **DRINKING & NIGHTLIFE**

10 William Street 143

A
A.B. Hotel 112
Annandale Hotel 113
Aquarium 157
Argyle 64
Arq 127
Arthouse Hotel 94
Australian Hotel 64

B
Bambini Wine Room 92
Bank Hotel 113
Bavarian Bier Café 94, 165
Baxter Inn 92
Beach Road Hotel 157
Beauchamp Hotel 127
Beresford Hotel 125
Blu Bar on 36 64
Bootleg 137

C
Cargo Bar 104
Clovelly Hotel 157
Coogee Bay Hotel 157
Corner House 156
Corridor 113
Courthouse Hotel 113
Cricketers Arms Hotel 125
Crystal Bar 94

D
Darlo Bar 127

E
Eau-de-Vie 126
Empire Hotel 113
Establishment 92
Exchange Hotel (Balmain) 79
Exchange Hotel (Darlinghurst) 127

F
Flying Fish 104
Fortune of War 64
Friend in Hand Hotel 112

G
Gazebo Wine Garden 137
Golden Sheaf Hotel 79
Good God Small Club 92
Grandma's 92
Grasshopper 92
Green Park Hotel 127
Greenwood Hotel 79

H
Harbour View Hotel 64
Hero of Waterloo 64
Hinky Dinks 125
Hive 114
Home 104
Hotel Hollywood 125
Hotel Steyne 165

I
Icebergs Bar 157
Imperial Hotel 114
Ivy 92

J
Jester Seeds 113
Jimmy Lik's 137

K
Kings Cross Hotel 135
Kit & Kaboodle 136

L
Loft 104
London Hotel 79
Lord Nelson Brewery Hotel 64

M
Manly Wharf Hotel 164
Marble Bar 92
Marlborough Hotel 113
Midnight Shift 127

N
North Bondi RSL 156
Northies 156

O
Old Fitzroy Hotel 137
Opera Bar 64
Orbit 92
Oxford Art Factory 125
Oxford Hotel 127

P
Paddington Inn 143
Palms on Oxford 127
Pocket 126
Pontoon 104

R
Ravesi's 154
Redoak Boutique Beer Cafe 94
Rose of Australia 114
Royal Hotel 143
Ruby Rabbit 127

S
Sandringham Hotel 113
Shady Pines Saloon 125
Shakespeare Hotel 125

Slip Inn & Chinese
Laundry 92
Sly Fox 114
Soho 136
Spice Cellar 92
Stitch 92
Stonewall Hotel 127
Sugarmill 136

Tanks Stream Bar 94
Tilbury 137
Tio's Cerveceria 125

Vanguard 113
Venue 505 125
Victoria Room 125

W
Waterbar 137
Watsons Bay Hotel 78
Winery, The 125
World Bar 136

Z
Zanzibar 113
Zeta 94

☆ ENTERTAINMENT

A
Australian Ballet 65
Australian Brandenburg
Orchestra 95
Australian Chamber
Orchestra 65

B
Bangarra Dance Theatre 65
Basement 66
Bell Shakespeare 66
Belvoir St Theatre 128
Bondi Openair Cinema 151

C
Capitol Theatre 95
Chauvel Cinema 144
City Recital Hall 94

D
Dendy Newtown 114
Dendy Opera Quays 66

E
Enmore Theatre 114
Ensemble Theatre 79
Event Cinemas George
St 95

G
Gaelic Club 128
Govinda's 128

H
Hayden Orpheum Picture
Palace 79
Hordern Pavilion 145
Hoyts Entertainment
Quarter 144-5

I
IMAX Cinema 104

L
Lyric Theatre 104

M
Metro Theatre 94
Moonlight Cinema 144
Musica Viva Australia 95

N
New Theatre 114

O
Old Fitzroy Theatre 137
Open Air Cinema 66
Opera Australia 65

P
Palace Verona 144
Performance Space 114
Pinchgut Opera 95

S
SBW Stables Theatre 128
Seymour Centre 114
Starlight Cinema 79
State Theatre 94
Sydney Comedy Store
144-5
Sydney Conservatorium
of Music 65
Sydney Dance Company
65
Sydney Entertainment
Centre 95
Sydney Opera House 66

Sydney Philharmonia
Choirs 65
Sydney Symphony 65
Sydney Theatre 66
Sydney Theatre
Company 65

W
Wharf Theatre 66

🛍 SHOPPING

A
Andrew McDonald 145
Ariel 145
Art of Dr Seuss, the 147
Artery 129
Australian Wine Centre 66

B
Balmain Market 79
Beehive Gallery 116
Berkelouw Books 115, 145
Best Little Bookshop In
Town 156
Better Read than Dead 115
Blue Spinach 129
Bondi Markets 157
Bookshop Darlinghurst 129
Broadway Shopping
Centre 115

C
C's Flashback 129
Calibre 146
Capital L 129
Chifley Plaza 97
Collette Dinnigan 147
Corner Shop 145

D
David Jones 96
Deux Ex Machina 115
Dinosaur Designs 146
Dymocks 96

E
Easton Pearson 146
Egg Records 116
EQ Village Markets 147
Everleigh Artisans' Market
115

F
Faster Pussycat 115
Frolic 116

G
Gertrude & Alice 158
Glebe Markets 115
Gleebooks 115
Gould's Book Arcade 115
Grandma Takes a Trip 128

H
Herringbone 147
Hey Presto Magic
Studio 96
Hogarth Galleries 146
Holy Kitsch! 128
House of Priscilla 129

I
Iain Dawson Gallery 146

J
Jurlique 97

K
Kemenys 158
Kidstuff 147
Kings Comics 96
Kinokuniya 96
Kirribilli Markets 79

L
Le Cabinet Des
Curiosities 116
Leona Edmiston 146
Lesley McKay's Bookshop
147
Love+Hatred 96

M
Market City 97
Mecca Cosmetica 145
Mr Stinky 129
Myer 96

N
Newtown Old Wares 115

O
Opal Fields 66
Original & Authentic
Aboriginal Art 67
Oxford 116

P
Paddington Markets 145
Paddy's Market 97

INDEX SPORTS & ACTIVITIES

Poepke 145
Puppet Shop at The Rocks 67

Q
Queen Victoria Building 95
Quick Brown Fox 116

R
Ray Hughes Gallery 129
Red Eye Records 96
Rip Curl 158
RM Williams 96
Rocks Market, The 67
Roslyn Oxley9 Gallery 146

S
Sass & Bide 146
Sax Fetish 129
Scanlan & Theodore 146
Stills Gallery 146
Strand Arcade 95
Strand Hatters 96
Surfection 157
Surry Hills Market 128
Sydney Antique Centre 128

V
Victoria's Basement 116

W
Westfield Bondi Junction 157
Westfield Sydney 95
Wheels & Dollbaby 128
Willow 146

Z
Zimmerman 145

SPORTS & ACTIVITIES

A
Andrew 'Boy' Charlton Pool 97
Audley Boat Shed (Royal National Park) 175

Sights 000
Map Pages 000
Photo Pages 000

B
Base 165
Bike Buffs 67
Blue Mountains Explorer Bus (Blue Mountains) 173
Blue Mountains Walkabout (Blue Mountains) 173
Bondi Golf Club 158
Bonza Bike Tours 67
BridgeClimb 55

C
Captain Cook Cruises 80
Centennial Park Cycles 148
Centennial Parklands Equestrian Centre 148
Clovelly Bowling Club 158
Coastal Walking Trail (Royal National Park) 176
Cook + Phillip Park 97

D
Darling Harbour Road Train 104
Dive Centre Bondi 158
Dive Centre Manly 165
Dripping Wet 165

E
Eastsail 81
Ecotreasures 165

G
Golden Stairs Walk (Blue Mountains) 173

H
Harbour Jet 80

I
I'm Free 97
Inner City Cycles 116

J
James Craig 80

K
Kalkari Discovery Centre 177
Kitepower 158

L
Lady Carrington Drive (Royal National Park) 176

M
Magistic Cruises 80
Manly Bike Tours 165
Manly Kakak Centre 165
Manly Surf School 165
Matilda Cruises 80

N
Natural Wanders 80
North Sydney Olympic Pool 81

P
Peek Tours 67
Pro Dive 165
Pylon Lookout 55

R
Rocks Ghost Tours, The 67
Rocks Walking Tours, The 67
Rollerblading Sydney 81
Royal Randwick Racecourse 148

S
SCG Tour Experience 148
Skater HQ (Manly) 165
Skater HQ (Paddington) 148
Sydney Architecture Walks 97
Sydney by Sail 80
Sydney by Seaplane 81
Sydney Cricket Ground 147
Sydney Flying Squadron 81
Sydney Football Stadium 147
Sydney Harbour Kayaks 80
Sydney Showboats 80

T
Tribal Warrior 80
Trolley Tours (Blue Mountains) 173

V
Victoria Park Pool 116

W
Walks Around Blackheath (Blue Mountains) 173
Waves Surf School (Royal National Park) 176
Wentworth Park 116
Whale Watching Sydney 80
Wylies Baths 158

Z
Zig Zag Railway (Blue Mountains) 174

SLEEPING

101 Addison Road 189

A
Adina Apartment Hotel Sydney 186
Alfred Park 187
Alishan International Guest House 185
Arts 188

B
Backpackers HQ 188
Beaufort at the Beach 189
Bed & Breakfast Sydney Harbour 182
Big Hostel 186
Billabong Gardens 185
Blue Mountains YHA 173
Blue Parrot 187
Blue Sydney 187
Bondi Beach House 189
Bondi Beachhouse YHA 189
Bonnie Vale Camping Ground 174
Bounce 185
Broomelea Bed & Breakfast 173

C
City Crown Motel 186
Cockatoo Island 183
Coogee Beach House 189
Cronulla Beach YHA 190

D
Diamant 187
Dive Hotel 189

E
Elephant Backpacker 188
Establishment Hotel 184
Eva's Backpackers 188

G
Glebe Point YHA 185
Glebe Village 185
Glenferrie Lodge 183

H

Hilton 183
Hotel 59 187
Hotel Altamont 186
Hotel Bondi 189
Hotel Stellar 186
Hughenden 188
Hyde Park Inn 184

I

Ibis Sydney Airport 190

J

Jackaroo 187
Jemby-Rinjah Eco Lodge 173

K

Kathryn's on Queen 188
Kirketon Hotel 186

L

Lane Cove River Tourist Park 190

Lord Nelson Brewery Hotel 182

M

Maisonette Hotel 188
Manor House 186
Mariners Court 188
Medina Grand Harbourside 185
Medina Grand Sydney 184
Medusa 186
Meriton Serviced Apartments Kent St 183
Meriton Serviced Apartments Pitt St 184

N

North Era Camping Ground 174
Novotel Sydney Manly Pacific 190

O

Observatory 182
O'Malleys Hotel 188

Original Backpackers Lodge 188
Outback Lodge 190

P

Park Hyatt 182
Park8 184
Pensione Hotel 185
Periwinkle 190

Q

Quay Grand 182
Quay West 182

R

Radisson Blu 184
Railway Square YHA 184
Ravesi's 189
Royal Sovereign Hotel 186
Russell 182

S

Savoy Hotel 183
Shangri-La 183
Simpsons of Potts Point 187

Sir Stamford 182
Sydney Central YHA 184
Sydney Harbour YHA 182

T

Tara 185

U

Uloola Falls Camping Ground 174

V

Vibe Hotel North Sydney 183
Vibe Hotel Sydney 184
Victoria Court Hotel 187
Vulcan Hotel 185

W

Wake Up! 184
Waldorf Woolloomooloo Waters 187
Watsons Bay Hotel 183
Westin Sydney 183
Windermere 190

INDEX SLEEPING

Sydney Maps

Map Legend

Sights
- Beach
- Buddhist
- Castle
- Christian
- Hindu
- Islamic
- Jewish
- Monument
- Museum/Gallery
- Ruin
- Winery/Vineyard
- Zoo
- Other Sight

Eating
- Eating

Drinking & Nightlife
- Drinking & Nightlife
- Cafe

Entertainment
- Entertainment

Shopping
- Shopping

Sleeping
- Sleeping
- Camping

Sports & Activities
- Diving/Snorkelling
- Canoeing/Kayaking
- Skiing
- Surfing
- Swimming/Pool
- Walking
- Windsurfing
- Other Sports & Activities

Information
- Post Office
- Tourist Information

Transport
- Airport
- Border Crossing
- Bus
- Cable Car/Funicular
- Cycling
- Ferry
- Metro
- Monorail
- Parking
- S-Bahn
- Taxi
- Train/Railway
- Tram
- Tube Station
- U-Bahn
- Other Transport

Routes
- Tollway
- Freeway
- Primary
- Secondary
- Tertiary
- Lane
- Unsealed Road
- Plaza/Mall
- Steps
- Tunnel
- Pedestrian Overpass
- Walking Tour
- Walking Tour Detour
- Path

Boundaries
- International
- State/Province
- Disputed
- Regional/Suburb
- Marine Park
- Cliff
- Wall

Geographic
- Hut/Shelter
- Lighthouse
- Lookout
- Mountain/Volcano
- Oasis
- Park
- Pass
- Picnic Area
- Waterfall

Hydrography
- River/Creek
- Intermittent River
- Swamp/Mangrove
- Reef
- Canal
- Water
- Dry/Salt/Intermittent Lake
- Glacier

Areas
- Beach/Desert
- Cemetery (Christian)
- Cemetery (Other)
- Park/Forest
- Sportsground
- Sight (Building)
- Top Sight (Building)

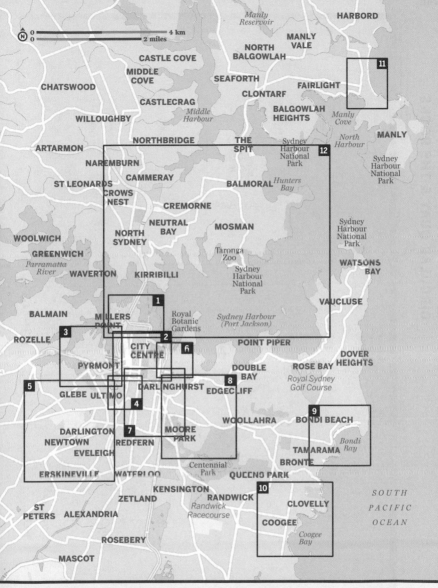

MAP INDEX

1 Circular Quay & The Rocks (p248)

2 City Centre (p250)

3 Darling Harbour & Pyrmont (p254)

4 Haymarket (p255)

5 Inner West (p256)

6 Kings Cross & Potts Point (p259)

7 Surry Hills & Darlinghurst (p260)

8 Paddington & Centennial Park (p264)

9 Bondi (p266)

10 Coogee (p267)

11 Manly (p268)

12 Sydney Harbour (p270)

CIRCULAR QUAY & THE ROCKS

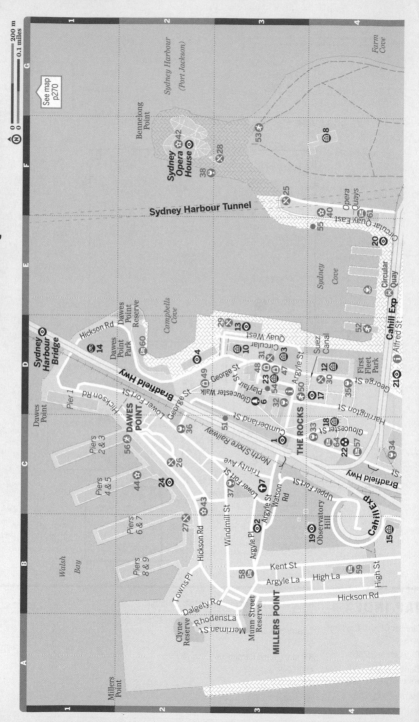

CIRCULAR QUAY & THE ROCKS

Top Sights (p54)
Royal Botanic Gardens ...G5
Sydney Harbour Bridge ...D1
Sydney Opera House F2

Sights (p57)
1 Argyle Cut C3
2 Argyle Place B3
3 Cadman's Cottage.........D3
4 Campbell's Storehouses..D2
5 Customs House E5
6 Foundation Park...........D3
7 Garrison Church............C3
8 Government House F4
9 Justice & Police
   Museum E5
10 Ken Done Gallery..........D3
11 Macquarie Place D5
12 Museum of
   Contemporary Art D4
13 Overseas Passenger
   Terminal C3
14 Pylon Lookout D1
15 SH Ervin Gallery B4
16 St Patrick's Church C5
17 Suez Canal D4
18 Susannah Place
   Museum C4
   Sydney Conservatorium
   of Music.............(see 41)
19 Sydney Observatory......B4
20 Sydney Writers Walk.....E4
21 Tank Stream Fountain...D4
22 The Big Dig..................C4
23 The Rocks Discovery
   Museum.....................D3
24 Walsh Bay.....................C2

Drinking & Nightlife (p64)
32 Argyle D3
33 Australian Hotel............C4
34 Blu Bar on 36 ....C4
35 Fortune of War D4
36 Harbour View Hotel........C2
37 Hero of Waterloo
   Lord Nelson Brewery
   Hotel ....(see 58)
38 Opera Bar F2

Entertainment (p65)
   Bangarra Dance Theatre (see 44)
39 Basement D5
40 Dendy Opera Quays.......F4
41 Sydney
   Conservatorium of
   Music..........................F5
   Sydney Dance Company (see 44)
42 Sydney Opera House......F2
43 Sydney Theatre C2
44 Sydney Theatre
   Company D3

Eating (p62)
25 Aria.............................F3
26 Cafe Sopra C2
   Cafe Sydney ....(see 5)
27 Firefly..........................B2
28 Guillaume at
   Bennelong F3
29 Quay............................D3
30 Rockpool......................D4
31 Sailors Thai Canteen D3

   Wharf Theatre ....(see 44)

Shopping (p66)
45 Australian Wine Centre...D5
46 Opal Fields...................D5
   Original & Authentic
   Aboriginal Art ......(see 47)
47 Puppet Shop at The
   Rocks..........................D3
48 FM Williams..................D3
49 The Rocks Market..........D2

Sports & Activities (p67)
50 Eorza Bike Tours...........D3
51 BridgeClimb..................C3
52 Captain Cook Cruises D4
53 Chcochoo Express F3
   Matilda Cruises .....(see 52)
54 The Rocks Walking
   Tours D3
55 Tribal Warrior...............E4
56 Walsh Bay Heritage
   Walk............................C2
   Whale Watching Sydney (see 55)

Sleeping (p182)
57 Bed & Breakfast
   Sydney Harbour...........C4
58 Lord Nelson Brewery
   Hotel B3
59 Observatory..................B4
60 Park Hyatt...................D2
61 Quay Grand.................F4
62 Quay West...................C5
   Russell...................(see 35)
   Shangri-La.............(see 34)
63 Sir Stamford E5
64 Sydney Harbour YHA......C4

Information (p227)
   Sydney Harbour National
   Park Information
   Centre ....(see 3)

CITY CENTRE

MILLERS POINT

Grosvenor St

Lang Park

Lang St

Bridge St

National Australia Bank House

31

42 75

52

York St

AAP Centre

Jamison St

Westpac Bank

Bond St

3

Gresham St

Loftus St

Spring St

Margaret St

George St

82

O'Connell St

Bligh St

Wentworth Hotel

Clarence St

27

Wynyard

Carrington St

Wynyard La

46

32

Pitt St

Hunter St

35

33

Qantas Centre

Shelley St

Sussex La

King Street Wharf

Erskine St

30

28

Ash St

54

Angel Pl

Hosking Pl

Colonial Centre

4

Western Distributor

Western Distributor

Sussex St

Slip St

Medina Grand Harbourside

Lime St

51

York St

7

11

5

50

Castlereagh St

Elizabeth St

83

Sydney Wildlife World

49

29

40

Theatre Royal

King St

Sydney Aquarium

Kent St

48

41

45 69

71 70

58

Eastern Suburbs Railway

Pitt St Mall

72

St James Rd

60

61 57

65

George St

66

24

Market St

22

See map p254

Day St

Cockle Bay

Market St

15

53

76

Sydney Hilton & Capital Centre

39

8

Cockle Bay Wharf

34

Druitt Pl

44

Clarence St

York St

Market Row

67

68

47

38

81

Westbound Cross City Tunnel

Druitt St

64

Park St

Western Distributor

Day St

26

Town Hall

Park St

Druitt La

Kent St

74

17

Eastbound Cross

Bathurst St

80

78

Spurs St

Sussex St

37

55

Wilmot St

63

Tumbalong Park

Albion Pl

Central St

36

Chinese Garden of Friendship

79

Liverpool St

43

See map 255

George St

56

World Tower

77

Museum

Elizabeth St

Liverpool St

Harbour St

Day St

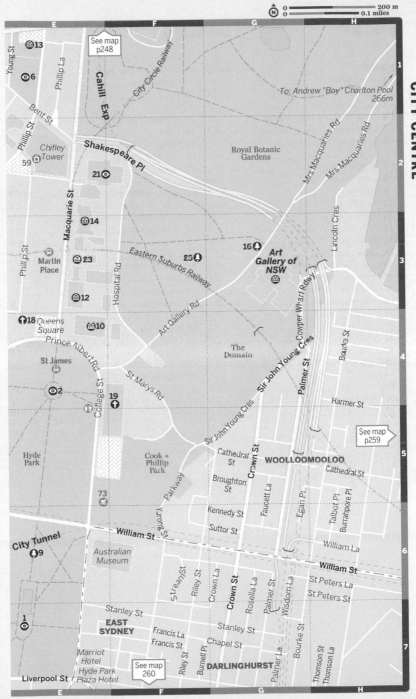

N
0   200 m
0   0.1 miles

See map p248

Young St

13

6

Phillip La

Cahill Exp

City Circle Railway

To: Andrew "Boy" Charlton Pool 266m

Bent St

Phillip St

Shakespeare Pl

Royal Botanic Gardens

Mrs Macquaries Rd

Mrs Macquaries Rd

Chifley Tower

59

21

Macquarie St

Lincoln Cres

Phillip St

14

Martin Place

23

Eastern Suburbs Railway

25

16

Art Gallery of NSW

Hospital Rd

12

18 Queens Square

10

Art Gallery Rd

The Domain

Sir John Young Cres

Cowper Wharf Rdwy

Palmer St

Bourke St

Prince Albert Rd

St James

2

College St

19

St Marys Rd

Sir John Young Cres

Harmer St

See map p259

Hyde Park

Cook + Phillip Park

Parkway

Cathedral St

Crown St

WOOLLOOMOOLOO

Cathedral St

Broughton St

Fauett La

Egan Pl

Talbot Pl

Burahpore Pl

73

Kennedy St

Suttor St

William La

City Tunnel

9

William St

Australian Museum

William St

Stream St

Riley St

Crown La

Crown St

Rosella La

Palmer St

Wisdom La

St Peters La

St Peters St

1

Stanley St

EAST SYDNEY

Francis La

Francis St

Riley St

Burnell Pl

Chapel St

Stanley St

Rosella La

Bourke St

Palmer La

Wisdom La

Thomson St

Thomson La

Marriot Hotel

Hyde Park Plaza Hotel

Liverpool St

See map 260

DARLINGHURST

CITY CENTRE *Map on p250*

◎ Top Sights (p84)
Art Gallery of NSW.....................................G3

◎ Sights (p85)
1 Anzac Memorial...E7
2 Archibald Memorial Fountain..................E4
3 Australia Square...C1
4 Commonwealth Bank branch D3
5 Commonwealth Bank Building D3
6 Governors Phillip & Macquarie
    Towers...E1
7 GPO Sydney C3
8 Great Synagogue.......................................D5
9 Hyde Park E6
10 Hyde Park Barracks....................................E4
11 Martin Place...C3
12 Mint..E3
13 Museum of Sydney.....................................E1
14 Parliament House.......................................E3
15 Queen Victoria Building C5
16 Speakers' Corner.......................................G3
17 St Andrew's Cathedral...............................C6
18 St James' Church..E4
19 St Mary's Cathedral...................................F4
20 St Philip's..B1
21 State Library of NSW E2
22 State Theatre...C4
23 Sydney Hospital..E3
24 Sydney Tower Eye.......................................D4
25 The Domain..F3
26 Town Hall C6
27 Wynyard Park...C2

⊗ Eating (p90)
28 Ash St Cellar...C2
29 Bistrode CBD B3
30 Central Baking Depot................................B2
    Din Tai Fung ....(see 24)
31 est...C1
32 Felix...C2
33 Rockpool Bar & Grill...................................D2
34 Sepia..B5
35 Spice Temple...D2
36 Sydney Madang...C7
37 Tetsuya's...B6

◎ Drinking & Nightlife (p92)
38 Arthouse Hotel...C5
39 Bambini Wine Room D5
40 Bavarian Bier Café......................................C3
41 Baxter Inn...B4
    Crystal Bar ....(see 7)
42 Establishment..C1
43 Good God Small Club.................................B7
44 Grandma's..B5
45 Grasshopper...C4
46 Ivy..C2
47 Marble Bar..C5
    Orbit..(see 3)
48 Redoak Boutique Beer Cafe......................B4
49 Slip Inn & Chinese Laundry......................B3
50 Spice Cellar..D3
51 Stitch...B3
52 Tank Stream Bar..D1
53 Zeta..C5

✪ Entertainment (p94)
54 City Recital Hall...C2
55 Event Cinemas George St........................C7
56 Metro Theatre..C7
   State Theatre....................................(see 22)

🛍 Shopping (p95)
57 Alannah Hill..C4
58 Bettina Liano...C4
59 Chifley Plaza...E2
60 David Jones...D4
61 Dymocks...C4
62 Hey Presto Magic Studio........................D2
   Jurlique...(see 61)
63 Kings Comics..C7
64 Kinokuniya...C5
65 Love+Hatred..C4
66 Myer...C4
67 Queen Victoria Building...........................C5
68 Red Eye Records...C5
69 RM Williams...C4
70 Strand Arcade...C4

71 Strand Hatters..C4
72 Wayne Cooper..C4
   Westfield Sydney.............................(see 24)

⊕ Sports & Activities (p97)
73 Cook + Phillip Park....................................E5
74 I'm Free..C6
   Sydney Architecture Walks............(see 13)

🛌 Sleeping (p183)
75 Establishment Hotel..................................C1
76 Hilton...C5
77 Hyde Park Inn...D7
78 Medina Grand Sydney...............................B6
79 Meriton Serviced Apartments
   Kent St..B7
80 Meriton Serviced Apartments Pitt
   St...C6
81 Park8...D5
82 Radisson Blu...D2
83 Westin Sydney..C3

CITY CENTRE

DARLING HARBOUR & PYRMONT

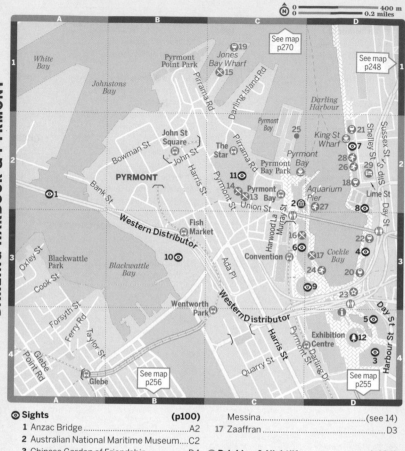

◎ Sights (p100)
1 Anzac Bridge A2
2 Australian National Maritime Museum....C2
3 Chinese Garden of Friendship D4
4 Cockle Bay Wharf D3
5 Darling Walk D4
6 Harbourside..C3
7 King Street Wharf D2
Madame Tussauds ....(see 8)
8 Sydney Aquarium................................D2
9 Sydney Convention & Exhibition
    Centre...D3
10 Sydney Fish Market............................B3
11 The Star...C2
12 Tumbalong Park.................................D4
Wild Life Sydney...............................(see 8)

✕ Eating (p102)
13 Adriano Zumbo C2
14 Café Court..C2
15 Cafe Morso C1
Din Tai Fung ....(see 11)
16 Kazbah C3

Messina...(see 14)
17 Zaaffran D3

◎ Drinking & Nightlife (p104)
18 Cargo Bar D2
19 Flying Fish..C1
20 Home...D3
21 Loft D2
22 Pontoon D3

✪ Entertainment (p104)
23 IMAX Cinema D3
Lyric Theatre....................................(see 11)

◎ Sports & Activities (p104)
24 Harbour Jet D3
25 James Craig C2
26 Magistic Cruises D2
27 Sydney by Sail...................................D2
28 Sydney Showboats D2

▣ Sleeping (p185)
29 Medina Grand Harbourside D2

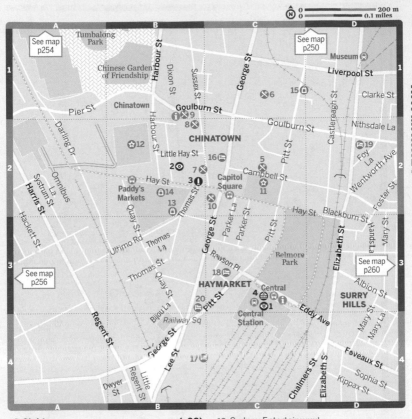

⦿ Sights (p90)
1 Central Station...C3
2 Chinatown...B2
3 Golden Water Mouth....................................B2
4 Rail Heritage Centre...................................C3

⊗ Eating (p92)
5 Chat Thai...C2
6 Din Tai Fung...C1
7 East Ocean..B2
8 Golden Century...B2
9 Mamak...B1
10 Marigold Restaurant..................................C2

⊕ Entertainment (p95)
11 Capitol Theatre..C2

12 Sydney Entertainment
   Centre..B2

🛍 Shopping (p97)
13 Market City..B2
14 Paddy's Markets...B2
15 Red Eye Records...C1

🛏 Sleeping (p183)
16 Pensione Hotel..C2
17 Railway Square YHA...................................B4
18 Sydney Central YHA....................................C3
19 Vibe Hotel Sydney..D2
20 Wake Up!...B3

INNER WEST

Key on p258

400 m
0.2 miles

See map
p255

See map
p254

Exhibition
Centre

ULTIMO

Harris St

William Henry St

Quarry St

Bulwarra Rd

Jones St

Wattle St

Mountain St

Abercrombie St

Broadway

CHIPPENDALE

Balfour St

Pine St

Myrtle St

Cleveland St

Shepherd St

Ivy St

Wentworth Park Rd

Cowper St

Wentworth St

Mitchell St

Queen St

Glebe St

Bay St

Greek St

Francis St

Grose St

Lake
Northam

GLEBE

St Johns Rd

Campbell La

Glebe Point Rd

Derwent La

Derwent St

Talfourd St

Westmoreland St

Mt Vernon St

Catherine St

Science Rd

City Rd (Princes Hwy)

Barff Rd

Eastern Ave

Fisher Rd

Manning Rd

University
of Sydney

Western Ave

Glebe

Bridge Rd

Hereford St

Wigram Rd

Boyce St

Charles St

Minogue Cres

Ross St

Parramatta Road (Great Western Hwy)

FOREST
LODGE

Sparkes St

CAMPERDOWN

Royal
Prince
Alfred
Hospital

Missenden Rd

Briggs St

Fowler St

Mallett St

Camperdown
Park

Lewis
Hoad
Reserve

The Crescent

Hogan
Park

Nelson La

Trafalgar La

Nelson St

Susan St

Johnstons Creek

Gordon St

Cardigan St

Pyrmont Bridge Rd

Barr St

To Bikescape
645m

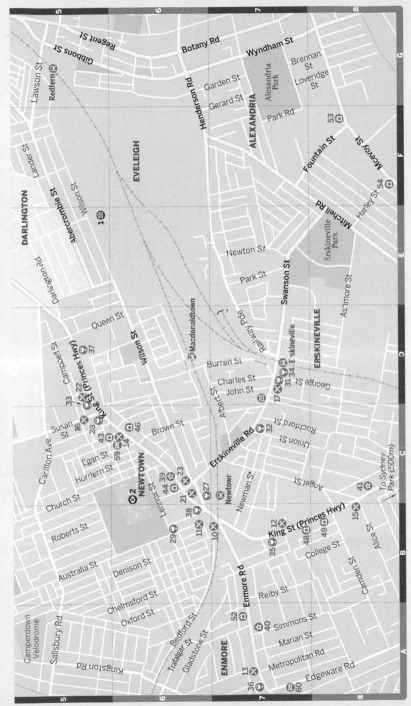

INNER WEST Map on p256

⊙ Sights (p107)
1 Anna Schwartz Gallery.....................E5
2 Camperdown Cemetery....................C6
Carriageworks........................(see 1)
3 Macleay Museum.............................E3
4 Nicholson Museum............................E3
5 Powerhouse Museum.......................G1
6 University Art Gallery.........................E3
7 University of Sydney..........................D4
8 Victoria Park.....................................E4
9 White Rabbit.....................................G3

⊗ Eating (p110)
10 Beach Burrito Company......................B7
11 Black Star Pastry..............................B6
12 Bloodwood..B7
13 Cow & The Moon........................(see 16)
Campos......................................A7
Deus Cafe...................................(see 47)
Eveleigh Farmers' Market...........(see 1)
14 Guzman y Gomez................................C6
15 Kingfish Bistro....................................B8
16 Luxe..C5
17 Maggie's..D7
18 Mecca Espresso.................................G2
19 Sappho Books, Cafe & Wine Bar.........E2
20 Sydney Kopitiam.................................G2
21 Thai Pothong......................................C6
22 Thanh Binh...D5

23 Vargabar Espresso.............................C6
24 Yuga..D2

⊙ Drinking & Nightlife (p112)
25 A.B. Hotel..D1
26 Annandale Hotel.................................A4
27 Bank Hotel...C6
28 Corridor...C5
29 Courthouse Hotel...............................B6
30 Friend In Hand Hotel...........................E2
31 Hive...D7
32 Imperial Hotel.....................................C7
33 Jester Seeds......................................D5
Marlborough Hotel.....................(see 28)
34 Rose of Australia................................D7
35 Sandringham Hotel.............................B7
36 Sly Fox..A7
37 Vanguard...D5
38 Zanzibar...B6

⊙ Entertainment (p114)
39 Dendy Newtown.................................C6
40 Enmore Theatre.................................A7
41 New Theatre.......................................C8
Performance Space.....................(see 1)
42 Seymour Centre..................................F4

⊙ Shopping (p14)
Beehive Gallery..........................(see 48)

43 Berkelouw Books................................C5
44 Better Read Than Dead......................C6
45 Broadway Shopping Centre.................F3
46 C's Flashback.....................................C6
47 Deus Ex Machina................................B3
Egg Records...............................(see 27)
Eveleigh Artisans' Market...........(see 1)
48 Faster Pussycat..................................B7
49 Frolic...B8
50 Glebe Markets....................................E3
Gleebooks.................................(see 19)
51 Gleebooks, Glebe................................D2
Gould's Book Arcade..................(see 37)
52 Le Cabinet des Curiosities..................A7
Newtown Old Wares....................(see 48)
53 Oxford..F8
Quick Brown Fox.........................(see 21)
54 Victoria's Basement............................F8

⊙ Sports & Activities (p116)
55 Inner City Cycles...............................E2
56 Victoria Park Pool...............................E3
57 Wentworth Park..................................F1

⊙ Sleeping (p185)
58 Alishan International Guest House........E2
59 Billabong Gardens..............................C6
60 Tara...A7
61 Vulcan Hotel.......................................G2

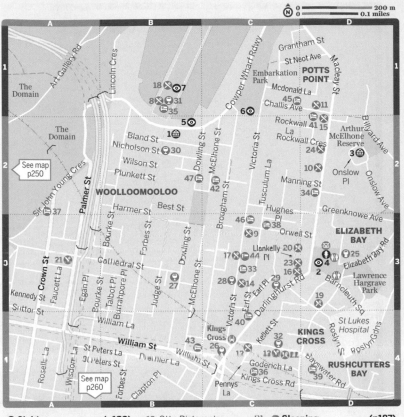

N 0 ─── 200 m
   0 ─── 0.1 miles

⊙ Sights   (p132)
1 Artspace......................B2
2 El Alamein Fountain......D3
3 Elizabeth Bay House D2
4 Fitzroy Gardens D3
5 Harry's Cafe de
   Wheels......................B2
6 McElhone Stairs...........C1
7 Woolloomooloo Finger
   Wharf.......................B1

⊗ Eating   (p132)
8 Aki's B1
9 Cafe DOV.....................C3
10 Cafe Sopra..................D2
11 Fratelli Paradiso...........D1
12 Guzman y Gomez C4
13 Hugo's Bar Pizza..........C4
14 Jimmy Lik's.................C3
15 La Buvette & Spring
   Espresso...................D2
16 LL Wine & Dine............C3
17 Ms G's........................C3

18 Otto Ristorante.............B1
19 Piccolo Bar..................D3
20 Room 10......................C3
21 Toby's Estate...............A3
22 Uliveto.........................C4
23 Wilbur's Place..............C3
24 Zinc............................D2

⊙ Drinking & Nightlife (p135)
   Bootleg................(see 28)
25 Gazebo Wine Garden....D3
   Jimmy Lik's...........(see 14)
26 Kings Cross Hotel........C4
   Kit & Kaboodle.....(see 29)
27 Old Fitzroy Hotel B3
28 Soho............................C3
29 Sugarmill.....................C3
30 Tilbury.........................B2
31 Waterbar......................B1
32 World Bar.....................C4

⊙ Entertainment   (p137)
   Old Fitzroy Theatre (see 27)

⊙ Sleeping   (p187)
33 Backpackers HQ C3
34 Blue Parrot..................D2
35 BLUE Sydney...............B1
36 Diamant.......................C4
37 Elephant
   Backpacker.................A2
38 Eva's Backpackers........C3
39 Hotel 59......................D4
40 Jackaroo......................C4
41 Maisonette Hotel..........D2
42 Mariners Court.............C2
43 O'Malley's Hotel B4
44 Original
   Backpackers
   Lodge........................C3
45 Simpsons of Potts
   Point.........................C1
46 Victoria Court Hotel......C3
47 Waldorf
   Woolloomooloo
   Waters.......................B2

SURRY HILLS & DARLINGHURST

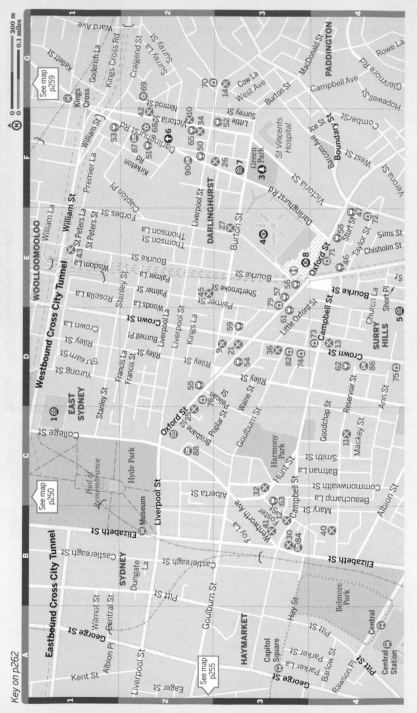

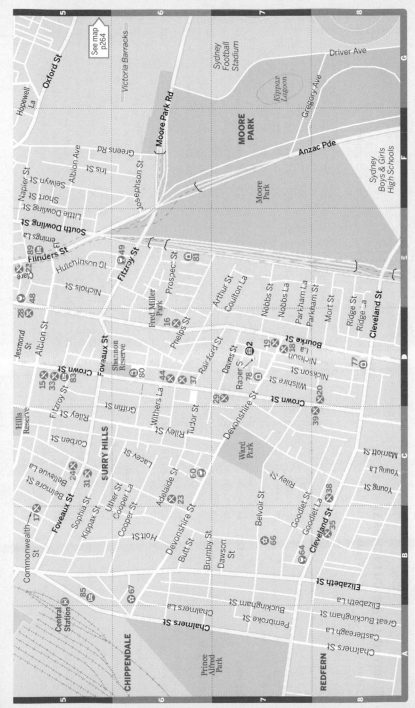

See map p264

Oxford St
Hopewell La
Victoria Barracks
Moore Park Rd
Sydney Football Stadium
Driver Ave
Kippax Lagoon
Gregory Ave
MOORE PARK
Anzac Pde
Moore Park
Sydney Boys & Girls High Schools

Albion Ave
Iris St
Napier St
Selwyn St
Short St
Little Dowling St
Greens Rd
Josephson St
South Dowling St
Flemings La
Flinders St
Hutchinson St
Fitzroy St
Prospect St
Arthur St
Coulton La
Nobbs St
Nobbs La
Parkham La
Parkham St
Mort St
Ridge St
Ridge La
Cleveland St

Clare 22 89
48
28
Jesmord St
Albion St
Nichols St
10 St
Fred Miller Park
16
Phelps St
Crown St
15 33 83
Foveaux St
Shannon Reserve
80
44 37
Rairford St
Davies St
Raper S
78
Wilshire St
Nickson St
2
19
18
Bourke St
Nichau La
77
29

Hills Reserve
Fitzroy St
Riley St
Corben St
Griffith St
Withers La
Tudor St
SURRY HILLS
Lacey St
Devonshire St
Crown St
20
39
Marriott St
Young La
Young St

Belmore St
Bellevue La
24
31
17
Foveaux St
Sophia St
Kippax St
Uther St
Cooper La
Cooper St
Adelaide St
23
60
Holt St
Devonshire St
Butt St
Brumby St
Dawson St
Belvoir St
Riley St
Ward Park
Goodlet St
Goodlet La
38
35
66
64
Cleveland St
REDFERN

Commonwealth St
Central Station
85
67
CHIPPENDALE
Chalmers La
Chalmers St
Pembroke St
Buckingham St
Great Buckingham St
Elizabeth La
Elizabeth St
Castlereagh La
Chalmers St
Prince Alfred Park

SURRY HILLS & DARLINGHURST Map on p260

◎ Sights (p119)
1 Australian Museum.....................C1
2 Brett Whiteley Studio................D7
3 Green Park.................................F3
4 National Art School....................E3
5 Object Gallery.............................D4
6 St John's Church.........................F2
7 Sydney Jewish Museum.............F3
8 Taylor Square.............................E3

✕ Eating (p121)
9 13b...D3
10 A Tavo a....................................F2
11 bangbang..................................C4
12 Bar H..B3
13 Bentley Restaurant & Bar.........D4
14 bills...G3
bills..(see 33)
15 Billy Kwong................................D5
16 Bistrode......................................D6
17 Bodega.......................................B5
18 Book Kitchen.............................D7
19 Bourke Street Bakery.................D7
20 Caffe Sicilia...............................D8
21 Don Don.....................................D3
22 Duke..E5
23 El Capo.......................................C6

24 El Loco.......................................C5
25 Falconer......................................C2
26 Fish Face....................................F3
27 Forbes & Burton.........................E3
28 Formaggi Ocello........................D5
29 fouratefive..................................D7
30 House..B3
31 Le Monde....................................C5
32 Longrain......................................C3
33 Marque..D5
34 Messina.......................................F2
35 Norfolk on Cleveland.................B8
36 Pablo's Vice................................D3
37 Pizza Birra...................................D6
38 Porteño.......................................C8
39 Red Lantern................................C8
40 Single Origin Roasters...............B4
41 Spice I Am..................................B3
42 Spice I Am - The Restaurant.....F2
43 Ten Buck Alley............................E1
44 Toko...D6
45 Universal.....................................E2

◎ Drinking & Nightlife (p125)
46 Arq...D3
47 Beauchamp Hotel.......................E4
48 Beresford Hotel...........................E5

49 Cricketers Arms Hotel................E6
50 Darlo Bar....................................F2
51 Eau-de-Vie..................................F2
Exchange Hotel............................(see 55)
52 Green Park Hotel.........................F3
53 Hinky Dinks.................................F1
Hotel Hollywood..........................(see 63)
54 Midnight Shift.............................D3
55 Oxford Art Factory.....................D2
56 Oxford Hotel...............................E3
57 Palms on Oxford........................E3
Pocket...(see 9)
58 Ruby Rabbit................................E4
59 Shady Pines Saloon....................D3
60 Shakespeare Hotel.....................C6
61 Stonewall Hotel..........................D3
62 The Winery..................................D4
63 Tio's Cerveceria.........................C3
64 Venue 5C5...................................B7
65 Victoria Room.............................F2

✪ Entertainment (p128)
66 Belvoir St Theatre.......................B7
67 Gaelic Club.................................B6
68 Govinda's....................................F2
69 SBW Stables Theatre.................G2

◎ Shopping (p129)
Artery..(see 51)
70 Blue Spinach..............................G2
71 Bookshop Darlinghurst...............E4
72 Capital L.....................................E4
73 C's Flashback.............................D4
74 Grandma Takes a Trip................D3
75 Holy Kitsch!................................D4
76 House of Priscilla........................D2
77 Mr Stinky....................................D8
78 Ray Hughes Gallery....................D7
79 Sax Fetish...................................E3
80 Surry Hills Markets.....................D6
81 Sydney Antique Centre..............E6
82 Wheels & Dollbaby....................D3

◎ Sleeping (p85)
83 Adina Apartment Hotel Sydney...D5
84 Big Hostel...................................B3
85 Bounce..B5
86 City Crown Motel........................D4
87 Hotel Altamont...........................F2
88 Hotel Stellar................................C2
Kirketon Hotel..............................(see 51)
89 Manor House...............................E5
90 Medusa.......................................F2
Royal Sovereign Hotel.................(see 50)

PADDINGTON & CENTENNIAL PARK Map on p264

⊙ Sights (p140)
1 Australian Centre for Photography..........D4
2 Centennial Park..........F6
3 Entertainment Quarter..........C7
4 Federation Pavilion..........G7
5 Juniper Hall..........C4
6 Moore Park..........A6
7 Neild Avenue Maze..........C2
8 Paddington Reservoir Gardens..........C4
9 Queen Street..........F5
10 Rushcutters Bay..........D1
11 Sherman Contemporary Art Foundation..........D3
12 Victoria Barracks..........B4

⊗ Eating (p141)
13 bills..........F5
14 Bistro Moncur..........F5
15 Buzo..........E5
16 Centennial Parklands Dining..........E7
17 Chiswick Restaurant..........G4
18 Four in Hand..........E3
19 La Scala on Jersey..........E5
20 Neild Avenue..........D1
21 Simon Johnson..........F5
22 Sonoma..........D3

⊙ Drinking & Nightlife (p143)
23 10 William Street..........D4
Light Brigade Hotel..........(see 19)

24 Lord Dudley Hotel..........F4
25 Paddington Inn..........D4
26 Royal Hotel..........D3
27 Wine Library..........E5
Woollahra Hotel..........(see 14)

⊙ Entertainment (p144)
28 Chauvel Cinema..........C4
29 Cinema Paris..........C7
30 Hordern Pavilion..........C7
31 Hoyts Entertainment Quarter..........C7
32 Moonlight Cinema..........G6
33 Palace Verona..........A3
34 Sydney Comedy Store..........C7

⊙ Shopping (p145)
35 Andrew McDonald..........D4
36 Ariel..........B3
37 Berkelouw Books..........A3
38 Calibre..........D4
39 Collette Dinnigan..........F5
40 Corner Shop..........D4
41 Dinosaur Designs..........D4
42 Easton Pearson..........B3
43 EQ Village Markets..........C7
Herringbone..........(see 39)
44 Hogarth Galleries..........C3
45 Iain Dawson Gallery..........E5
46 Kidstuff..........F5

47 Leona Edmiston..........D4
Lesley McKay's Bookshop..........(see 13)
48 Mecca Cosmetica..........B3
49 Oxford..........D4
50 Paddington Markets..........D5
51 Poepke..........D4
52 Roslyn Oxley9 Gallery..........E3
Sass & Bide..........(see 48)
53 Scanlan & Theodore..........B3
54 Stills Gallery..........C2
55 The Art of Dr Seuss..........E5
56 Willow..........B3
57 Zimmermann..........B3

⊙ Sports & Activities (p147)
58 Centennial Park Cycles..........F7
59 Centennial Parklands Equestrian Centre..........C7
Centennial Stables..........(see 59)
Eastside Riding Academy..........(see 59)
Moore Park Stables..........(see 59)
60 Skater HQ..........C7
61 Sydney Cricket Ground..........C6
62 Sydney Football Stadium..........C5

⊙ Sleeping (p188)
63 Arts..........B3
64 Hughenden..........E5
65 Kathryn's on Queen..........E5

PADDINGTON & CENTENNIAL PARK

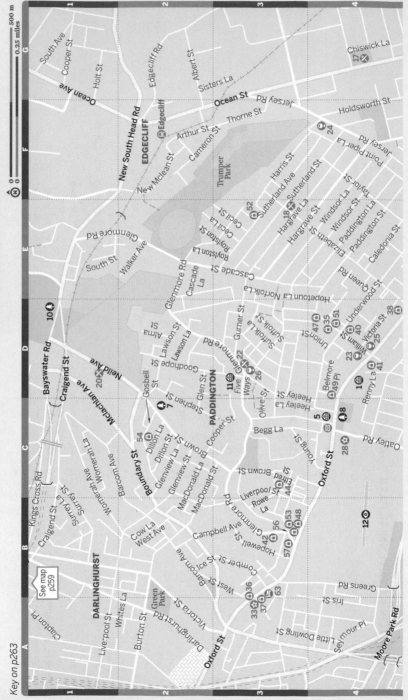

See map p259

500 m
0.25 miles

DARLINGHURST

EDGECLIFF

PADDINGTON

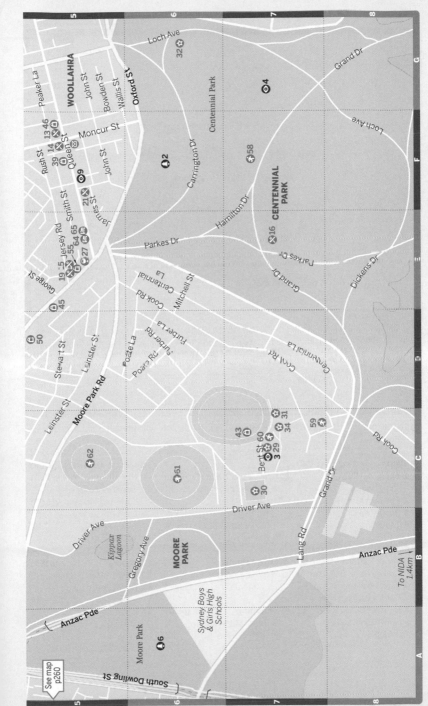

BONDI

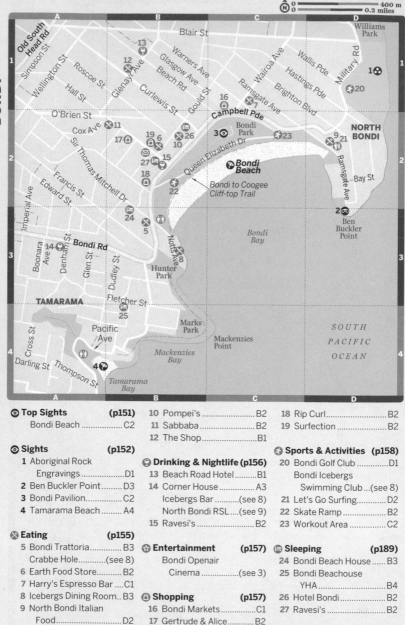

Top Sights (p151)
Bondi Beach C2

Sights (p152)
1 Aboriginal Rock
  Engravings D1
2 Ben Buckler Point D3
3 Bondi Pavilion.............. C2
4 Tamarama Beach A4

Eating (p155)
5 Bondi Trattoria.............. B3
  Crabbe Hole............(see 8)
6 Earth Food Store........... B2
7 Harry's Espresso Bar C1
8 Icebergs Dining Room.. B3
9 North Bondi Italian
  Food........................... D2

10 Pompei's B2
11 Sabbaba B2
12 The Shop..................... B1

Drinking & Nightlife (p156)
13 Beach Road Hotel B1
14 Corner House A3
   Icebergs Bar ....(see 8)
   North Bondi RSL ....(see 9)
15 Ravesi's B2

Entertainment (p157)
Bondi Openair
  Cinema ....(see 3)

Shopping (p157)
16 Bondi Markets C1
17 Gertrude & Alice........... B2

18 Rip Curl.......................... B2
19 Surfection B2

Sports & Activities (p158)
20 Bondi Golf Club D1
   Bondi Icebergs
   Swimming Club ...(see 8)
21 Let's Go Surfing............. D2
22 Skate Ramp B2
23 Workout Area C2

Sleeping (p189)
24 Bondi Beach House B3
25 Bondi Beachouse
   YHA............................. B4
26 Hotel Bondi.................... B2
27 Ravesi's B2

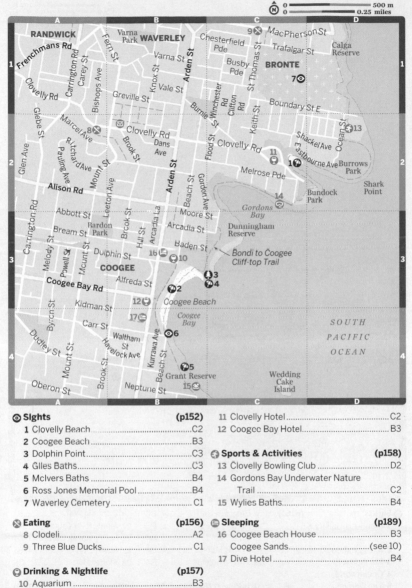

COOGEE

◎ **Sights** (p152)

1 Clovelly Beach C2
2 Coogee Beach B3
3 Dolphin Point C3
4 Giles Baths C3
5 McIvers Baths B4
6 Ross Jones Memorial Pool B4
7 Waverley Cemetery C1

✖ **Eating** (p156)

8 Clodeli A2
9 Three Blue Ducks C1

◉ **Drinking & Nightlife** (p157)

10 Aquarium B3

11 Clovelly Hotel C2
12 Coogee Bay Hotel B3

◆ **Sports & Activities** (p158)

13 Clovelly Bowling Club D2
14 Gordons Bay Underwater Nature
    Trail C2
15 Wylies Baths B4

◻ **Sleeping** (p189)

16 Coogee Beach House B3
    Coogee Sands .... (see 10)
17 Dive Hotel B4

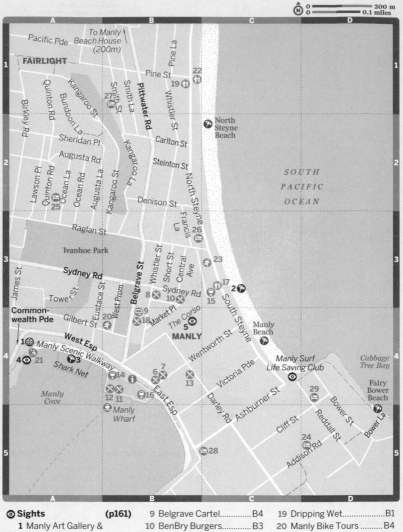

⊙ Sights   (p161)

1 Manly Art Gallery &
   Museum A4
2 Manly Beach C3
3 Manly Cove A4
4 Oceanworld A4
5 The Corso B4

⊗ Eating   (p163)

6 Adriano Zumbo B4
7 Barefoot Coffee
   Traders B4
8 Barefoot Coffee
   Traders B3

9   Belgrave Cartel B4
10 BenBry Burgers B3
11 Chat Thai B4
12 Hugos Manly B4
13 Pure Wholefoods B4

● Drinking & Nightlife (p164)

14 Bavarian Bier Café B4
15 Hotel Steyne C3
16 Manly Wharf Hotel B4

● Sports & Activities (p165)

17 Base C3
18 Dive Centre Manly B4

19 Dripping Wet B1
20 Manly Bike Tours B4
21 Manly Kayak Centre A4
22 Manly Surf School B1
23 Skater HQ C3

⊜ Sleeping   (p189)

24 101 Addison Road D5
25 Beaufort at the Beach A2
26 Novotel Sydney Manly
    Pacific B3
27 Outback Lodge B1
28 Periwinkle C5
29 Windermere D4

SYDNEY HARBOUR *Map on p270*

◉ **Sights** (p72)
1 Admiralty House C6
2 Balmoral Beach...F2
3 Cobblers Beach...G2
4 Cremorne Point...D5
5 Cremorne Reserve D5
6 Dr Mary Booth Reserve Foreshore
   Walkway...B5
7 Fort Denison..C6
8 Kirribilli House...C6
9 Kirribilli Point..C5
10 Luna Park..B5
11 Mary MacKillop Place..............................A4
12 May Gibbs' Nutcote..................................C4
13 Nielsen Park & Shark Beach H5
14 Obelisk..G3
15 Sydney Harbour National Park................F6
16 Taronga Zoo F5

✴ **Eating** (p78)
17 Bathers' Pavilion.......................................F2
   Ripples...(see 25)

◷ **Drinking & Nightlife** (p78)
18 Greenwood Hotel B4

✴ **Entertainment** (p79)
19 Ensemble Theatre......................................B5
20 Hayden Orpheum Picture Palace.............D3
21 Starlight Cinema..B3

◉ **Shopping** (p79)
22 Kirribilli Markets B5

✦ **Sports & Activities** (p80)
23 MacCallum Pool...D5
24 Natural Wanders B5
25 North Sydney Olympic Pool......................B5
26 Rollerblading Sydney.................................B5
27 Sydney Flying Squadron B5

◉ **Sleeping** (p183)
28 Glenferrie Lodge..C6
29 Vibe Hotel North Sydney...........................B5

Key on p269

SYDNEY HARBOUR

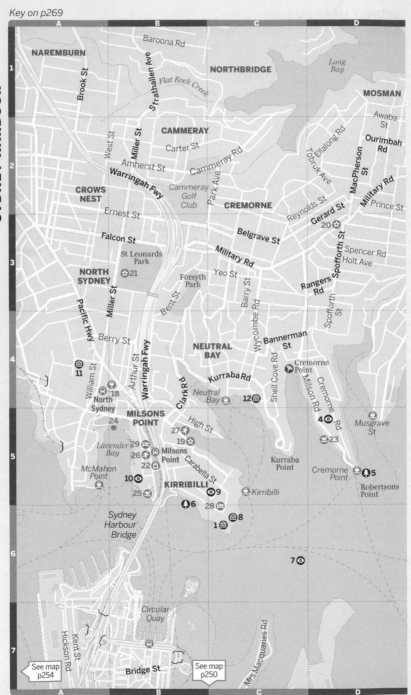

See map
p254

See map
p250